CP cloth 1st h⁵⁰

06-17⁰⁰

Anglo American
and the Rise
of Modern South Africa

Anglo American
and the Rise
of Modern South Africa

Duncan Innes

MONTHLY REVIEW PRESS
NEW YORK

Copyright © 1984 by Duncan Innes

Library of Congress Cataloging in Publication Data

Innes, Duncan.
  Anglo American and the rise of modern South Africa.

  Bibliography: p.
  Includes index.
  1. Anglo American Corporation of South Africa, Ltd.—
History. 2. South Africa—Economic conditions.
3. Mineral industries—South Africa—History. 4. South
Africa—Industries—History. I. Title.
HD9506.S74A534   1983   338.7′622342′0968   83-42523
ISBN 0-85345-628-3
ISBN 0-85345-629-1 (pbk.)

Monthly Review Press
155 West 23rd Street
New York, N.Y. 10011

Manufactured in the United States of America

10 9 8 7 6 5 4 3 2 1

*For my father, and to the
memories of my mother and sister*

Contents

List of Tables

List of Figures

Acknowledgements

This study began as a D. Phil. thesis in Comparative Politics at the University of Sussex. Since then it has gone through a series of revisions designed in the main to reduce its length. What must surely have ranked initially as one of the world's longest theses is now, I hope, a manageable book. Two substantial sections of the original thesis not included here have been published elsewhere.

In its earlier stages the thesis was financed by a scholarship from the International University Exchange Fund (IUEF). After a not uneventful few years of existence, this organization has now passed into obscurity. My sincere gratitude to the members of this organization for the financial support afforded me is tinged with a certain regret that such an association should have contributed to my being imprisoned briefly in South Africa. Life, it seems, is nothing if not full of surprises!

Through the many years that this work was in progress one person has been an immense source of emotional and intellectual support. Francine de Clercq has shared with me so many of the experiences of production involved in this work that I really owe her a debt of gratitude which supersedes all else. Her contribution was important not only in sharing some of the work load of the book but also in taking on additional burdens to give me space in which to write. Without her help, this book might not have materialized.

Another person whose contribution I have valued greatly is my former supervisor at Sussex, Geoff Lamb. His assistance in helping me to come to grips with the theoretical issues involved, in helping me to keep an extremely unwieldy topic manageable and in encouraging me to finish were both welcome and necessary. I am also grateful to my former student colleagues at the University of Sussex, and in particular to Dan O'Meara, for the stimulating intellectual environment they helped to provide when this work was in its formative stages. Much of the later writing on this work was done while I was employed as a Research Fellow in Sociology at the University of Warwick. In working through and developing many of the ideas used in this work I benefited from discussions and debates with my colleagues at the university, especially Bob Fine and Martin Legassick.

Finally, a special word of thanks is also due to all those with whom I have carried out joint work; to those who assisted me during my field-work, often under difficult conditions; and to Ann Kelly who typed three versions of the manuscript with care and without ever despairing.

Introduction

It is common knowledge that the Anglo American Group of companies is a major force in the economic, political and social life of South Africa. In virtually every major sphere of mining, financial and industrial activity in the country the name of Anglo crops up either as the dominant authority, such as in gold and diamond mining, or at least as an important influence. Overall, the consolidated value of the Group's investments makes it easily the largest single company in the country. Translated into social terms this means that the Group wields an awesome degree of power. Nor does the extent of Anglo's power stop at South Africa's borders: the company's interests extend deep into the economic heart of Africa and, further afield, Anglo companies are constantly forging new links and putting down roots in regions as far afield as Europe, North and South America, Australia and Asia.

Because of the extent of its interests and power the Group has naturally generated a wide range of journalistic, political and academic interest and many millions of words have been spent over the years describing its activities. Much of this work has concentrated on specific areas of Anglo's activities or just on keeping abreast with its expansion in certain branches of industry in one or other country. There is, however, surprisingly little that has been written on the Group as a whole and relatively few attempts have been made to gauge the extent of its influence in world affairs. The most substantial work in this regard is undoubtedly Theodore Gregory's large and cumbersome book, *Ernest Oppenheimer and the Economic Development of Southern Africa* (1962), which traces the Group's origins and involvement in gold, diamond, coal and copper mining in southern Africa until the mid-1950s. An essential reference source, this work none the less suffers from two important failings: an over-zealous commitment to the indiscriminate presentation of technical and economic detail (particularly as far as the diamond industry is concerned) so that the wood becomes well and truly buried in the trees; and an overarching admiration for the achievements of the Group's first chairman, Sir Ernest Oppenheimer, which results in the work being devoid of any serious criticism at all (no mean achievement for a book of over 600 pages). It should be said at the outset, though, that Gregory is not alone in reproducing these shortcomings. The aura that surrounds most wealthy families, not to mention respect for the power they wield, has led many to romanticize the Oppenheimers' role in society (see, for instance, Gary Hocking's *Oppenheimer and Son*, 1973) rather than to subject it to close and critical scrutiny. Similarly, the scope of Anglo's involvement in so many different branches of industry has caused many a serious researcher to become irretrievably bogged down in a morass of technical detail. Failure to overcome these kinds of danger must seriously impair any overall analysis and, though Gregory's is undoubtedly an important work, it is particularly weak in precisely the area in which a work of this kind should be strongest: that is, in assessing the Group's strength and influence in South Africa's economic and political life.

Since Gregory's book was published, two serious attempts have been made to get to grips with this question. The first was initiated by the South African government when in 1964 it established a commission to inquire into the affairs of the Anglo American Group (the so-called Hoek Report). Regrettably, the commission's findings have never appeared in public, although they were submitted in 1966 to the then Prime Minister, B. J. Vorster. Consequently, both the findings and the reason for their failure to appear in public must remain a matter for speculation. The second (although far more limited in scope) was a Special Survey carried out by the *Financial Mail* of South Africa, entitled 'Inside the Anglo Power House' (4 July 1969). Though journalistic in orientation, and therefore descriptive rather than analytical, this survey is an extremely useful introduction for anyone wishing to come to terms with the Group, providing a clear and readable account of the major areas of Group activity and a concise outline of its structure. However, the survey makes no attempt to explain the Group's influence in South African society other than telling us that because it is big, therefore it is also influential. This latter approach is, of course, extremely common. Almost everyone with more than a passing interest in South Africa knows that Anglo is a powerful influence in the country and that this influence derives from its immense economic strength. However, from this observation a strange conclusion is sometimes drawn: namely, that therefore there is nothing more to be said on the subject! Such is the potency of ideology in our society that the more prominently power displays itself, the less obvious it seems to some that it should be examined. Such an approach is entirely unacceptable. It is not enough to affirm that Anglo is powerful. Before that statement can have any meaning at all we have to know the conditions and extent of that power, what form it takes, how it works and what are its limitations. These are the crucial questions one has to answer before any real assessment of Anglo's role in South Africa can be made.

This work attempts to address these questions. It attempts to present a considerable amount of empirical material on the Group and its activities, not just for the sake of empirical description, but in order to enhance our understanding of the nature of the Group's role in South African society and, in the process, to throw some light on the nature of that society itself. Though intended partly as a historical study of the Anglo American Group, this work is also fundamentally concerned with an analysis of South African society, seeking to understand both the nature of the society in which Anglo came to develop and also how that society has changed over time.

Such a task is, to say the least, ambitious and I am conscious of the fact that the end result falls short of the original goal. When this work started I had hoped to include a full account of Anglo's activities, not only in South Africa but on a world scale, not only economically but politically as well. Not surprisingly, the scope of such an undertaking proved too time-consuming and unwieldy and the focus had, therefore, to be narrowed down. Anglo American is a multinational combine actively involved in exploiting the resources of over 45 countries of the world, many of these in Africa—and yet the reader will find no serious analysis here of the Group's operations outside South Africa (though most of these are indicated). Similarly, Anglo American is actively involved at a number of levels in influencing the direction of political change in southern Africa—yet there is little here which deals with this question other than at the level of establishing the general relationship between Anglo and the South African state. Again, Anglo's labour policies and practices have at times deviated significantly from those of its colleagues in the Chamber of Mines—and yet there is no analysis here of specific aspects of Group labour policy. These, and other areas of study, must await further research and investigation. Until they are carried out no analysis of Anglo American can pretend to be complete.

What I have done here is to try and trace the Group's historical origins and subsequent expansion in South Africa and to identify and explore the patterns that emerge in terms of their relevance for the development of capitalism in South Africa. Thus a major part of this analysis is concerned with examining and describing the process by which Anglo rose to a position of dominance in the South African mining industry and with tracing from there its diversification into those sectors of South African industry, commerce and finance in which it is today prominent. However, such an analysis, necessary though it is to constructing a coherent picture of the Group and its major spheres of economic activity, cannot in itself provide an answer to the fundamental question posed earlier: that of understanding what this awesome display of economic activity actually means for South African society. To answer that, one needs to link the various aspects of company growth and activity to the wider processes of social change and development in the society as a whole. That is, one has to locate the development of the Anglo American Group in the changing social relations of South Africa and be able to identify the evolutionary processes which that society itself is undergoing. Of course, these two aspects of the analysis are not inseparable: Anglo American has emerged both as a product of the evolving social relations in South Africa and as an important influence on them. But this dialectical relationship should not obscure the fact that the evolution of the firm and the evolution of society are analytically separate.

To understand the nature of South African society we need to be able to identify its motivating forces: how it develops, what form it takes and, most important of all, why it develops. Thus we need to lay bare the fundamental laws of motion of capitalist society in general so as to expose the real nature of South African society. It is only when we have established the true character of capitalist society and the various historical phases it passes through that we can attempt to locate the development of the firm in relation to it. Thus, though we may characterize Anglo American as a monopoly institution from, say, its formal inception in 1917, this moment in time need not necessarily correspond with that at which we identify capitalist society in South Africa as evolving to its monopoly stage. The characterization of a particular society as monopoly capitalist is not synonymous with the existence of monopoly firms within it, though the latter is a necessary precondition for the former.

At what stage, then, can such a characterization be made? There is in fact a considerable body of literature encompassing different schools of thought, which attempts to provide theoretical answers to this question. Much of this literature is rooted in the debates which took place around the turn of the century between the liberal economist J. A. Hobson and, in the Marxist camp, V. I. Lenin, Rosa Luxemburg and Nikolai Bukharin. These authors tried in one way or another to explain and come to terms with the immense social changes which were taking place before their eyes as the phase of competitive capitalism gave way to monopoly capitalism or imperialism. Since then the character of monopoly capitalist society has undergone profound changes and the world we live in today is not the same as that which these authors tried to define. Yet much of what they said then continues to inform the analyses of those who write today, such as in the works of Paul Baran, Paul Sweezy, J. K. Galbraith, Ernest Mandel and Andre Gunder Frank to name but a few of the more modern theorists of imperialism. This debate remains open-ended and riven with contention—as well it must in a world characterized by the most rapid and uneven social development known to humankind. Yet, within the ambit of these divergent views, there is a measure of broad agreement as to the general characteristics of monopoly capitalism. Foremost among these are the five characteristics which Lenin (1973b, pp. 105–6) identified as being the most 'basic features' of monopoly capitalism. These are:

1   The development of the tendencies of concentration of production and capital to the stage where monopolies emerge which play a decisive role in economic life;
2   the merging of bank capital with industrial capital to create finance capital giving rise to the emergence of a financial oligarchy;
3   the increasing importance of the export of capital (as opposed to that of commodities);
4   the rise of international monopoly combines which share the world among themselves; and
5   the complete territorial division of the world among the major capitalist powers.

The above rather simple description is of course far from adequate as a basis for a detailed analysis of the phenomena of monopoly capitalism and imperialism. There have been strong disagreements among theorists over precisely how these five features should be ranked, whether they are not now outmoded, whether new features should not be added, what these should be, and so forth. Others have drawn attention to difficulties which emerge from a closer look at some of the concepts utilized in the description: How, for instance, does one define the 'decisive' role which monopolies play in economic life? How precisely is 'finance' capital to be defined in relation to the various forms of investment and money capitals? Does the 'export of capital' include the export of capital goods and, if so, how then can it be opposed to the export of 'commodities'? And, of course, how does the notion of 'the complete territorial division of the world' among the major capitalist powers square with modern notions of 'spheres of influence' both between east and west and among western powers themselves? These and other criticisms represent a serious challenge to the usefulness of the above criteria as tools of analysis. Yet undoubtedly the description does capture at least some of the more prominent features of capitalist society in its monopoly or imperialist phase of development. As such it provides a useful general guide to the kinds of features we need to look for in South African society before we can identify it as having reached the monopoly phase.

But even if we now have a general guide for developing our characterization of South African society, we still have the problem of identifying the main motivating forces of the society we are attempting to characterize. In other words, while we can now identify the major features by which we can assess whether a particular capitalist society has passed from its competitive to its monopoly phase, we still have not identified the method by which we can define the social forces which are largely responsible for motivating this transformation. Here again the debate is wide open and there are any number of different possibilities to be explored. The specific debate which we would like to address briefly is that between those who believe that it is the economic processes of capitalism which produce the transition and those who believe that it is the struggle between the two great classes of capitalist society, the capitalist class and the working class.

At a general level the question we are here addressing is that of understanding the way in which the most important defining features of monopoly capitalism (as outlined above) are related to the concepts of 'class conflict' and 'politics' and 'economics' in capitalist society. For instance, it is often argued in Marxist theory that it is the movement of the purely *economic* processes of capital accumulation, such as the rising organic composition of capital, which give rise to conditions of monopoly capitalism (producing *inter alia* the tendencies towards concentration of production and capital and that of the export of capital). While such arguments are correct within the confines of economic theory, it should be noted that they have been abstracted for analytic purposes from the social realm. That is, the 'organic composition of capital' is an abstract concept which refers, in value terms, to what Marx called the 'technical composition of capital'. This latter term is specifically intended to describe social reality (as opposed to its abstract 'reflection' which is described in economic or value terms) and is intended to refer, in Marx's words, to 'the mass of means of production employed, on the one hand, and the mass of labour necessary for their employment on the other' (Marx, 1974, vol. I, p. 574). Phrased in these social (or, as Marx calls them, 'material') terms, the notion of the antagonism between classes, which is only implicit in the abstract economic argument, immediately becomes obvious, since when we talk within the confines of capitalist production about the relationship between tools and machinery on the one hand and workers on the other we are actually talking about the 'exploitation' of one class by another. Thus abstract economic concepts, such as the 'organic composition of capital', which are phrased in value terms, in fact embody social and, especially, class relations no less than do the more obviously social or material concepts themselves. It is the failure to recognize this 'hidden' class aspect in many of Marx's more abstract economic concepts which often leads to the emergence of economistic forms of argument.

This same point may be illustrated by looking at the other end of the process involving the rising organic composition of capital. Just as this rise is accompanied by the emergence of some of the more prominent features of monopoly capitalism (such as the increasing concentration of production and capital), so it is also accompanied by the emergence of other tendencies, such as a falling rate of profit. Here again, though not perhaps immediately obvious in the term itself, the notion of class conflict appears as crucial if we examine the question from a social point of view. A falling rate of profit implies a relative weakening of the economic base of accumulation as far as the capitalist class is concerned and therefore has to be countered. The most effective way of doing this from an abstract economic point of view is by increasing the rate of surplus value. In social terms this means increasing the rate of exploitation of the working class. To carry this through, the capitalist class needs to wage a successful assault against the working class—an assault which will usually take not only an economic form, as particular capitalists strive to force down wage rates in 'their' factories, but also a political and ideological form as the state and cultural forms of organization of capital enter the fray on behalf of the capitalist class as a whole. Thus at every stage of the forward movement of the abstract economic processes of capital accumulation we find the social forces of class and class conflict predominate. Every theoretical concept within the Marxist vocabulary—even the most abstract economic term—is imbued with this notion of class conflict. It is therefore this conflict, and the struggle which it generates, which determine the movement of social forces and the development of social relations within the evolution of capitalism.

Having identified the main driving force of capitalist society, the next problem is that of explaining the relation between the notion of class conflict and those of 'economics' and 'politics'. There are of course heated arguments about the way in which this relation should be conceptualized, ranging from the rather mechanistic view of Mandel that political relations are simply economically determined, to Althusser's more sophisticated determination 'in the last instance' or to Poulantzas's 'relative autonomy' of economic and political spheres which veers between Althusser and pluralism. (See, for instance, Mandel, 1968; Althusser, 1969; Poulantzas, 1973.) These interpretations all, in my opinion, fail to conceptualize the problem correctly and consequently cannot provide an adequate solution to the question. (For an important critique of some of these arguments, see S. Clarke, 1977, and Clarke *et al.*, 'Althusserian Marxism', 1981.) Briefly, it seems to me theoretically incorrect to try and establish a *directly* determinant relation between economics and politics in capitalist society precisely because they are separate in our society. Any theoretical attempt to establish such a relationship between them (including Althusser's 'in the last instance') can only negate the separation which quite clearly exists in the material world. However, to say that they appear separate in the material world is not to say that they are not determined nor even that they are not ultimately linked, but *only that one cannot determine the other.*

In capitalist society both economic and political relations appear as contradictory. The contradictions in these relations exist precisely because they express or embody class relations—and it is in these class relations that the real contradictions lie. Consequently, in substance economic and political relations are no more than separate or different forms of class relations. While they clearly appear as separate in our societies, these forms are unified by the capitalist social relations which they embody (and to which they give phenomenal expression)—which is why they appear as specifically *capitalist* forms. This formulation therefore not only maintains the notion of *class determination,* it also establishes the nature of the link between economics and politics as being *indirectly* mediated through class relations. It is for this reason that we shall subsequently refer to economic and political relations 'corresponding' with one another, rather than one 'determining' the other (as in Mandel, Althusser or Poulantzas) or (as with the pluralist model) their being 'autonomous' from one another.

The above remarks have important implications for the general focus of this work. Much of the detail to follow, involving as it does a dissection of the activities of the Anglo American Group, will seem to produce a heavy economic bias. However, as the above discussion indicates, economic relations not only embody class antagonisms but are also, albeit indirectly, inextricably bound up with political relations. Consequently, a detailed analysis of the Anglo American Group affords us the opportunity both to assess the class character of a leading producer in South Africa and also to assess it in relation to the policies and actions of the South African state. To this end we will seek at all stages of the analysis to locate the Group's historical expansion within the context of the economic, political and social struggles which have characterized the history of capital accumulation in South Africa. In order to carry this out—and in order to ascertain the nature and character of the accumulation process in South Africe—we need to commence our study, not with an account of the historical origins of the Anglo American Group, but rather with an account of the historical origins of industrial capitalism in South Africa. We therefore begin with a broad analysis of the conditions of accumulation in the mining industry in the very early period of capitalist production.

CHAPTER 1
The Rise of the De Beers Monopoly in Diamonds

There is clear evidence that mining was carried on in southern Africa by many of the communities that inhabited the region prior to the arrival of the Dutch in 1652. But it was in 1852 that the first significant *capitalist* mining venture was undertaken in southern Africa when Messrs Phillips and King, a Cape firm, began mining copper in Namaqualand (in the remote western part of the Cape Colony) (Noble, 1875, pp. 78–81). However, the slight impact made on the social relations in the colony by these relatively small-scale copper mining ventures was completely overshadowed by the revolutionary changes which followed the discovery of a diamond in Hopetown in 1867. By 1871, only four years after the first diamond had been discovered, the largest diamond-producing mines in the world had been established around the area known as Kimberley. The five largest of these mines, which were to become the basis of South African production, were: the De Beers Mine, the Kimberley Mine, the Dutoitspan Mine, the Bultfontein Mine and, further afield, the Jagersfontein Mine. Diamond production rose extremely rapidly. It took only four years for South Africa to become the world's largest diamond producer: as the value of production rose from £500 worth of diamonds to £403 349. The following year output leapt to over £1.6m and thereafter continued to rise fairly consistently, reaching £4.3m in 1889.[1] (Table 1.) To understand how these increases were achieved it is necessary to analyse the important changes which occurred in the form of capital accumulation in the industry during the early part of its history.

CAPITAL RESTRUCTURING IN THE DIAMOND INDUSTRY:1867–1902

Three distinct phases may be identified in the period of accumulation discussed here: the era of small independent capitals or petty-bourgeois production, 1867–73; the phase of transition or of company production, 1874–85; and the period of monopoly organization and control of production, 1886–1902. Similar conditions and phases may be identified broadly in the relations of exchange.

Petty-bourgeois production and exchange, 1867–73

The very earliest stages of diamond production in South Africa occurred under conditions of small-scale competitive capitalism: that is, production was organized on the basis of numerous independent capitalists, each in control of small resources of capital and in fierce competition with one another. At first these petty-bourgeois relations of production were reproduced politically on the diamond fields by the producers themselves—the era of 'Diggers' Democracy'—and then, as production expanded and wage-labour became increasingly generalized, through the state: for instance, both the number of claims that an individual could hold and the size of each claim were limited.

Although the international market for diamonds was ultimately controlled by large merchant interests in the centres of capitalism, specifically in London and Amsterdam, exchange relations in South Africa were not dissimilar from those that characterized production: a plethora of small dealers, both legal and illegal, operated in the immediate vicinity of the diamond fields and around the ports of Cape Town and Port Elizabeth. These small dealers often bought the diamonds from the producers and sold them to the main European dealers, although some of the larger dealers, such as Mosenthal and Co., did have branch offices in South Africa and bought stones directly from the diggers. Thus the marketing relations in the industry in the period immediately following the discovery of diamonds were objectively constituted by both large-scale capitalist interests based predominantly in Europe and numerous small entrepreneurs based in South Africa. There was of course some individual mobility between the two groupings. Occasionally, some of those who arrived in Kimberley as representatives of the larger firms of European dealers set themselves up in business independently. One such case (which will be of relevance to our subsequent analysis) was that of Anton Dunkelsbuhler, who arrived at Kimberley in 1872 as a representative for a firm of London dealers, Mosenthal and Co., and, after returning to London, set up his own firm, Dunkelsbuhler and Co., in 1878 (Gregory, 1962).[2]

There was also a degree of mobility between dealers and diggers. Some dealers, such as Barnato, bought up claims on the Kimberley fields and engaged in production as well, while a few producers, like Rhodes, became dealers as well. But this individual mobility does not affect the distinction between producers' capital and merchants' capital—a distinction which was firmly grounded in the material conditions of the industry and which reflected itself in the different forms in which contradictions emerged in production and exchange. For instance, while the producers were confronted with the problems of organizing and maintaining production with minimal capital resources, poor technology and the virtual absence of infrastructural facilities, dealers had to contend with the vagaries of a highly sensitive world market. Very often these differences brought producers and dealers into conflict with one another for while producers sought to sell as much of their output as soon as they could, dealers were wary of buying new stones before ridding themselves of their existing stock. Though this conflict may exist in any industry where there is a low level of vertical intergration between producers and merchant capital, the particular form of the diamond market intensified the contradiction.[3]

In the nineteenth century diamonds were essentially a luxury commodity, whose sales depended upon the maintenance of the good fortunes of the ruling classes of Europe, Russia and the United States of America. Any economic or political crisis affecting these classes would profoundly disturb the diamond market. Also, being a luxury commodity, the maintenance of the diamond price was heavily influenced by relations of supply and demand. Over-production rapidly undermined the credibility of diamonds as rarities, wreaking havoc with their price. Production of South African diamonds had already severely strained the market in this regard. It took South Africa only four years to surpass Brazil as the world's largest diamond producer and by 1872, after the discovery of the four major diamond 'pipes', South African production was almost six times as great as the annual rate of Brazilian production. (Table 1.) Continuous increases of this kind posed serious problems for the diamond market.

This then was the initial form of the early industry—a form which, as we shall see, was to undergo rapid and fundamental changes over the next two decades. The term 'Diggers' Democracy' refers to the fact that in this period the individual small digger was paramount and the regulations the diggers drew up and the legislation later enacted by the state reflected that paramountcy. In particular, the size of claims was limited to 30 × 30 Cape ft and the number of claims limited to two per person so as to allow for maximum participation by the largest number of diggers. Thus in 1871 there were 3588 claims on the Kimberley 'pipes' alone: 620 on the De Beers Mine; 460 on the Kimberley Mine; 1067 on Bultfontein; and 1441 on Dutoitspan.[4] These limitations clearly restricted those with more capital from buying up vast numbers of claims—that is, the regulations prevented the concentration and centralization of capital and consequently prevented the development of the industry based on techniques of large-scale mining.

Under the social conditions prevailing in southern Africa at the time, such a development was in any event highly improbable. Even had there been at this stage greater knowledge of the depth and extent of the diamondiferous area, the labour force necessary for large-scale mining was not readily available. Few white diggers were prepared to become wage-labourers since, having some capital of their own, they preferred to seek their fortunes in prospecting; similarly, though having lost some of their land, African communities in general were still able to subsist on the land which remained to them and consequently had no need for wage-labour. The absence of a large readily available proletariat therefore ensured that initially the form of production relations which emerged in the industry remained petty-bourgeois in character. This period of petty-bourgeois production is thus characterized by an absence of the generalized form of wage-labour—and coincides with an absence of the capitalist form of the state in the administration and organization of the diamond fields. It is only with the generalization of wage-labour on the fields that the political era of 'Diggers' Democracy', in which the diggers were literally a 'law unto themselves', is superseded by the direct intervention of the colonial state in all aspects of political life. In other words, it is only when the need for capitalist domination of labour becomes generalized in a specific location that it becomes necessary for production on the one hand and the administration and control of production on the other to become 'separated' into the different forms of 'economics' and 'politics'.

During the phase of petty-bourgeois production the method of production and the form of the labour process were both crude:[5] mining was based on the method of open-cast quarrying and was carried out by the claim-holders themselves using picks and shovels and buckets. They dug down into their claims, through the top layer of 'yellow ground' to the middle layer of main diamond-bearing 'blue ground' below. As the pits became deeper, roadways about 4.5 m (15 ft) wide were left unquarried so that the earth could be hoisted to the surface in buckets and carried by wheelbarrow or cart to the nearby sorting grounds, known as 'floors'.

Clearly, the deeper the pits went the more difficult it became for claim-holders to work the claims alone, and consequently a demand for labour began to emerge. The actual supply of labour to the mines was, however, slow in coming forth and in fact came about only as a result of a two-fold process of dispossession. First, attempts were continuously made to dispossess African claim-holders of their claims, especially on those occasions when there were shortages of claims, and some of those dispossessed were subsequently forced into wage-labour as a means of survival.[6] Secondly, African migrants from neighbouring and outlying areas were beginning to flow in increasing numbers to the diamond fields in search of work following the intensification of the process of conquest. Van der Horst writes that in the period 1871–3 open quarrying and sorting was carried on primarily by 'European' diggers employing two or three African workers to assist them. In 1871 there were some 10 000–12 000 'Europeans' on the mines and some 30 000 blacks. (Kallaway, 1974, p. 14, note 16; see also Simons and Simons, 1969, p. 35; van der Horst, 1942.) Consequently, the capital-labour relation in the industry very quickly began to take on a racial form, with ownership a 'European' or white preserve and wage-labour predominantly, though not completely, black.

This phase in the history of the diamond industry thus saw the beginning of the formation of a class of wage-labourers whose origins need to be examined in some detail. Many South African historians have sought to explain this phenomenon by arguing that the migrants were attracted to the field by the prospect of earning cash wages to enable them to purchase guns with which to kill each other and/or Europeans (see *inter alia* Angove, 1910; Doxey, 1961; de Kiewiet, 1937). These arguments, however, are at bottom simply descriptions of social reality at that time and do not explain that reality. Certainly Africans *were* buying guns to an increasing extent but the gun trade itself needs to be situated, and can only be understood, within the context of the expansion of capitalist relations in South Africa and of the threat these posed to pre-existing precapitalist relations.

European colonization was only achieved in South Africa in the first instance by forcing the African communities off much of their traditional land. Despite these setbacks, however, the African communities had continued to provide for most of their subsistence requirements through working the land that remained to them, even on occasions producing substantial surpluses. This was particularly true of the Basotho who, in the period 1830–65, had produced large surpluses for trade with other African communities and with the colonists. But in 1865 the colonists in the Orange Free State responded to the rising productivity of the Basotho by waging war against them. The war lasted until 1869 when the Basotho king, Moshoeshoe, called on the British colonial state to secure a 'truce'. As a result the Basotho lost most of their western grazing and grain land and, following the inevitable overcrowding and disruption that ensued, some districts began the inevitable drift into poverty. As a result Basotho peasants were increasingly forced to migrate to the diamond fields for short periods of wage-labour so as to supplement their declining rural income. In order to intensify and speed up this process of migratory labour, especially with regard to those districts which continued to export grain, the British colonial administration imposed a hut tax of 10s. on the Basutoland Protectorate in 1870 (Ginsberg, 1974, p. 2).[7] By 1873 approximately 30 000 Basotho had been forced, under the twin pressures of dispossession and taxation, to seek work outside Basutoland, and especially on the Kimberley mines. By the mid-1880s migrant labour had become an integral part of Basutoland's economic life and had become a necessary feature of life for the Basotho people.

Thus by the 1880s the form of Basutoland's integration with South African capitalism had been completely transformed. Although still expressed through relations of exchange, these had been transformed from trade relations (agricultural commodities for seed, guns, technology) to relations of exploitation (labour-power for wages); that is, Basutoland had become a reservoir of labour for capitalism in southern Africa.

This process of proletarianization was not of course confined to the indigenous inhabitants of Basutoland. By 1878 the effects of land deprivation on the economies of the local Griqua communities had become so severe that in that year the Griqua rose up in revolt and were only crushed at great financial expense by the armed forces of the British colonial state. Further afield in the north-eastern Transvaal the Bapedi, under the leadership of Sekhukhune, suffered a similar fate. The Bapedi had migrated to the mines in relatively large numbers to obtain wages with which to buy guns so as to defend their lands against the encroachment of the Transvaal colonists. As a result they managed to maintain control of their land and were able to sustain themselves until 1879 when a combined army of British and Boer troops, supplemented by Swazi units, forced them to surrender much of their land to the colonists. Taxes were imposed on the defeated people and, consequently, the flow of Bapedi migrants to the Kimberley mines increased: by 1884 Bapedi workers comprised 40 per cent of the black labour force on the Kimberley and De Beers mines (van der Horst, 1942, p. 84). This pattern was repeated after the defeat of the Zulu under Cetywayo in 1879. Zululand was dismembered into thirteen chieftaincies and, after the military intervention of the Transvaal Boers, a vast tract of Zulu territory was ceded to the Transvaal in 1884. From 1884 onwards there is a significant increase in the flow of Zulu migrants to the mines at Kimberley (see van der Horst, 1942, p. 84; Kallaway, 1974, p. 10; and Ginsberg, 1974, p. 3).

The early period of the extension of capitalist relations in southern Africa thus produced intense resistance from the indigenous communities which, particularly from the mid-1860s onwards, took the form of armed struggle in certain regions as these communities based on pre-capitalist forms of production sought to defend themselves against the encroachment of capitalism. The defeats which most of these communities suffered intensified the process of proletarianization and produced an absolute surplus-population on the land, thereby creating a reserve army of labour which was essential to the expanded reproduction of capitalism.[8]

However, the process of dispossession was uneven and though over the long term it secured the necessary labour supply for the expansion of capitalism, over the short term capitalists faced acute problems of labour shortages in certain key sectors of the economy. For instance, in the diamond industry in the 1870s—that is, before the effects of dispossession were being most starkly felt by the African communities— labour shortages were at their worst. Both the discovery of the diamond 'pipes' in 1871 and the increasing depths of the pits thereafter added to the pressures on claim-holders to secure more labour.[9] Despite the fact that between 1871 and 1875 some 300 000 Africans came to work on the mines (averaging around 10 000 at any one time), the diamond industry continued to be plagued by labour shortages (Doxey, 1961, p. 15).[10]

African mine-workers were not slow in grasping the advantages which the labour scarcity conferred on them. Desertion became a common occurrence on the diggings as workers sought to secure better wages and working conditions for themselves. As a result, wages on the mines began to rise.[11] From 1869 to 1870—that is, prior to the discovery of the main diamond 'pipes'—African wages were around 2s. 6d. per man per week on the diggings; in 1871, the year of the discovery of the 'pipes', they jumped to 7s. 6d. per man per week and in addition rations valued at around 5s. 6d. each per week were provided; by 1874 wages had reached around 10s. per man per week plus rations (van der Horst, 1942, p. 71).

This remarkable advance raises the whole question of workers' militancy and forms of struggle at this time. Although it is clearly true that, as the Simonses have argued, mine-workers at Kimberley at this time should be regarded as 'peasant workers', it seems incorrect to infer, as the Simonses do, that therefore these workers did not develop 'an outlook and organization to cope with the effects of industrialism' (1969, p. 46). The Simonses support their conclusion by pointing out that 'the men in the compounds never combined' and that 'compound life consequently tended to perpetuate tribal superstitions and antagonisms'. But this seems to suggest a misunderstanding of the real nature of the conflict in southern Africa at the time. It is not just that 'peasant workers' were trying 'to cope with the effects of industrialism'; rather, the African communities were struggling to preserve their precapitalist social relations against the onslaught of capitalist relations. This struggle involved fighting on two fronts: on the one hand, developing and defending production in the rural areas and, on the other, using wage-labour as a means of acquiring purchasing power so as to buy guns to defend their land and to buy seeds, implements and so on to raise productivity. The African peasants adopted forms of struggle appropriate to these ends. As peasant workers on the mines they negotiated over wages and deserted in order to squeeze higher wages and better working conditions out of their employers. In this context, desertion needs to be understood as a form of withholding labour, even though no formal combination of workers is involved. As peasants in the rural areas they sought to increase production and, when threatened, they rose in armed revolt against the invaders. Clearly, these peasant workers then understood only too well the dangers that the advances of capitalism (of 'industrialism') meant for them. To argue, as do the Simonses, that the fact that they did not develop *fully prole-tarian* forms of struggle shows that they failed to understand indus-trialism, conflates the two stages of the struggle. The first stage of their struggle was *against proletarianization*, and the forms of struggle they evolved, such as desertion, armed struggle and so on, are manifesta-tions of their struggle against that process and reflect clearly their awareness of the dangers that 'the effects of industrialism' posed for their traditional way of life. It was only *after* they had lost the struggle to preserve access to the land—that is, in the second stage—that their struggle was to begin to manifest itself in a more fully proletarian form.

The form of struggle adopted by African workers in the early 1870s posed serious problems for small claim-holders. Profits on the diggings were low and many could not afford to pay higher wages (van der Horst, 1942, pp. 64, 68). In addition, claim-holders were encountering serious technical problems in the pits. As the pits went deeper the narrow roadways collapsed and could not be built up again. A system of aerial ropeways was evolved to hoist the 'blue ground' from the indi-vidual claims to the edges of the mine. However, reefs continued to collapse and water began to accumulate in the bottom of the pits. At a time when a more plentiful and better disciplined labour force was required to enable the claim-holders to overcome these problems the workers refused to accept the discipline of capital. All attempts to impose further labour controls simply had the effect of intensifying the labour shortage. For instance, officials pointed out that the colonial administration should be careful not to harass Africans too much lest they refused to sell their labour-power at all (Kallaway, 1974, p. 12).[12]

In general the relative weakness of the position of the diggers and the state at this time in relation to African workers was an expression of the low level of advance of the proletarianization process. Conquest had not progressed sufficiently by the mid-1870s (the major assaults against the Bapedi, Zulu, Xhosa and Sotho were still to come): Africans still had access to agricultural land—they still had viable economic bases—and as a result were in a comparatively powerful position in relation to capital.

By the period 1873–4 serious pressures were thus emerging on capitalists engaged in the production of diamonds. The contradictions that they generated could not be resolved without restructuring the labour supply in such a way that either the supply be increased or the demand decreased. These were the only ways in which wages could be reduced and the necessary discipline imposed on the African work-force. The financial and economic crisis that hit the capitalist world in 1873 was to provide the immediate stimulus for mining capital to embark upon such a restructuring.

The phase of transition, 1874–85

We noted earlier that an economic crisis would have a serious and immediate impact on the diamond market since in a crisis luxury commodities are the first to suffer. Pressure on the diamond market had been building up since the start of production on the diamond 'pipes' in South Africa. With the onset of the crisis, under the simultaneous and in this case separate pressures of over-production and contraction of demand, diamond sales plummeted immediately and the market collapsed. Caught between falling prices and rising costs the small digger, without the necessary financial resources to sustain him through the crisis, was faced with impending ruin. At one time in 1874 African wages were reported to have risen as high as 30s. a week while, in addition to the wage increases, costs were rising as a result of the new technical problems encountered in the pits, such as flooding and falling reef.

Events moved swiftly on the diamond fields. During and immediately after the crisis increasing numbers of claims belonging to weaker diggers were becoming available for take-over by the more successful diggers.[13] At the same time it was becoming necessary to merge adjacent claims in an effort to solve the pressing technical problems in the pits.[14] But the laws in existence at the time were expressly designed to prevent take-overs and mergers by restricting the size and number of claims each person could hold. The more successful claim-holders began to mount a campaign against these laws, demanding in addition the withdrawal of the Statute Law of Griqualand West of 1872 which confirmed the right of Africans to hold claims, the introduction of a vagrancy law and the more effective implementation of the revised Masters and Servants Act of 1872. Thus they put forward demands for legal reforms which, if granted, would lead on the one hand to the increasing centralization of producers' capital and on the other to an intensification of forms of labour control. The state, however, was only prepared to concede in 1874 to a modification of the law relating to claim-holdings so as to allow one person to hold up to ten claims (Ordinance no. 10 of 1874; section I, 18). This concession proved inadequate and the claim-holders now mounted an offensive against the state which culminated in the Black Flag Rebellion of 1875. An immediate consequence of the rebellion was the removal from office of the lieutenant-governor, J. Southey. Following his removal all restrictions on claim-holding were withdrawn (Ordinance no. 12 of 1876);

black claim-holders were bought out by Europeans and disappeared from the fields; the Masters and Servants Act was more effectively administered; and in 1880 Griqualand West was incorporated into the Cape Colony, thereby extending the Cape's Vagrancy Act to the diamond fields. The demands of the more successful claim-holders had thus been fully met. (For a detailed analysis of the events surrounding the rebellion see Ginsberg, 1975.)

The Black Flag Rebellion represented an important turning-point in the history of capital accumulation on the diamond fields. The rebellion was much more than just the climax of a struggle by some capitalists to change and introduce particular laws. It was part of a more fundamental process to restructure the form of legal and political relations to correspond more closely with the changing conditions of accumulation in the industry. The original form of law, expressed perhaps most clearly in the laws restricting take-overs and mergers, and the local form of political organization which had developed on the diamond fields in the early years (Diggers' Democracy), arose in conjunction with relations of petty capitalist production. The changing conditions of accumulation, manifested most starkly in the intensification of workers' struggles and in the new technical problems of production, imposed on the capitalist class as a whole the necessity to restructure the relations of production and the corresponding political and legal relations. Consequently, the state's concession of 1874 failed to halt the momentum for change since what was required was not just the modification of a particular law, but the transformation of the forms of legal relations and of the state so as to strengthen the capitalist class in its struggle against labour. The success of the rebellion ushered in the new forms of these relations: the diamond fields were absorbed under the direct authority of the more powerful Cape colonial state, thereby enhancing the political power of the capitalist class; and the legal relations were restructured to allow for the increased centralization of capital among the producers through the emergence of joint-stock companies. Through this process of restructuring, the capitalist class was to strengthen itself sufficiently to once again gain the initiative in its struggle against labour.

The 1873 crisis engendered similar pressures to restructure the market relations which prevailed in the industry at that time. Just as the crisis spelt ruin for those independent diggers who had insufficient financial resources to sustain them, so on the marketing side many of the small dealers found themselves unable to ride out the crisis. Mergers and take-overs increased in the period immediately following the crisis, enhancing the domination of large merchant interests and leading to pressures on the state to restructure the relevant legal relations. In 1874 legislation was passed which legally confined the diamond trade to diamond dealers who paid an annual fee of £50 and brokers who paid £25, thereby increasing the pressures on the small dealers. In this way the centralization of capital proceeded in the sphere of exchange and a more 'rationally' articulated diamond market under the leadership of large capitalists began to emerge.

The result of these processes was that conditions of competitive capitalism based on separate units of production and exchange were gradually transformed through the increasing lateral combination of units of production and exchange in the industry.[15] The tendency towards the increasing centralization of producers' capital thus occurred in conjunction with a similar tendency in merchants' capital.

Regarding producers' capital, the sweeping aside of the small independent digger heralded the introduction of important changes in the labour-process, thereby paving the way for a transition in the method of production itself. The mergers and take-overs that occurred resulted in the joint-stock company emerging as the dominant form of capitalist economic unit on the fields: in the decade 1871–81 the number of claims on the Kimberley mines was reduced from 3588 to 71 (Houghton and Dagut, 1972). The new economies of scale to be gained from centralization made it possible to restructure the labour-process in such a way as to cope with the technical problems involved without increasing the demand for labour. Production could now be rationalized through *inter alia* the increasing mechanization of the labour-process and through raising the level of capital-intensity in the industry. As early as 1874, when the two-claim law was lifted, mechanical instruments of production had begun to appear on the diamond fields: the horse-whim was introduced in that year to replace ropes and buckets as a means of hoisting the 'blue ground' to the surface of the pits; in the same year washing machines were introduced to replace shovels as a means of breaking down the 'blue ground'; and in 1875 the first steam-engine arrived for use (van der Horst, 1942, p. 78).

These changes were to have far-reaching consequences for the relations of power between the contending classes in the industry. In the first place, the changes enabled capitalists to begin, albeit erratically, to stabilize the demand for labour: the rapid increase in the size of the labour force to 10 000 in 1874 (from the time of the industry's inception in 1867) was gradually brought under control, so that, despite wide fluctuations over individual years, it averaged out at only a little over 10 000 between 1874 and 1890 (van der Horst, 1942, p. 85).

However, the erratic nature of this stabilization process meant that the rise in wage levels could not be contained. During the period 1879–82 black wages on the mines were reported to be between 15s. and 30s. per week (van der Horst, 1942; Ginsberg, 1974, p. 6). Both the high level of the wages and the wide wage differential suggest that at times over this period black workers were still able to negotiate from a position of strength. Furthermore, black workers continued to desert on a large scale: the civil commissioner of Kimberley reported that of the estimated 30 000 Africans who left the diamond fields in 1882, only 12 000 had obtained passes to do so (van der Horst, 1942, p. 74n). However, the growing centralization of capital under the form of the joint-stock company was leading capitalists to investigate new methods of disciplining the African labour force. In particular, convict labour became increasingly popular since not only was it cheap but it also made desertion extremely difficult. Thus, while many African workers continued over this period to challenge the domination of capital, at the same time new techniques were being evolved through which capitalists could impose a harsh discipline on at least a portion of the workforce. In 1884 one of the largest joint-stock companies, the De Beers Mining Co., built and began operating its own convict station which housed some 400 convicts and 25 guards. The superintendent of the De Beers convict station estimated in 1887 that the maximum cost of supplying a prisoner with clothes and blankets was £21s. 7d. per annum and that the cost of food was 8d. per man per day, while the Committee on Convict and Gaols reported that these convicts 'appear to be very tractable and docile' (Kallaway, 1974, p. 9). Some 67 000 prisoners are estimated to have passed through the Kimberley gaol in the period 1873–87, suggesting that this system directly affected a significant proportion of African workers (Matthews, 1887, p. 112). Yet the historical significance of this form of labour coercion lies not so much in its direct importance at the time as in its impact on future forms of labour control, for the convict system was the precursor of the compound system. In the words of the Inspector of Mines: 'In the convict barracks, or [De Beers] branch gaol, the perfection of the compound system may be said to have been reached. The only important difference being that between compulsory and voluntary service.'[16] The development of the convict system was thus an attempt to evolve a form of discipline over labour which would break the resistance of African workers and force down both wage levels and the rate of desertion.

The various forms of restructuring which occurred at this time were accompained by changes in the skill component of the labour force. The tendency towards increasing mechanization demanded a higher complement of skilled workers, many of whom came from Europe. But the arrival of large numbers of white skilled workers ensured that gradually the division of labour based on skills became racially demarcated. Kallaway (1974, p. 13) has pointed out that 'by 1880 it was established practice that Blacks were largely (unskilled) labourers, and mechanics and overseers were white to a man'. As a result the industry came, in the second phase of its development, to be racially stratified, not only in the capital–labour relation, where capital had become a white preserve, but also in the skill differential within labour where skilled work became dominated exclusively by whites. As accumulation proceeded blacks were ejected from one sphere of production after another, eventually being confined to the lowest sphere where working conditions were hardest and economic rewards lowest.

The increasing centralization of capital under the form of organization of the joint-stock company thus served to stabilize the demand for labour, to allow for the development of new forms of labour control and to introduce a racial division of labour based on differentials of skill. The impact of these changes on production is reflected in the following figures: the value of diamond output rose from £1.5m in 1876 to £4.3m in 1887. (Table 1.)

Thus it is in this second phase that the relations of exploitation and domination which were to characterize the mining industry over its later years began to emerge most clearly. African resistance to these changes continued to manifest itself initially in the forms discussed earlier. However, both the conditions of increasing centralization of capital and of increasing concentration of workers at the point of production,[17] combined with the military defeats suffered by the African communities in the rural areas, gradually led to the development of more authentic forms of proletarian struggle. In 1884 white miners had gone on strike over the issue of 'searching' and, following state intervention against them, had formed a union to defend their interests. The first authentic strike involving black workers occurred in 1889 and was followed by another in 1894 in which six workers were killed by police and 300 dismissed from their jobs (Simons and Simons, 1969, pp. 3, 13). Thus the early restructuring of capital was accompanied by indications of a change in the form of workers' struggle—a threat which capitalists sought to meet by completing the process of restructuring.

During the 1880s the effects of conquest were beginning to make themselves felt on the African communities and the numbers of black workers on the mines began to rise. Yet the relatively slow rate of the increase and the intense competition for labour between the mining companies enabled black workers to resist attempts to reduce wage levels. Further amalgamation among the companies would, however, serve to diminish competition in this critical area. Furthermore, continued amalgamations would facilitate the evolution among employers of a joint strategy to overcome the desertion problem. In addition to these pressures towards further amalgamation, which arose directly from the form of class struggle at that time, there were also pressures of a more technical kind.

As the open pits reached depths of 120m (400 ft) and more the problems of falling reef and flooding reasserted themselves in a more serious form, ushering in a revolution in the method of production itself: the transition from open-pit quarrying to underground mining.

As one pit after another had its operations restricted by disastrous reef falls (at one stage the whole of the Bultfontein pit bottom was buried by fallen reef) new equipment was brought in and shaft-sinking and underground rock tunnelling began (van der Horst, 1942, pp. 77–8). This transition encouraged further amalgamations among the producers both because small proprietors were ruined by the persistent rock falls and because of the chaotic nature under which shaft-sinking and tunnelling originally occurred—in 1885 there were four different systems of underground mining operational in the Kimberley Mine and six different shafts had been sunk in the De Beers Mine (Noble, 1875, pp. 340–1).

As a result of these various pressures amalgamation—and therefore the centralization of capital—continued throughout the 1880s. Although in 1881 there were seventy-one claim-holders on the diamond fields, production was in fact dominated by twelve joint-stock companies with a combined capital of some £2.5m—that is, almost a third of the total producer's capital.[18] It was these large companies which grew most rapidly through the amalgamations. Commenting on the progress of the De Beers Diamond Mining Company at this time, the chairman, Cecil Rhodes, claimed that it had 'progressed with extraordinary success, expanding its range of ownership, absorbing step by step its floundering neighbours'. The capital of De Beers in fact increased from £200 000 in 1880 to £841 550 in March 1885—an increase of 321 per cent in five years.[19] As a result company production levels rapidly reached unprecedented heights: the number of diamond loads treated by De Beers rose from less than 100 000 per annum in 1882 to 500 000 in 1887 (Noble, 1875, p. 342).

However, as is always the case given the contradictory nature of capitalist accumulation, the resolution of one set of contradictions inevitably involves the generation of a new set. In this case the resolution of contradictions at the level of production generated a set of contradictions at the level of the market. Restructuring the relations of production had achieved a markedly higher rate of increase of output which in turn intensified the pressures of over-production on the highly sensitive market. Between 1883 and 1887 the value of diamond sales rose by almost 80 per cent from £2.4m to £4.3m (Table 1). The question which posed itself in the mid-1880s was, how much longer could the market continue to absorb the increase? In the highly volatile situation which prevailed these pressures began to manifest themselves as contradictions on the share market. The successful amalgamations and attendant increases in efficiency and profits had produced a speculative boom in share prices, which the banks actively contributed towards by making advances against scrip. In 1886 the inevitable happened: the share market crashed and a serious depression ensued in the Cape Colony. This depression, which ruined many of the smaller and more speculative joint-stock companies and weakened many more, provided the impetus which was to usher in the third phase of early accumulation in the industry: amalgamation under a single control.

The emergence of monopoly conditions, 1886–1902

The crisis of over-production which the industry faced was a manifestation of the contradiction within capitalism and arose in part out of the conditions of class struggle. Pressures from labour had played an important part in forcing the capitalist class to reorganize the method of production and restructure relations of production in the industry, enabling the mine-owners to mount a counter-attack against labour which manifested itself especially in the development of new forms of controls over black workers and in a general stabilization of the demand for labour. But the counter-attack did not *solve* the contradiction: rather, it forced it to emerge in a new form—that is, to manifest itself now in the form of a crisis of over-production. Thus even in its new form the crisis could not be resolved in the interests of capital without an intensification of the class struggle—that is, without an intensification of the attack on labour. At least one astute commentator at the time understood the form which that attack would take:

> What on earth Kimberley was thinking about when she allowed these diamond combinations to be inaugurated or carried through we cannot understand. Ere long the whole proved diamondiferous country will be under one or two controls, who can start works or stop them *a discretion* . . . Suppose the Rothschild group [i.e. De Beers] one of these days elects to put quotations up by shutting the properties down. Thousands of workmen—niggers mostly—would be discharged, and the industries of the town would have an awful blow. (Bellairs, 1889, pp. 23–4)

That is, in order to resolve the crisis, the mine-owners needed to limit production, which involved an attack on the working class through large-scale retrenchment of labour. Yet not only did the resolution of the immediate crisis in the interests of the capitalist class demand an attack on labour, it also involved resolving the question of which of the particular capitals would have to be sacrificed in the interests of capital in general. The further concentration of capital through the centralization of control would assist in securing both these ends: first, because it would centralize authority among the various particular capitals, thereby reducing the degree of intra-capitalist competition; and, second, because it would enable the capitalists to centralize and extend the machinery for labour control. As we shall see, the successful resolution of the crisis demanded that these measures be carried to their ultimate conclusion—that is, so fierce were the struggles that they could only be overcome through the complete centralization of producers' capital in the industry under a single control. The struggle in effect passed through two phases: first, that of intra-capitalist rivalry, and then the struggle waged by capital in its newly constituted form against labour.

The depression of 1886 opened the way for the first phase of the resolution in that it substantially weakened some capitals in relation to others, thereby stimulating a further round of take-overs and mergers. By 1887 all the mines on the De Beers Mine had been brought under the centralized control of one company, the De Beers Co., under the chairmanship of Rhodes, while in the following year the whole of the Kimberley Mine was brought under the centralized control of the Kimberley Co., under the chairmanship of Barnato. (Centralization on the other two mines, Bultfontein and Dutoitspan, had not as yet progressed to the same extent.) The issued share capital of the two giants stood in 1888 at: De Beers, £2 509 620; Kimberley, £1 748 190 (Frankel, 1938). Competition between the two companies remained fierce as neither would agree to terms to limit production and neither was strong enough to impose terms on the other. Yet competition between the two had to be eliminated if the market was not to collapse. This danger of course not only affected the producers in Kimberley, but was of importance to the large dealers in Europe as well, since they also stood to suffer from a collapse of the market. Consequently, the monopoly Rothschild group, the dominant interest in De Beers, secured the support of other major dealers, including Jules Porges and Co. which was led by Wernher and Beit and which controlled the French Co., to provide the necessary finance for De Beers to take over the Kimberley Co. Thus it was an alliance of powerful dealers with interests in the leading producing companies, De Beers and the French Co., which made the take-over of the Kimberley Co. possible. The market value of the Kimberley Co. at the time of the take-over (£8 036 000) was such that not only was this the largest amalgamation in South Africa's history, but it could never have been possible without the financial intervention of the European monopoly combines. Out of this amalgamation the De Beers Consolidated Mines Ltd emerged in 1888. Virtually the first act of the new company was to extend the area of its control by buying up most of the companies on the Dutoitspan and Bultfontein mines (these properties were valued at £4.5m). Thus the first phase in the struggle to resolve the crisis ended with the extension of conditions of monopoly capitalism throughout the sphere of diamond production in Kimberley.

The second phase, involving a concerted attack on labour, was begun immediately the first phase had been completed. While production on the De Beers and Kimberley mines was continued, most of the operations on the Dutoitspan and Bultfontein mines were immediately suspended. As a result the value of total diamond sales was immediately reduced from £4.3m in 1889 to £3.8m the following year and

£3.6m in 1891. (Table 1.) (The Dutoitspan and Bultfontein mines were in fact left practically unworked until after the turn of the century.) This means of resolving the crisis through controlling and limiting production saw a sudden and dramatic upturn in retrenchment levels in the industry. During the year 1888–9 37 per cent of the workers on the diamond mines lost their jobs: 2770 Africans and 240 whites (van der Horst, 1942, p. 85). It is clear from these figures that it was black workers who bore the brunt of the capitalist attack.

Yet this was only the first stage of the offensive against labour and in particular against black labour. The reduction in the demand for labour immediately shifted the balance of forces in wage bargaining from labour to capital, enabling the mine-owners at last to stop the upward drift of wages. After 1886 black wages were gradually reduced to a uniform level of between 7s. 6d. and 15s. per week plus food and accommodation (from 15s. to 30s. per week plus food and accommodation in 1882) (Doxey, 1961, p. 19; Kallaway, 1974, p. 12). Between 1889 and 1898 working costs as a whole were reduced by 50 per cent on the Kimberley diamond fields (Simons and Simons, 1969, p. 43). Furthermore, it was in this period that the compound system was introduced throughout the industry as the most suitable means by which the mine-owners could discipline the black labour force. By 1887 the compound system was being used by the De Beers Co. and five years later, following amalgamation under a single control, the system had been extended to include twelve compounds in Kimberley.

The closed compound system, modelled as it was around the principles of convict labour,· ensured the total isolation of African workers from all forms of social contact beyond the mines. Consequently, it prevented the workers from negotiating with different employers about their wages; it prevented, or at any rate substantially reduced, the possibilities for desertion; it increased the efficiency of the workers by regimenting them even during non-working hours and by controlling their alcohol intake, thereby preventing loss of work-time caused by excessive drinking; and, finally, it provided a new source of revenue for capitalists since workers were forced to spend their wages on food and supplies sold by company-owned stores. Thus the implementation of the system enabled the capitalist class to extend its control over virtually all aspects of the workers' lives, so as to reduce their ability to struggle to the absolute minimum.

Although strikes and other forms of struggle continued to manifest themselves among black workers after the generalized extension of the system (such as the strikes of 1889 and 1894), there can be little doubt that the imposition of the system represented a serious defeat for African mine-workers. Yet the defeat, carried through in the wake of this restructuring, was more than just a defeat for African mine-workers at Kimberley; it was a defeat for the whole South African working class in that it formed part of a drive by a section of the capitalist class to restructure the labour market in South Africa in a form which ensured a structural division between 'free' and 'unfree' workers. This division, characterized as it is in racial terms (with white workers relatively 'free' and African workers 'unfree'), has been one of the most potent weapons in the capitalist struggle to maintain the relations of exploitation and oppression on which accumulation depends in South Africa. This phase of the resolution of the crisis in the diamond industry thus brings us to a critical point of reference for accumulation in other sectors of the economy and for accumulation in general in South Africa.

The restructuring which occurred at this time was not, however, confined to producers' capital alone, but manifested itself also among merchant interests in the industry. We have already seen the important role which merchant capital played in securing the necessary amalgamations which gave rise to the emergence of De Beers Consolidated in control of South African production. Although this enabled the capitalists to limit production and therefore prevent the immediate saturation of the market, in itself the imposition of monopoly control over production was insufficient to resolve all the contradictions which manifested themselves on the market. For instance, the sensitivity of the market meant that it was subjected to considerable and frequent price fluctuations. The problem the dealers faced was that when the price rose they usually had insufficient diamonds in stock to benefit from the increase, while when it fell they were often forced to stockpile diamonds imposing a serious strain on their financial resources. What was required was a marketing organization which was financially strong enough to be able to hold sufficient stones to be released when prices rose and to be able to hold back stones when prices fell. In other words, what was required was a marketing organization—a lateral combination of dealers—which could implement measures to control the price of diamonds.

Centralization of control over production paved the way for the introduction of these measures on the market, since there was now one producer from whom all dealers obtained their stones. Those dealers who were most involved in the establishment of De Beers—for example, Wernher, Beit, the Barnatos and the Mosenthals—were influential in establishing the first Diamond Syndicate in 1889 whose purpose was to buy up and market all of De Beers's output for a limited period of three months. The success of this scheme enabled ten companies, each with a specific quota, to form a new syndicate in 1890 on the same basis.[20] This syndicate in fact collapsed under internecine strife but was eventually re-formed in 1902, after some 'rationalization' had occurred, with a membership of eight companies.[21] Under the new contract the syndicate agreed to the principle of division of its profits with

De Beers, expressing formally for the first time the extent to which monopoly conditions were embracing all spheres of capital. Yet both the degree of lateral integration which had been achieved among dealers and the degree of vertical integration between producers and dealers were grounded in the establishment of centralized control over production. Without that control there was every likelihood that the force of competition would reassert itself between particular capitals— both between producers and dealers and among dealers themselves— threatening to smash the institutions that linked them together formally. If the monopoly conditions and relations which united capitalists in *production* could not be maintained it was inevitable that the institutions which gave expression to that unity would cease to exist. Events during the first two decades of the twentieth century were to show just how precarious the conditions for that unity in the diamond industry really were.

MONOPOLY CAPITALISM AND DE BEERS

In the space of a mere 35 years the diamond industry in Kimberley had been radically transformed: relations of small-scale competitive capitalism which characterized the industry in the period from its inception in 1867 had, by 1902, given way to their opposite—monopoly relations. However, these critical transformations in the relations of production and exchange in the industry were based essentially on the monopolistic control which De Beers Consolidated exercised over diamond production in Kimberley. Outside the Kimberley area of South Africa and, indeed, in other parts of the diamond-producing world, no such monopoly existed. Consequently, it is important to emphasize that, although by the turn of the century monopoly relations had developed in the industry, these were by no means generalized throughout the industry as a whole. Hence the centralization of production under single control on the Kimberley mines represented only a phase in the development of monopoly relations throughout the industry as a whole.

The tenuous monopoly which De Beers exercised in the industry rested on the company's capacity to ensure that no other major producer emerged to challenge its domination. Consequently, De Beers had secured significant interests in the Jagersfontein and Koffiefontein diamond mines of the Orange Free State, the only other major producers in South Africa, as well as establishing an agreement with the South West Africa Co. which was *inter alia* engaged in diamond prospecting in the German colony. At the same time it was the policy of the De Beers directorate to ensure that the company bought up all actual or potential diamond-bearing ground, often so as *not* to work the diamond areas in order to avert the dangers of over-production. In this way De Beers sought to ensure 'a finger in every pie' as a means of protecting her monopoly position and De Beers's chairman, Rhodes, could claim: 'You may be quite sure whenever you hear that a new mine has been discovered, that if De Beers are not there they are very near the spot.'[22]

Yet De Beers, at this stage of its development, was too weak both in terms of financial and technical requirements to ensure success for this policy and in 1902 the inevitable happened: an important discovery near Pretoria led to the establishment of the Premier (Transvaal) Diamond Mining Co., whose owners refused either to sell out to De Beers or to sell through the syndicate, forming their own selling organization in London instead. The rise of this powerful competitor immediately imposed a strain on the relationship which had been established between De Beers and the syndicate, since the latter now became wary of carrying large stocks under conditions where the market was faced with the threat of over-production. The recession from 1907 to 1909 intensified these strains as the average value of diamonds on the world market fell from 23s. 1d. per carat to 12s. 6d. per carat, doing immense damage to De Beers, the syndicate and the Premier Co.

The recession and attendant crisis were not even over when, in 1908, production began on the diamond fields of German South West Africa—again independently of De Beers—and a single selling agency, the Diamond Regie, was rapidly formed to market these stones abroad. Unable to continue with a price war, which was undermining its own position as much as that of its competitors, De Beers sought instead to reach separate marketing agreements with both the Premier and South West Africa companies, based on the principle of partial limitations of output. The uneasy truce continued for a few years but was not a sound basis for market sharing, consisting as it did of a number of separate agreements between the various competing parties. In 1914 the South African government invited the contending parties to a conference to try and thrash out a joint agreement. Five days before war broke out an agreement was reached: a diamond pool of producers, based on a quota system, was established which would sell an agreed output to the syndicate: De Beers's quota would be 48 per cent, Premier's 31 per cent and the Diamond Regie's 21 per cent.

These clashes reflect the extent to which competitive conditions still prevailed in the industry as a whole in the early years of the twentieth century. Yet, equally, the form which this resolution took indicates the extent to which production relations in the industry had progressed from the earlier years. Production on both the Premier and South West African mines was, virtually from the start, relatively highly centralized as was their system of marketing. Consequently, although De Beers's absolute monopoly had been broken by the end of the first decade of this century, monopoly conditions continued to entrench themselves in the industry. These conditions were reflected in the agreements over limitation of output and division of markets which were reached among the major producers immediately prior to the war. It is interesting to note, too, that the joint agreements were only reached *after* the political unification of South Africa had been achieved under the form of the unitary capitalist state and that the state itself played an important role in bringing the agreements about. This illustrates one of the important economic roles which the state comes to play in capitalist society: that of securing the conditions for the expanded reproduction of capitalism even—and especially—when particular capitalist groupings are on the point of destroying themselves.

The joint agreement between De Beers and the other monopoly combines in the diamond industry (an agreement, incidentally, which was dissolved by the First World War) was, however, only one aspect of the extent to which production relations in South Africa were being transformed under the impact of international monopoly capitalism. We have traced in some detail the changing form of the relations of production in the diamond industry and have seen how large capitalist groupings emerged at the expense of smaller capitals. We have seen, too, how these large groupings, following the international contours of capitalist relations in the diamond industry, were themselves threaded into the network of international monopoly capitalism: the take-over of the Kimberley Co. by the De Beers Co., for instance, was made possible only by the financial intervention of the giant Rothschild group and other European monopoly financial institutions. De Beers Consolidated thus emerged from the take-over not only, as we have seen, as a more potent force in the class struggle in South Africa, but also as the localized institutional expression of international monopoly capitalism. Consequently, De Beers became one of the most important institutional means through which monopoly capitalism began to expand in southern Africa at this time.

In particular, De Beers was linked, through cross-shareholdings and other means, to some of the other important monopolies in the region and participated together with them in a number of important ventures designed to expand the area of capitalist production. In 1889, the year in which De Beers Consolidated was formed, some of its more important shareholders had participated in the establishment in London of the British South Africa Co. This company was given the Royal Charter to 'open up' the interior north of the Limpopo River for capitalist development and the De Beers directorate took out shares in the company to help finance its railway-building programme to Rhodesia. In this way De Beers came to have a 20 per cent holding in the British South Africa Co. (Farnie, 1956; also Gann, 1965, p. 83) in addition to the personal shareholdings of individuals on the De Beers board. By 1901 De Beers had acquired shareholdings in at least two Rhodesian gold mines as well (van Onselen, 1976, p. 27). Similarly, De Beers pumped capital into Gold Fields of South Africa, the London-based company Rhodes had formed in 1887, to help finance its programme of gold expansion (Gregory, 1962).

But it was not only in conjunction with other large institutions that De Beers participated in expanding capitalist relations locally. Through its own ventures this company came to be recognized as a formidable force in the local economy: for instance, prior to 1900 De Beers alone was responsible for the production of half of the exports of the Cape Colony (Gregory, 1962). Partly in order to promote its policy of buying up all diamondiferous areas in South Africa the Trust Deed of De Beers Consolidated had been framed in such a way as to give it wide powers for investment outside the strict confines of the diamond industry. Thus by the turn of the century De Beers had become a great ground landlord, owning 538 000 acres (217 000 ha) of land regarded as either actually or potentially diamondiferous. On this land the company became involved in cattle-raising, horse-breeding and fruit and wine farming (the Rhodes Fruit Farms Ltd still operates today). In addition to these interests a considerable amount of De Beers's capital was ploughed into ventures related to the requirements of the diamond industry: for instance, the company invested in collieries to provide the industry with cheap fuel; in railways and telegraph to build up necessary infrastructure; and in explosives to circumvent the high cost of explosives which arose out of the 'dynamite monopoly'. Furthermore, the company quickly moved into other related areas, such as general finance, banking and other mining.[23]

Thus by the early years of this century the wide range of De Beers's interests in various branches of production in southern Africa meant that the company had itself come to closely resemble the monopoly combines which had spawned it initially. The spread of its investments ran from agriculture through banking and industry (mainly explosives, but also cold storage, bricks and tiles and jam and wine), railway-building, telegraphs and the press to coal and copper mining and, above all, gold mining. In many of these areas De Beers's influence was extremely powerful, extending and consolidating throughout southern Africa the power and influence of international monopoly capitalism. Nowhere, however, was the extension of monopoly capitalism more strongly felt at this time—and nowhere was the influence of the diamond magnates who controlled De Beers more powerful—than in the emerging gold mining industry in the Transvaal Republic.

NOTES

1. By 1972 the total value of *recorded* sales from diamonds produced in South Africa was £910 209 275. (See Table 1.) The *actual* total is undoubtedly much higher since diamonds smuggled out are not recorded.

2. This firm prospered and was to play a crucial role in the establishment of the Anglo American Corp. of South Africa.

3. Vertical integration refers to the undertaking by a single company or companies of successive stages in the process of producing and marketing a single commodity.

4. Union of SA, *Official Year Book of the Union of SA*, no. 1, 1917, p. 451.

5. The term 'method of production' is used throughout this work as a general term to define broad phases in the development of the labour process in an industry or society: for example, the transition from small-scale manufacturing production to large-scale industrial production. The term 'labour process' refers to the actual process of production in specific factories, mines, farms, and so on. Consequently, relatively small or isolated changes in the labour process do not imply a change in the overall method of production in a society or industry; such a change only occurs when the labour process throughout an industry or society has been thoroughly revolutionized.

6. According to Matthews (1887): 'A great deal of animosity towards the natives existed about this period [*c*. 1872]. Part of this feeling was originated, I think, from many white men not possessed of claims being jealous of their black brethren digging at Du Toit's Pan and Bultfontein' (p. 209). See also Simons and Simons (1969), pp. 36–8, Kallaway (1974), pp. 4, 5.

7. From the Report of the Commission Appointed by the Secretary of State for Dominion Affairs, *The Financial and Economic Position of Basutoland*, January 1935, p. 16.

8. For a theoretical discussion around the concept of 'surplus-population' (both 'absolute' and 'relative') and its relation to the 'reserve army of labour', see Legassick and Wolpe (1976).

9. By 1876 the average digger was employing 'a gang of about twenty Natives and a European overseer', compared with two or three African workers in 1874 (van der Horst, 1942, p. 79).

10. The labour shortage which prevailed at this time was not just confined to the diamond mines, but, according to van der Horst (1942), extended to the 'coastal colonies where the construction of railways and harbours and the needs of the growing towns competed with the farmers in the market for Native Labour' (p. 64).

11. Writing in 1872 the German digger, Von Weber, claimed that: '. . . as the influx of kaffirs does not keep pace with the growing demand for labour, and as no kaffir will stay in service if someone else offers him a shilling a week more, wages rise from month to month'. (Quoted from Doxey, 1961, p. 18. See also Ginsberg, 1974, p. 5.)

12. From government paper: G20-81, p. 130.

13. The capitalist law of uneven development operated with devastating effectiveness on the diamond fields. While some producers, like Rhodes, 'struck it rich' relatively quickly, others dug for long periods with little or no success; hence the division which emerged between 'weaker' and 'more successful' diggers. For example, only 40 per cent of the original 801 claims on the Kimberley Mine ultimately proved to be workable on a profitable basis. (Ginsberg, 1975, p. 14.)

14. Each claim-holder dug at his own pace and consequently the pit 'bottom' consisted of numerous different levels. This increased the dangers of falling reef and made a solution to the problem of flooding more difficult, leading to demands to 'rationalize' digging operations.

15. Lateral combination or integration refers to the amalgamation of companies engaged in the same stage of production of the same commodity.

16. The Inspector of Mines Report for 1885, G40, 1886, p. 12. Cited in Kallaway (1974), p. 8.

17. By 1887 the De Beers Co. alone employed 18 000 workers: 15 000 Africans and 3000 whites. (Matthews, 1887, p. 183.)

18. Of these 71 companies 13 were in the De Beers Mine (total capital, £1 334 000); 13 in the Kimberley Mine (capital, £2 685 000); 18 in the Dutoitspan Mine (capital, £2 220 750); 16 in the Bultfontein Mine (capital, £871 100); and 11 in 'outside mines' (capital, £923 000). (Frankel, 1938.)

19. Three of the most prominent joint-stock companies operating at this time were: the De Beers Diamond Mining Co., formed in 1880 from the combined claims of Rhodes, Rudd, Maguire, Stow and others on the De Beers Mine with a capital of some £200 000; the Kimberley Central Diamond Mining Co. registered in 1880 and operating on the Kimberley Mine under the control of the Barnato brothers; and the French Co. (Compagnie Française des Mines de Diamant du Cap de Bon Espérance) with interests in the major mines and under the control of Jules Porges and Co. whose leading members included Wernher and Beit. These companies were all linked to prominent merchant interests: the De Beers Co. was closely linked to the powerful Rothschild financial empire in London, while both Barnato Bros Ltd and Jules Porges and Co. were among the leading dealers at the time. (Frankel, 1938.)

20. Anton Dunkelsbuhler and Co. was a member of the syndicate with a quota of 10 per cent. (Gregory, 1962.)

21. Dunkelsbuhler's quota was now 12 per cent. (Gregory, 1962.)

22. C. J. Rhodes, Address to Shareholders, De Beers Cons. Mines Ltd, Annual General Meeting 1898.

23. Hobson (1928) has analysed the conditions under which monopoly combines find it necessary to invest outside the confines of their immediate area of production. These conditions would seem to be particularly apposite in the case of the diamond industry—with its strict need to regulate and control output—and, hence, to De Beers:

> The profitable management of a trust depends primarily upon regulation of output, which involves a limitation on the employment of capital . . . it is thus impossible for a trustmaker to find full continuous employment for the high profits he makes by extending the plant and working capital of his own business—such a policy would be suicidal. He must look outside his own business for fields of profitable investment for his profits . . . Thus the profits arising from specific monopolies are logically forced into the more general regions of finance. They form a large and growing fund of free capital which naturally associates itself with the free funds held by bankers.

CHAPTER 2
Forging the Monopoly Group System in Gold

EARLY TRANSFORMATIONS IN CAPITALIST RELATIONS

The formation of an international gold standard in 1816 to regulate exchange relations on a world scale formally established gold's role as the money-commodity. As European capitalism expanded during the mid-nineteenth century, so the demand for gold increased, encouraging the growth of prospecting activities. Many of these prospectors made their way to southern Africa and before too long the first discoveries of gold deposits were reported in the South African Republic: near the Olifants River in 1868; near Pietersburg and in the Murchison Range in 1870; near Sabie in 1872; and in the Barberton District in 1875. By 1883 the value of Transvaal gold production stood at a modest £30 457.[1]

These relatively small finds were supplemented by others, such as the discovery of the rich Sheba Reef at Barberton in 1885. But it was in 1886 that the main gold-bearing reef of the Witwatersrand was discovered. Geological conditions on this new field were substantially different from those on the other South African gold fields. Previously, gold had been found usually in relatively rich nuggets or in alluvial deposits and where an underground reef was discovered, such as at Barberton, it was uneven, patchy and contorted. On the Witwatersrand, however, gold was present in hard conglomerate beds known as 'banket', which were unique in that they ran in relatively long and unbroken sequence. At certain points the reef reached the surface of the earth and it was these 'outcrops' which were first discovered and mined with the use of picks, shovels and pans by the early prospectors and diggers. The discovery made very soon after digging had commenced that the reefs dipped steeply downwards—that the 'outcrop' was in fact only the top extremity of the beds—saw the start of shaft-sinking to find and reach the gold-bearing rock. The new shaft-sinking operations were to usher in a period of revolutionary change in the method of gold mining production on the Witwatersrand.

When the gold fields were first proclaimed in 1886 there were some

3000 people active in the area, most of whom were prospectors who worked 'with a view to selling claims at enhanced prices' (Letcher, 1936, p. 80). In most cases mining was carried on by a lone digger employing two or three Africans to help crush and wash the gold-bearing rock: picks, shovels, pans and a stamp (to crush the ore) were the most common tools in use on the fields. At that stage shaft-sinking was still in its infancy: by the end of the year only four shafts had been sunk to any significant depth, three small mills were in operation and arrangements were under way to erect two more (Letcher, 1936, p. 80). The method of production on the gold fields and the form of labour process were in general not dissimilar from those on the diamond fields at Kimberley between 1867 and 1873. Again, as on the diamond fields, political relations were organized through a Diggers' Committee. Yet the Gold Law enacted in July 1886 by the Volksraad (Legislative Assembly) of the South African Republic contained a number of paragraphs which ensured that the phase of independent 'non-racial' petty-bourgeois production would be short-lived on the gold fields. Paragraph 39 effectively incorporated the Diggers' Committee under the overall control of the state, thus denying it the form of independence which had initially prevailed at Kimberley. Paragraph 61 introduced a formal racial stratification in gold mining whereby the owners of the means of production were to be exclusively white and 'non-whites' were tolerated on the fields only if they were 'in the service of white men'. But most important of all from the point of view of large capital was the stipulation that any 'European', on payment of license fees, could acquire any number of claims (see Houghton and Dagut, 1972, vol. II, p. 15). The process of amalgamation on the gold fields could not be hampered as it had been initially in Kimberley by legal restrictions and consequently petty-bourgeois relations of production were to disappear on the Witwatersrand even more rapidly than had been the case in Kimberley.

In July 1886—before the gold fields had even been proclaimed—a piece of gold-bearing ore was taken to Kimberley and exhibited before a group of leading diamond magnates (they included Rhodes, Rudd, Beit, Eckstein and Robinson). Within a week most of these gentlemen were on the Rand inspecting the fields and busily buying up farms throughout the area. Within a few months Rhodes was proposing to some of the other magnates with whom he was associated that they should amalgamate the claims and interests which they had acquired. In 1887 the first London-registered South African gold mining–finance house, the Gold Fields of South Africa Ltd, was formed with an initial capital of £125 000 out of the amalgamated claims of Rhodes, Rudd and Caldecott.

Thus while conditions of competition similar to those which had prevailed in Kimberley in the late 1860s also characterized the earliest period of Witwatersrand gold production, the important difference between the two was that monopoly capital, personified by the diamond magnates, was introduced to the Rand from the very beginning. This did not of course mean that competition disappeared from the fields: on the contrary, it continued on a larger and often more vicious scale as monopoly capitalists sought to out-manoeuvre each other to gain possession of the richest areas on the fields. What it did mean though was that *petty-bourgeois* relations of competition had virtually disappeared. Consequently, the Witwatersrand gold fields came to be dominated, almost from their inception, by monopoly forms of capitalist relations. Thus the organizational form of the dominant unit of production on the gold fields rapidly passed from that of the individual digger to that of the mining-finance house: following the formation of Rhodes's Gold Fields Company, the house of Eckstein was formed in 1887, as was the house of G. and L. Albu, the house of Wernher and Beit, the house of Messrs Ad. Goerz; while Barnato formed Johannesburg Consolidated Investments (JCI) in 1889. These houses were essentially the organizational forms through which the diamond magnates secured the necessary financial support from Europe to buy up as much of the potentially gold-bearing ground as they could. It was a period of cut-throat competition characterized largely by speculative investment as capitalists vied with one another to gain access to, and control over, the potential gold-bearing ground rather than a period of large-scale exploitation of the fields. However, the form which that exploitation was to take would be conditioned by the relations of monopoly capitalism established in this period.

Although it was established relatively quickly that the gold-bearing reef extended down into the earth, there was no certainty as to how far the beds extended nor as to how rich they were. The first task for the mining houses was to find answers to these questions. Consequently, shaft-sinking operations proliferated under the control of the mining houses, ushering in a revolution in the method of production. Picks and shovels gave way to mechanized forms of production: shafts were erected and equipped with haulage gear for sinking and driving tunnels underground; pumping machinery was brought into operation; and machine-crushers were used to crush the greater quantities of ore produced (see Glanville, 1888; Noble, 1892, pp. 500–3; Letcher, 1936, pp. 95–7). Mechanization brought with it soaring levels of production: output rose from 254 kg of fine gold in 1886 to 1240 in 1887, 7084 in 1888 and 10 915 in 1889. (See Table 2.) Mechanization also brought with it the further centralization of capital and concentration of production on the Rand and with it came the potential for sinking ever deeper shafts. In 1892 the mining houses found the answer to their first question when a diamond drill borehole was sunk 2343 ft (714 m) into the earth's crust at which point it intersected the conglomerate beds of

Witwatersrand banket. The Main Reef had been 'proved': subterra-
nean deposits of gold were now known both to be abundant and also to
persist to great depths. The industry's evolution had entered a new
phase.

Yet the waves of optimism that this, and subsequent intersections at
even greater depths, generated on the international capital markets
were subdued by other reports to emerge from these borehole
findings: these were that the gold-bearing rock of the Witwatersrand
was of a particularly *low-grade* quality.[2] Thus while the period of investigation of the long-term gold mining potential of the Witwatersrand
had been successfully concluded (in that the abundance of the Reef had
been established), the accomplishment of the next stage—that is, the
profitable exploitation of the field on the basis of generalized deep level
underground mining methods—was hardly likely to be a simple undertaking. While every capitalist is faced with the problem of how to
reduce costs to their utmost in order to maximize profits, the specific
conditions of the gold mining industry in the South African Republic in
the early 1890s meant that this problem took a particularly severe
form. Not only were these problems of a geological and technical kind,
but they were also critically related to questions of labour supply and
control as well as to the overall structure of the industry and its inser-
tion in a specific political and social milieu.

GOLD MINING COSTS AND THE EVOLUTION OF THE GROUP SYSTEM

The establishment of the international gold standard as the means by
which currency exchange values could become accurately known in
terms of one another meant that Britain, as the world's leading economic and political power, bought up all the gold which was offered for
sale on the international market at a fixed price. The importance of this
cannot be over-emphasized since it implied a condition which applied
to no other commodity: that is, that there was an *unlimited market* for
gold as the money-commodity. The unique role which gold played in
the international monetary system thus afforded it certain special 'attri-
butes' which differentiated it from other commodities and which influenced the form of development of the industry as a whole. This
influence was felt not only in the special form of the marketing system
which evolved, but also in the specific form of the production relations.

The specific nature of the international market for gold had contradictory implications for the future development of the industry. On
the one hand, conditions of an unlimited market at a fixed price meant
that the gold industry would not be hampered as others, and especially
the diamond industry, had been by market fluctuations and restrictions: the market for gold was unlimited and therefore the threat of

over-production did not exist, while the existence of a fixed price meant that capitalists could plan production on the basis of assured returns on the sale of the commodity.[3] On the other hand, a fixed price meant that if costs rose capitalists were unable to transfer the cost rise to the price of the commodity and profits sank accordingly. In other words, under these special marketing conditions the cost restraint made itself felt more directly and acutely than in other industries.

This restraint assumes special significance when the long lifespans of the mines are taken into consideration. With a fixed price for gold severe cost inflation in the industry over time can lead to mines being forced to close down even though substantial deposits of gold still remain underground, since it is no longer profitable for the company to go on producing. The so-called 'physical' limitations to gold production are in fact socially determined: that is, when we read that the gold fields are 'drying up' this does not mean, as is often supposed, that there is no gold left underground, but rather that a point is being reached at which it may no longer be profitable to go on producing it. This point is known in mining circles as the pay limit—the minimum limit at which ore can be profitably mined. The lower the pay limit, the more ore becomes available in the reserves for profitable production and the longer the mine's lifespan; conversely, the higher the pay limit, the less ore is available in reserves and the shorter the life of the mine. Thus if costs are kept low the pay limit will be low and there will be a greater potential for long-term profitability. But if costs rise substantially during the mine's lifetime, capitalists who have foregone quick returns on their investments will find themselves denied their longer-term 'rewards' as well.

The significance of these conditions is that they emphasize how important it is for capitalists to be able to secure and maintain a low cost structure in the gold mining industry. The next question, then, is: what were the most important elements in the cost structure of the industry and how could these best be regulated or controlled?

Gold mining costs in fact fall into two main categories: expenditure on *labour* and on *stores and equipment*. Establishing a 'deep level' gold mine of course requires considerable capital expenditure on the latter item, since in the initial stages shaft-sinking equipment has to be erected, as well as the gold milling and extraction plant and housing, offices and other infrastructure. It is only then that underground 'development'—that is, shaft-sinking and tunnelling to open up bodies of gold-bearing reef—and organized production proper commences in the form of 'stoping'. It is at this latter stage of a mine's life that its cost structure will come to reflect the relation between expenditure on stores and equipment on the one hand and labour on the other which will characterize the period of actual production itself. During this phase labour is by far the largest component of total costs. This was particularly true for the first two decades of the industry's life when expenditure on labour accounted for approximately 60 per cent of the industry's total costs.[4] Since expenditure on labour was such an important element in the cost structure, capitalists could be expected to look to the question of determination of the price for labour-power as the sphere in which the greatest relief from the cost constraint could be gained. It was, as we shall see, this question which dominated relations within gold mining during the last decade of the nineteenth century— that is, during the period in which 'deep level' underground mining was organized on a systematic scale throughout the Witwatersrand.

The specific problem facing the mine-owners at this time was how to secure a sufficiently large labour force to exploit the known quantities of ore without provoking a massive wage explosion. Here again, geological conditions—that is, the very low grade of the ore—meant that a large volume of ore had to be removed from the earth in order to extract a relatively minute quantity of gold.[5] These conditions led, in the period prior to the 'proving' of the field, to a demand on the one hand for a relatively large supply of cheap labour whose main productive function was to remove the gold-bearing ore and waste rock, transport it to the surface and crush the ore—that is, to engage, as we shall see, in unskilled menial labour—and, on the other, for a much smaller component of skilled labour to operate and maintain the machinery and supervise the unskilled workers. This relatively more skilled group of workers was drawn essentially from overseas and consisted, in the main, of experienced miners already in possession of various skills who demanded relatively high wages. Development of the underground mines on the basis of a highly mechanized method of production would inevitably lead to an increase in the demand for this kind of expensive labour and would contribute to a rising cost structure in the industry. However, developing the mines on the basis of a more labour-intensive method of production would only be possible if a large supply of cheap labour could be obtained to carry out the unskilled work.

We have already seen how the phase of military conquest (from 1865 to the end of the nineteenth century) led to a marked increase in the numbers of migrant workers who made their way from the African reserves to the centres of capitalist production. The commencement of gold production in the Transvaal, with its growing appetite for labour, was to add yet another focal point to which migrants were drawn as the process of impoverishment in the reserves intensified. However, this flow of labour was neither large nor fast enough to satisfy the needs of the gold mining industry after the discovery of the Witwatersrand reef and the transition to 'deep level' underground mining. From as far back as the 1850s the Natal colony had been making use of African migrant labour from the Delagoa Bay area in the Portuguese colony of

Mozambique and a regular flow of migrant workers had been established. Now with the commencement of gold production in the
Transvaal many of these migrants began to move down to the gold
mines and by 1890 there were 8750 Mozambicans employed on the
gold mines of the Rand out of a total of 15 000 African workers.[6]

Commenting on this phenomenon, Sir Percy Fitzpatrick remarked
that 'the Portuguese East Coast has been the salvation of the Rand'.[7]
This was true in a double sense: first, in that Mozambique supplied the
majority of the African labour force on the Rand mines (approximately
58 per cent of the total) in the early years of deep level mining; and
second, in that the existence of this absolute surplus-population within Mozambique made it possible for capitalists to develop the gold
mines on the basis of labour-intensive methods of production. Thus,
not only the development of the gold mining industry of the Rand, but,
more specifically, the development of the gold mining industry on the
basis of a labour-intensive method of production has its origins in the
creation of this absolute surplus-population and its capacity for absorp-
tion by the industry. 'Foreign' sources of African labour supply have
thus exerted a critical influence on the industry from its inception.

By 1890 then a system of labour supply had emerged on the gold
fields which was based essentially on the exploitation of an army of
unskilled African migrant workers. However, as had been the case in
diamonds, conditions of labour shortage persisted as the industry expanded. This phenomenon was worsened considerably by the growth
of other economic sectors competing for labour (especially coal mining
in Natal, farm production and the expansion of infrastructure). African
migrants quickly utilized these 'favourable' conditions to press for wage
increases on the gold mines, a development which led to escalating
wage rates on the Rand gold mines: wage rates of 63s. per month for
Africans on the gold mines of the Witwatersrand in October 1890
compared with 33s. per month on the Barberton mines, 27s. at Pil-
grim's Rest and around 20s. per month on the farms at that time
(Harries, 1976, p. 64). Mining capitalists reacted with alarm to this
situation as it posed a serious threat to the industry's low cost structure
and, consequently, to the whole rationale for basing the industry's
development upon African migrant labour. The result of this alarm was
the combination in 1889 of the most important gold mining interests on
the Rand under the umbrella of the Witwatersrand Chamber of
Mines.[8]

Although a Diggers' Committee representing gold producers had
been formed as early as 1886, the Chamber of Mines was a very different form of producers' organization. It was in a very real sense an
integral part of the *monopoly* relations which had been established on
the Rand and as such bore little relation to the earlier Diggers' Committee which was essentially a product of petty-bourgeois relations of

production. Initially, the Chamber underwent a number of 'teething troubles': for a start, one of the most important mining-finance houses on the Rand, J. B. Robinson and Co., refused to join;[9] secondly, the Chamber's initial attempts at tackling the question of escalating African wage rates—the prime reason for its formation—failed dismally. Following its establishment, the Chamber immediately reduced the African wage rate from 63*s*. to 44*s*. a month, which led to an immediate and substantial decline in the total number of African workers on the mines—from about 15 000 in 1890 to 12 500 in 1891 (the Mozambican section of the labour force declined from 8750 to 7000).[10] Faced with this expression of African workers' resistance (probably the first case of a large-scale withholding of African labour on the gold fields), the Chamber had little option but to acknowledge defeat and to abandon its earlier wage determination. The effect was immediate: as wages rose so African migrants, predominantly Mozambicans, returned to the mines—by 1893 the total African labour force on the mines stood at 29 000, of whom probably about 75 per cent were Mozambicans (between 19 500 and 22 100).[11]

Although the Chamber's first salvo against African workers had ended in its defeat, it began over the following years to develop a more systematic approach to the question of African labour, which in the end was to secure the conditions for the expanded reproduction of capitalism through the industry. This development was exemplified in the establishment in 1893 of a Native Labour Department with a mandate to 'systematically organize the native labour supply' and to 'tackle the native problem, and endeavour, while lowering the rate of native wages, to secure an ample supply of labour'. However, these changes, and the gradual consolidation of the Chamber itself, were occurring under new conditions, different to those which had prevailed in 1889.[12] In particular, the rapid expansion of 'deep level' mining in the early 1890s and the 'proving' of the Witwatersrand field in 1892 had made conditions for combination far more favourable in the industry. Before proceeding with our analysis of the Chamber's role in the struggle against African migrants we need to examine the implications of these changing conditions, and especially of the group system itself, for the future of organized collusion among capitalists in the industry.

The importance of 'proving' the field in 1892 was that it established both that the industry had a potentially long-term future and that, given the low-grade quality of the gold-bearing rock, it would require a particularly low and tightly controlled cost structure to maintain profitability over the long term. It was through the establishment and subsequent development of the group system that the mine-owners were able to realize these dual goals. Henry Clay has succinctly summarized the benefits which this system brought to capitalists in the industry:

The Gold Mining Industry may claim to provide a working model of a 'rationalized' industry. Through the group system of control of separate mining companies and the close co-operation of the whole industry through the Chamber of Mines and its subsidiary services, it has substituted for the blind selection by competition of the fittest to survive, a conscious and deliberate choice of methods, equipment, areas and personnel on the basis of an extremely detailed comparative study of results . . . (Cited in Frankel, 1938, pp. 81–2)

But how was it possible for capitalists in the gold mining industry to carry through this transformation? It is of course true that the evolution of conditions of monopoly capitalism in the industry imply the transformation of competition into its opposite, monopoly, thereby providing the objective basis for collusion among different capitalist groupings. But this argument, though correctly identifying an important general tendency within monopoly capital, does not explain why these changes took the specific form of the group system. As Clay himself points out, in the British coal mining industry at that time there were over 1000 separate units of production, compared with 33 on the Rand. Clearly, the conditions under which capitalists had to organize production on the Rand were critical determinants: here we can mention especially the large outlays of capital expenditure on machinery and equipment which were necessitated by the need to organize deep level underground production over a long period as well as the need to secure a vast army of labourers at low cost. But while these conditions imposed on capitalists the necessity to exert a rigid and tight control over the industry, they do not completely explain why that control took the form of the group system. For the key to answering that question we have to return to our argument concerning the unique marketing structure of the industry.

The unique function which gold fulfilled as the money-commodity at this time meant that, unlike any other commodity, there was an unlimited market for gold. This factor in turn reduced the role which competition played in the industry, since capitalists did not need to vie with each other to hold on to or increase their respective shares of the market. Of course, this did not mean that competition was totally absent from the industry: competition made its presence felt particularly in the attempts to secure access to gold-bearing ground as well as in the manoeuvrings over scarce labour resources. The point, though, is that the reduction in influence of competition in production meant that the monopoly tendency towards 'collusion' became the dominant factor in determining the form of organization of capitalist production of gold—that is, in determining the evolution of the group system.

The precursor of the group system was the mining-finance house or joint-stock company. Although a large number of financial, property, prospecting and mining companies operated on the Rand at this time,[13] it was a mere handful of these which gradually came to dominate the gold fields. Although these mining-finance houses were all separate companies, each with its own board of directors, relations between the capitalists who controlled them were already relatively close, especially since most of them were, in one way or another, involved together in the diamond industry through the single organization of De Beers Consolidated. But it was the specific relations of production and marketing in the gold industry which provided the conditions for the close collusion and high degree of inter-penetration of capital which came to characterize this branch of the industry over the next few years. Unlike the diamond industry in which the existence of diamonds underground did not necessarily mean that capitalists could embark immediately upon maximum exploitation of the fields (on the contrary, the dangers posed by over-production led, as we saw, to limitations being placed on production), in the gold industry the unlimited market meant that maximum exploitation of existing resources was immediately possible. Consequently, the only limitations imposed on capitalists were those of finding sufficient capital to finance production, securing a sufficient supply of low-cost labour-power and maintaining a low cost structure overall.

Existing resources of capital under the control of the capitalists on the gold fields were inadequate for the large-scale development of the deep level mines and needed to be supplemented by capital drawn from the capital markets of Europe.[14] Consequently, investment in gold mining had to be made as attractive as possible to the overseas investor which meant, in the final analysis, promising high returns at low risk. The former could be achieved through maintaining a low cost structure and the latter through spreading the risk over a number of ventures. The group system emerged as the organizational form through which both of these objectives could be achieved. By merging a number of mining-finance houses together into distinctive 'groups' and thus bringing a large number of producing mines (sometimes as many as sixteen) under a single control, the Rand capitalists were able to spread the risks of investment in mining considerably. (It should be borne in mind that not only is investment in the early stages of a mine's life a highly speculative venture since little is known of the conditions to be encountered in practice underground, but in addition it involves a considerable period of time—at least two years in those days—before any returns are earned and, consequently, only a relatively tiny sector of the 'investing public' was at that time able to afford investments in the industry.) Furthermore, the group system made it possible for these newly created giant companies to diversify their investments into other industries, and indeed other countries, thereby spreading the risk even further.

The group system also met the second requirement of being a suitable organizational form through which a low cost-structure could be imposed on the gold mining industry. As Ernest Oppenheimer put it in 1930:

> Where, as in the case on the Rand, there are many companies whose properties adjoin or are adjacent to one another, all engaged in the same class of work, the existence of a central organization for the supply of expert advice and information on matters of common interest, is clearly of incalculable value. It certainly ensures the companies great economies . . . (Cited in Gregory, 1962)

Through the group system a single centre was established for the provision of those technical and administrative facilities which comprised the common necessities of a group of producing units, thus supplanting a system according to which each producer had to find and pay for its own necessities. This increased the possibility of not only achieving greater economies of scale (through buying stores in bulk for instance) but also achieving technical breakthroughs (through the pooling of scientific and technical skills and resources), thereby lowering the cost-structure and literally prolonging the industry's lifespan.

The initiation of deep level underground mining on a large scale throughout the industry was accompanied therefore by important transformations in the organizational and institutional form of monopoly capital on the Rand as the mining houses gave way to the system of groups. One by one, the various mining houses merged with one another, taking over smaller companies in the process, until they had been more or less completely replaced by the giant groups. In 1892 the Gold Fields Co. was transformed into Consolidated Gold Fields of South Africa Ltd; the House of Eckstein gave rise in 1893 to the Rand Mines Ltd; in 1895 General Mining emerged out of the House of G. and L. Albu; the House of Wernher Beit expanded considerably at this time, changing its name to Central Mining in 1905; and Messrs Ad. Goerz and Co. became Union Corporation in 1918.[15] Though it did not change its name, Johannesburg Consolidated Investments Ltd underwent a similar path of development. These six groups, whose expansion in every case was based on the transition to deep level forms of production, thus emerged during the 1890s to dominate the entire field of gold mining operations on the Rand, though a number of smaller groups (such as Lewis and Marks, J. B. Robinson and Co., Abe Bailey and Co. and Transvaal Mining) also functioned effectively. Furthermore, one of these six, Wernher Beit and Co. (subsequently Central Mining), emerged as the most powerful of the groups in effective control of Rand Mines,[16] and closely associated with Consolidated Gold Fields and some of the smaller groups.

Before moving on to an analysis of the extension of the group system through the transformation of the Chamber of Mines, it would be useful to comment briefly on the relations of control within the group. The merging together of a number of mining-finance houses, each controlling their own mining, exploration and prospecting companies, resulted in a single mining-finance company emerging as the 'parent' concern in the group. The 'parent' company did not itself participate directly in the actual search for and production of gold—this was the exclusive concern of the 'subordinate' mining and prospecting companies—but instead saw to the financial requirements of its member companies, either raising capital for them or providing the capital itself, as well as centralizing their administrative and technological requirements. In the early days of gold mining each 'parent' company usually had two boards of directors, one in London and one in the Transvaal. Control over the 'parent', and thus over the group as a whole, was exercised through the standard procedure of a majority shareholding in the company, reflected in a majority of seats on the London board of the company. However, the relations of control *within* the group were not as straightforward, since the 'parent' company virtually never held a majority shareholding in its member concerns.

When a group's prospecting companies confirmed a gold find the decision of whether or not to float a mining company rested, and still rests, with the 'parent' concern. If the decision is positive then the 'parent' applies to the government for a lease to mine the area, which is inevitably granted. The 'parent' company then concerns itself with arrangements for the provision of finance for the mining company being formed, as well as seeing to the appointment of the technical and administrative staff: mine managers, consulting engineers, buyers, secretaries and so on. It is at this point that control is exerted, for the 'parent' company has the right, which it almost invariably exercises, to delegate members of its own staff to carry out these functions. Hence it is through the managerial, engineering, secretarial and other contracts which it receives from the newly formed mining company—or, more precisely, through the contracts which it awards to itself—that it secures a *monopoly over information* in the new mine which enables it to exercise control over the subsequent planning, development, operation and management of the mine. Of course, in addition to securing these contracts for itself, the 'parent' will have a substantial minority shareholding in the new company and so will be well represented on the mine's board. But the important point is that, in view of the system of awarding contracts, it is not necessary for the 'parent' company to have a majority shareholding in order to exercise effective control, which therefore helps to keep the 'parent' liquid to finance further exploration and development projects. The bulk of the remainder of the new company's shares will then usually be taken up by some or all of the other groups, leaving a minority proportion for 'public' consumption. In this way the group system has enabled a handful of large companies to dominate the gold fields since, through their monopoly over information, they have been able to secure the most profitable mines for themselves, leaving the remainder for 'public' consumption (and for consumption by companies outside the oligarchical network).

This restructuring of the organizational form of monopoly capital on the Rand thus implied important changes in the financial, technical and control relations of the industry. Yet these organizational changes did not just affect the form of the dominant capitalist units of production on the Rand, the groups, they also affected the form of the organizational relations between them. That is, the evolution of the group system at this time also implied important changes in the Chamber of Mines as the institutional expression of the combination of particular capitals 'for fighting purposes in politics and economics' (Hobson, 1900).

THE CHAMBER OF MINES, THE STATE AND THE ASSAULT ON LABOUR

The three problems which had to be overcome to secure maximum exploitation of the gold fields were: to find sufficient capital to finance production; to secure a sufficient supply of low-cost labour-power; and to maintain a low cost structure overall. We have seen how the group system evolved as the means by which capitalists overcame the first of these—that is, as the means by which they were best able to attract capital to the Rand to finance production. We turn now to an examination of the means by which capitalists sought to overcome the latter problems. It should be stressed that we are primarily concerned with the problems posed by the need to secure a sufficient supply of low-cost labour-power since, as we have argued, it was only on the basis of successfully overcoming this limitation that profitable exploitation of the fields would be assured. In this sense, although the evolution of the group system as an organizational form pre-dates the 'resolution' of the labour question, this latter question none the less required 'resolution' before the group system could consolidate itself on the Rand.

Commenting on the evolution of the gold mining industry in its first few decades of existence, Gregory (1962) wrote:

> The group system itself has undergone a steady process of integration, in as much as the number of groups has declined, their scope has become larger and their interrelations have become closer. Moreover, with the steady increase in the power of the State and the complexity of the problems which the mining industry has had to face in the field of labour relations, legislation, monetary policy, etc., the significance of the Chamber of Mines, as the representative and consultative body of the industry, has also grown.

Just as the groups arose to centralize production and administration among a number of producing units, so the Chamber of Mines arose to co-ordinate relations among the groups and as such represented the highest organizational expression of the monopoly tendency of *collusion* on the Rand. Yet, as we shall see, the successful maintenance of collusion among the groups depended on overcoming working-class resistance to the domination of monopoly capital, for it was that resistance which generated competitive tendencies among the groups threatening to disrupt capitalist domination on the Rand. In fact, the process of integration of the group system, to which Gregory refers, was far from being as 'steady' in its development as he suggests. Rather, it was achieved only through a process of intense struggle and as such was characterized by severe upheavals and significant restructuring of the capital relation. It was only by the end of the first decade of the twentieth century, after the black working class in particular had suffered a number of important defeats at the hands of capitalists and the state, that integration was successfully secured and the group system under the leadership of the Chamber firmly established.

We have seen how the transition to deep level underground mining immediately generated a demand for labour on an unprecedented scale in South Africa and how, subsequently, wages soared on the gold fields. In response to this situation the various groups had combined to form the Chamber of Mines, whose first act was to try and force down African wages. Although black workers' resistance (through the withholding of their labour-power) forced the capitalists to abandon their wage determination, which in turn immediately produced an upward drift in wages, they did not abandon the organization that they had established (the Chamber of Mines) to defend their combined interests.

The contradiction which this early failure emphasized was that it was not possible for the mine-owners to control the price of African labour-power unless the supply could also be controlled. In fact at the same time as mining capitalists were formulating plans through the Chamber for a direct assault on wage rates, they were also appealing to the state for support in securing control over the supply of labour to the mines. In 1890 the Chamber wrote to the Kruger government that: 'Private enterprise has repeatedly failed in attempting to organize and maintain an adequate supply of Kaffirs. The task must be undertaken by the public authorities, and the Chamber trusts that the Government will lend it their indispensable assistance.'[17] Although the government replaced the old Gold Laws of the 1880s with formal mining regulations in 1891, they did nothing to respond to the capitalists' plea for measures to control the supply of labour. What the mine-owners specifically sought from the state was participation by government officials in the recruitment drives in the rural areas; more stringent application of the Pass Law; an end to the activities of labour touts *en route* to the mines; and the establishment of depots along the main routes to shelter migrant workers. The state's refusal to intercede on the mine-owners' behalf led the latter to take matters into their own hands: in 1893 the Chamber established its own Native Labour Department to 'systematically organize the native supply'.

The resistance posed by black workers, however, exposed a major weakness in the mine-owners' position: that is, that the department lacked the means of *enforcing* a common policy on the industry as a whole. More than anything, this failure reflected the difficulties monopoly capital faced in integreating itself in the early years of its evolution. Although the organizational forms of such integration (or collusion) were emerging, monopoly capital was not yet sufficiently strong in relation to labour to enable its organizations to operate effectively. As black workers continued to resist enforced controls over their employment by deserting in large numbers in order to bargain for higher wages and better working conditions elsewhere, competition between capitalists again emerged with mine managers and their labour 'touts' seeking to outbid each other. The result was the upward drift of wages: by 1895 African wages varied between 40s. and 60s. a month, with skilled African drillers often earning as much as 70s. Furthermore, conditions had deteriorated to such an extent for the mine-owners that by that time no two mines operated with the same wage rate (van der Horst, 1942, p. 130).

The seriousness of these conditions for the mine-owners was eased initially by the boom in share prices which took place in Europe in 1894–5, enabling windfall profits to be earned on market transactions. However, the boom ultimately contributed to the crisis for it became apparent that as soon as the boom ended many of the marginal mines which had been floated at this time would be unable to continue profitable production unless a significant reduction in costs was achieved. These conditions, combined with the ill-fated Jameson Raid, eventually produced the collapse of the share market in 1896. There was no way in which capital could secure its position in the long run without an overall assault against the working class.

However, conditions at the time prevented mining capitalists from directing their attack against the *whole* of the working class on the mines. In particular, it was not desirable for them to try and secure a substantial reduction in the wage rates of white workers—despite the immense financial benefits such a course of action could bring them if successful.[18] First, the bulk of these white mine-workers came from Europe with a tradition of trade unionism and very quickly organized themselves into unions to defend their position. (For instance, the Witwatersrand Mine Employees' and Mechanics' Union was formed by workers from Cornwall, Lancashire and Scotland as early as 20 August 1892.) An attack on these workers meant an attack against *organized* labour which was not an attractive proposition from the capitalist point of view in the early years of monopoly organization in the industry. Secondly, white labour, with its attendant skills, was at that time concentrated in the construction and development side of mining (especially in the establishment of deep level mines) rather than in actual production itself. The strategic importance of their work in this sphere of mining—especially because of the time-lag which existed between flotation of a mine and commencement of production—placed these workers in a particularly strong bargaining position at this time. Finally, political factors—and in particular the capitalists' desire to cultivate the support of the 'Uitlanders' (many of whom were of course white miners) in their tussle with the Republican government—formed a further inducement to them to avoid a large-scale open confrontation with white workers at this time. (For instance, the mine-owners collaborated closely with the Transvaal National Union, which was formed in 1892 to campaign for equal franchise rights for all white men in the Transvaal.)[19]

But while these conditions mitigated against the mine-owners launching an overall attack against the whole of the working class, or indeed concentrating their attack on white workers, no such mitigating conditions existed in relation to African workers. On the contrary, the large-scale development of the gold mines on the basis of labour-intensive methods of production made it inevitable that the mine-owners would need to establish stringent controls over that section of the labour force which was to provide the overwhelming mass of labour-power for the mines.[20] These controls involved not only immediate questions such as organizing the channels of supply to the mines and securing control at the point of production, but on a far wider social scale they involved gaining conscious control over the process of proletarianization itself.

Once it became clear that the mines required a mass of labour-power on a scale far larger than hitherto envisaged, it became equally clear that the existing form of the migrant labour system was inadequate for these purposes. Although the process of conquest had increased the flow of migrants to both the diamond fields of the Cape and the gold mines of the Transvaal, large-scale labour-intensive gold mining required a *permanent reserve army of labour* from which it could draw its labour supply. The process of conquest, which had confined the bulk of the African population to tiny 'reserves' within South Africa, had created the political and economic conditions for the location of that proletariat in the rural areas rather than around the points of production themselves. These conditions provided a crude framework which was suitable for the development of monopoly capitalist relations of labour control: first, because they enabled the capitalist class to ease the political dangers inherent in the concentration of a massive proletarian army at the point of production; and second, because they provided the mine-owners with an ideological rationalization for a low-wage economic policy. However, in the 1890s these conditions were not adequate to meet the rising needs for labour-power. It was therefore in order to restructure and extend the social relations through which a permanent proletariat could be created and controlled in the rural areas that the mine-owners appealed to the state in the South African Republic. As we shall see, that form of state, corresponding to quasi-feudal/petty-bourgeois relations of production, proved inadequate to the task of restructuring those overall conditions on a basis that met the requirements of monopoly capital. It was only through the direct intervention of the imperialist state that the requirements of monopoly capital were finally met and the proletariat decisively defeated.

The first major attempt by mine-owners and the state to mount a combined assault against African labour came in the mid-1890s amid conditions of mounting crisis in the industry.[21] The first salvo in the attack was fired when the state passed the Pass Law of 1895. This act, which had actually been drawn up by the Native Labour Committee of the Chamber of Mines, was designed to increase the mine-owners' control over the movement of black workers, so as in particular to curb the high rate of desertion on the mines. Specifically, the law provided a rudimentary form of influx control in areas proclaimed as labour districts (which were invariably gold mining areas): Africans were prevented from seeking work in a labour district unless they were in possession of a District Pass and, on obtaining employment, were issued with an Employers' Pass (numbered metal arm badges were originally used); Africans without a pass were liable to arrest and it was an offence for employers to engage Africans without District Passes (van der Horst, 1942, pp. 133–4). (This law was supplemented by the Republic's original Pass Law as well as by the Master and Servants Act.) The next salvo in the attack came with the agreements reached within the Chamber of Mines in 1896 and 1897 to secure a reduction in African wage rates: black wages were cut by 30 per cent overall. However, this time the Chamber moved beyond simply reducing the actual monetary price of the wage and sought in addition to standardize both hours of work and rations supplied on the mines (by introducing agreed minimum hours of work and maximum rations) in order to try and prevent mine-owners from manipulating these competitively against one another. A further important area of the attack involved an extension in the Chamber's sphere of activities with the formation of the Rand Native Labour Association (NLA) at the end of 1896. This organization was intended to establish a monopsony over labour recruitment and as such was an essential element in the overall strategy to emasculate African workers.[22]

Thus by centralizing recruiting operations through the NLA the Chamber sought to establish the conditions for a further overall reduction in labour costs, both by extending the catchment area from which black labour could be drawn (thereby increasing the size of its reservoir of labour-power so as to undermine the bargaining position of black workers) and, at the same time, by eliminating 'touts' and other middlemen and centralizing administration. However, such a system of control over recruitment would be ineffective unless labour could simultaneously be disciplined at the point of production. Thus the success of the NLA depended as much on the state's ability to prevent desertions through effective application of the Pass Law as it did on the ability of the Chamber to organize effective recruiting machinery. Similarly, the Chamber's chances of maintaining its recent wage determination were critically dependent upon black workers being prevented, again through state administration of the Pass Law, from leaving the mines before their contracts had expired.

Despite the varied array of legislative, industrial and organizational machinery which the mine-owners and the state amassed against black workers, the latter refused to be cowed, resorting again to the strategy of withdrawing labour-power. Following the 1897 wage reductions the Secretary of the Chamber of Mines reported that: 'consequent on this action, a rather greater number of Natives than usual are leaving the Rand'. By June 1899 the black labour shortage was estimated to be as high as 12 000, despite efforts by the NLA to recruit labour from as far afield as Sierra Leone, the Gold Coast and Liberia (Hobson, 1900). Under these kinds of pressure, competitive tendencies reasserted themselves among capitalists and overall wage rates began to rise (van der Horst, 1942, p. 131). Capitalists had no hesitation in apportioning the blame for these conditions on the state's failure to prevent the withdrawal of labour-power by black workers. Jennings outlined the mine-owner's case before the Industrial Commission of Inquiry:

> We have a most excellent law, namely the Pass Law, which should enable us to obtain complete control over the kafirs. As at present administered, the Pass Law gives us no such protection . . . As the matter now stands, we import kafirs who sign a contract to serve us for twelve months; many leave after a couple of weeks, and it is impossible to recover them.

The state's failure to effectively carry through its share of the assault was crucial in undermining the success of the whole strategy. The shortage of labour at the point of production, which was engendered by the state's failure to prevent black workers from withdrawing their labour-power, not only affected conditions on the mines themselves but also undermined the recruiting activities of the NLA in the rural areas.[23] The NLA failed both in its efforts to centralize recruiting operations and to secure a monopsony over recruiting (though it had a certain success in Mozambique).

Though the state appointed an Industrial Commission of Inquiry to investigate the grievances of the mine-owners in 1897 and though the government-controlled newspaper continued to express a certain sympathy with the mine-owners' position, the manifest failure of the state to actually meet the requirements laid down by monopoly capital and expressed through the demands of the mine-owners resulted in the initial frustrations of the mining capitalists turning into open hostility. As Hammond put it to Consolidated Gold Fields: 'With good government there should be an abundance of labour, and with an abundance of labour there will be no difficulty in cutting down wages . . . ' (cited in van der Horst, 1942, p. 11). The war clouds which built up and eventually erupted in 1899 thus had their origins in the contradiction between the political requirements of monopoly capital for an effective system of labour control and the capacity (or rather, incapacity) of a quasi-feudal/petty-bourgeois form of state to meet those requirements.

Although production on the gold fields virtually ground to a halt during the war, in 1900—even before the war was over—the Chamber of Mines put forward a request that the new British administration should take over responsibility for black labour recruitment for the gold mines. Although the regime refused this specific request, it did set about reforming the Pass Laws and securing their more effective administration, authorizing municipalities to segregate Africans in locations and hiring out convict labour to the mines. The 1902 survey, 'The Gold Mines of the World', jubilantly proclaimed:

> Because of the new Government there can now be an organized labour supply all over South Africa . . . there will be an efficient pass-law *(sic)*, ensuring no loss to the mines by desertion: there will be no premiums except of official agents: the sale of liquor will be regulated, or stopped: the natives will work on a longer contract . . . it will be possible to reintroduce hand labour in stoping instead of rock drills, and the mines will be bound down not to outbid each other for workers as in the past.

This jubilation expressed itself most profoundly on the stock exchange: the gold boom which followed the close of the war saw 299 new gold mining companies floated on the Rand (van der Horst, 1942, p. 162).

However, it is important to exercise caution in interpreting the relationship between the mine-owners and the 'new' state in the post-war period. Certainly it was true that the capacity of the imperialist form of state to carry through a major assault on black labour corresponded more closely with the requirements of monopoly capital than had been the case with the Republican government before the war; but does this mean, as Hobson argued it would, that 'the mining magnates . . . rule the Transvaal'? The answer to that, and any similar crudely economistic formulations, must be a decisive 'no!' If we were to adopt such a position, then we would be unable to explain certain important measures adopted by the new Transvaal administration which were bitterly resented by mining capitalists on the Rand: such as the increase (above prewar levels) of direct taxation on mining revenues; the increase from 5 to 10 per cent of the Republican profits tax (legislated in 1898, it had never actually been collected under the Kruger regime); the extension of the municipal boundaries of Johannesburg which rendered the residential property of many mines liable to local rates; and the establishment of an inspectorate in the Native Affairs Department to police living and working conditions for labour on the mines.

The purpose of the imperialist state's intervention through the war was not simply to provide the conditions within which mine-owners could earn easy profits, but more fundamentally to secure the conditions within which the expansion of capitalist relations could be facilitated throughout southern Africa as a whole. While this expansion would inevitably be based largely on the mining industry, thereby making preservation of capital's interests in this industry a primary concern of the state, it did involve promoting other sectors of the economy as well: in particular, it involved the provision of large-scale stimulants to agriculture, given the ravaged state of agriculture in the two Boer republics after the war. Furthermore, precisely because the mining industry was to provide the backbone of capitalist expansion, it was inevitable that the state would seek to secure the bulk of its revenue from that source.

The measures referred to above, such as reform and effective administration of the Pass Laws, segregation of Africans into locations and hiring out convict labour, were clearly introduced by the state to assist the mine-owners in their struggle to break the back of the resistance being waged by black workers. In addition other measures, such as modifications to the Master and Servants Act and the Liquor Law (which forbade the sale of liquor to Africans), were introduced in an effort to curb the desertion rate on the Rand. It is important to note, though, that most of these measures were *modifications* of the pre-existing legal and administrative machinery and had in fact originally been introduced by the Republican government. In no case did they reflect a fundamental breach with previous attempts to control labour. The point is worth repeating that the failure of the previous state lay not in its failure to *establish* the necessary machinery for labour control, but rather in its failure to *administer* it effectively.

However, not all of the new measures were to the liking of all the mine-owners. In particular, the establishment of an inspectorate in the Native Affairs Department to police conditions on the mines caused considerable resentment among some mine-owners and provides an important illustration of the way in which the capitalist state can act to curb the 'excesses' of particular capitalists in order to further the interests of the capitalist class as a whole. It had long been apparent that the appalling working and living conditions of Africans on the mines were a major cause of the high desertion rate.[24] However, because of their perception of Africans as no more than the embodiment of the commodity, labour-power, capitalists were unwilling to spend a part of their wealth on improving these conditions—even though such improvements were in their longer-term interests. It was at this point—to secure the longer-term interests of the capitalist class itself—that the state intervened through the newly constituted inspectorate to press for reforms in the compound system. A degree of government control over compound managers was established through the requirement to hold government licences; mortality statistics and compound reports were compiled; and in 1905 a Coloured Labourers' Health Ordinance was enacted which prescribed minimum compound conditions as well as giving the state the legal power to enforce compliance. However, as has been pointed out, these measures were administered with extreme caution:

> . . . the department treated the mines with great leniency. They were given considerable time to carry out the improvements. They were assured that there would be no premature publicity. Low grade mines or mines nearing the end of their productive life were not required to effect improvements involving the expenditure of large capital sums. (Jeeves, 1975)

These measures, though unpopular with certain mine-owners, were thus not in any way designed to place serious impediments in the way of capital accumulation in the industry. Rather, they were designed to introduce more scientific and rational methods of control over African labour in order to secure the expanded reproduction of capitalism.

With the establishment by the state of a more effective discipline over the black labour force at the point of production, it was possible for the capitalists, through the Chamber, to return to the dual problems of reducing the wage rate and organizing the supply. In 1900 the Chamber established the Witwatersrand Native Labour Association (WNLA) to replace the earlier Rand Native Labour Association as a centralized recruiting agency. The regulations of WNLA were framed to give it monopsonistic powers over recruitment for the Rand: 'No Company, whilst a member of the Witwatersrand Native Labour Association, will be allowed under any circumstances to engage any but white labour, except through the agency of the Association.'[25] In July 1900 WNLA obtained an official monopsony over all recruitment within Mozambique from the colonial regime in that country and at the same time reduced the wage rate for African workers to a maximum of 35s. and a minimum of 30s. per month. (This compared with an average wage rate of 49s. 9d. for Africans in 1899.) The response of African workers was immediate: their numbers fell from a peak of 96 704 in 1899 to 42 587 in 1902 (a drop of 56 per cent) (van der Horst, 1942, pp. 164–5). Although the cut-back in mining operations imposed by the war must have accounted for a large part of this drop, nonetheless worker resistance also played a part, and in 1902 WNLA was forced to concede temporary defeat and wages were raised to a maximum of 50s. per month. Even at this new rate, strong resistance prevailed among black workers with the number employed rising to only 64 454 in 1903 (still a third lower than the number employed in 1899), so that during that year the wage rate was again raised to between 50s. and 60s. per month.[26]

The mine-owners' response to the crisis was again to turn to the state for support—and this time the new state was able to provide that support! The government immediately instituted measures designed both to overcome the short-term shortage of labour and to seek ways of 'resolving' the problem over the long term. The state had already arranged a *modus vivendi* with the colonial regime in Mozambique to secure access to the section of the reserve army located there and it now instituted the Transvaal Labour Commission, whose Majority Report found that there was 'no adequate supply of labour in Central and Southern Africa' to meet the labour requirements of the Transvaal. Although the possible use of 'European' labour in 'unskilled' grades of work was contemplated for a while, the campaign waged by the Chamber of Mines to overcome the shortage through the importation of Chinese labour eventually won the day when in 1904 the Transvaal Legislative Council authorized the importation of indentured Chinese labourers. The Chamber of Mines set up a special company, the Chamber of Mines Labour Importation Agency, to control the flow: between February 1904 and November 1906, 63 296 Chinese men were contracted and shipped to South Africa at an average cost of about 50s. a month plus food and quarters (Richardson, 1977, p. 86). By bringing in large quantities of labour-power from outside the existing catchment area of central and southern Africa, the size of the industrial reserve army was substantially increased, thus undermining the position of black workers. (Between June 1903 and January 1904 the African wage rate fell from 55s. per month to 51s. 11d.) It is primarily for this reason that the importation programme constituted such a significant attack on the resistance of black workers.[27]

While the importation of Chinese labour was designed to ease the short-term contradictions in the mining industry (output in fact regained prewar levels at 117 291 kg in 1904), the state established the South African Native Affairs Commission (1903–5) to investigate the 'native problem' over the longer term, so as to make recommendations for future 'native policy' in South Africa. The commission is important because its recommendations were subsequently to form the basis for the 1913 Native Lands Act. Essentially what it argued was:

> that certain restrictions upon the purchase of land by natives are necessary, and recommends: that purchase by natives should in future be limited to certain areas to be defined by legislative enactment; and that the purchase of land which may lead to tribal, communal or collective possession or occupation by natives should not be permitted.[28]

Here was the conceptual framework for racial segregation on a national scale in South Africa—that is, for the essential political means through which a reserve army of labour could be created and reproduced in the rural areas as the prerequisite for capitalist expansion. Although the commission's findings resembled earlier pieces of state legislation (such as the Glen Grey Act of the Cape Colony which was also concerned with creating a rural-based African proletariat), the significance of this commission's recommendations lay in its determination to use *economic* forms of coercion to secure the permanent reproduction of labour-power:

> It cannot but be an advantage to the natives to be induced *without compulsion* to become more industrious. Economic pressure and the struggle for existence will be felt by many of them at no very distant date and an industrious people will be better fitted for such conditions—which are now even arising.[29]

But before the commission's recommendations could be enacted, capital was again to be plunged into crisis—this time as a result of the commitment by the newly elected Liberal government in Britain to end the recruitment of Chinese labour.

This decision was accompanied by a further withholding of labour-power by African workers in South Africa: the numbers employed decreased from 107 756 in April 1905 to 90 420 in July 1906 (the year the importation of Chinese labour ended) (Jeeves, 1975). The combined force of these conditions engendered immediate panic among mine-owners and resulted in the re-emergence of significant competitive tendencies within their ranks as individual mine-owners, arguing that WNLA was incapable of securing a sufficient supply, sought to recruit their own labour in Mozambique and elsewhere: in April 1906 a new recruiting organization, the Transvaal Mines Labour Co., emerged in close association with J. B. Robinson and Co. to recruit in Mozambique; later that year WNLA's monopsony over recruitment in Mozambique was broken when the new organization received a licence to recruit there; the Robinson Co. was forced to withdraw from WNLA and resigned from the Chamber as well; elsewhere, WNLA's monopsony also broke down as most of the mine-owners began their own recruitment operations throughout British South Africa, forcing WNLA to release its members from the recruiting agreement in the Cape, Northern Transvaal and Basutoland. Faced with the increasing divisiveness and competitiveness that prevailed within the ranks of the mine-owners, the state emerged as the only force capable of forging the necessary unity to sustain the cheap labour system for the mines. In 1907 the Transvaal government intervened to bring the warring factions together so as to preserve recruitment 'through a single organized body'. The results were: the re-establishment of WNLA's monopsony in Mozambique, the return of the Robinson Co. to the Chamber and WNLA, and the closer collaboration of the state as a regulating influence in the work of WNLA. By 1908 the total number of African workers on the mines had reached 149 000 (from 81 000 in 1905 (Table 3) and 106 000 in 1907 (van der Horst, 1942, p. 216). However, it was not until as late as 1912, with the formation of the Native Recruiting Corporation, that the Chamber was able to re-establish its monopsony within South Africa itself. In that year the total number of African workers on the mines reached 191 000 (Table 3).

Thus the direct intervention of the state had preserved the necessary unity of the mine-owners in the face of working-class resistance, thereby enabling them to retain control over the supply of labour. At the same time, the increasing effectiveness of state administration over the machinery of labour control at the point of production had enabled the capitalist class to emerge from the crisis with its low-cost labour policy intact: average African wages, which had risen to 56s. per month in 1906 (during the crisis), had been reduced to 54s. 1d. by 1910 (van der Horst, 1942, p. 206). Under these conditions, the resistance of African workers began to crumble, reflected in the rising level of workers on the mines. The direct intervention of the imperialist state had caused the initiative in the struggle to pass from labour back to capital.

With the immediate labour crises of the post-war period 'resolved', the state was able to consolidate the power of monopoly capital over labour: the 1910 Act of Union established a juridically unified form of capitalist state in South Africa, so as to facilitate political domination for capital; the 1913 Administration of Persons to the Union Regulation Act formally classified 47 per cent of South Africa's African mine labour force as 'foreign', thereby enabling the state to extend its control over these workers through a further denial of rights;[30] the 1913 Native Lands Act, enacting the recommendations of the Native Affairs Commission of 1905, legally confined Africans within South Africa to live on 8.8 per cent of South Africa's land space, thereby establishing the legal conditions for the reproduction of a vast reserve army of labour in the rural areas of South Africa itself; and the Native Labour Regulation Act of 1913 increased the legal provisions for control over both the 'internal' and 'external' supplies of labour to the points of production inside South Africa.

It was this barrage of legislation, intensifying and extending the state's control over African labour (through controlling the conditions of its reproduction as well as the conditions of its access to the points of production), which laid down the broad legal framework for present-day apartheid South Africa. It was in response to this barrage of legislation that the Native National Congress was formed in 1912 (later to transform itself into the African National Congress of South Africa). Forty years later, under the leadership of this organization, the working and oppressed classes were to launch their most powerful assault yet against the state in South Africa. Out of the defeat suffered by the African workers and peasants in the early part of this century arose the phoenix of the future.

CONCLUSION

The gold mining industry in South Africa is, even today, the bulwark of the country's economy and as such continues to exert a profound influence on the economic, political and social life of the country. The early years of the industry's development were thus formative, not only in terms of establishing the capitalist relations of production which were to be the basis of subsequent growth in the industry itself, but also in terms of conditioning the form of evolution of wider social relations in the country, including such phenomena as the migrant labour system, the character and form of the state and the system of race relations.

Yet neither the specific form of capitalist production relations in the industry nor those of the wider social relations can be regarded as totally indigenous to South African society. It was in fact the export of capital, technology and skilled labour from the major centres of international capitalism which stimulated the process of massive social transformation in the southern African region. Thus the specific economic, political and social forms to develop in and around South Africa's mining industry originated under the contradiction generated by the impact of international monopoly capitalist relations on pre-capitalist and mercantile capitalist relations already located in the region. This contradiction took the form of intense social struggles as both indigenous local communities and settler colonial communities sought to resist the revolutionary transformations initiated by the advancing forces of capitalism. In the end, these local communities were to lose these struggles: the African communities were swept off their lands and herded into tiny reserves where they could be contained; while the Boer republics were ground down and their political and military strength broken so that a unitary capitalist state under British influence could be established in South Africa. Yet though the domination of capitalism was established the specific features and forms of the 'new' society bore witness to the struggles and resistance of the defeated communities.

It is not always appreciated in commentaries on this period of South African history—particularly by those who interpret it in terms of a conflict between modes of production—that the key to understanding why events unfolded as they did lies in recognizing the specific form of the international capitalist relations involved: that is, in recognition that they were relations of *monopoly* capitalism. It is this which explains why the gold mining industry developed on such a large scale in South Africa: why it was possible for gold ore of very low grade, buried deep in the earth's crust under thick layers of hard rock, to be removed and profitably exploited; why it was possible for the resistance of millions of black people to be broken; why it was possible not only to control these people but also to discipline them so that their labour would be sufficiently cheap for the industry to develop on a profitable basis; why it was possible to prevent the advantages secured by highly paid, organized skilled workers from permeating through to other sectors of the workforce; how it was possible for the labour and other economic needs of the mining industry to be secured without destroying other local industries, such as agriculture and infrastructure, on which mining also depended; and, finally, how it was possible to secure all this while at the same time securing sufficient political influence in the region to ensure the social and political stability on which the future reproduction of the industry was equally dependent. These were no mean achievements. They amounted to no less than the greatest social revolution ever carried out on the African continent. Their effect is still felt today in the daily lives of many millions of people.

Had international capitalism, and especially British capitalism, not been in its monopoly phase of development at the time the effects of its intrusion in the southern African region would undoubtedly have been very different. We saw how rapidly the involvement of the diamond magnates in the affairs of gold mining led to the eclipse of the digger—the petty-bourgeois capitalist—and the emergence of the great monopoly institutions, such as the joint-stock companies or mining-finance houses and groups. Without the involvement of these magnates or others like them, who can doubt that the era of petty-bourgeois production and of Diggers' Democracy would have had a far longer existence? And what would have been the effect on wider social relations? Would the Republican governments have fallen? With relations of petty-bourgeois production entrenched on the gold fields there would probably have been no conflict between their needs and the capacity of the state to meet those needs. And with the labour requirements of the industry substantially diminished, what then would have been the fate of South Africa's black population? The fact that these and many other similar questions must remain hypothetical attests to the crucial role which monopoly—as opposed to competitive—capitalism played in shaping the destiny of the region at this time. (Even in the earlier period of the development of the diamond industry, without the involvement of the great European financiers and banks in guiding the destinies of the De Beers, Kimberley and French companies, their power would have been only a fraction of what it actually was, presuming that they were able to come into existence at all.)

In stressing the importance of monopoly capitalism in influencing the development of South African society at this stage of its history we are not of course arguing that monopoly relations were established in *all* branches of production and distribution in the economy. On the contrary, what we have sought to do in this and the preceding chapter is to examine the way in which monopoly relations first came to be forged in the region through the mining industry. Outside this industry relations of competitive capitalism and pre-capitalist relations continued to prevail in commerce, other industries and, most important of all, agricultural production. Yet the future of these pre-monopoly relations was undoubtedly limited by the triumph of monopoly relations in mining (though they were to endure historically for some time yet). The point at which we have terminated this phase of our analysis is that at which the forces of monopoly capitalism, through the associated institutions of the groups and the Chamber of Mines and with the assistance of the imperialist state, had achieved for themselves a position of relatively secure dominance in the mining industry. This point has been defined as that at which the conditions for an adequate supply of cheap labour-power, in the form of largely unskilled African migrant labour, were secured. From here on South African society was to undergo important transformations as monopoly relations were consolidated in the mining industry and then spread gradually to other branches of production and distribution. This process was far from smooth; on the contrary, as we shall see, major struggles lay in store for those who owned and controlled the means of production in mining. None the less, the close of the first decade of this century saw an important phase in South Africa's history draw to a close: that of the struggle to *establish* and *entrench* monopoly relations in the mining industry. From now on the struggles that were to be fought would take place *within* the parameters already defined by these monopoly relations.

NOTES

1. S. W. Silver and Co. (1891), p. 519.
2. Whereas the average grade of ore mined on the Rand was about 6.5 pennyweight (dwt) per ton, that for Canadian gold mines was 10 dwt per ton and for Australian mines 13 dwt. (Johnstone, 1970a.)
3. From the end of the Napoleonic wars in 1816 to 1914 the price of gold remained stable at 84s. 11d. (£4 4s. 11d.) per fine ounce. For a detailed analysis of the history of gold's role in the monetary system see Innes (1981a).
4. This is only a rough approximation since estimates of the precise relation between these two elements of costs for this period vary from van der Horst's high for labour of 67 per cent of the total in 1894 to Hobson's figure of 55 per cent for the same year and Wilson's 55 per cent for 1911. However, Hobson's and Wilson's figures refer only to salaries and wages and do not include other components of labour costs, such as foodstuffs, social service costs for white workers and recruitment costs for African workers. (See van der Horst, 1942, p. 128; Hobson, 1900; and Wilson, 1972, p. 160.)
5. A mine was regarded as producing a 'high grade' of ore if it recovered half an ounce of gold from every ton of gold-bearing ore. Furthermore, in addition to the gold-bearing ore that had to be removed, the mine had to remove another half a ton of waste rock for every ton of gold-bearing ore.
6. These figures do not include Mozambicans recruited after they had crossed the Transvaal border, nor those on other Transvaal mines. (Witwatersrand Chamber of Mines, *Second Annual Report, 1890*, pp. 65, 76.)
7. *Report of the Transvaal Labour Commission* (1903), p. 119.
8. As the *First Annual Report* (1889) of the Chamber of Mines put it:

   So long as the total supply is deficient it is to be feared that eager competition between managers to secure labourers will be inevitable. This competition has in some cases taken the regrettable form of overt attempts to bribe and seduce the employees of neighbouring companies to desert their employers. Even without resort to actual attempts to bribe, a manager finding himself short of labour which is urgently required, has standing alone scarcely any other remedy than to raise his rates of pay. The result has necessarily been a steady rise of rates all round, which is adding a very heavy additional expense to the working of the mines. (p. 9)

9. When the Chamber was formed in 1889 all the leading mining-finance houses, with the exception of J. B. Robinson and Co., joined it. Robinson held out alone against the Chamber until 1895 when, supported by two other large companies which had previously been members of the Chamber (Ad. Goerz and Co. and G. and L. Albu and Co.), he formed a rival combination, the Association of Mines. In 1898, how-ever, Goerz and Albu were enticed back to the Chamber and the subsequent collapse of the Association forced Robinson into the Chamber shortly afterwards. (Hobson, 1900.)
10. Witwatersrand Chamber of Mines, *Third Annual Report, 1891*, p. 50.
11. Witwatersrand Chamber of Mines, *Fifth Annual Report, 1893*, p. 182.
12. By 1892 there were 95 members of the Chamber of Mines representing 59 com-panies on the Witwatersrand and 8 members representing 4 companies in other districts of the Transvaal. (Letcher, 1936, p. 106.)
13. According to Frankel (1938), there were 642 such companies on the Rand in 1889, of which 315 had offices in London. However, Frankel makes the point that: 'These figures involve much duplication since Investment and Exploration companies rein-vested moneys in Mining and Land companies.'
14. During this period the most important source of capital investment in the peripheral countries was Britain. Joseph Chamberlain had just launched his new policy of 'Constructive Imperialism' which was a deliberate attempt to promote capital in-

vestment in the British Empire. Commenting on this phenomenon, Frankel (1938) writes:

> A remarkable complex of financial institutions was evolved to further the process of international investment. The huge British commercial banks, financing commodity movements throughout the world, had long been the greatest source of short-term credit. Alongside them, there developed the public, private and imperial banks of the British Dominions. Around them grew up that unique security market for investment in long-term ventures which functioned through highly specialised groups of financial, promoting, underwriting and investment companies.

Between 1885 and 1900 the total value of Britain's long-term foreign investments rose from £1602m to £2485m, compared with a rise from £678m to £1068m for France and from £390m to £986m for Germany. (In 1900 the total value of US long-term foreign investments was only £103m.) (Frankel, 1938.)

15. Messrs Ad. Goerz and Co. was incorporated under German law. However, following the First World War the German-held portion of its issued capital became classified as 'enemy' shares and was re-sold to shareholders in the Allied countries, excluding France, and its name was changed.
16. The two groups became collectively known as the Corner House Group.
17. Cited in Chamber of Mines, *Second Annual Report, 1890*, p. 61.
18. Although there were more than seven times as many African workers as whites employed on the gold mines in 1895, white wages were on aggregate higher than those for black workers.
19. These arguments should not be taken to mean that no struggles occurred between capitalists and white workers at this time. As early as 1890 Lionel Phillips wrote:

> The wages paid to [skilled] miners and artisans are enormous . . . I shall insist on heavy reductions being made at once. . . . To avoid a possible strike, I shall advise Managers, in informing their men of the reduction, to say that they not only have definite orders to reduce pay, but to reduce the staff. The fact of a few men being dismissed from each company simultaneously (even though the staff be reduced for the moment a trifle below requirements) will have a good moral effect on those kept on. (Cited in Fraser and Jeeves, 1977, p. 37)

20. The following account neatly illustrates the role which black workers fulfilled in the labour process on the mines in 1894–5.

> All purely manual and certain kinds of skilled work are performed by natives. The classes of work for which they are mainly engaged are: in the mines— hand-drilling, shovelling, filling, tramming, also assisting machine drillmen, track layers, timbermen, etc.; on the surface—landing, dumping and filling trucks, tramming, ore-sorting, stoking and assisting enginemen, carrying coal, lumber, etc., pick and shovel work, assisting millmen, filling and emptying tailing vats, and generally all work carried on under strict supervision. In some cases natives, and more often half-castes and Indian coolies, have learned a trade and work as mechanics, smiths, engine-drivers, etc. (Hatch and Chalmers, cited in Houghton and Dagut, 1972, p. 316)

21. Output, which had climbed at an exceptionally fast rate during the period of transition to deep level underground mining suddenly dropped in the mid-1890s: for instance, whereas between 1893 and 1894 the rate of increase was 28 per cent (from 40 130 kg to 56 142 kg), between 1894 and 1895 the rate of increase fell to 10.5 per cent (to 62 758 kg) and between 1895 and 1896 it slumped to a mere 0.4 per cent (to 63 005 kg). (Table 6.)
22. In his evidence to the Transvaal Labour Commission in 1903, Fitzpatrick explained the relationship between the wage cuts of 1896–7 and the formation of the Native Labour Association:

You must understand this, that the necessity for the reduction in the rate of wages arose from the fact that there was competition among ourselves and that little by little one employer bid against another until finally the average became too high and the whole industry took it in hand and tried again to make a fresh start. That is my recollection of it, and that was what prompted us to form the Native Labour Association. You see we could not pool the supply, so we pooled the demand. The employers agreed to divide the supply among ourselves, that is, what they could get.

23. According to the Report of the Rand Native Labour Association for 1898:

From the northern districts of the Transvaal we have succeeded in getting 12 233 natives. Here the opposition was of a far more serious nature than on the East Coast. Companies, some of which are members of the Association, instead of allowing me to collect boys for them at prices obtained during the latter months of the year 1897, sent their own representatives to compete against mine. These circumstances account for the price of Northern boys being raised to £10s. 0d. per head. (Chamber of Mines, *Tenth Annual Report, 1898*, p. 446)

24. Jeeves (1975) has estimated that the death rate among Africans on the mines at this time was probably between 80 and 100 per thousand per annum.
25. Transvaal Chamber of Mines, *Report for 1900 and 1901*, p. 112.
26. Evidence of the effect of this resistance on production is provided by the *Report of the Transvaal Labour Commission* (1903):

In August, 1899, there were 6240 stamps at work in the Transvaal, which, according to the Chamber of Mines' report, produced gold worth £1 720 907, equal to £20 650 884 per annum. In July of this year, of the 7 145 stamps erected on the Rand, 3725 were being worked and produced gold to the value of £1 028 250, the output for the whole of the Transvaal being £1 068 917, equal to £12 827 004 per annum. The remaining 3420 stamps are idle because of lack of native labour, and the producing 3725 stamps are working at a serious economic disadvantage. Moreover, the annual loss to the industry in dividends on the basis of the present stamping power is estimated by the Chamber of Mines at £2 924 947. . . (p. xiv)

27. Richardson (1977) lists three other reasons why the Chamber adopted this strategy: it would serve to further fragment and divide the working class; it allowed the mining houses more leverage in their fight against the rising cost of stores; and it eased pressures on the Mozambican labour market (p. 90).
28. *Report of the South African Native Affairs Commission, 1903–1905* (1905).
29. ibid., our emphasis.
30. That is, workers from Mozambique, North and Southern Rhodesia and Nyasaland. Workers from Bechuanaland, Basutoland and Swaziland were not affected by this act.

CHAPTER 3
Class Conflict and the Birth
of Anglo American

By 1898 South Africa had become the largest gold producer in the world, ahead of the USA and Australia. Although she lost that position during the Anglo-Boer War, by 1904 prewar production levels had been regained and from then on, although a gradual slow-down occurred in the rate of increase, there was an unbroken period of rising output until 1912 (Table 2). However, in 1913 and 1914 the industry was hit by a series of strikes. Led by white miners, the strikes of June 1913 (in which some 18 000 whites on 63 mines participated) and January of the following year (the general strike) left capitalists and the state in no doubt as to the militancy of important sections of the labour force.[1] Although the general strike was eventually crushed by the armed intervention of the state and the rule of capital restored, mining capitalists had only a brief two-year respite before the level of output in the industry went into a serious decline which lasted for six consecutive years (Table 2). Although not the only cause, workers' struggles played a critical role in engendering these latter conditions and, as we shall see, it was only when their resistance had been smashed that the conditions for enhanced expansion could be reimposed on the industry.

The immediate cause of the decline in output recorded in 1917 was, however, a product of the war in Europe rather than the result of a resumption of workers' resistance. The outbreak of war caused an increase in the price of mining materials, especially stores and raw materials, both because European production had switched over to meet war requirements and because the supply of materials from abroad had become more erratic. The value of stores consumed in gold production suddenly began to rise during the war: from £10.2m in 1914 to £10.9m in 1915, £12.3m in 1916, reaching £14.4m in 1920.[2] Between July 1914 and July 1918 the working costs per ton of ore milled on the gold mines of the Witwatersrand rose by 28 percent (from 16s. 8d. to 21s. 4d.).[3] Nor did these increases abate during the period of high inflation

Table A   Witwatersrand Gold Mines

	July 1914	July 1917	July 1918
Number of companies	43	40	38
Revenue per ton *(s. d.)*	25/1	24/2	25/1
Working costs per ton *(s. d.)*	16/8	19/–	21/4
Gross profit per ton *(s. d.)*	8/5	5/2	3/9

Source Constructed from Cons. Gold Fields of SA, Report of the Manager in Johannesburg, 30 June 1918.

that followed the end of the war: by July 1921 working costs per ton had risen 54 per cent above the 1914 level (to 25 *s.* 7*d.*).[4]

The significance of these increases can only be fully appreciated if it is borne in mind that, throughout the period of the war, revenue per ton milled did not rise (and in fact fell slightly during part of the period) on the central Witwatersrand, where most of the Transvaal mines were located (see Table A). Consequently, gross profits per ton were cut by a drastic 55.4 per cent on the Rand during the war years, while five mines actually had to cease production (see table). Of course, given the different geological and other conditions under which various mines operated, each group was affected somewhat differently by these cost increases. But, overall, the period was one of significant cost inflation in the price of stores which inevitably led to a rise in the pay limit of the industry as a whole, thereby reducing the gold reserves—and potential life expectancy—of the Rand.

Although the rising cost of stores was the immediate cause of cost inflation in the industry at this time, the major cause over the longer term came from labour, which constituted the largest proportion of costs. While the conditions of oppression which existed in both the industry itself and in the wider social relations had enabled the mine-owners to hold black cash wages to a relatively low level of increase (they rose from £29 per annum in 1911 to £30 per annum in 1916 and by 1921 had reached only £33 per annum), white cash wages had soared after the war, rising from £333 per annum in 1911 to £355 in 1916 and reaching £496 in 1921 (a rise of 40 per cent between 1916 and 1921) (F. Wilson, 1972, p. 46). Although the high rate of inflation in South Africa at this time meant that in real terms both white and black earnings actually declined,[5] as far as the mine-owners were concerned these wage increases, and especially those won by white workers, were intolerably high. The largest group on the Rand, Central Mining, reported that white wages had been the major source of cost inflation in the group between 1915 and 1920, rising by 43 per cent compared with an overall cost rise of 32 per cent (black wages rose by only 13 per cent; mining materials by 33 per cent and 'Other Costs'—that is, Sundries—by 28 per cent).[6]

Representatives of capital on the Rand expressed increasing concern about these conditions, especially as more and more mines came to be seriously affected. As early as 1918 the manager of a leading group had reported:

> In July, 1914, thirteen Witwatersrand companies were making a working profit of 5/- or less per ton crushed, whereas today 31 companies come under that category: that is to say, that three-fifths of them, milling 63.2% of the total tonnage, and producing over 50% of the total gold output of the Rand, are making a gross profit of only 2/3d [sic] per ton; and as from this low margin of working profit payments have to be made for Miners' Phthisis levies, Debenture interest and redemption, Taxation charges, Capital expenditure, etc. it will be realized how precarious is the position of many of these companies.[7]

It was clear that the mine-owners would not be prepared to tolerate a continuation of these conditions indefinitely. What was even worse from their point of view was the escalating level of resistance which was taking place among workers in the industry.

The major threat in this regard was posed by the rising militancy of the black labour force on the mines. Although black mine-workers had embarked on a number of actions against their employers over the preceding years, they had failed to achieve any significant improvements in their living or working conditions.[8] However, as the inflation rate spiralled in the immediate postwar period, so the militancy with which workers pressed their demands intensified: in July 1918 black miners again struck on the Rand and this time had to be driven down the shafts by armed mounted police. Despite the intervention of the armed forces of the state, resistance continued to mount and in December the following year the Chamber of Mines was forced to concede a small wage increase (based on a bonus system). This proved inadequate to quell the demands of the workers and in February 1920 the Chamber was forced to concede a further increase—this time in the basic wage rate—of 3*d.*, representing an increase of 11 per cent for underground workers and 14 per cent for surface workers. But the militancy of the workers could not be bought off so easily: during the month of February 1920 some 71 000 black workers (out of 173 000) were engaged in a massive strike that affected 22 of the 35 operating mines on the Rand.[9] Although the strike was eventually crushed and only a few piecemeal reforms won, the event of such a massive display of solidarity among those workers who were the backbone of the mining industry caused considerable consternation among capitalist circles.

Summing up these events, the Simonses (1969) wrote:

> The strike was a well planned, disciplined campaign and not an 'instinctive revolt'. It showed that many thousands of men from a wide variety of

regions and peasant communities could combine effectively. It was a 'new phenomenon', remarked Sir Evelyn Wallers, president of the Chamber of Mines, this first 'native strike in the true sense of the word'. The 'absolutely peaceful cessation from work' indicated that the African 'was advancing more rapidly than we had anticipated', and would not remain satisfied for very long with his position in industry. (p. 232)

Thus by 1920 the mine-owners found themselves under attack from two quarters: by the increasing militancy and organization of black workers and by the spiralling cost structure in which white wage increases were the major factor.[10] The long-term solution which they were to seek to impose on the industry was to shake the very fabric of white racial domination in South African society before its success was assured.

THE RESPONSE OF MINE-OWNERS AND THE STATE

There were broadly speaking only two avenues open to the capitalists if they were to restore profitability in the mining industry: they could either attempt to reduce the cost of inputs to the industry or they could attempt to increase the revenue on gold sales. In the end, both avenues were utilized but in the initial stages of the mounting crisis mine-owners sought the latter course of action.[11]

Capital and the gold price

Gold sales were governed by a fixed price and it was thus not possible for capitalists in the mining industry to employ the standard monopolists' technique of simply agreeing a price rise among themselves: they had to obtain the approval of those states (primarily Britain) responsible for the management of the international monetary system. In 1918 they began exerting pressure to this end when a committee was formed by mining interests to discuss 'the very complex question of the price of gold' with the British government and other pressure was brought to bear on the government in South Africa.[12] Although both governments initially resisted these pressures, the contradiction they, and especially the British state, faced left little room for manoeuvre: while the state could not be pressured into tampering with the price of the money-commodity itself simply because the profits of a section of capital were being eroded, at the same time it was precisely because gold was the money-commodity that its production, and consequently the profits of that section of capital which organized its production, had to be protected. The crisis which mining capitalists faced in 1919 meant that the reproduction of international capitalism could not be secured unless the interests of the gold producers were protected. In July 1919 the

British state gave way and a free market was introduced for gold produced in South Africa and Rhodesia.

The result of the new arrangement (known as the gold premium) was an immediate increase in gold mining revenue and, consequently, working profits. In 1919, the year of its introduction, the gold premium added approximately 53 per cent (£3 500 000) to the standard working *profit* of the Witwatersrand gold mines (£6 603 509).[13] Regarding working *revenue*, the improvements were also substantial: in 1920, the first full year in which the premium operated, it added 7s. 1d. per ton of ore mined to the standard revenue of 28s. and the following year it added 6s. 5d. per ton to the standard revenue of 28s. 7d. (in both cases the final revenue was 35s. per ton).[14]

Capital and mining stores

The support provided by the state at this time gave mining capitalists the 'breathing space' they needed to see them through the immediate postwar crisis. However, the premium did not last—nor was it ever intended to last—and clearly mining capitalists still had to put their own house in order. They therefore turned their attention to the other avenue open to them: that of seeking reductions in the cost of inputs to the industry. Here again, though, they were somewhat hamstrung in that in one area at least—that of stores—the question of reducing costs was beyond their immediate influence over the short term. However, it is worth noting that mining capitalists did not accept completely the argument put forward by manufacturers in Britain that disruptions caused by the war were responsible for the continued price rises after the war. They pointed to another tendency which they saw as contributing to the price rises: that of the acceleration of monopoly conditions in postwar Britain. For instance, the managing directors of a leading monopoly institution on the Rand, Consolidated Gold Fields, complained:

> Today, owing to a lack of competition, the purchaser of any manufactured stores which are required by the industry is more or less forced to accept what is offered, and pay whatever price is asked. Today, the manufacturers and producers of several of the most important commodities necessary to the mines have formed rings and combines, and the consumers suffer accordingly.[15]

However, since monopoly conditions also existed in the gold industry, the mine-owners were able to take steps to counter to an extent the effects of these monopolistic tendencies. A number of the groups began to invest in local industry around this time, orienting their investments in particular towards those industries which could serve the mining industry in one way or another. At the same time the Chamber of Mines established a scheme to manufacture certain stores in South Africa, utilizing scrap metal and reworking old material where possible, so as to lessen dependence on imports.[16] This development was to provide an important boost to South Africa's embryonic engineering industry.[17] Another important change, though this affected the other pole of the production continuum, was the decision taken by the mineowners at the end of the war to build a gold refinery and establish a mint in the Transvaal. This was intended to further reduce their dependence on monopoly institutions beyond their immediate control in Britain—this time in the handling of their product.[18]

Capital and labour

But while these changes brought some alleviation to the problem of spiralling costs,[19] they did not have an immediate impact and neither did they affect the major area of cost increase: that of white labour. It was by securing reductions in this area that mine-owners stood to gain the most. Following the 1920 African mine-workers' strike capitalists had begun to review the position of black workers in the industry. A memorandum issued after the strike by the board of management of the Chamber's internal recruiting organization, the Native Recruiting Corporation, put forward the germ of a solution to the problems posed by both black and white workers in the industry:

> If the semi-skilled class of native labourers referred to can be allowed to even partially obtain their justifiable aspirations for advancement in industrial life the danger of recurrent strikes with their attendant losses and disorganization may be largely prevented. The semi-skilled native justly treated should prove a useful asset to the industry in assisting to guide the mass of unskilled labourers employed. (Bonner,1979)

By training some African workers to semi-skilled positions and then using them to replace white workers in those positions, both aspects of the labour problem could be tackled: wage rates for semi-skilled African workers could be raised, thus neutralizing at least one section of the black labour force who could be used to replace some white workers in the supervision or 'policing' of lower-skilled black workers; while at the same time the overall wage bill of white workers could be reduced. The only problem with this strategy was that, unless it could be related to productivity increases, it would simply lead over the longer term to a rise in the total wage bill for black labour. The way in which this particular contradiction could be overcome was through the wider application of the jack-hammer drill throughout the industry.

However, what this strategy involved was not only a restructuring of the labour process but also a reorganization of the racial forms which capital had itself imposed on the industry at an earlier stage of its development. The actual strategy which the Chamber employed was to seek to *modify* the existing colour bar in the industry rather than to abolish it altogether. There were in fact two aspects to the colour bar: the statutory—that is, legally enforced—colour bar which protected 32 job categories for white workers in which 7057 whites were employed on the mines; and the 'conventional colour bar' (the so-called 'status quo agreement' reached in 1918 between the mine-owners and white workers) which protected 19 job categories in which 4020 white workers were at that time employed. The Chamber in fact confined its attack largely to this latter category, seeking to bring black workers into jobs covered by the 'conventional colour-bar'. In so doing it sought on the one hand to drive a wedge between white workers, thereby preventing a united opposition to its attack, and on the other to groom a 'privileged section' of the black proletariat to the task of assisting in the oppression of the mass of the labour force. But while the strategy was *seemingly* directed against only a section of the white labour force, it was *actually* an assault on the whole labour force in the industry, though it affected sections of that labour force differentially. What the mine-owners sought to gain, through the modifications to the colour bar and the wider application of the jack-hammer drill in the labour process, was not only the expulsion of a section of white labour from production, but also a more general process of de-skilling among white workers as a whole and in particular a rise in the level of exploitation of black workers. Had the mine-owners simply extended the use of the jack-hammer drill without restructuring the racial forms, organized white labour would no doubt have sought wage increases to match the productivity gains. It was thus essential to capital that the restructuring of the labour process occurred under conditions of increasing utilization of unorganized and cheap (which meant black) labour. At the same time, had the racial forms been modified and higher paid black labour been used to an increasing extent without restructuring the labour process, this would simply have resulted in an overall increase in the total black wage bill without any corresponding increase in productivity. These two elements in the strategy—restructuring the racial forms and restructuring the labour process—were thus both crucial to the overall success of the assault on the labour force.

The precise moment of the attack was determined by the decline in the gold premium: the price of gold fell from an average of 111s. per fine ounce between July 1920 and June 1921 to 97s. 9d. per fine ounce in December 1921. In November of that year the mine-owners gave notice of their intention to break the 'conventional colour bar' and reoganize underground work, arguing that in so doing they sought to fulfil the 'justifiable aspirations for advancement' of black workers. By presenting the assault in this way the mine-owners hoped to secure the compliance of the black section of the labour force in the dispute. However, the owners were well aware that their actions were likely to lead to strong resistance from white workers and they had therefore sought the support of the state before embarking on any action. In October 1921 the mine-owners had met Prime Minister Smuts and, in the words of Sir Lionel Phillips, informed him 'that whatever we may do may involve some industrial trouble for which the Government must be prepared' (Fraser and Jeeves, 1977, p. 327). Although Smuts was initially reluctant to commit the forces of the state so unconditionally, the capitalists would not be deterred: 'strike or no strike', wrote Lionel Phillips, 'we shall get our costs down'.[20] By December, it seems the state had guaranteed that support. According to Phillips:

> There is, of course, a fair hope that everything will be accomplished without a big strike. If it comes, however, it has got to be faced once and for all . . . as long as disorder is treated with vigour from the beginning, there is really nothing to be feared . . . The great thing is that the framework is properly organized and, I believe, that is being done. (Fraser and Jeeves, 1977, p. 331)

On 2 January 1922 white coal miners came out on strike and eight days later, on the 10th, the white gold miners followed suit: the Rand Revolt had begun.

It is not necessary to deal in any detail with the events of the strike itself as these have been covered adequately elsewhere (see especially Johnstone, 1976). Suffice it to say that before the strike was eventually brought to an end on 16 March martial law had been proclaimed, 250 lives had been lost and 4758 people arrested. This was how the manager of one of the leading groups on the Rand, Consolidated Gold Fields, perceived the events leading up to the strike:

> The price of gold which, for the twelve months ended 30/6/21, had averaged 111/- per fine ounce, fell steadily during the next six months to 97/9d in December 1921, and, since the beginning of 1922, the average price realized has been in the neighbourhood of 94/-, and is now about 92/6d. In the face of this steady fall it had become obvious that, if a disaster of great magnitude was to be avoided, there was an urgent need for the effecting of large economies in working. A certain amount of relief was to be expected in the cost of commodities as the industrial conditions of producing countries returned to normal. Certain economies could be brought about by the reduction of wages . . . The main direction, however, in which the industry had to look for economy was that of the reduction in the number of persons employed (both European and Native) and an improvement in the productivity of the remainder, and for these purposes it was essential to restore the authority of the Mine Manager upon the Mine so that he might be in the position of being able to bring about such economies unhampered by any considerations other than those of efficiency. Nothing proved so prejudicial to the efficient working of the Mines previous to the strike as

the restrictive policy of the Unions and their interference with managerial functions.[21]

As the above statement suggests, capitalists were well aware that the
power of *organized labour* would have to be broken before it would be
possible to carry through the reforms in the organization of production
and the labour process which were deemed necessary to secure the
higher exploitation of labour. By 16 March 1922 that power had been
broken and the mine-owners could implement their changes.

The effect was immediate. A comparison of working costs on the
Witwatersrand mines for the month of July 1921 with those of the
following July shows a fall of £400 000.[22] 'These reduced costs,' wrote
the manager of Consolidated Gold Fields, 'are principally due to more
economic use of labour.'[23] Costs per ton milled fell from 25s. 7d. in July
1921 to 21s. 1d. in July 1922 (and by 1923 had fallen even further to 20s.
4d.), while the number of tons milled rose slightly (from 2 010 236 to
2 057 895) over the same period.[24] Overall, the value of salaries and
wages in the gold industry fell from £16.7m in 1921 to £13.3m in 1923
(a drop of 20.4 per cent), while the value of dividends distributed by the
industry rose from £7.3m in 1921 to £8.5m in 1923 (a rise of 14 per
cent).[25] These major savings in wages were achieved partly through
the expulsion of white labour from the mines and their replacement by
black workers: the number of white workers employed during the
months of July 1921 and July 1922 fell from 21 562 to 16 865—a drop of
21.8 per cent or 4697 workers; while the number of African workers
employed during those same months rose from 176 507 to 183 645—a
rise of 3.8 per cent or 7138 workers.[26] Nor were those white workers
who retained their jobs exempt from the ravages of the capitalist onslaught: the average wages of white miners were reduced by 10s. a shift
to 32s. 6d.—a fall of 23.5 per cent. Nor were these declines of only a
temporary nature. Between 1921 and 1922 white wages in three job
categories (machine stoping, onsetters and skipmen, and fitters) fell
from 33s. 5d., 25s. 9d. and 29s. per day to 21s., 16s. 6d. and 20s. 9d.
respectively. In 1930 these wage rates were still as low as 21s. 8d., 18s.
2d. and 23s. 7d. respectively and it was not until 1949 that machine
stopers regained their 1921 wage levels, 1950 for fitters and 1953 for
onsetters and skipmen.[27] At the same time as white wages were being
slashed black workers' wages increased marginally from an average of
£33 in 1921 to £33.50 in 1926 (F. Wilson, 1972, p. 46). Again taking an
overview, the total value of salaries and wages in the industry did not
reach its 1921 level until 1932—a decade after the Rand Revolt.[28]

These far-reaching inroads into the standards which white workers
had attained for themselves are, however, only one aspect of the overall gains secured by the mine-owners. While white labour certainly
bore the brunt of the assault on total wage costs, it was as we shall see

the black workers who were to bear the brunt of the assault on the productivity of labour. It was as a result of the gains secured in the sphere of raising the productivity of black labour, while at the same time reducing the total wage bill through the assault on white wage rates, that the mine-owners won their greatest advances in increasing the exploitation of the whole labour force.

Capital and the labour process

In 1923 the directorate of the Central Mining Group reported on certain important advances their mines had achieved in 'mining practice':

> In several directions a distinct advance has been made in mining practice, and, as a consequence, for the first time in the history of the Rand, it may be said with confidence that periodical shortages of native labour will, in future, exercise less influence on operations than in the past. The average price of gold has been lower than in the preceding year, but the introduction of mechanical and metallurgical improvements, together with greater efficiency, resulted in increased output and reduced working costs, which more than compensated for the lower price of the metal.[29]

The 'mechanical' improvements referred to involved in particular the wider application of drilling machines underground. The group's consulting engineer reported:

> As a result of prolonged research, our mines are gradually replacing hammer boys and the larger types of drilling machines by small 'jack-hammer' machines. Owing to the comparative ease with which the latter can be handled underground, two (or even, with the latest improved type, one) of them can drill as much in an ordinary shift as a whole gang of hammer boys. Although the old type of jack-hammer machine could only drill about 16 ft [4.9m] per shift, the latest pattern, utilizing drill steel which has been heat-treated and accurately gauged by the special methods introduced as a result of the foregoing investigations, is capable of drilling as much as 63 ft [19.2m] during the same period. The translation of such an improvement into actual working practice is necessarily a gradual process, but a remarkable reduction of breaking costs has already been effected in our Group.[30]

These transformations, then, enabled fewer black workers to drill further in a given time-period, thereby both reducing the number of workers necessary to drill per shift and increasing the drilling capacity of each shift. Nor did the improvements stop there. The following year (1924), Central Mining reported 'a further improvement in efficiency, in consequence of which working costs were again reduced.'[31]

Although perfected by the Central Mining Group (the leading group on the Rand at that time), these technical improvements were not confined to that group alone but were immediately passed on through the Chamber of Mines to the other groups in the industry, thus enabling them to share in the spoils.[32] It was the unique marketing conditions in the industry, which substantially reduced the impact of competitive tendencies among capitalists, that made these forms of *technical* collusion possible. Under more 'normal' marketing conditions, of course, each company seeks to effect productivity gains at the technical level in order to reduce the amount of labour-time necessary for the production of its commodity so as to undercut its rivals. Consequently any breakthroughs achieved by one company in the sphere of technical knowledge are jealously guarded by the company concerned. But in the case of gold mining, where the concept of undercutting in the sense used here is not applicable, the reverse conditions applied. By pooling the technical information and resources acquired by the individual groups, it became possible for mining capitalists as a whole to advance at a faster rate.[33]

As a result of the pooling of technical resources the groups were able to move extremely rapidly in applying the machines to underground work. In 1924 the Consolidated Gold Fields report related the group's improved mining results to 'the development of the Jack Hammer Machine', arguing that: 'The extended use of these machines has been accompanied by a marked increase in efficiency, the fathoms broken per machine shift having been recently just under two fathoms as compared with less than half this figure for the previous year.'[34] The following year the chairman of the Anglo American Group, Ernest Oppenheimer, stated in his annual report: 'No review of the year's work on the Rand would be complete without some reference to the remarkably increased efficiency of rock breaking. . . . Pride of place now belongs to the Jackhammer without which the efforts to improve the fathomage broken could not have been so successful.'[35] During 1923 and 1924 the number of jack-hammer drills employed in the Central Mining/Rand Mines Group rose by 56 per cent (from 1594 to 2478), while the number of reciprocating machines in use—these are the old type of rock-breaking machines—declined by 95 per cent (from 796 to 43).[36] Within the jack-hammer category it was the 'wet' jack-hammer that achieved the major productivity improvements. During 1923 alone the number of 'wet' jack-hammers employed on the group's mines rose by 111 per cent (from 742 to 1563).[37] As a result the average volume of machine fathomage broken by jack-hammers on mines within the Group rose from 24 per cent in January 1923 to 83 per cent in January of the following year.

Following these changes productivity rates per man rose sharply. Central Mining reported that, while the average efficiency level of 'hammer boys'—that is, African workers *not* using the jack-hammer drill—remained constant at 2.1 fathoms per African per month between January 1923 and December 1924, overall the average number of fathoms broken per month per African worker (including those using jack-hammers) rose from 5.1 to 9.6 over the same period.[38] Table 4 reveals that between 1921 and 1926 productivity in the gold mining industry as a whole increased by 15.2 per cent or 6.08 fine ounces per man (from 40.06 ounces to 46.14 ounces). This rise indicates the important impact which the changing nature of the labour process was having on the industry's productivity. In the words of the Central Mining Group's consulting engineer: 'It can be fairly said that the methods of breaking rock in the mines have been revolutionized.'

It is worth recalling at this point the words of Ernest Oppenheimer in 1925:

> It must not be overlooked that without the reorganization of underground work dating from the 1922 strike and without the introduction of over-lapping shifts the industry could not have attained the results of which they are now justly proud. The improved fathomage broken is not only due to the better types of machines and drills now used, but also largely to the fact that the effective drilling time has been practically doubled.[39]

In other words, the mine-owners could not have achieved the major improvements described above without first smashing the resistance of organized labour. The benefits which the groups derived from the large-scale application of the jack-hammer drill were not a product of the 'marvels of modern technology' (though these provided the technical means to that end), but were a product of the capitalists' ability through struggle to prevent organized workers in the first instance from participating in those benefits and in the end to secure them at the expense of labour. It was the outcome of these struggles which largely determined the particular forms in which the labour process was restructured—that is, the forms in which the new technologies were integrated with, and transformed, the existing relations of production.

However, the fact that, as a result of these favourable conditions, capital in the industry was able to appropriate larger quantities of surplus value does not necessarily mean that all sections of capital engaged in South African mining benefited equally. On the contrary, the generation of a rising quantity of surplus value in the industry at this time led to significant changes among the individual capitals able to benefit from appropriation of this surplus value, based primarily on their differential access to the sources of expanded value. Thus the struggles waged between capital and labour in the industry can be said to have had far-reaching consequences for the relations among the different capitals engaged in mining production. It is to the origins and nature of the changes among the various capitals in the industry that we direct our attention in the next section.

THE FAR EAST RAND GOLD FIELD
AND THE ANGLO AMERICAN GROUP

Profitability in the South African mining industry is far from uniform. There are rich, average and poor mines—a categorization which, though not solely determined by the extent and grade of the ore reserves of particular mines, is none the less related to these geological conditions. But in addition to this differential among *mines* there are also important differentials among the various geographical *fields* in which mining is conducted, based again at least partially on the richness of the gold-bearing reef in particular areas. In this section we will examine certain critical aspects of the differential between the Far East Rand gold field and the rest of the Witwatersrand.

Although it had been known for some time that the Far East Rand contained deposits of gold, during the late nineteenth and early twentieth centuries the region was exploited primarily for its coal resources and it was not until 1917 that it was actually proclaimed a gold field.[40] The major difficulty in attempting to exploit the region's gold resources was that the reef lay considerably deeper underground than in any other part of the Rand and, consequently, production costs seemed to be prohibitively high, especially in the context of inflationary cost increases during the war.[41] However, the availabilty of new mechanical means of production, especially the jack-hammer drill which could speed up development work considerably, led the state to accept the recommendation of the government mining engineer that 'the Far East Rand should be rapidly opened up'.

The high cost of development work required on the new field ruled out the possibility of expansion through small-scale production. It also meant that even the large monopolies had to approach the question of new investments in the field with extreme caution. However, those groups which did invest in the new field were in the end able 'to show grades and profits well above the average of the Rand'.[42] Referring to the 'phenomenal increase' in the profits of the Far East Rand mines, Consolidated Gold Fields pointed out that whereas in July 1914 the Far East Rand gold mines were contributing only 20 per cent of the profits of the gold mines of the Witwatersrand as a whole, by July 1917 they were contributing 48 per cent of the total profits and by July of the following year a massive 59.7 per cent.[43] By 1919 the eleven gold mines which had been established on the Far East Rand and which, between them, were crushing only 27 per cent of the Witwatersrand's total tonnage, were paying out almost 70 per cent of the total distributed dividends in the industry as a whole. These figures and Table B give an indication of the profit differential which existed between the eleven newly formed mining companies on the Far East Rand and the remaining 38 mining companies on the Rand.

Table B   Gold Mines on the Rand Compared

	Gold mines on the Far East Rand			Other gold mines on the Witwatersrand		
	July 1914	July 1917	July 1918	July 1914	July 1917	July 1918
Number of companies	9	12	11	43	40	38
Revenue per ton *(s. d.)*	30/2	35/–	36/8	25/1	24/2	25/1
Working costs per ton *(s. d.)*	17/3	19/4	30/5	16/8	19/–	21/4
Gross profits per ton *(s. d.)*	12/11	15/8	16/3	8/5	5/2	3/9

Source Compiled from data in Cons. Gold Fields of SA, *Report of the Directors*, 31 December 1919.

The table shows not only the much higher gross profits among mines on the Far East Rand, but more significantly it shows that the profit differential between mines on the Far East Rand and those on the rest of the Rand actually increased over time: from 4*s*. 6*d*. per ton in 1914 to 12*s*. 6*d*. per ton in 1918. This was due both to the rising profitability of Far East Rand mines (up by 26 per cent) and to the consistently declining profit levels of mines on the rest of the Rand (a decline of 56 per cent.) Thus, although the mines on the older fields of the Rand continued to make the greatest contribution to the industry's output, it was clear by the end of the war that the centre of gravity, in terms of the industry's profitability, had shifted markedly towards the mines on the new Far East Rand field.

Nor did this tendency abate in the postwar years. By 1920 the crisis had forced another seven mines to close down outside the Far East Rand, bringing the number of closures since 1914 to thirteen.[44] Although the rise in revenue for the whole industry secured through the gold premium after 1919 enabled those mines outside the Far East Rand to fare considerably better than they had done previously, Table C shows the extent to which the Far East Rand consolidated its position as the most important field on the Rand during the early 1920s.

The table shows clearly that profitability on the Far East Rand mines was considerably higher than the level for the industry as a whole: the average working profit per ton milled on the Far East Rand over the three years being 18*s*. 11*d*. compared with 9*s*. 9*d*. for the whole of the Rand. Both the declared working profits and dividends of the mines on the Far East Rand improved over the period covered by the table, with these mines paying out 66.6 per cent of the total dividends distributed by the industry in 1923 and 63.6 per cent the following year. Furthermore, by 1924 the Far East Rand's share of the value of total Witwatersrand gold production had risen to 45.3 per cent (from 25 per cent in 1918),[45] indicating that the industry's centre of gravity was rapidly swinging towards the Far East Rand in terms of output as well

Table C   *Far East Rand Statistics Compared with Statistics for the Industry as a Whole[a]*

	Far East Rand			Whole of Witwatersrand		
	1921	1923	1924	1921	1923	1924
Tons milled	6 860 110	8 183 700	10 351 600	23 400 605	26 538 875	28 209 073
Yield (in fine oz)	3 030 257	3 502 687	4 232 294	7 924 534	8 898 731	—
Average price of gold (per fine oz) (s. d.)	106/10	90/3	91/10	106/10	90/3	91/10
Revenue (per ton milled) (s. d.)	43/1	37/7	37/7	35/2	29/5	29/10
Costs (per ton milled) (s. d.)	24/5	18/1	19/2	25/8	20/-	19/7
Working profit (per ton milled)	18/8	19/6	18/5	9/6	9/5	10/3
Declared working profit (£)	6 410 849	7 408 362	9 536 644	11 102 935	12 508 510	9 544 516
Declared dividends (£)	4 929 213	5 602 175	6 067 659	7 163 941	8 411 970	—

[a]Those statistics that refer to the *whole* of the Witwatersrand are not immediately comparable with those in the previous table which refer to the *rest* of the Witwatersrand. Statistics for 1922 have been omitted from this table as they were distorted that year as a result of the white miners' strike.

Sources Table compiled from data in the following: Cons. Mines Selection Co., *Report of the Directors,* 31 December 1921, p. 5; Anglo American Corp. of SA, Minutes of the Proceedings at the Seventh Ordinary General Meeting, 27 May 1924, p. 3; Anglo American Corp. of SA, *Eighth Annual Report* for year ended 31 December 1924, p. 4.

as profitability. It was thus clear by the mid-1920s that the Far East Rand, despite all the risks and difficulties involved in mining at great depths, had established itself as the new centre and most lucrative area of gold mining in South Africa.

A shift of this nature, of course, had far-reaching consequences for the relation between capitals or groups which together controlled the mining industry in South Africa. Given the lucrative nature of Far East Rand production, compared with that on the rest of the Rand, it is clear that those capitals which had emerged in control of the Far East Rand field would benefit substantially from their position and would have the potential capacity to expand relatively faster than those capitals tied up in the less lucrative low-grade producers on the rest of the Rand. As we shall see, the proclamation of the field in fact heralded the emergence of the capitalist group which was ultimately to come to dominate not only the South African mining sector but also vast sectors of production and distribution within South Africa as a whole.

By the time the full extent of the gold-bearing reserves of the Far East Rand had become clearly known, one group of companies was found, largely fortuitously, to be in control of the best areas in the field. This group was headed by the Consolidated Mines Selection Co., which had been established in Britain in 1897 at the time of the great monopoly formations in South Africa's gold mining history. However, Consolidated Mines had been one of the less lucrative monopolies operating in South Africa as it had no significant investments on the central Witwatersrand, which was the hub of gold mining activity at the time. In an era of speculative investment in which mining-finance houses cast their nets wide in the hope of 'striking it rich', the company had begun after the Anglo-Boer War to buy up mineral rights further afield. As part of this programme they had bought the rights to a number of properties in the region now known as the Far East Rand. These properties, which were subsequently to give rise to the immensely rich Springs and Brakpan gold mines, had been part of the portfolio of the Transvaal Coal Trust Co. (established in 1889) which owned a number of coal mining properties in the region. However, because of the problems related to establishing a gold mine on the Far East Rand, progress in developing these properties was relatively slow and the company was soon in financial difficulties. In 1905 the Consolidated Mines Selection Co. was taken over by A. Dunkelsbuhler and Co., an old-established diamond trading concern which had been an influential member of the Diamond Syndicate since 1890 and was also an important shareholder in the rich Premier (Transvaal) Diamond Mining Co. A. Dunkelsbuhler and Co. was controlled by the Oppenheimer family.[46]

When drilling and other exploratory investigations began to reveal the full gold potential of the Far East Rand, the Oppenheimers used Consolidated Mines to extend their interests in the field by buying up substantial shareholdings in the Transvaal Coal Trust (TCT)—the largest property owner in the region. By 1916, the year in which the field's true potential became public knowledge, the take-over of the TCT had been completed and the company was renamed the Rand Selection Corporation. Primarily through their interests in these three companies,[47] the Oppenheimers came to control the richest gold-bearing areas in the richest gold field in South Africa.

Although these investments afforded the Oppenheimers vast *poten-*

tial to expand their base of accumulation, at that time the group was not particularly well placed to develop that potential. In the first place the immense capital requirements of development work could not be met by the group's own financial resources, strained as these were by the recent acquisition of the TCT.[48] Nor could war-torn Europe be expected at that time to furnish the needs of developing gold mines in South Africa and so the Oppenheimers turned their attention to the expanding capital markets of the USA, which afforded great possibilities if they could be tapped. However, here the group ran into difficulties in that Consolidated Mines, which was legally in control of the gold-bearing properties, was in 1916 not particularly well placed to raise capital in the United States since approximately one-third of the company's shares were held by German companies or individuals—a connection which was hardly helpful at that time.[49] In order to overcome this problem the group decided to float a new company whose specific purpose would be to tap the American capital market for finance to develop the Far East Rand mines without having to run the risk of being labelled as a company under the control of 'enemy' shareholders. The man chosen to head the new company was Ernest Oppenheimer, already a director of Consolidated Mines, Rand Selection and some of the smaller companies in the group—and the company which he founded was the Anglo American Corporation of South Africa.

The formation of the Anglo American Corporation was thus a key element in the strategy worked out by a particular group of European capitalists to gain access to the capital markets of the United States in order to proceed with development of the Far East Rand gold field which was largely under their control. When the new company was formed on 25 September 1917 the board of six directors reflected the coalition of interests that had given rise to its birth and was necessary to sustain its growth: Ernest Oppenheimer, as chairman and managing director, represented the interests of the Oppenheimer family; W. Honnold (formerly a director of Consolidated Mines Selection) was the Oppenheimer family's liaison with American financial interests, specifically linking the Oppenheimers with the giant US banking firm of J. P. Morgan and Co. who were important shareholders in Anglo American; C. Hamilton Sabin represented the interests of the major US corporation, Guaranty Trust, which became banker to Anglo American; W. Boyce Thompson represented the interests of another giant US concern, this time the mining combine, the Newmont Mining Corporation; the Hon. F. C. Hull, Minister of Finance in the first Union government of South Africa, was highly regarded both by British financial interests in South Africa and by important functionaries of the South African state itself; and finally, the Hon. H. Crawford, an MP in South Africa and also a representative of the National Bank of South Africa.[50]

As the above list illustrates, the Anglo American Corporation was to be the institutional form through which *monopoly* capital in the USA and Britain would be channelled into the further exploitation of mineral resources in South Africa (this time focusing on the new gold field). It was conceived during the phase of international domination of monopoly capitalism in order to extend that domination over yet another field of mineral production in South Africa. Both its own formal financial strength and the financial and political power of its backers marked it off from the very beginning as a monopoly concern. For instance, when it was formed in 1917 it had an issued share capital of £1m (half of which was subscribed in the United States and the remainder in Britain and South Africa), which the directorate had the power to increase to £2m.[51] As Ernest Oppenheimer's son, Harry, has noted: 'This capital was substantial at the time and from the beginning the Corporation was planned as a major new mining house' (1967, p. 97).

In addition to the direct links with other powerful monopoly combines and the state which Anglo American acquired and which were reflected on the company's directorate, the group sought and secured backing for the new company from other influential quarters as well. For instance, Herbert Hoover (later to become President of the United States) was an important contact, having been closely associated with Ernest Oppenheimer and Honnold in raising American financial support for the corporation. Furthermore, before floating the corporation, Ernest Oppenheimer had carefully sought to obtain informal backing for the venture from important functionaries of the state in South Africa, thereby preparing the ground politically as well as economically. In particular, he had sought the backing of the Prime Minister, General J. C. Smuts, by insisting that the company be registered in South Africa so as to emphasize its South African character (though this move would seem to have had as much to do with the tax benefits which could be derived from a South African registration as with any gestures to economic nationalism in South Africa). Oppenheimer undoubtedly was concerned that the new company's significant American backing should not raise fears in South African state circles of *American* domination of South Africa's natural resources and he actually presented the pro-British Smuts with a confidential statement outlining 'the American connection'. As a result, Oppenheimer was able to report that Smuts 'welcome[s] the idea of American financiers taking an interest in South African development and generally looks upon the formation of our Company with considerable favour' (cited in Gregory, 1962).

Thus the considerable financial backing and political support which Anglo American received, both within the United States and Britain on the one hand and within South Africa on the other, provided Ernest Oppenheimer with a good deal of justification for the ambitious programme he was sketching out for the company even before it was formed:

> The first object I have in view is to secure for our company a fair share in the business offering on the Far East Rand. Once this is accomplished I shall steadily pursue the course of bringing about an amalgamation of Consolidated Mines and Rand Selection with our own company. We have already travelled some considerable distance towards an amalgamation between Mines and Rand Selection . . . it does not seem too optimistic to think that we shall be able, within a reasonable time, to bring about a willing combination of the three Eastern Rand holding companies which would straightaway make us the most important gold group in Johannesburg. There is, moreover, no reason why our new company should not grow in other directions than in gold development. It may for instance play a part in the diamond world. What South Africa wants (for diamonds) is enterprise and money and I believe our new company will supply both.[52]

These words were, of course, to prove prophetic. Yet in assessing their impact as prophecy it is important that we do not confuse Oppenheimer's undoubted ability to make a reasonable assessment of his company's potential, based on his knowledge of its position in production, with an idealized view of him as a sort of visionary guided by unfailing entrepreneurial skills. Most interpretations of Anglo American's history, including especially that by Gregory, tend towards the latter interpretation (and are reinforced by a vast battery of company propaganda). Yet in the era of monopoly capitalism there is little room for the entrepreneur and even less for the visionary. Given the considerable background experience in diamonds of those who controlled the corporation and given the corporation's grounding in production on the rich gold fields of the Far East Rand, there is little likelihood that the course of the company would have been significantly different under another chairman. The only factor which could have *significantly* changed the course of its history would have been a different outcome to the struggles being waged between capital and labour in the mining industry as a whole, since it was these which established the conditions for accumulation in the industry. But the conclusion of these struggles in capital's favour after 1922 paved the way for the company to expand along its designated course. Oppenheimer's real strength lay in his down-to-earth ability to correctly gauge that course and in his determination to steer the company along it.

94 Anglo American

NOTES

1. Although the 1913 strike was led by white miners, African workers also participated on a significant scale. (See Simons and Simons, 1969, pp. 156–60.) The implications of this were not lost on the capitalist class. The *Report of the Economic Commission* drew attention 'to the danger in South Africa under existing conditions of industrial unrest', noting in particular 'what serious effects such disturbances have upon the native mind'. According to the report:

> A Government inspector deposed thus:—'Some natives are realizing that it is in their interests to form a combination, and they are engaged in bringing into existence what they call "The Native Workers Union"' . . . In answer to the question whether he thought that the natives had learned lessons in combination from the events of last July, the Inspector replied: 'I am sure of it.' (para. 95)

2. Union of SA, *Official Year Book of the Union of SA*, no. 1, 1917, pp. 430–4; no. 2, 1918, pp. 469–77; and no. 8, 1925, pp. 484–92.
3. Cons. Gold Fields of SA, Report of the Manager of the Company in Johannesburg, 30 June 1918.
4. New Cons. Gold Fields, *Report of the Directors*, 30 August 1921, p. 21.
5. Taking 1936 as base year (100), white cash wages fell in real terms from 102 in 1911 to 94 in 1916 and 90 in 1921. The decline in real black cash wages is even more marked: base year (100) 1936: from 100 in 1911 to 90 in 1916 to 69 in 1921. Consequently, the ratio in the earnings gap between white and black workers rose from 11.7:1 in 1911 to 12.0:1 in 1916, reaching 15.0:1 in 1921. (F. Wilson, 1972, p. 46.)
6. Calculated from Central Mining and Investment Corp. *Report of the Proceedings at the Fifteenth Ordinary General Meeting*, 18 June 1920, p. 13.
7. Cons. Gold Fields of SA, Report of the Manager of the Company in Johannesburg, 30 June 1918.
8. A strike of black mine-workers in June 1913 was followed by a spate of strikes in December 1915 and January and February 1916. In 1917 black miners embarked on a mass boycott of mine shops because of the high prices of goods they carried (see Bonner, 1979).
9. Even most of those mines at which black workers did not strike were 'affected' since in many cases troops had to be used to prevent miners from going on strike. (Bonner, 1979.)
10. Nor should these events be isolated from the general trend towards militancy among workers throughout the society at this time. The number of white trade union members in the country rose from 10 500 in 1915 to 132 000 in 1920; the number of strike actions rose from 12 in 1914 to 47 in 1919 and 66 in 1920 (Simons and Simons, 1969, p. 220); in 1919 the first large-scale organization of African workers and peasants, the Industrial and Commercial Workers' Union (ICU), was formed; and in 1921 the Communist Party of South Africa was formed.
11. Under the conditions of white labour shortage which applied during the war, the mine-owners were unlikely to succeed with a strategy to reduce costs in that quarter at that time. Similarly, they could not hope to achieve any significant reductions in the price of stores, most of which were beyond their control.
12. Cons. Gold Fields of SA, *Report of Manager in SA*, 30 June 1918, p. 4.
13. Cons. Mines Selection Co., *Report of the Directors*, 31 December 1919, p. 4.
14. Central Mining and Investment Corp., *Report of the Directors*, December 31 1920; and Cons. Mines Selection Co. *Report of the Directors* for year ending 31 December 1921, p. 5.
15. Cons. Gold Fields of SA, *Report of the Managing Director*, 30 June 1920, p. 15.
16. New Cons. Gold Fields, *Report of the Directors*, 30 June 1921, p. 25.
17. As early as 1919 the Gold Fields Group reported that 57.5 per cent of the total spent on stores for group mines was spent on locally produced goods (that is, £790 000 out

of a total of £1 380 000), with the remainder being imported. (Cons. Gold Fields of SA, *Manager's Report,* 17 September 1919, p. 14.)

18. Report of Sir Evelyn Wallers, Director, in Central Mining and Investment Corp., *Report of the Directors at the Twentieth Ordinary General Meeting,* 31 December 1924, p. 13.

19. The cost of stores, which had averaged £14 402 000 between 1920 and 1921, declined to an average of £13 601 500 between 1923 and 1924 (1922 excluded because of the interruption to production caused by the Rand Revolt). (Union of SA, *Official Year Book of the Union of SA,* no. 8, 1925, pp. 484–92.)

20. In November 1921 Lionel Phillips wrote: 'Smuts accused me of wanting a strike. This is, of course, furthest from my desire, but there are worse things than a strike (deplorable as it may be) viz:—to sit supinely by and watch ruin overtake half the industry . . . Smuts's argument against a strike is that it is impossible to foresee its course or end.' (Fraser and Jeeves, 1977, pp. 327–30.)

21. New Cons. Gold Fields, 30 June 1922, pp. 19–20.

22. ibid., p. 21.

23. The manager added: 'The prospects of the Industry for the future are today much brighter than has been the case for many years past.' (New Cons. Gold Fields, Report of the Manager, 29 November 1923, p. 21.)

24. New Cons. Gold Fields, *Report of the Proceedings at the Ordinary General Meeting,* 29 November 1923, p. 20.

25. Union of SA, *Official Year Book of the Union of SA,* no. 8, 1925, pp. 484–92.

26. New Cons. Gold Fields, *Report of the Ordinary General Meeting,* 29 November 1923, pp. 28–9. Before the strike the mine-owners had promised the unions that 'not more than 2000' white workers would be retrenched, 'and then only as a temporary measure pending the return to the former level of profits'. (Simons and Simons, 1969, p. 278.)

27. SA Bureau of Census and Statistics, *Union Statistics for Fifty Years* (1960).

28. Union of SA, *Official Year Book of the Union of SA,* no. 13, 1930–1, pp. 426–35; and no. 17, 1934–5, pp. 505–16.

29. Central Mining and Investment Corp., *Report of the Directorate,* 31 December 1923, p. 4.

30. Central Mining and Investment Corp., *Report of the Consulting Engineer,* 31 December 1923, p. 11.

31. Report by Sir Evelyn Wallers, Director, in Central Mining and Investment Corp., *Report of the Directors at the Twentieth Ordinary General Meeting,* 31 December 1924, p. 11.

32. In 1923 Central Mining reported: 'Our technical advisers' detailed investigation of rock drilling methods . . . was energetically continued during the year, and has furnished results of outstanding importance, which we have recently communicated to the industry generally, through the medium of the Witwatersrand Mine Managers' Association and the South African Institution of Engineers.' (Central Mining and Investment Corp., *Report of the Consulting Engineer,* 31 December 1923, p. 11.)

33. This tendency within gold mining capital was further encouraged by the fact that the groups themselves were already closely linked through cross-shareholdings and interlocking directorships.

34. New Cons. Gold Fields, *Report of the Directors,* 30 June 1924, p. 19.

35. Anglo American Corp. of SA, *Report of the Proceedings at the Eighth Ordinary General Meeting,* 16 May 1925, p. 4.

36. Central Mining and Investment Corp., *Report of the Directorate,* 31 December 1923 and *Report of the Consulting Engineer,* 31 December 1924, p. 19.

37. According to the Directors' Report, one 'wet' jack-hammer could be operated by two Africans and could break as much ground as 15 to 20 'hammer boys'. (Central Mining and Investment Corp., *Report of the Directorate,* 31 December 1923.)

38. Central Mining and Investment Corp., *Report of the Consulting Engineer,* 31 December 1924, p. 19.
39. Anglo American Corp. of SA, *Report of the Proceedings of the Eighth Ordinary General Meeting,* 16 May 1925, p. 4.
40. Between 1898 and 1911 the Far East Rand produced some 6.4 per cent of the total output of the Witwatersrand compared with 83.9 per cent for the Central Rand.
41. Sir Robert Kotze, Government Mining Engineer, Memorandum on the Far East Rand, Department of Mines, 1916.
42. Cons. Mines Selection Co., *Report of the Directors,* 31 December 1917.
43. Cons. Gold Fields, *Report of the Directors,* 30 June 1919, p. 17.
44. Cons. Mines Selection Co., Minutes of the Ordinary General Meeting, reproduced in *The Mining World* (28 May 1921), p. 2.
45. Anglo American Corp. of SA, *Eight Annual Report,* 31 December 1924, p. 4.
46. Originally of German descent but subsequently naturalized British, Anton Dunkelsbuhler had arrived in Kimberley in 1872 as a representative of the diamond dealing firm of the Mosenthals. In 1878, however, he set up his own firm, A. Dunkelsbuhler and Co. The firm prospered and two of Dunkelsbuhler's cousins, Louis and Ernest Oppenheimer, were subsequently brought into the business (Ernest following his elder brother in 1896). In 1902 Ernest was sent to South Africa to run the company's Kimberley office and it was he who persuaded the company to take a large interest in the successful Premier Mine. Both Ernest and Louis eventually became partners in the Dunkelsbuhler Co. and, after Anton died, controlled the company, together with their cousin Walter Dunkels. (Gregory, 1962.)
47. These were: Anton Dunkelsbuhler and Co., which was controlled by the Oppenheimers and which in turn controlled the Cons. Mines Selection Co., which in its turn controlled the Rand Selection Corp. The Oppenheimers also had interests in a number of other smaller companies, but these three were by far the most important.
48. In 1917 the authorized capital of the Cons. Mines Selection Co. was only £600 000 (issued capital £552 500), while the issued capital of the Rand Selection Corp. was only £550 000. (Cons. Mines Selection Co., *Directors' Report* for the year ended 31 December 1917, p. 1.)
49. German shareholdings amounted to 33.5 per cent of the company's total issued share capital (from 'a letter to the Shareholders of the Consolidated Mines Selection Company Ltd from Sidney S. Kennedy', dated 16 May 1918). In fact the German connection resulted in a concerted attack being waged on the company in the British press following the outbreak of war.
50. In addition to this central board of directors there was also a New York committee, under the chairmanship of Honnold and consisting of the above mentioned US directors plus T. W. Lamont, and a London committee consisting of a number of directors of Cons. Mines Selection, including Louis Oppenheimer. (All data derived from Anglo American Corp. of SA, *Third Annual Report of the Directors,* for the year ending 31 December 1919, p. 1.)
51. Comparative figures for the authorized share capital of other groups on the Rand in 1918 are as follows (from Gregory, 1962):

Cons. Gold Fields of SA:	£4.5m
Johannesburg Cons. Investments:	£4.5m
Central Mining and Investments:	£3.4m
General Mining:	£1.9m
Goerz and Co. (Union Corp.)	£0.88m

52. Letter from E. Oppenheimer to Honnold, dated 25 May 1917, and cited in Gregory (1962).

CHAPTER 4

The Marriage of Gold and Diamonds: Anglo Absorbs De Beers

By the time the Far East Rand was actually proclaimed a gold field the Oppenheimer Group had three gold mining companies operating in the area—Brakpan Mines, Springs Mines and Daggafontein Mines— and was in control of two other mining areas, Schapenrust Claims and Geduld Deep Mynpachten.[1] Initially, these companies were under the direct control of Consolidated Mines Selection and Rand Selection, and when Anglo American was formed it, too, acquired shares in all three. At the same time the new company embarked upon a fierce battle with the JCI Group for control over two other important mining areas in the field, the West Springs Area and the new State Areas Lease. Although Anglo American was successful in winning control over the first of these areas, subsequently forming its own mining company (West Springs Ltd) to develop it, Anglo failed in its bid for the latter area.

By 1918 the Oppenheimer Group had control over four of the eleven mining companies on the Far East Rand (with minority interests in others). No other single mining group, except for JCI, controlled more than one Far East Rand mine. Furthermore, as Oppenheimer himself declared in his Chairman's Report of 1920: 'The gold mines in which we are largely interested are classified as "high grade" propositions . . . We have considerable investments in several properties which, although not yet productive, give promise of great potential value.'[2] Table D clearly illustrates the high profitability of Anglo American's Springs Mine in both 1917 and 1918 when compared with the average on the Far East Rand and on the Rand as a whole. In 1918 the Springs Mine recorded a profit per ton which was 22 per cent higher than the average for the Far East Rand and a massive 213 per cent above that for the Witwatersrand as a whole.[3]

Thus, with its interests confined largely to 'high grade propositions' on the Far East Rand the Oppenheimer Group, and Anglo American in particular, stood in a favourable position in relation to the other groups active on the Witwatersrand. Although not as yet in a position to challenge the dominance of the old groups, such as Central Mining

Table D   Comparison of Profitability of Springs Mine with Mines on the Far
East Rand and Witwatersrand

	Anglo American Group Springs Mine		Average for mines on Far East Rand		Average for mines on Witwatersrand	
	1917	1918	1917	1918	1917	1918
Revenue per ton *(s. d.)*	39/–	42/4	35/–	36/8	—	27/11
Costs per ton *(s. d.)*	22/1	22/6	19/4	20/5	—	21/7
Profits per ton *(s. d.)*	16/11	19/10	15/8	16/3	—	6/4

Source Cons. Mines Selection Co., *Report of the Directors,* 31 December 1917, 31
December 1918 and 31 December 1919.

which controlled twenty mines and milled 44 per cent of the industry's
total tonnage, or Gold Fields with its fourteen mines, none the less the
foothold which the Oppenheimers had gained in the lucrative new
growth area in the industry was to provide them with a profitable and
secure basis from which to launch further expansion. Their first move
in this direction, when it came, was of such a scale that it left no room
for doubt that the Group was about to become a force to be reckoned
with in southern African mining.

ANGLO AMERICAN AND NAMIBIAN DIAMONDS

Because of their heavy investment programme on the Far East Rand
the leadership of the Anglo American Group had expressed a reluc-
tance to embark upon any major new investment programme unless
'new business of any really tempting nature' should happen along.
Early in 1920, however, in a brief circular to the shareholders of the
Anglo American Corporation, Ernest Oppenheimer announced that he
had given way to temptation and had acquired a new diamond company in Namibia.[4] The speed of the acquisition and the secrecy with
which it was surrounded indicates just how effective Oppenheimer's
pre-flotation preparations for Anglo American had been, for it was the
'inside' contacts that he had secured in the state which enabled him to
clinch the deal before his competitors even knew of the proposition.

   What in fact happened was that the Namibian diamond fields, which
by 1914 were producing 21 per cent of southern Africa's total diamond
output, were taken over by the Custodian for Enemy Property during
South Africa's occupation of the German colony. After the war pressure
was brought to bear on the German companies in the colony to sell
their diamond interests to companies which would be more sym-
pathetic to the promotion of British interests in the region. While this
pressure was being exerted, the former Finance Minister in South
Africa, F. C. Hull, who was also a director of Anglo American, entered

into secret negotiations with the South African government for Anglo American to buy up these companies. By the time these negotiations were discovered by De Beers, the sale of these companies to Anglo American had virtually been secured. Although the Oppenheimer Group's own financial resources were inadequate for them to carry through this coup over De Beers alone, Anglo American was able to draw on the financial resources of the giant J. P. Morgan Group in the United States to carry it through (Gregory, 1962, p. 117).

This acquisition is crucial to a consideration of the Group's future evolution, and especially of Anglo American's role within it. The Group had long been involved, via Dunkelsbuhler and Co., in the diamond industry, but this involvement had proved to be far from satisfactory, leading Ernest Oppenheimer to express the wish that Anglo American should extend its activities in diamonds.[5] With its existing diamond interests confined largely to the sphere of trade the ideal course for the Group was to gain control over a major diamond producer as this would strengthen its position in relation to the Barnato–Breitmeyer–De Beers group which exercised an uneasy hegemony over the industry. The Namibian acquisition gave the Oppenheimer Group access to precisely the source of power in production which it needed to strengthen its position.

Although the *sale* of diamonds had been centralized in Namibia under German control, *production* had not and Anglo American's initial investment had involved buying up eleven mining companies that controlled production in Namibia. However, no sooner was this completed than Anglo set about centralizing production under a single company, Consolidated Diamond Mines of South West Africa, formed specifically for that purpose.[6] To carry through the thorough reorganization of production relations necessary to reap the benefits of economies of scale, CDM had to seek government approval for the scheme. But, as Harry Oppenheimer delicately put it, 'Hull had been working quietly in this matter' (1967, p. 98), and by 1922 Ernest Oppenheimer was able to report:

> The negotiations with the South West Africa—Administration, for bringing about an agreement for working the whole of the Company Fields as one unit, and for consolidating the various sales of Royalties, have now been brought to a successful conclusion . . . In broad outline, the result is that your Company has, *inter alia*, the sole and exclusive right to win diamonds for a very lengthy period of years, within the area of the Sperregebiet [approximately 27 000 sq. km/10 400 sq. miles], except only on certain Fields held by other Diamond Companies [about 98 sq. km/38 sq. miles in all]. furthermore, all production within this area can now be treated as one unit and mining carried on in the most economical manner, irrespective of any other consideration.[7]

By the beginning of the 1920s, then, CDM seemed set to make a major contribution to the revenue of the Group as a whole—and monopoly penetration of the Namibian economy had entered a new phase.

However, the recession which rocked the capitalist world in 1920 and 1921 hit the diamond industry, as usual, particularly severely and, far from proving a boon to the Group at this time, CDM became a liability on Group resources. CDM's contribution to world production fell from 16.8 per cent in 1920 to 11.5 per cent in 1921 and 10.3 per cent in 1922, during which time all dividend payments ceased and the Anglo American Corporation was forced to enter into a Financial Support Agreement to help the diamond company through the crisis.[8] Backed by the income from its holdings in the Far East Rand, as well as by its overseas financial supporters, Anglo American was able to sustain CDM through the crisis, thus enabling the diamond company to survive a period in which, under conditions of small-scale capitalism, it would probably have collapsed. CDM immediately cut back on production, expelling thousands of workers from production and maintaining only a skeleton labour force: the number of workers employed by CDM fell from 285 whites and between 2583 and 3816 blacks during 1920[9] to 58 whites and 166 blacks in January 1922.[10]

By 1922, however, the crisis had abated and the diamond market began to recover: the value of CDM's diamond sales, which were only £18 017 in the first quarter of the year, had reached £524 700 by the end of that year and the Financial Support Agreement with Anglo American was automatically terminated. By the end of 1923 the total value of CDM's diamond sales had reached £1 404 161 and the company's contribution to world production had climbed to almost 13 per cent.[11] This improvement was, of course, only made possible by drawing labour back into production again, a trend which is reflected in the rise in employment figures: by December 1923 274 white workers and 4429 black workers were employed by the company and the general manager was complaining of a severe shortage of black labour.[12] The following year (1924) Anglo American reported that the diamond market was 'firm and active' again: CDM had successfully weathered its first storm.

Thus it was Anglo American's position as part of a monopoly conglomerate which was the key to its successful take-over of diamond production in Namibia: first, because it had access to the financial resources of overseas monopoly groups which gave it the financial power to buy the rights to virtually all the diamondiferous areas in Namibia; secondly, because it had the organizational capacity to centralize production on the diamond fields, thereby increasing the scope of production and profitability in the area; and thirdly, because it had other sources of income in gold production which it could draw on to sustain its diamond producers through the crisis of the international depression. The fact, too, that these alternative sources of income were in *gold* production needs to be stressed because in a capitalist crisis (such as occurred between 1920 and 1922), while the price of most commodities fell, or at the very least fluctuated dangerously, the price of the money-commodity, gold, remained relatively stable. (In fact, the gold premium which operated at this time gave the gold price a boost.) Hence, while most capitalist businesses were unstable and insecure during the crisis, those engaged in gold production had a stable source of revenue which provided them with a bulwark of support.

ANGLO AMERICAN AND GROUP CONTROL

The acquisition of CDM had important ramifications for the control structure within the Oppenheimer Group as a whole. Although the seat of control within the Group rested in A. Dunkelsbuhler and Co., controlled exclusively by the Oppenheimer family, it was the Consolidated Mines Selection Co. which, since its take-over by the Oppenheimers in 1905, had been the leading or 'front' company in the Group—that is, it was from this company (and not the Dunkelsbuhler Co.) that the Group's major subsidiaries sprang. The establishment in 1917 of the Anglo American Corporation as a group holding company did not initially alter this pattern since the new company joined Rand Selection and the smaller New Era Consolidated as major subsidiaries of Consolidated Mines. (See Figure 1.)

However, the acquisition of CDM which was carried through by the Anglo American Corporation on behalf of the Group raised this latter company's standing in the Group, especially in relation to Consolidated Mines. Not only was Anglo American in a stronger position financially than Consolidated Mines, but with roots in the major branches of mineral production in South Africa it was more securely placed. It was rapidly becoming clear that as a largely under-capitalized speculative concern, Consolidated Mines was not a particularly suitable vehicle to lead the Group through the period of heavy development work on the South African properties which lay ahead; Anglo American, on the other hand, in a much stronger financial position, seemed better placed to carry through these tasks.[13]

The first phase in the transfer of Group leadership to Anglo American began when the chairman of Consolidated Mines announced the take-over by Anglo American of the Rand Selection Corporation.[14] To carry through the deal Anglo American increased its authorized share capital from £2m to £4m, of which £3 320 000 was issued. At the same time provision was made to raise the number of directors on the Anglo American board from six to a possible twelve so as 'to provide additional seats on the Directorate as the interests of your [Anglo American] Corporation extend and become more varied'.[15] Through this take-over the Anglo American Corporation emerged in practice as the leading company in the Group.

Shortly after the take-over the depression broke, hitting Consolidated Mines particularly badly. Grossly under-capitalized and heavily overcommitted to a large development programme in South Africa, the company was thrown headlong into a financial crisis.[16] There was now no alternative but for Anglo American to step in and save its ailing partner. On 17 October 1922 the directors of Consolidated Mines called an Extraordinary General Meeting: 'For the purpose of submitting to the Shareholders an agreement for the sale of the South African assets of the Company to the Anglo American Corporation of South Africa Ltd.' The agreement was ratified at the meeting, although not without some strong criticisms being raised, and Consolidated Mines Selection passed into virtual obscurity, retaining only 'a number of small interests of a speculative character' of its own, the book value of which amounted to a mere £55 000.[17]

The depression which rocked the capitalist world in the early 1920s was thus the final stimulus to the rationalization of the Group's control structure. With its sound financial backing, authorized share capital of £4m and lucrative investments in southern Africa's gold and diamond mines, the Anglo American Corporation had emerged with virtually the whole of the productive resources of the Oppenheimer Group concentrated under its control. (See Figure 2.) Although from this point onward it is the Anglo American Corporation which inevitably holds the centre of the stage within the Group (reflected in the fact that the Group as a whole came to be known by its name), sheltered behind the giant corporation and still exercising control over it stood as always the Oppenheimer family's own company, A. Dunkelsbuhler and Co.

ANGLO AMERICAN AND THE STRUGGLE FOR DE BEERS

Virtually from its inception, capital in the South African mining industry had exhibited a strikingly high degree of centralization, with control over all the major branches of production and distribution in the industry centralized in relatively few hands. The major organizational form this inter-penetration took was for groups to emerge holding important interests in both gold and diamonds. For instance, the Central Mining Group had major interests in both the gold and diamond industries through its holdings in the Central Mining Corporation (mainly gold) and L. Breitmeyer and Co. (diamonds). Similarly, following Barnato's death Solly Joel had combined Barnato's interests with his own, thus not only giving him control over important gold (through JCI) and diamond (through Barnato Bros) interests, but also making him the largest single shareholder in De Beers Consolidated, the

Jagersfontein Mine and the Premier Diamond Mining Co. The Oppenheimer family had moved along the same well-trodden path: from the position they held in diamonds through the Dunkelsbuhler Company, they had penetrated the gold industry through Consolidated Mines, Rand Selection, New Era and Anglo American; their acquisition of CDM then took them back into diamonds.

Although this close inter-penetration of capital existed, relations of control among the major owners of production in the industry were relatively loosely organized. Hence, no one particular group of monopoly capitalists had managed to gain a firm control over *all* aspects of mining activity. Certainly one could speak of a loose coalition of interests (combining Central Mining in gold, De Beers Consolidated in diamond production, and Breitmeyer and Barnato's in diamond dealing) as exercising a leadership position in the industry. But this coalition, effectively amounting to an alliance between two distinct groups (the Central Mining–Breitmeyer Group on the one hand and the JCI–Barnato Group on the other) was far from secure in this position. Not only was it relatively weak at the core, having no clearly defined operational centre, but also large areas of diamond and gold production fell beyond the sphere of its control and therefore its effectiveness throughout the industry was limited. We saw earlier that it was the seizure of some of these areas of production beyond the sphere of control of the hegemonic Group alliance (the Far East Rand in gold and Namibian production in diamonds) which had enabled the Anglo American Group to develop from relatively ineffectual beginnings into an important force in the industry. The question which this development posed was: what effect would the emergence of this dynamic new Group-force have on the existing relations of power and control in the industry?

The implications of this question were far less severe for the gold industry than for diamonds. The defeat of the miners' strike in 1922 had shown that centralization was sufficiently advanced to defend capitalists in the gold sector against the combined onslaughts of the working class and weak market conditions. Under these most intense of pressures, the alliance among the groups had held firm and enabled them to overcome the crisis of the early 1920s. There seemed no real reason why this alliance could not accommodate a shift in the balance of power among some of its leading members. However, conditions for capital in the diamond industry were far less secure and, consequently, a change in the balance of power in this industry threatened to initiate severe disruptions. In particular, there was the danger that unless new producers were co-opted into the existing relations of control in the industry, a destructive price war would develop which could shatter the sensitive market. Events over the following few years were to show just how fragile the 'unity' in the diamond industry had become.

When Anglo American gained control over CDM in 1919 pressure was immediately exerted on it to enter into agreement with the other South African producers, which it did.[18] However, as events rapidly unfolded, it became clear that the Anglo American Group was far from satisfied with either the terms of their agreement with the other producers or with their relations, on the selling side, with the syndicate.[19] Yet, with control of the syndicate firmly held by the Breitmeyer and Barnato companies and De Beers exerting a dominant influence over the South African producers, the Anglo Group was too weak to initiate the changes which it sought in order both to expand Namibian production and to develop the sales side of its operations through the Dunkelsbuhler Company.[20]

The discovery of six major new areas of diamond production after the war provided Anglo American with the opportunity to expand its productive base, and therefore its power, in the industry. All these fields—in Angola, the Congo, West Africa, British Guiana and, within South Africa, in Namaqualand and Lichtenburg—were outside the sphere of control of De Beers and the syndicate and thus needed to be brought within the ambit of their control in order to ensure stability for the market. Yet in the early 1920s when these fields began expanding production the controlling interests in the syndicate and De Beers were not well-placed to bring this about. The depression of 1920–2, which had hit the diamond industry particularly severely, had forced De Beers and the leading syndicate firm of L. Breitmeyer and Co. to shy away from new investments.[21] Nor did the financial links which the Breitmeyer company held with Central Mining alleviate this position, since this latter company's gold mines were among the least profitable at the time. Although the Anglo American Corporation's diamond interests were also damaged by the depression, her lucrative gold mines on the Far East Rand as well as her important American connections put her in a much stronger financial position than her competitors in diamonds.[22] In 1922 the Anglo American Corporation, together with the syndicate firm of Barnato Bros, reached an agreement for the purchase of Congolese diamonds; and the following year Anglo American announced the acquisition of the Companhia de Diamantes de Angola.

These coups enabled the Oppenheimers to increase their influence over both the Diamond Syndicate and De Beers. In return for handing over the contract for the purchase of Angolan and Congolese diamonds to the syndicate Anglo American was granted an 8 per cent holding in that organization. (Combined with the Dunkelsbuhler company's 12.5 per cent, this gave the Group as a whole a stake of just over 20 per cent in the syndicate.) At the same time the Anglo American Corporation gradually began buying shares in De Beers Consolidated; it acquired an interest in the diamond fields of West Africa, arranging to purchase all diamonds produced in these fields, and also entered into an agreement to purchase 'quite a proportion of the trade' in British Guiana diamonds.[23] The output of these fields (Angola, the Congo, West Africa and British Guiana), combined with that from Namibia, amounted in 1924 to some 38 per cent of total world production.[24] Anglo American's position in the industry had been substantially enhanced.

But Anglo American's competitors in De Beers and the syndicate were alive to the danger this posed to their position: in 1922 they tried to clip the company's wings by initiating a reduction in the price of diamonds—a move which Ernest Oppenheimer thought 'would cripple South West Africa permanently'.[25] The Oppenheimers responded by attempting to establish their own syndicate in open competition with the existing organization. But relations between the original syndicate and the South African producers proved too strong for the Oppenheimers to break and in the end it was only CDM and the other non-South African producers (all of which were already in the Oppenheimer camp) which joined the Oppenheimers' organization in 1925.

The establishment of the Oppenheimer syndicate had brought the battle into the open. But since the battle took the form of a price war between the two syndicates, it threatened to bring about the collapse of an already unsteady market. At this point the state intervened, as it had in a similar situation in 1914, to force a 'solution' on the contending parties in their own long-term interests. What the state in fact did was to introduce the Diamond Control Act (no. 39 of 1925) which in effect gave the state sweeping powers to take over the sale and production of diamonds in South Africa.[26] The reasons behind the Act's introduction were spelt out by the Minister of Mines:

> The whole object of this bill is not to carry out everything that is stated in it, but to have a sword of Damocles hanging over combinations and combines like the Syndicate. It is not intended to attack producers in South Africa: the main object is to protect producers . . . the object of the bill is further to stimulate competition . . . I cannot conceive of any hon. member saying that the producers in South Africa are in every respect capable of minding their own business and looking after their own interests, because if that statement is made, I challenge it at once. (Cited in Gregory, 1962)

While both De Beers and Central Mining spoke out strongly against the Act, accusing the government of 'interference in the conduct of the diamond business',[27] Ernest Oppenheimer adopted a far more conciliatory position, using his position in Parliament to secure an amendment to the bill (which was incorporated into the Act) that in the event of any dispute the government would give preference to *local* purchasers of diamonds. As a result the final version of the legislation favoured the locally registered Anglo American Corporation since the companies comprising the original syndicate were all registered abroad.

Under the combined pressures of the Anglo American syndicate and the state, the original syndicate split wide open: Solly Joel, who controlled Barnato Bros and was influential in JCI, transferred his allegiance to the Oppenheimer syndicate. The newly enlarged syndicate then made an offer to purchase the total output of De Beers and the other South African producers, which the original syndicate was unable to match. The offer was accepted on 30 July 1925. Having lost control of the output of the South African producers the original syndicate collapsed and in October of that year was taken over by the Oppenheimer syndicate.[28]

The take-over of the syndicate's business was a major landmark for the Oppenheimer Group in their campaign to exert a dominant influence in the diamond industry, since it ensured that as dealers the Group could no longer, in Harry Oppenheimer's words, be 'pushed around'. However, control over the syndicate meant more to the Group than just control over the *sale* of diamonds; it meant an important step forward in their campaign to secure control over *production* as well.

However, under the leadership of De Beers the three South African producers remained hostile to any attempt by the Oppenheimer Group to undermine their position in production (though in recognition of the power Anglo American had acquired in the industry Ernest Oppenheimer was appointed to the De Beers board in July 1926). The proclamation in 1926 and 1927 of two new and relatively rich diamond fields within South Africa (Lichtenburg and Namaqualand) gave Anglo American the opening it needed: by the end of 1927 the Group had brought the most important diamondiferous areas in the new fields under its control. A confrontation between Anglo and De Beers was now inevitable. In May 1927 the Anglo American Group made a bid for De Beers. Although the bid was rejected by the De Beers board, it was becoming increasingly apparent, in the face of the mounting international crisis which was threatening to engulf capital throughout the world, that centralization of control in the diamond industry was an urgent necessity.[29] Through the Morgan Grenfell Co. Anglo secured the financial backing of the giant Rothschild Group in its bid to take over De Beers and on 19 December 1929—just after the Great Depression had broken—De Beers capitulated. The following day Ernest Oppenheimer was unanimously appointed chairman of De Beers Consolidated Mines.

The timing of the take-over was thus directly linked to the Great Depression itself. Faced with the severe disruptions which the Depression initiated, capitalists in various industries throughout the world were forced to restructure the relations of production in their industries so as to resolve the contradictions caused by massive over-production. In the diamond industry this meant establishing a rigidly centralized control sructure through which drastic cut-backs in production could be enforced. As the new leader in the diamond industry, the task fell to the Anglo American Group to carry this through.

The first step was to carry through a thorough reorganization of the institutional control structure in the industry. The basis of this reorganization was, on the one hand, to bring De Beers firmly under the control of the Anglo American Group and, on the other, to extend the control of De Beers both over the other producers and over the sale of diamonds.[30] These changes, carried through during the Depression, brought the whole of the industry under Anglo American's tight control. (See Figures 3 and 4.) This control was exercised at three different levels: through the majority shareholding which the Anglo American Corporation and Barnato Bros had acquired in De Beers; through the control which De Beers exerted over the Diamond Corporation; and through the direct participation which the Anglo American Corporation and the Dunkelsbuhler Co. held in the Diamond Corporation.[31] The Anglo American Group had thus succeeded in bringing under its control all of the known diamondiferous resources in the capitalist world. From then on the Group's influence would be felt in every corner of the world, including the USSR, where diamond production for the international market occurred.

The second step was to drastically reduce output so as to resolve the crisis of over-production which was the root cause of the crisis in the industry. Although De Beers had emerged in control of the diamond industry this in itself was not sufficient to resolve the contradiction— what was needed was an assault on the working class. The form the capitalist attack took was to attempt to bring about the virtual cessation of diamond production throughout the world. As a first step De Beers, in the face of some opposition from the South African government, brought production on the Dutoitspan Mine to a halt and imposed a four-day week for white workers and a six-day (as opposed to seven-day) week for black workers on the Premier and Jagersfontein mines.[32] At the same time arrangements were made with the other non-South African producers to suspend deliveries of stones. However, the Depression did not abate and in 1932 De Beers sought to bring all its southern African mines to a halt. For a while the government tried to resist these moves, but Ernest Oppenheimer disparagingly swept their objections aside.[33] By December 1932 Oppenheimer could report:

> This means that, with the exception of the State diggings and the alluvial production, all production of diamonds in the Union of South Africa and in South West Africa has ceased for the time being. The producers outside the Union have co-operated with the producers in the Union in

bringing about material reductions in production and prospecting work, and in reducing or ceasing deliveries of diamonds and to this is due the small improvement in the diamond market which has been evident for the last three months. (Cited in Gregory, 1962, p. 284)

The gradual recovery of the diamond market which accompanied the lifting of the Depression saw conditions of profitability slowly return to the industry. Stocks held by the Diamond Corporation began to decline during the mid-1930s as sales increased: stocks fell from £15.1m in 1932 to £9.9m in 1937, while sales rose from £1.5m to £9.2m over the same period (Gregory, 1962, pp. 248, 311). In January 1935 conditions were suitable for De Beers to recommence production at CDM in Namibia and the following year Dutoitspan recommenced underground production. Although by this time the crisis was clearly past, De Beers refused to reopen the Jagersfontein and Premier mines, preferring to transfer their quotas of output to De Beers's other South African mines. This decision, which enabled De Beers to secure considerable financial advantages from economies of scale, led to the permanent loss of thousands of jobs. At the same time a further intensification of the control structure took place in the industry when the South African government, which held certain diggings in Namaqualand, joined the other southern African producers (De Beers, Premier, Jagersfontein, CDM, the Cape Coast Co. and the Diamond Corporation) in the Diamond Producers Association (formed in 1934). By the time the Second World War broke out the diamond industry was both strong and vibrant and the substantial increase in the demand for industrial diamonds which developed during the war ensured an expanding market thereafter.

CONCLUSION

In concluding our analysis of this phase of Anglo American's history it would be useful to comment on both the character of the Group and on the implications of its rise for the evolution of monopoly relations in South African society. Both these questions are important in assessing the key role which the Group has come to play in capital accumulation in South Africa.

Regarding the former, the Anglo Group is often regarded as being somehow 'more South African' or, conversely, less of an international group than its competitors in the mining industry. This argument is then used to explain why it was that Anglo, rather than one of the other mining companies, developed such a strong orientation towards involvement in South African political and economic affairs, expressed for instance in: its heavy South African investment bias; its early decision to register and establish a head office in South Africa; and the prominent role which it has played in the political life of the country.

Thus, according to this view, Anglo American becomes clearly differentiated from the other mining groups on the grounds that it is a South African rather than an international institution. In similar vein and contributing to this view is the ideology which Anglo itself has generated that it has been a pioneer in the struggle for economic nationalism in South Africa.

However, a more thorough examination suggests that this interpretation is far from accurate. For instance, although at the time Ernest Oppenheimer did present the South African registration of the Anglo American Corporation as a move in support of economic nationalism in the country, a few years later this same man, responding to the taxation system which the Smuts government had recently imposed on the mining industry, was presenting a very different explanation for local registration of the company:

> It is a matter of regret, however, that the dual taxation at present imposed upon companies by the Union Government and the Provincial Council has not been abolished. Apart from the unsettling effect of being at the mercy of two taxing authorities, there is always the danger that the two taxes together will be greater than the tax imposed upon companies in England, and that it would be more advantageous for companies to be floated in England instead of in South Africa. One of the chief reasons which made it possible for us to float the Anglo American Corporation in Johannesburg was that the Company would be subject to taxation only by the Union Government and that this taxation compared very favourably with the English Companies Tax.[34]

Thus in registering itself in South Africa the Group was clearly doing no more than any international firm would do: that is, seeking to secure an advantageous tax position for itself.[35] Furthermore, to argue that Anglo has played a more prominent role in South Africa's political life than the other groups assumes that these latter are concerned only with their profits and not with the broader economic and political issues in the country. This is clearly not correct: the fact that the Chamber of Mines arose, in Hobson's words, as 'the concentration of the entire industry for fighting purposes in politics and economics' shows unambiguously that *all* sections of monopoly capital on the Rand in fact displayed a very serious concern with these broader questions. Indeed, could one possibly expect anything less from capitalists exploiting the world's largest gold reserves?

We have argued that it was the monopoly phase in capital's evolution that produced the European financial conglomerates which gave rise to the giant monopolies or groups that dominate South Africa's mining industry. As we have seen, in its origins and form the Oppenheimer Group was no different from any of the others, being primarily located as far as shareholdings and financial backing were concerned in Britain, Germany and the United States of America, but largely located as far as production was concerned in diamonds and gold in South Africa. As an essential component of the Group, the Anglo American Corporation can clearly not be characterized in any other sense than as a European-based international company with strong American associations.[36]

However, it is true that there are important differences among the various groups, for instance in terms of the spread of their investments and their relations with the state in South Africa. In particular, the Oppenheimer Group stands out as being far more tightly linked to South Africa than any of the others. For instance, while in 1918 the interests of the Anglo American Corporation were all in South Africa, the South African interests of the second largest group on the Rand, Consolidated Gold Fields, accounted for less than 50 per cent of their total investment portfolio.[37] Similarly, while in 1920 all of the Anglo American Corporation's investments were tied up in South Africa and its colony, Namibia, less than 40 per cent of the investments of the largest mining group on the Rand, the Central Mining–Rand Mines Group, were in South Africa, the rest being spread throughout the world (*inter alia* in Nigeria, the Sudan, Trinidad, Britain, India, Burma and the United States).[38] An examination of the investment portfolio of the leading company in the Oppenheimer Group at this stage, Consolidated Mines Selection, reveals a similar tendency to that within Anglo American: in 1917 over 86 per cent of its investments were in South Africa and in 1919 over 88 per cent.

In order to explain the high concentration of Oppenheimer Group investment in South Africa in the period prior to the end of the First World War we need look no further than the financial difficulties which beset a small group involved in a considerable development programme on the Far East Rand. All available finance which the Group could secure in these early years was ploughed into development of these mines, hence the high concentration of South African investment compared with other groups. After the war it was, of course, the nature of the investment opportunity which arose—control over the rich Namibian diamond fields—and its close relation to the existing interests of the Group which determined its future investment programme. At a time of international instability it would have been foolish indeed for the Group to embark upon a programme of expansion on a world scale while such a tempting proposition as these diamond resources (in a sphere in which the Group had already developed considerable financial, technical and marketing skills) arose on its very doorstep. Given these investment decisions it is, of course, not at all surprising to find the Group's financial commitment to the region expressing itself in ideological and political terms as well. The 'South African nationalism' which the Group espoused was as much a product of its historical evolution as a means to protect and expand its interests in the future. More than any other, the future of the Oppenheimer Group was bound up, during this period, with the political, economic and social reproduction of capitalism in South Africa. Seen in this light, it is not surprising that representatives of the Group should have concentrated so much of their energies on seeking to influence the state directly and over and above the influence they could exert through institutional channels established by the industry as a whole, such as the Chamber of Mines. Ernest Oppenheimer himself entered Parliament, as did his son, Harry, and after him his son-in-law, Gordon Waddell.

The second point concerns the relationship between Anglo's rise and the evolution of monopoly relations in the country. In this and the preceding chapter we examined the way in which Anglo American came to concentrate some of the most important mineral resources in the region under its control, moving from a position of financial strength in the gold mining industry to a position of absolute control in the diamond industry. In carrying through this campaign the Group was forced, by the wider conditions of the industry, to introduce important reforms in the industry's control structure. However, it is worth emphasizing that in so doing the Group was not acting as a free agent nor in any sense autonomously—that is, it was not acting, as Gregory has argued, almost solely on the initiative of its chairman, Ernest Oppenheimer. Rather, the Group was responding to the underlying tendencies of concentration and centralization of production and capital which characterize monopoly capitalism. It was these monopoly tendencies which were forging greater unity between the different branches of mineral production in South Africa; Anglo American merely gave organizational and institutional expression to that unity. That is, the real unity created by these tendencies manifested itself organizationally in the form of the leadership role played by the Anglo American Group. Hence, Oppenheimer's 'genius' lay in the fact that he correctly perceived the fundamental tendencies of the time and recognized the favourable position his Group held (for example, the resources of the Far East Rand, American financial support, skills in the diamond industry, close links with the South African state) in relation to those tendencies.

This phase of the history of South Africa's mining industry, incorporating both the opening up of major new gold and diamond fields and the unification of large sectors of the industry under a single institutional control, was one in which the monopoly capitalist relations which had been established earlier were consolidated. As we have seen in this and the preceding chapter, consolidation was not carried through without the eruption of severe economic crises in both branches of the industry; without an intensification of open class conflict through the launching of savage onslaughts against workers in gold (in 1922) and diamonds (during the depressions); and without the development of considerable internecine strife and restructuring (especially in diamonds). Though the end result was at no stage predetermined—that is, at no point were the capitalists ever certain of winning through—in the end they did win, and handsomely at that. The defeat suffered by workers on the gold mines provided the conditions for capitalists to reorganize production relations in that industry so that, as we shall see, when market conditions favoured expansion during the 1930s they were able to make good the opportunities they were afforded. As far as diamonds were concerned, the retrenchments carried out during the Great Depression and, most important, the reorganization of the institutional control structure which followed the take-over of De Beers laid the basis for a new era of stability and expansion in the industry.

This phase of consolidation was thus crucial in terms not only of strengthening the relations of monopoly control in the industry, but also of bringing new areas of production under monopoly domination. Some of the areas covered in this and the preceding chapter, such as the Far East Rand gold field and the Lichtenburg and Namaqualand diamond fields, were inside South Africa's political borders, while others, such as the diamond fields of Namibia and Angola and, farther afield, those of the Congo and West Africa, fell beyond these borders. Yet, as we have seen, this political barrier provided no obstacle to Anglo American in its efforts to expand its productive base and extend the sphere of its control.

The point here is that while the phase of South Africa's mining development covered in our first two chapters ended in about 1910 with the firm establishment of monopoly relations, by the end of the Great Depression a phase of monoploy consolidation had been carried through which had involved *inter alia* the opening up of new areas of production in both major branches of the South African industry, the reorganization of the industry under stricter control and the extension of that control to new areas of production beyond South Africa's borders. These classical features of monopoly capitalism—the concentration of ever larger areas of production under increasingly centralized forms of control—point unequivocally to a substantial strengthening of monopoly capitalist relations in the mining industry at this time. As we shall see, this phase was to prove the precursor to the greatest period of expansion in the industry since its inception. But before proceeding with this aspect of our analysis it would be useful to look at the impact of these monopoly tendencies on branches of production outside the strict confines of the mining industry. As we noted earlier, though by the time of Union the influence of monopoly control in South Africa's mining industry was being felt throughout the region, whole areas of production and distribution still remained organized on pre- or petty-capitalist lines. We turn now to an examination of South Africa's growing manufacturing industry at this time to see what impact, if any, the strengthening of monopoly relations in mining was having on the evolution of this branch of production.

NOTES

1. The Brakpan Mine had begun producing well before 1917, while production on the Springs Mine began in that year. Daggafontein was, however, still only in the development stage and it was to be some time before this mine was to commence profitable production. Both Brakpan and Springs, however, became extremely prosperous relatively quickly. (Cons. Mines Selection Co., *Director's Report* for year ended 31 December 1917.)
2. Anglo American Corp. of SA, Fourth Ordinary General Meeting, Minutes of the Proceedings, 31 December 1920, p. 5.
3. Cons. Mines Selection Co., *Report of the Directors,* 31 December 1917, 31 December 1918 and 31 December 1919. In 1916 Anglo's Brakpan Mine recorded a profit per ton of 11s. 8d.; in 1917 it was 14s. 3d. and in 1918 16s. 8d. (Cons. Mines Selection Co., *Report of the Directors,* 31 December 1917 and 31 December 1918.)
4. The circular read as follows:

   Your Corporation and those associated with it hold the control of the new company, the Consolidated Diamond Mines of South West Africa. Your Corporation's interest exceeds one-third of the total capital of the new Company . . . Your Corporation and those associated with it are represented by five Directors (out of nine) on the Board of the new Company . . . The Anglo American Corporation of South Africa Ltd. will take charge of the London and Johannesburg offices of the Consolidated Diamond Mines of South West Africa Ltd. (Ernest Oppenheimer, Circular to Shareholders, Anglo American Corp. of SA, 24 February 1920)

5. Harry Oppenheimer (1967) remarked that at this time the Oppenheimer Group was being 'pushed around and [having] its share of the business unfairly limited by its larger and richer partners' (p. 97).
6. Shortly before the outbreak of war Professor Kaiser, a German geologist, had been commissioned to report on the Namibian diamond fields. He reported after the war as follows:

   If one examines the results of the actual exploitation of the fields and the prospecting work carried out so far, then, in the light of these experiences one arrives at the result that the content of the fields is for certain 14 million carats, and that it will probably amount to 16½ million carats, and this does not exhaust all the possibilities of the fields . . . It is quite possible that several million—possibly even many millions—of carats may be recovered from the diamond areas in excess of the above estimate. I must still add that in consequence of the amalgamation into one big company, many deposits which a small company could not exploit economically may now prove profitable. (Cited in Cons. Diamond Mines of SWA, *First Annual Report* for year ending 3 December 1920, p. 3)

7. Cons. Diamond Mines of SWA, *Third Annual Report* (Deputy Chairman's Report), 31 December 1922, p. 2.
8. Union of SA, *Official Year Book of the Union and of Basutoland, Bechuanaland Protectorate and Swaziland,* no. 12, 1927–8, p. 518. These percentages do not

reflect accurately the extent of the crisis in production in that they include the sale of accumulated stock.

9. Cons. Diamond Mines of SWA, *First Annual Report*, 31 December 1920, p. 8.
10. Cons. Dimaond Mines of SWA, General Manager's Report, pp. 6–7, *Third Annual Report*, 31 December 1922. Within South Africa De Beers adopted a similar policy in relation to workers on its producing mines. In 1921 the De Beers *Thirty-third Annual Report* stated: 'Since last year the world generally has been passing through a period of severe depression, which has been felt most acutely in the diamond industry [and which has] unfortunately necessitated the retrenchment of a large number of employees, both European and Native. All mining work was stopped, and expenditure in every department was greatly reduced.' (30 June 1921, p. 2.)
11. Anglo American Corp. of SA, *Seventh Annual Report*, 31 December 1923, p. 4.
12. Cons. Diamond Mines of SWA, General Manager's Report, *Fourth Annual Report*, 31 December 1923, p. 5.
13. The relative financial strengths of the two companies was reflected in their capital position in 1919: the authorized share capital of Cons. Mines, which was fully issued, stood in that year at £600 000; while that for Anglo American was £2m, of which only £1m had been issued. (Cons. Mines Selection Co., *Directors' Report*, 31 December 1919, p. 1, and Anglo American Corp., *Third Annual Report*, 31 December 1919, p. 3.)
14. Cons. Mines Selection Co.'s *Report of the Directors* (31 December 1919) stated:

> . . . The Anglo American Corporation of South Africa has made an offer to the Shareholders of the Rand Selection Corporation to exchange their holdings on the basis of eleven Anglo American Corporation shares for every five Rand Selection Corporation shares. Your Directors have enquired closely into the merits of the above offer, and it has been decided to take advantage of same, as far as the holding of the Consolidated Mines Selection Company in the Rand Selection Corporation is concerned. An important element in deciding on this course is the fact that the Anglo American Corporation has secured a very large interest in the management of the diamond mining industry of South West Africa, thus opening a new field of operations independent of the vicissitudes of South African gold mining. (p. 10)

(This latter point was elaborated on at some length in the Chairman's Report.)
15. Anglo American Corp. of SA, Circular to Shareholders, 2 March 1920.
16. The 1922 Chairman's Report of Cons. Mines Selection Co. outlined the problem as follows:

> The outstanding facts for Shareholders in the accounts are that the profit carried to balance-sheet is about £100,000 less than the corresponding figure a year ago; and that we have drawn on the reserve account to the extent of £100,000 in order to keep the valuation of our various assets on the usual safe basis for the future. The absence of a dividend . . . will have prepared you for the disappointing character of this year's report . . . Unfortunately the market price of some of our assets showed a heavy depreciation and it was necessary for safety to write off an amount of £151,996. To meet this depreciation in part we had to draw on the reserve account to the extent of £100,000 . . . It is with regret that we trench on the reserve account built up in preceding profitable years. (Printed in *The Mining World*, 27 May 1922)

17. As one irate shareholder pointed out, despite the fact that the Company's issued capital was only £600 000: 'between the years 1916 and 1920 inclusive you [the Directors] have provided or guaranteed the provision of a sum exceeding £5m for your subsidiary companies . . . What I understand is that this agreement [with Anglo American] is partly owing to the difficulties those guarantees have occasioned. I do not think it is a subject of congratulation if you have only £600 000 and you guarantee £5m.' (Cons. Mines Selection Co., Minutes of the Extraordinary General Meeting held on 17 October 1922, *The Mining World*, 4 November 1922, pp. 2–4.)

18. De Beer's quota was 51 per cent, Premier's 18 per cent, Jagersfontein's 10 per cent and Namibia's 21 per cent. (Gregory, 1962, p. 113.)
19. In 1920 Anglo American appealed to the state against the size of the Namibian quota. As a result the state granted a small increase of £200 000 per annum, with which Anglo expressed its continued dissatisfaction.
20. A. Dunkelsbuhler and Co. held a 12.5 per cent interest in the Diamond Syndicate, which allowed it the same proportion of participation in syndicate business. The two groups which together controlled the syndicate, Barnato Bros and JCI on the one hand, and L. Breitmeyer and Co. and Central Mining on the other, each held 35 per cent of the syndicate after the war. (Gregory, 1962, pp. 111, 136.)
21. As late as 1923 the De Beers Report was still commenting gloomily on the impact which 'this blighting and disastrous depression' was having on the diamond industry and outlining an extremely cautious policy to protect the company from the crisis:

    It is hardly necessary for me to remind you of what the people directly and indirectly dependent on the diamond industry have suffered and are still suffering. We have taken stock of the position, and have tried to read the future, and we have come to the conclusion that we must husband our resources, limit our activities to the principal object of the Company, cut away all unprofitable expenditure on outside ventures and undertakings, and economise wherever possible, and thus arm ourselves against evils that may arise from the unsettled and unsavoury conditions still prevailing in Europe and insure [sic] the future of your Company as far as human foresight can. Don't misinterpret our actions; we are not alarmists, but we are not going to shut our eyes to conditions the continuation of which makes the prospect of a complete restoration of the 1919–20 demand remote. It is better to face possibilities of depression . . . (De Beers Cons. Mines, *Thirty-fifth Annual Report*, 30 June 1923, p. 32)
22. In November 1921 Ernest Oppenheimer had written to his American associates thus:

    Further to this, from the very start, I expressed the hope that besides gold, we might create, step by step, a leading position in the diamond world, thus concentrating by degrees in the corporation's hands the position which the pioneers of the diamond industry (the late Rhodes, Wernher, Beit, etc.) formerly occupied. Such a position is most difficult to attain, requiring intimate knowledge of the diamond trade, pluck and a great deal of patience, but, above all, the support of powerful financial groups who would be prepared to play the part which Messrs. Rothschilds played vis-à-vis the original leaders, at the time of the De Beers amalgamation. It is quite evident to my mind that eventually an amalgamation of the four big diamond producers (De Beers, Premier, Jagersfontein and Consolidated Diamonds) will be brought about, and I see no reason, if we continue our diamond policy, why we should not play a leading role in such an operation. (Cited in Gregory, 1962)
23. Letter from Ernest Oppenheimer to M. Hodgson, dated 6 March 1924.
24. Union of SA, *Official Year Book of the Union of South Africa and of Basutoland, Bechuanaland Protectorate and Swaziland*, No. 10 1927–8
25. Letter from Ernest Oppenheimer to Louis Oppenheimer, January 1922.
26. In terms of the Act the government gained the right *inter alia:* to fix quotas and minimum prices; to create a Union Diamond Board with powers to purchase, sell, deal in and hold stocks of diamonds, and to export diamonds from the Union; in addition the Board could 'demand and receive diamonds from any producers . . . for export and sale on their behalf'; and could 'create a monopoly of sale and export through the Board'.
27. Central Mining and Investment Corp., Twentieth Ordinary General Meeting, Report of the Proceedings, 20 May 1925, p. 9.
28. Ernest Oppenheimer became chairman of the new syndicate, in which the Anglo American Corp. and A. Dunkelsbuhler and Co. held jointly a 45 per cent interest,

while Barnato Bros. held 45 per cent and JCI 10 per cent. The leading concern in the original syndicate, L. Breitmeyer and Co., was not represented on the new syndicate, although some of the smaller firms in the old syndicate subsequently became sub-participants in the new.

29. As early as July 1929, when the impending crisis was beginning to manifest itself on the world market, the Kimberley directorate of De Beers noted in a letter to the London Board that: '. . . in a business of the nature of that under discussion [the take-over bid by Anglo American] there are of course many factors which require careful consideration, and not the least of these is that of the general financial position of the world . . ." At the same time, Ernest Oppenheimer told Parliament that: '. . . there is at the present moment a considerable falling off in the demand for diamonds and the diamond trade requires the most careful handling to prevent the present lull from assuming serious dimensions'. (Cited in Gregory, 1962, p. 213.)

30. In July 1930 the Anglo American Corp.'s 59 per cent in CDM, as well as Barnato Bros' holding in Jagersfontein, were transferred to De Beers in return for shares in that latter company, giving Anglo American a controlling interest in De Beers and De Beers (which already held a controlling interest in the Premier Mine) control over CDM and Jagersfontein. With the four 'conference producers' now unified under a single control, Anglo American began to reorganize the control structure in sales so as to bring the selling institutions within the sphere of control of the producers. The Diamond Syndicate was enlarged to make way for the South African producers, who together owned 50 per cent of the new organization (known as the Diamond Corp.), while De Beers had the right to appoint the organization's chairman, who held a casting vote. In this way the South African producers, and ultimately De Beers, came to exercise control over the Diamond Corp. which was formed on 18 February 1930 with a capital of £2.5m. The Anglo American and Barnato companies then transferred their holdings in the Lichtenburg and Namaqualand fields to the Diamond Corp., thereby increasing the extent of their control over that organization. (A. Dunkelsbuhler and Co. and Barnato Bros were appointed as sole agents of the Diamond Corp.) The syndicate then transferred both its stock of diamonds and its contracts with the South African producers to the Diamond Corp. at the beginning of 1931 (as a result of which the corporation's capital was doubled to £5m) and then dissolved itself, leaving the Diamond Corp. in undisputed control of diamond sales throughout the world. Furthermore, the corporation was vested with the sole power to deal with all non-South African diamond stocks and to secure all future acquisitions of such diamonds. The Diamond Corp. thus emerged as the only institution through which diamonds could be sold on the international market and therefore, through their control over the Diamond Corp., De Beers and the other southern African producers now came to exert a powerful influence over producers throughout the rest of the world. (See Figure 4.)

31. Ernest Oppenheimer, who had become chairman of De Beers in December 1929, also became chairman of the Diamond Corporation in March 1930.

32. The government made some protestations to De Beers at the 'unfair treatment' afforded to white workers but Ernest Oppenheimer told the Minister of Mines: 'I am not going to be pointed to as the Chairman of De Beers company who saw it brought to bankruptcy and who kept their Europeans employed to ruin the shareholders.' (Gregory, 1962, p. 250.)

33. The Minister of Mines pointed out: 'We have had the spectacle in South Africa that there is one man who is chairman of all the producing companies in South Africa, that the same man is chairman of the Diamond Corporation. He alone is the centre of the whole diamond industry, and moreover, he advocates his own case in this House. The fact is that the Hon. Member for Kimberley can juggle, manipulate and deal with all the diamonds as he pleases . . ." Although the government actually set up a Commission of enquiry into 'the diamond industry in all its aspects and branches', the Anglo American Group refused to allow any section of the industry to

give evidence before the commission and it was subsequently withdrawn. (Gregory, 1962, pp. 264–84.)

34. Anglo American Corp. of SA, Eighth Ordinary General Meeting, Report of the Proceedings, 16 May 1925, p. 5.

35. Over the following years in fact most of the other groups followed Anglo American's example and registered themselves in South Africa.

36. In fact, as we saw earlier, about three-quarters of the initial £1m capital of this supposedly 'South African' concern was subscribed abroad: £500 000 in the USA and £250 000 in England.

37. Cons. Gold Fields of South Africa, *Report of the Directors,* 30 June 1918, Schedule no. 1. The Gold Fields Group in fact had a large expansion programme in the USA and in 1919 they changed the name of the holding company in the group from Consolidated Gold Fields of South Africa to New Consolidated Gold Fields.

38. Central Mining and Investment Corp., Report of the Proceedings at the Ordinary General Meeting, 18 June 1920, p. 3.

CHAPTER 5
Industrial and Mining Growth Between the Wars

THE ORIGINS OF THE CAPITALIST MANUFACTURING INDUSTRY

Inevitably, South Africa's incorporation into the imperialist system as a major exporter of minerals stimulated other sectors of the local economy, producing rapid growth and transforming their relations of production and distribution. Expansion of the local market initiated far-reaching changes in the relations of production in agriculture, encouraging the emergence of specific forms of capitalist relations in certain areas. Major developments occurred in infrastructure through expansion in means of transport (especially road and rail), telecommunications, electricity, water supply and so on. At the same time substantial changes began to manifest themselves within the country's nascent manufacturing industry. The mining industry not only provided a major *direct* market for manufactured commodities, it also *indirectly* provided new markets through the changes which it wrought in other sectors of the economy. Initially, the major imperialist powers supplied most of the manufactures for these markets, but before long South Africa's own manufacturing sector began to respond: existing small-scale craft and artisanal industries transformed themselves into capitalist enterprises, while a few foreign-owned companies established plants locally.[1] By the end of the Anglo-Boer War local manufacturing was supplying explosives, boots, steel, cement and candles for consumption on the mines, while clothes, textiles, brick, tiles, bakeries, soap and other locally produced light commodities were finding a wider internal market.[2]

However, in the face of competition from the imperialist powers, local capitalist manufacturing production was unable to make any substantial progress other than in a few limited areas. Although the state did provide some form of protection in 1906 (for *inter alia* boots and shoes, biscuits, confectionery, sugar, soap, blankets and rugs, printing and harness and saddlery) and although in 1910 the Cullinan Commission, which was appointed to investigate the possibilities of developing local industries, did recommend further protection (implemented by the state in 1914), the manufacturing sector remained relatively poorly developed, contributing only 7 per cent to the National Income in 1911–12 compared with 28 per cent for mining and 16 per cent for agriculture.[3] However, the outbreak of the First World War was to have important implications for this sector of the economy and for the future course of capitalist development in South Africa.

The outbreak of war caused considerable disruption to the existing system of international trade. On the one hand, the demands of the war forced the major European powers to move over to 'war production', generating acute shortages in a wide range of industrial and household commodities; while, on the other, the disruption to overseas trade routes caused by enemy harassment to shipping rapidly intensified these shortages. The overall result was not only a shortage of a whole range of commodities but also rampant price inflation. However, the increased cost of imported manufactured commodities immediately made local manufacturers more competitive on the South African market, while the shortages in a wide range of manufactured goods created a vacuum which local manufacturers, wherever possible, rushed to fill. The result was the rapid expansion of the local capitalist manufacturing sector: gross industrial production rose by 173 per cent in seven years (from £22m in 1910–11 to £40m in 1915–16, £49m in 1916–17 and £60m in 1917–18); the number of employees in the sector rose by 126 per cent over the same seven years (from 55 000 to 124 000 of whom 63 per cent were African); and the sector's contribution to the National Income rose to 9.6 per cent (compared with 21.6 per cent for agriculture and 20.3 per cent for mining).[4] South Africa thus emerged from the war with the nucleus of an industrial structure whose main pillars were electricity, steel, engineering (mainly maintenance and repair work), chemicals and fertilizers, construction materials, clothing and the processing of agricultural goods.

It should be noted at this point that, although much of South Africa's manufacturing production occurred independently of the mining industry, none the less capital from the mining industry did play an important role in the strategic industries referred to above. The engineering industry was, of course, closely linked to mining, while the mining house, Lewis and Marks, was involved in a wide range of manufacturing activities (see Note 1). Similarly, as we saw in Chapter 1, De Beers Consolidated had embarked upon a programme of manufacturing investment as long ago as the 1890s. The most important of these investments was in the explosives industry where, in response to the higher prices which flowed from the dynamite monopoly established by the Nobel–Dynamite Trust, De Beers had formed the Cape Explosives Works in 1903. In 1909 after another British firm, Kynochs, had established an explosives factory in the country, the South African market was 'divided' exclusively among these three producers.[5] The Central Mining and Investment Corporation controlled both the Pretoria Portland Cement Co. and the Cape Portland Cement Co., as well as having control in the Hume Pipe Co. (South Africa) and a brick and tile works.[6] The mining and property conglomerate, African and European (controlled by Lewis and Marks), owned a controlling 43 per cent stake in the largest steel producer in the country, the Union Steel Corporation of South Africa, which cast the first ingot of South African steel in 1913.[7] But probably most important of all was the mine-owners' role in the electrification of South Africa. In 1906 the Transvaal Chamber of Mines agreed to support the Central Mining and Gold Fields groups in the establishment of the Victoria Falls and Transvaal Power Co. in order to supply electricity to the mines. This company in effect monopolized the electricity supply in South Africa from its inception in 1906 until the establishment of the Electricity Supply Commission (ESCOM) in 1922.[8] Thus not only were mining companies involved in all those industries which formed the main pillars of the country's emerging industrial structure, but sometimes, as in the case of electricity and explosives, that involvement was linked to monopoly control.

Although it was the outbreak of war which triggered off this burst of industrial activity in South Africa, the cessation of hostilities did not automatically lead to a return to prewar conditions. In the immediate aftermath of the war the local industrial sector continued to expand: between 1917–18 and 1920–1 the value of gross industrial production rose by 63 per cent to stand at £98m (which meant a contribution of 12.3 per cent to the National Income, compared with 18.2 per cent for agriculture and 15.7 per cent for mining (Pearsall, 1937, p. 414). Although some of this increase is probably exaggerated by the inflationary conditions of the immediate postwar period, the actual volume of output in the industrial sector grew by a substantial 43 per cent between 1916–17 and 1920–1 (Pearsall, 1937, p. 414). This rapid rate of expansion is also reflected in the rising number of employees in the sector, reaching 180 000 in 1920–1, which was an increase of 45 per cent over 1917–18 and of 227 per cent over 1910–11. Between 1910–11 and 1920–1 the value of wages in the sector increased by 340 per cent (from £5m to £22m), while over the same period the value of fixed capital increased by only 120 per cent (from £20m to £44m) (Pearsall, 1937, p. 414). This would suggest, as is to be expected during a war when there is a shortage of capital goods for industry, that this industrial boom was labour-intensive in character.

But the question remains of how South Africa could sustain this level of industrial growth after the war, when one would have expected the resumption of industrial production in Europe to wipe out a number of the less competitive local industries. In fact, Europe's industrial recovery was seriously delayed by the escalation of militancy among the European working classes and by chaotic postwar economic conditions.[9] The period of rampant inflation which these conditions produced gave South Africa's industrial sector a further breathing space. In the words of the Secretary of the Department of Mines and Industries in South Africa:

> . . . having regard to the economic position of the world today, the present is undoubtedly a favourable opportunity for the investor to put capital into the development of Union resources. Great possibilities lie in the direction of steel production, of coal by-product and maize by-product industries, of woollen manufacture, fibre and cotton production, shipbuilding and repairing, and the development of our deep-sea fisheries, to mention only a few of the most important which require large capital to be put into them.[10]

The possible implications of this change in South Africa's industrial fortunes were not lost on some of the mining groups in the country. Consolidated Gold Fields, already involved to an extent in industrial investment in South Africa, took a particular interest. In 1919 the Group's manager argued that: '. . . we should turn to a policy of fostering and encouragement of local manufactures (dependent as little as possible upon the importation of raw materials) with a view both to lessening our dependence on overseas industrial conditions and to being able, by creating internal industrial competition, to take full advantage of cheaper local manufacturing costs'.[11] What makes this argument of special relevance is that it occurs at a time when the major price increase on the mines came from the rising wage level of white miners. The strategy being advocated here therefore seems to involve in part an attempt to try and drive down the value of (predominantly white-owned) labour-power by reducing the value of the bundle of wage-goods required for its reproduction. The success of this strategy would lead to the production of relative surplus-value on a generalized and hitherto unparalleled scale in South African society.

Some of the mining companies did in fact expand their industrial interests during this period. The Gold Fields Group was particularly active in the field, acquiring *inter alia* an engineering and building concern, a furniture company, a brick and tile works, a rubber factory, a soap and oil manufacturer and constructing a sugar mill. By 1920 the value of Gold Fields' industrial interests in South Africa had grown to almost 10 per cent of the total value of their investments.[12] Other mining companies which expanded their industrial interests at this time included African and European, which enlarged its steel interests (this company also controlled the South African Breweries and the Vereeniging Milling Co.),[13] and De Beers, which constructed a new fertilizer factory under the control of the Cape Explosives Works.[14] However, this trend was rapidly brought to a halt in the early 1920s when South Africa's industrial sector began to exhibit signs of strain.[15]

By this time the European capitalist classes had managed to reassert a somewhat shaky dominance over their working classes and industrial production was beginning to expand, leading to a gradual lowering of world prices for manufactured commodities (see Hobsbawm, 1972, Chapter 11). The result was increasing pressure on industrial production in South Africa and other peripheral countries. Faced with these pressures individual capitalists, including the mine-owners, turned to the state to support their industrial investments.[16] In 1921 the Smuts government responded by establishing the Board of Trade and Industries to redraft the Customs and Excise Tariffs and 'to advise the government in respect of assisting and developing industries in the Union'.[17] As a result Tariff Protection was extended to a further sixteen industries. However, the response to these measures from individual groups of capitalists was less than enthusiastic and by about 1923 it seemed clear that the state's piecemeal approach to the issue of protection was inadequate to stave off the mounting pressure of overseas competition.[18]

In the elections of the following year, however, the Smuts government was swept from power. The new government which took office, the Pact government, was dedicated to the more thorough protection of local industries. In 1925 it enacted the Customs Tariff and Excise Duty Amendment Act, which provided a wide range of protection for local industries. This was followed by the introduction of a number of other measures, such as the establishment of the state-owned Iron and Steel Corporation of South Africa (ISCOR), which served to promote local industrial development (for details of these various measures see Davies, Kaplan *et al.*, 1976, pp. 9–10). Through these and other changes South Africa's manufacturing sector received the support it needed to sustain it through a difficult phase of its growth.

Yet this description of the South African state's success in protecting the emerging manufacturing sector from the ravages of foreign competition belies the complexity of the problem. If it was as straightforward as this then one wonders why other peripheral countries were not able to follow a similar course. True, some like Australia and Canada did, but the vast majority did not and we need to explain why South Africa should have been among the privileged few. Most Marxist analyses have tended to explain this phenomenon by arguing that the Pact government was fundamentally different from its predecessors in that it represented an 'anti-imperialist' alliance of local capitalist classes (with white workers in tow) which was dedicated to the industrialization of South Africa (see Davies, Kaplan *et al.*, 1976, p. 29; and for a detailed critique of this position see Innes and Plaut, 1978, pp. 51–61). While changing class alignments and their implications for South African state policy are clearly an important part of the explanation, this does not go far enough since it assumes an unwarranted degree of passivity and homogeneity on the part of 'imperialism'. In other words, any analysis of new class alignments in South Africa needs to locate itself within the context of a changing imperialist framework. If the argument is broadened in this way the policies of the Pact government will be seen to be far less 'anti-imperialist' than has often been assumed.

IMPERIALISM AND SOUTH AFRICAN INDUSTRY

Analysing the economic changes in Britain during the inter-war period, Hobsbawm (1972) has argued that:

> . . . . in 1914 Britain was perhaps the least concentrated of the great industrial economies, and in 1939 one of the most . . . Concentration first became noticeable during the Great Depression—in the 1880's and 1890's—but until 1914 its impact in Britain was strikingly smaller than in Germany and the USA. In its industrial structure Britain was wedded to the small or medium-sized . . . competitive firm, just as in its economic policy it was wedded to Free Trade. There were exceptions, notably in the public utilities and heavy industries (iron and steel, heavy engineering, shipbuilding) . . . the tendency to concentration undoubtedly existed, but it had certainly not transformed the economy. However, between 1914 and 1939 it did so . . . (pp. 214–15)

This transformation, brought about as a result of Britain's failure to compete with her more highly concentrated industrial competitors, occurred together with a shift towards capital goods production in British industry. The period of postwar reconstruction and innovation offered new opportunities for British *heavy* industry at a time when her traditional *light* industries were in decline (Francis, 1939, pp. 57–62). Metals and metal products, electrical goods, chemicals, as well as durable consumer goods like motor cars, aircraft, silk and rayon emerged as the new 'growth industries'.[19]

This change in the structure of British production was accompanied by important shifts in British ideology and state policy. Staunch supporters of the policy of Free Trade, like Sir Lionel Phillips, the chairman of the Central Mining Group, suddenly began to question the wisdom of Free Trade policy and to support calls for local industrialization in peripheral countries like South Africa which were within the 'British Empire'.[20] However, the *quid pro quo* for this support was the demand that *British* capital goods be used in the construction of the light industries being established in these countries. This demand was most clearly expressed in the Ottawa Agreement signed in 1932 between Britain and the countries comprising her 'Empire' (see Francis, 1939; and also Drummond, 1974, pp. 170–201). As far as the South African market was concerned, the agreement secured preferential

access for British-manufactured machinery used in all branches of mining, manufacture, agriculture and electricity, as well as for British-
manufactured cotton and rayon goods (Marais, 1960, p. 144). The
immediate effect of the agreement was that the value of South Africa's
imports of British goods receiving preference increased by 180 per
cent in four years (from £5m in 1932 to £14m in 1936) while the value of
South Africa's imports of industrial machinery from Germany fell by
233 per cent in one year (from 1 161 000 reichmarks in 1932 to 270 000
reichmarks in 1933) (Marais, 1960, pp. 147–8).

In the light of these important changes it seems wrong to assume
that the growth of industry, and particularly light industry, in peripheral countries like South Africa, necessarily contradicted the interests
of British capitalism or was necessarily 'anti-imperialist'. On the contrary, so long as Britain could gain preferential access to these industries, such a development would benefit her economy. The events
which occurred in South Africa's chemical industry during 1924 provide a useful illustration of the way in which British capitalists
benefited from the expansion of an important sector of South African
industry.

In the prewar period the South African explosives industry (at this
stage the most important industry within the chemical sector) was
dominated by three independent British-controlled producers: the
Nobel–Dynamite Trust, Kynochs and the Cape Explosives Works.
However, this situation did not last: in 1918 Nobel's secured a merger
between their South African subsidiary and the Kynochs subsidiary
and on 1 January 1924 the Nobel–Kynochs Co. merged with the Cape
Explosives Works, controlled by De Beers, to form the African Explosives and Industries Ltd (AE & I, subsequently to become AE & CI).[21]
In order to understand the forces behind these mergers, which central-
ized control over the production of explosives and fertilizers in South
Africa, we need to examine conditions within the chemical industry in
Britain.

Immediately following the war the British chemical industry was in a
relatively weak position. As competition from American and German
companies intensified, the British producers were deprived of a rising
share of their home market and also of sections of the Dominion and
South American markets (Reader, 1970, pp. 317–27, 398–404). Nowhere was Hobsbawm's argument about the under-concentration of
British industry more true than in the case of chemicals where, in
particular, the establishment of the German chemical giant, IG Far-
benindustie, represented a concentration of capital and power which
was massive even by American standards. In contrast to this the British
chemical industry was dominated by four separate firms, none of which
was strong enough on its own to compete with the German combine.
These conditions forced the British chemical industry into a thorough

restructuring which had important effects on its relationship with chemical companies in the Dominions in particular.

The British strategy was sketched out by Nobel's in 1926:

> . . . there are two considerations of prime importance from the point of view of the chemical industry of the Empire. First, the British chemical industry must be reorganized on broader lines in order that an Empire view may be taken. Secondly, it is inevitable that Australia, South Africa and Canada, and South America, will develop their own industries at as rapid a pace as population will allow. (Cited in Reader, 1970, p. 399)

The department recommended that the company should take 'a leading interest in these two movements'. Shortly afterwards Nobel's amalgamated with the three other major British producers, giving rise to the Imperial Chemical Industries Ltd (ICI), a company which, according to its chairman, was 'Imperial in aspect and Imperial in name'. ICI's policy towards the chemical industries in the Dominions was unequivocal: not to undermine their capacity for expansion, but to gain a position within them from which they could be dominated. Of course such a policy was not without certain short-term costs. As the ICI chairman, McGowan, put it when discussing the position in another Dominion: 'Australia will inevitably aim at becoming self-contained . . . and it may be necessary to sacrifice some immediate profit in order to consolidate our future position' (Reader, 1970, p. 402). But such were the conditions of international competition at the time that as far as ICI was concerned this was the only viable approach if the company was to maintain and enhance its competitive position.

That then was the international context within which the merger between the three major chemical producers in South Africa occurred. All these companies were British-controlled and their merging together to form AE & I under the joint ownership of ICI and De Beers should not be seen apart from the movement towards concentration in the British industry at the time.[22] Following the merger, arrangements were quickly entered into between AE & I and ICI to avoid any 'destructive' competition between them: ICI agreed not to compete on the South African market with any of the existing or future manufactures of AE & I, while the latter agreed not to expand into the markets of other countries where ICI operated. Thus through the merger and application of the monopoly principle of division of markets ICI was able to strengthen Britain's position in relation to her rivals. At the same time as British capitalism benefited from these developments, the stimulus given to local industrial development benefited South African capitalism as well. For a start, the South African mergers immediately brought about 'substantial economies' in the production of explosives, resulting in a lower price of explosives for the mines.[23] Secondly, the merger opened the way for AE & I to dominate the

South African market and, with British technical support, to play a major role in the subsequent development of South Africa's chemical industry.

This illustration is only one example of the coincidence of interests which existed between imperialists and locally based capitalists over the issue of industrialization in South Africa. In similar vein, the establishment in 1922 of the state-owned Electricity Supply Commission (ESCOM) brought major benefits to the British-based producers of electrical equipment as well as to South African capitalism (Christie, 1977). Of course, none of this negates the fact that South African capitalists had to struggle to win acceptance for their industries nor even that they were opposed by important British interests, especially those in light industries, which stood to lose from their advances. But the progress of capitalism is always contradictory and before one can claim that these developments seriously damaged the future of British capitalism their impact on the growth areas of British industry has to be assessed. Here, as our evidence suggests, there were substantial advantages to be gained from the growth of industry in South Africa. The result was a subtle, but none the less real, shift in British imperialist strategy to accommodate this industrial growth on the capitalist periphery (even at the cost of damaging Britain's own light industries) so as to turn it to Britain's own advantage. Such a shift in policy, embracing other countries as well as South Africa, implied a change in the form of imperialism itself—a transition to a higher stage in which imperialist domination was exercised through forms such as technical and marketing agreements, rather than through the wholesale destruction of peripheral industries. Underlying this change, and making it possible, was the large-scale transition to monopoly concentration and heavy industry production in the imperialist power itself.

THE STATE, LABOUR AND INDUSTRY

A number of academic studies have claimed that the key to explaining South Africa's industrial growth lies in the economic policies (such as protectionism, subsidies, etc.) which the Pact government introduced (see, for instance, Houghton, 1973; and Davies, Kaplan *et al.*, 1976). Though these measures are important, we would argue that they are not sufficient to explain the phenomenon of industrial growth. What these measures did was to provide space for industry, affording it a kind of cocoon within which to develop; but they cannot explain the growth process itself. The key to that explanation lies in laying bare the conditions of surplus value extraction in industry: of explaining how the capitalist class gained an adequate supply of labour and secured control over that labour force. An essential element in that process was the assault waged by the state against the working class during the 1920s, since this created the political conditions for the reorganization of labour supply and control in the economy.

The state's victory over white miners in 1922 produced widespread demoralization among white workers throughout the country.[24] The capitalist class immediately seized the initiative to consolidate its position through the introduction of a number of measures aimed at intensifying the oppressive and exploitative conditions of the labour force. In general, the strategy was to weaken the working class as a whole by entrenching racial divisions within its ranks. As far as the growing manufacturing sector was concerned, a more pliable and docile labour force was essential if the sector was to survive the troubled period of the mid-1920s.

The Industrial Conciliation Act of 1924, the Wage Act of 1925 and the establishment of the Department of Labour all aimed at incorporating white workers in a complex system of official bargaining and arbitration at the same time as African workers were explicitly excluded from participation in these procedures. The unemployment situation for white workers was eased through the state's 'civilized labour policy' (which sought to absorb unemployed white workers into the state sector) and through the Job Reservation Act of 1926, which protected white workers in certain job categories from being replaced by black workers. However, these attempts to win over white workers were accompanied by others specifically intended to drive down the cost of white labour-power in industry. Most important in this regard was the strategy to replace white semi-skilled workers with cheaper black labour, or alternatively to use cheaper forms of white labour (either female or juvenile) to replace white adult male labour in skilled and semi-skilled positions.[25] The effect of these replacements was to lower the overall cost of white labour and as such represented an attack on the position which the white section of the working class had previously won for itself.

The white workers' response to this two-pronged strategy took two distinct forms. Many of the existing craft or closed unions sought to defend their members' position by working within the new industrial relations machinery and ignoring the position of black workers. In so doing they isolated themselves from the mass of the working class and laid themselves open to co-option. Others, however, rejected this approach, choosing instead either to transform existing closed craft unions into open industrial unions or to organize 'parallel' unions for African workers. This latter form of defence oriented itself more towards developing and utilizing the growing strength of black workers and as such posed an alternative to the racial exclusiveness of the former approach. The South African Trade Union Congress (SATUC) was formed in 1925 to promote open industrial unions mainly among white workers and in 1928 the South African Federation of Non-

European Trade Unions emerged to co-ordinate organization among black workers.[26] Black workers had already shown signs of militancy and organization, especially through the 1920 mine strike and the activities of the Industrial and Commercial Workers' Union (ICU).[27] Gradually it was becoming clear that the possibility existed for an organized working relationship to be forged among sections of the racially divided industrial workforce.[28] At the same time the *political* militancy of black workers was asserting itself, especially in the more militant stance adopted by the African National Congress. By the late 1920s these developments posed a direct challenge to the state's strategy of entrenching racial divisions among the working class and to its overall political domination.

The state's response was to launch a 'campaign of terror' against the organized industrial and political power of the black workers and against those organizations, like the Communist Party and certain industrial unions, which were forging links among all sections of the working class. Under the legal umbrella of the Native Administration Act of 1927 and the Riotous Assemblies (Amendment) Act of 1930 the police acquired widespread powers of repression which they used to murder, imprison and beat up workers and their leaders, as well as breaking up meetings, assemblies and strikes (Simons and Simons, 1969, pp. 416–37). By 1932 the ICU had been destroyed as an organization, the ANC and Communist Party severely battered and many of the industrial unions had either been broken or were so weak that they were no longer able to mount any serious opposition to the state's racialist policies. The working class had been decisively defeated and its division along racial lines further entrenched.

In the wake of this defeat the state set about reorganizing the forms of labour supply to the economy. What it sought was to create a sufficient supply for all branches of production without either creating shortages in any one branch or without losing political control. To do so under conditions of labour-intensive production in mining and agriculture was in itself complex, but the additional requirements of an expanding manufacturing sector posed even greater problems. The result was a further range of repressive and racialist legislation through which the state sought to expand and control the supply of *black* labour.

The Native Service Contract Act of 1932 and the so-called Hertzog Bills of 1936 aimed at securing a captive African labour force for agriculture through increasing the farmers' control over labour tenants, curtailing squatting and preventing the flow of Africans to the urban areas. In this way the state promoted labour stability within capitalist agriculture. Through the 1931 and 1937 amendments to the Immigration Act and by lifting the ban on the recruitment of African labour north of latitude 22° the state, respectively, tied foreign African workers down on the mines for the duration of their contracts and opened the way for the Chamber of Mines to extend the catchment area of their recruitment. Through these means mining capitalists were encouraged to draw an increasing proportion of their black labour from outside South Africa.[29]

While these measures brought relief to the agricultural and mining industries, they also cut off important sources of labour supply to the urban areas, and especially manufacturing. However, the Native Land and Trust Act of 1936, which intensified the proletarianization process among the African peasantry by further restricting African land ownership, swelled the numbers of those forced to seek work in the urban areas where most manufacturing was located. At the same time the Native Laws Amendment Act was introduced in 1937 to curb the movement of African work-seekers from the reserves and rural areas, so as to try and limit the numbers entering the urban areas to the bare minimum required for labour. For those who did gain access to the urban areas there were further restrictions in store: the Urban Areas Act of 1933 severely curtailed the freedom of movement, residence and occupation of blacks within the urban areas, while amendments to the Pass Laws—and the greater ferocity of their application—made it extremely difficult for them to escape these draconian controls (Simons and Simons, 1969, pp. 467–8, 499).

The 1930s were thus a period of major social restructuring during which the state thoroughly reorganized the labour supply in three key areas: through increasing the size of the labour pool; through controlling labour's access to the points of production; and through disciplining it at these points. The defeat suffered by the working class at the turn of the decade had deprived it of the organizations necessary to lead it in opposition to these measures. Racially divided and disorganized, the working class became pliable in the hands of its rulers as they moulded it to meet their needs. The cost of skilled and semi-skilled white labour was reduced as militant white workers were neutralized through co-option, concessions and repression; the supply of semi-skilled and unskilled black labour was increased without producing wage inflation; and the political dangers associated with the concentration of a reserve army of black labour in the urban areas was averted through restricting access to these areas and tightening controls over those in them. Under these political conditions all the major sectors of capitalist production in South Africa flourished.

These political changes, though crucial to promoting economic expansion, were not *solely* responsible for the boom which followed. The *immediate* stimulus in fact came from a reorganization of the capitalist monetary system and from a series of initiatives by the South African state to capitalize on this reorganization. The Depression which broke in 1929 eventually forced a general devaluation of currencies on the world's capitalist states. The British government led the way in 1931 when it devalued sterling by abandoning the gold standard. Although the South African government clung to the old gold parity for some sixteen months, in the end it followed suit. The result was an immediate rise in the gold price: fixed at R8.495 per fine ounce between 1925 and 1931 (reaching R8.613 per fine ounce the following year), the gold price jumped to R12.473 per fine ounce in 1933, the year South Africa came off the old gold standard. The 47 per cent increase was followed by further increases each year until 1940 when the price was fixed at R16.8 per fine ounce—98 per cent above the 1931 figure.[30] Over this same period the value of South Africa's gold sales rocketed by 155 per cent (from R92.4m in 1931 to R236m in 1940) (Table 2, column 3) and the value of dividends in the industry rose by 147 per cent (from R17.2m in 1931 to R42.45m in 1940).[31]

However, it was not just capitalists in the gold mining industry who benefited from these developments. The higher revenue which accrued following the rise in the gold price provided a potential source of capital for investment in other branches of production as well. With the working class temporarily subdued and the state expanding the black labour supply, capitalists in both agriculture and manufacturing were particularly keen to gain access to these funds. However, in this they were opposed by the mine-owners who sought to appropriate this revenue for their own development programme. At this point the state intervened, first to impose on mining an Excess Profits Tax of 50 per cent of the gold price rise and then, under pressure from the mine-owners, to place a definite limitation on the tax yields over a five-year period.[32] The effect of these measures was to increase the circulation of capital through the economy without jeopardizing the development programme in mining. As the principal source of revenue in the economy, the gold mining industry had to be allowed to develop, hence claims for the state to appropriate a greater proportion of the industry's 'windfall' profits were rejected and, through the tax limitation scheme, the industry was *guaranteed* substantial revenue for long-term planning purposes. At the same time the state acceded to the argument of agriculturalists and manufacturers that the 'windfall' profits provided a potential source of capital which was crucial to their development needs. Thus through its intervention the state was able to reconcile the different capitalist interests involved and promote expansion in all sectors of the economy.[33]

Between 1933 and 1939 direct taxation of the gold mines accounted for one-third of all state revenue (£98.5m out of a total of £295.7m). State expenditure on agriculture and irrigation increased substantially at this time, while export subsidies and internal price subsidization measures were extended to agricultural commodities. The state pumped finance into the public electricity corporation, ESCOM, as well as into another state-controlled body, the South African Railways and Harbours (SAR & H). In 1940 the state introduced an important expansion programme for the public iron and steel corporation, IS-COR, and in 1942 established the Industrial Development Corporation (IDC) as a 'financial institution specializing in industrial finance, namely, in the systematic and thorough investigation of new propositions and the underwriting and selling of securities'.[34] Through these financial and other provisions, the state therefore sought to stimulate production in agriculture and manufacturing, while at the same time reorganizing the overall political conditions of labour supply and control.

The result was a resurgence of foreign investment in South Africa and, in particular, a significant rise in the level of both foreign and mining investment in manufacturing production. According to the Board of Trade and Industries 'large overseas concerns increasingly established branch factories' inside South Africa as a means of gaining access to the local market without running up against the protective tariffs. Prominent among these were many of the leading American and European monopoly concerns, like Nestlé's, Cadbury's, Ford, General Motors, McKinnon Chain (US), Dunlop, Firestone, Siemens, Babcock and Wilcox, Dorman Long, Stewarts and Lloyds, Davy Ashmore and General Electric. In addition, other foreign companies already established in South Africa, like ICI and Lever Brothers, expanded their local plant (Legassick, 1974a, p. 263).

South African mining interests also began to take 'a considerable interest in manufacturing undertakings',[35] thus renewing the tendency of diversification out of mining. While this interest, according to the Board of Trade, initially 'manifest [*sic*] itself mainly in the form of finding lucrative investments in existing factories rather than in establishing and nursing new industries', by the end of the decade a leading journal noted that 'mining houses have recently been responsible for the flotation of several large industrial concerns'.[36] Among the more important mining investments in manufacturing at this time were: De Beers's investments (with ICI) in fertilizer production; Anglo American's involvement in 1936 in the manufacture of mining equipment and high-speed drills; Union Corporation's investments in pulp and paper milling through SAPPI; and Anglo-Transvaal's involvement in engineering, glass, cement and fish processing. (See Chapter 7.)

By 1939 manufacturing was contributing 18 per cent to the country's GDP, which was almost as great as that of mining at 21 per cent, and well ahead of agriculture at 13 per cent.[37] But equally significant was the increasing involvement of monopoly concerns (both foreign manufacturers and mining houses) in this growth. However, before examining industry further, we turn to an analysis of the developments which were taking place in the mining industry, since these were to have major implications for the future of industry and the development of capitalism in South Africa.

ANGLO AMERICAN AND GOLD MINING EXPANSION

The 30 years between 1930 and 1960 produced remarkable changes in South Africa's mining industry. These included substantial improvements in gold output achieved through both technological advances and the development of three new gold fields. Over this period the volume of fine gold produced per annum rose by 99.7 per cent (from 333 000 kg to 665 000 kg) and the number of tons of ore treated rose by 131 per cent (from 29 million to 67 million) (Table 2). In addition, these years produced profound changes in the industry's power relations. From being a middle-ranked gold producer in 1928, Anglo American rose to become the industry's largest producer, responsible by 1958 for 27.6 per cent of South Africa's total gold output.[38] Though it was only in the post-Second World War period that this latter tranformation was actually achieved, its roots were firmly bedded in the events of the 1930s.

The gold mining boom which occurred during the 1930s—described by Frankel as 'the greatest boom' in South African mining history—owed its life to the rising gold price. The working profit in the industry, which had averaged RO.93 in the five years between 1928 and 1932, jumped to an average of R1.60 over the following five years (1933–7) (Table 6, column 3). A substantial proportion of these profits was ploughed back into the industry: between 1933 and 1936, 74 per cent of the new capital expenditure on producing gold mines was financed out of retained profits (Frankel, 1938). Much of the new investment was capital-intensive in character: expenditure on stores rose by 106.3 per cent in the nine years between 1932 and 1940, compared with a rise of only 17.2 per cent over the preceding nine years.[39] New mechanical methods of production were devised where none had existed before, such as using fans and refrigerator units for ventilation. Other mechanical devices, such as the scraper winch (used for the removal of ore) were brought in to replace hand tools. New extensions were added to existing equipment, such as in the methods of supporting tunnels and in drilling. And new sources of power to motivate machinery were introduced as steam-power began to give way to electric power (for details see MacConachie, 1967; Mennell, 1961, pp. 97–103; Black, 1960). While many of these technical changes were first introduced on the newer mines of the Far East Rand, they gradually spread to the older mines as well. Overall, their effect on underground productivity levels was to reverse the decline which had occurred between 1926 and 1931, producing an increase of 6 per cent between 1931 and 1936 and a further increase of 10.2 per cent between 1936 and 1941 (F. Wilson, 1972, Appendix 29, p. 190).

However, while these changes were important for the industry, the most important advances occurred in another sphere: that of prospecting. Using new methods and equipment, a huge prospecting programme was launched as the price of gold rose. Bettween 1932 and 1935 approximately 200 000 ft (61 000m) of borehole prospecting was carried out on the Rand which, according to one commentator, was 'many times as much as during the previous quarter of a century' (Stokes, cited in Gregory, 1962, p. 511). As early as April 1933 two companies were formed to investigate and assess the development prospects of the Far West Rand and Klerksdorp areas. These companies—West Witwatersrand Areas (West Wits), controlled by Consolidated Gold Fields with Anglo American as minority partner, and the Western Reefs Exploration and Development Co., controlled by Anglo—were to give birth to four new mines before the end of the decade: Venterspost in 1934, Libanon in 1936, Blyvooruitzicht in 1937 (all under Gold Fields' control) and Western Reefs in 1939 (controlled by Anglo). By April 1937 Anglo American had formed a new company, West Rand Investment Trust, to hold its expanding interests in the new growth area of the Rand.[40]

However, these developments were eclipsed by the discovery of a new gold field in the Orange Free State Province. There had been intermittent interest in the gold-bearing potential of this region since 1855, but by 1932 interest in the field was at a particularly low ebb. None the less, the wide sweep of prospecting activity in the early 1930s encompassed this area as well, and some encouraging new results were obtained. However, at this time the Orange Free State fields were governed by mining regulations which had been introduced during the nineteenth century and were aimed at hampering the operations of joint-stock companies and monopolies. Following the favourable results achieved in prospecting, in 1936 the state brought these regulations into line with the Transvaal mining code, thereby opening the way for the groups: from 1936 onwards the Anglo American Corporation, Union Corporation, Central Mining, Consolidated Gold Fields, Anglo-Transvaal, South African Townships and African and European Investments were all active in the Province. The scale of this post-1936 prospecting activity went way beyond anything that had occurred before[41] and within three years the main Basal Reef, which was to be the foundation of the Orange Free State gold field, had been discovered.

As it happened, Anglo American's initial prospecting ventures all proved to be of no real value and by 1939 (the year in which the Basal Reef was 'proved' in the Orange Free State) it looked as if Anglo

American would be effectively excluded from participation in the development of a potentially large gold field. But Anglo did have a foothold in the field via her minority interests in two smaller groups, South African Townships and African and European. These groups had gained control over important gold-bearing ground and over the next few years Anglo moved decisively to establish itself in the field through their interests. Initially, Anglo sought to buy up shares in Western Holdings, the company that held SA Townships' Free State interests, but was frustrated in 1941 when JCI put in a bid for control of SA Townships. Anglo immediately responded with a counter bid which was accepted in January 1942. Commenting on the SA Townships takeover, Ernest Oppenheimer noted that: 'The great thing is that we are now . . . back in the Free State.'[42]

The Group's next attempt to extend its holdings in the Free State was also frustrated early on. This time Anglo tried to buy into African and European, but was blocked by the parent company, Lewis and Marks, which refused all overtures from Anglo for partnership in the Free State. Despite this rejection, by 1943 Anglo had managed to gain both a minority stake in African and European (mainly through the holdings it acquired with South African Townships) and a 25 per cent interest in its Free State operations (Gregory, 1962, p. 562). But the news that African and European's Free State holdings were sufficiently valuable to develop three large gold mines proved too much for Anglo: in 1945 the corporation took control of Lewis and Marks through the acquisition of 149 850 shares (out of 150 000). Through this take-over Anglo gained control over *inter alia* African and European and all its Free State properties.[43] Thus through the acquisition of SA Townships and Lewis and Marks, Anglo American launched itself into a position of considerable power in the Orange Free State gold fields, after having been virtually out of the running in 1939.

Nor does the story stop there. Throughout the Second World War Anglo American extended its control over smaller companies with important holdings in the Free State. In this way Anglo acquired a 60 per cent holding in any potential mine to be developed within the areas controlled by the Blinkpoort Gold Syndicate and the Witwatersrand Extension Co. Thus by 1945 Anglo American was in direct control of four important gold-bearing areas in the Orange Free State held by South African Townships, African and European, Blinkpoort and Witwatersrand Extension. These areas, all located close together, were among the richest gold-bearing properties in the Orange Free State and were to become the most important growth points in South Africa's expanding mining industry, giving rise to 8 out of the 14 gold mines subsequently developed in the Province (Table 7). Of these 8 mines, Anglo actually controlled 7,[44] which put it well ahead of its competitors: Anglo-Transvaal controlled 2 Free State mines, while JCI,

Union Corporation, General Mining, Gold Fields and Central Mining controlled 1 each (Table 7). The control which Anglo had acquired over new sources of production in the Free State thus placed it, potentially, in an immensely favourable position in relation to the other groups, indicating that an important shift in the industry's power relations was about to take place.

Before analysing that shift, it would be useful to comment briefly on some of the reasons why Anglo American was able to achieve this position. In earlier chapters we have noted two factors which undoubtedly were influential in this regard: the financial strength of Anglo's backers, particularly in America, and the wealth of the Group's Far East Rand interests. However, there is a further aspect of Anglo's development which is of relevance to the Group's rise to prominence in the Orange Free State—and that is the sectoral diversification of its interests, and in particular its massive investments in diamonds. Commenting on Anglo's historical evolution, the corporation's former deputy chairman, R. B. Hagart, has noted (1967):

> Gold mining remains the main source of the Group's strength, but it is worth remarking how fundamental it is to the Group's success and development that there is this combination of gold mining, copper mining and diamonds, each subject to the somewhat different effects of fluctuating economic conditions in the world and each lending strength and stability, sometimes in unison, sometimes separately. (p. 108)[45]

A brief look at the Group's evolution during the late 1920s and early 1930s will illustrate just how important this sectoral diversification was in sustaining and, ultimately, promoting Anglo's growth throughout this period.

For a long time during the 1920s Anglo American was unable to develop one of its Far East Rand gold mines, Daggafontein, because its financial resources were being ploughed into the struggle for control of the diamond industry on the one hand and into developing the Group's Northern Rhodesian copper interests on the other. Although by the end of the decade Anglo had more or less entrenched itself in both these spheres, the Depression drastically reduced the price of both diamonds and copper, thus undermining Anglo's financial strength. However, since the price of gold remained stable during the Depression, Anglo tried to bring its Daggafontein gold mine to the production stage, so as to earn new revenue to see it through the crisis. But before this could be done the Group had to find another £50 000 to equip the mine for production. Both the principal banks in South Africa, Barclays and Standard, refused to provide the finance and Anglo American was forced to delve into reserves (between 1931 and 1932 over £2m was taken from the corporation's reserves). However, within three months of the money being provided, the Daggafontein mine was making a profit in excess of £50 000 per *month*—and subsequently became one of the mainstays of Anglo American's financial support throughout the rest of the Depression. The Group's diamond interests, however, continued to drain financial resources away as Anglo was forced to accumulate large stocks of diamonds in order not to break the market completely. In 1931 and 1932 the corporation recorded meagre profits of only £113 303 and £119 704 respectively (Gregory, 1962, p. 107). For six years during the 1930s the Anglo American Corporation received no dividends at all from its huge diamond interests and it was not until 1936 that the corporation received dividends from its Northern Rhodesian copper interests. Throughout this long period it was the Group's gold interests which saved it from bankruptcy.

However, the boom conditions which returned to the diamond industry during the mid-1930s enabled Anglo American to earn a surfeit of profits in that branch of production, which considerably enhanced the Group's financial strength.[46] This new source of revenue put Anglo in a favourable position in relation to its competitors in the gold industry, helping it to seize control of South African Townships and African and European, thereby leap-frogging its way back into control over the Orange Free State gold field at the same time as developing new mines on the Far West Rand and Klerksdorp fields. Thus the wide spread of the Group's investments played an invaluable role in Anglo's development at this time as the Group first used its gold interests to help it secure control over the diamond industry, and then used its diamond interests to help overcome its competitors in gold mining.

This diversification—and the relative ease with which the Group channelled surplus value from one branch of production to another—provide further evidence of Anglo's monopoly character as increasingly it took the form of an international conglomeration of interests. Organizationally, too, the Group began to change to take account of these developments. In particular, Ernest Oppenheimer began to decentralize the Group's control structure so as to avoid the dangers of over-centralization, which could hamper the effectiveness of local operations where specific skills and quick decisions were required. However, Oppenheimer was careful to secure his own position through maintaining the Anglo American Corporation as the clearly defined centre of the new structure. As a result the organizational form of the Group gradually came to resemble a 'solar system' in which a growing number of 'middle-tier' finance or holding companies (each of which was responsible to the parent concern for a specific sphere of Group productive activity) emerged, revolving around a central point (the Anglo American Corporation) and linking it to the producing companies. In this way clearly defined lines of control were established without impinging on specific local requirements and, most important, without tying down the Anglo American Corporation's finances in unnecessarily large shareholdings in subsidiaries (the 'middle-tier' companies all held interests in each other as well as in 'their' respective producers and in the parent concern) (Figure 5). Thus in 1928 the Group established Rhodesian Anglo American (RHOAM) to hold its interests in Rhodesia; in 1936 it formed the Anglo American Investment Trust (ANAMINT) to take over its diamond interests; in 1937 it established the West Rand Investment Trust (WRITS) to hold its gold interests on the Far West Rand and Klerksdorp fields; and in 1944 the Orange Free State Investment Trust (OFSITS) was formed to hold its Free State interests (Figure 5). It was through these developments that the form of organization of the Anglo American Group as we know it today began to take shape.

However, at the same time as Ernest Oppenheimer was reorganizing the Group around the fulcrum of the Anglo American Corporation, he also changed the name of the company through which his family exerted control over the Group as a whole. The firm of A. Dunkelsbuhler and Co., which had been founded as a diamond dealing concern in the earliest days of South Africa's diamond industry, had also and most importantly served as the organizational means of the Oppenheimers' control over the whole Group. (See Figures 1 and 2.) After the company's founder, Anton Dunkelsbuhler, died during the 1920s the company continued to flourish under the leadership of the two Oppenheimer brothers, Ernest and Louis, and their cousin, Walter Dunkels (the son of Anton). However, during 1935 the company disappeared from the scene to be replaced on 1 July 1935 by E. Oppenheimer and Son, which took over all the functions of its predecessor to become the new nucleus of the expanding Anglo American Group. (See Figure 5.) Through this company the Oppenheimer family to this day exercises control over the Group by means of a complicated network of financial arrangements which we will elaborate on later.

In conclusion it should be said that all of the above developments— the opening up of the new gold fields, Anglo's rise to prominence, the Group's diversified portfolio and changing organizational form—were in one way or another manifestations of monopoly forms of capitalist development and implied a deepening and intensification of these forms in South Africa's mining industry. The new gold fields that were opened up by the groups concentrated vast new resources of production and capital into the hands of a few large companies. Anglo's takeover of groups like SA Townships and Lewis and Marks was an important manifestation of the growing tendency towards increasing centralization of capital and control in the industry. The changing organizational form of the Anglo Group expressed its growing influence as a monopoly combine, facilitating its capacity to retain control over a diversifying base in production without inhibiting new expansion. These changes helped prepare the industry for a new phase of growth which was to surpass anything hitherto achieved in the field of gold mining. Out of that growth was to come a profound change in the form of South African capitalism.

NOTES

1. One commentator, writing at the time, summed up the situation as follows:

> A beginning has been made with manufacturing industry in the Transvaal, but as yet factories are few and unimportant. The great engineering works on the Rand have been called into existence by the requirements of the mines, and might properly be considered as part of the mining industry. They are extensive and well-equipped; some of the workshops can turn out heavy machinery well made and well fitted, and all can execute repairs, make castings, and fit in parts with efficiency and despatch. But so far the great cost of skilled labour, and other items of expenditure, have made it impossible to compete with home and American industry in machinery manufacture . . . Industries other than mining and its associated works have in the past had little encouragement from the Government, from Capital, or from the people of the Transvaal. The most considerable industries in the country are nearly all due to the enterprise of one firm, Messrs. Lewis and Marks [a foreign-owned concern]. Besides being distillers, and gold miners, and farmers, this wealthy house engages in coal-mining, jam making, candle-making, glass-and-bottle making, leather-making, brick-making, and pottery manufacture; and if in some matters their influence has not always been for the good of the state, they deserve praise of their encouragement of local industry. (Bleloch, 1901, pp. 236–7)

2. Board of Trade and Industries, Report no. 282, p. 102, para. 323.
3. ibid., p. 102, para. 323, and Table IV, p. 11.
4. ibid., p. 11.
5. De Beers Cons. Mines, *Thirtieth Annual Report* for the year ending 30 June 1918.
6. Central Mining and Investment Corp., *Report of the Directors*, 31 December 1923, p. 15.
7. African and European, *Directors' Report* for the eighteen months ended 31 December 1924.
8. Although the company was supported by some municipal enterprise in certain towns and by De Beers in Kimberley, its monopoly was in fact statutorily recognized in the Transvaal Power Act. Its annual output rose rapidly from 3m units of electricity in 1908 to 267m in 1911. ('The Development of the Use of Electricity in South Africa', Officially Contributed, *South African Journal of Economics*, vol. 16, no. 4, December 1948.)
9. Gross production in the industrial powers actually fell by 20 per cent between 1913 and 1921 and world trade in manufactured commodities did not regain its 1913 level until 1929. (Hobsbawm, 1972, p. 211.)
10. Cited in Cons. Gold Fields of SA, Manager's Report, 17 September 1919, p. 18.
11. ibid., p. 18.
12. Cons. Gold Fields of SA, *Report of the Directors*, 30 June 1920, p. 17; and the African Land and Investment Co., *Eighteenth Annual Report*, 31 March 1920, pp. 6–7.
13. African and European, *Report of the Directors*, 30 June 1920; and Chairman's Report in *The Mining World*, 31 December 1921.
14. De Beers Cons. Mines, *Report of the Directors*, 30 June 1920, p. 2.

15. According to the Cons. Gold Fields of SA *Report of the Directors* (30 June 1921): 'Competition from overseas has been severe and is likely to become increasingly keen in future' (p. 25).
16. Cons. Gold Fields of SA reported that: 'The Government of the Union has been urged to bring in a large measure of protection for the benefit of local industries, but although it has done something to assist certain manufacturers, it has stopped short of the general demands.' (*Report of the Directors*, 30 June 1921, p. 25.)
17. Board of Trade and Industries, Report no. 282, p. 102, para. 326.
18. Among the groups involved in criticizing state policy at this time were a number of leading mining houses, including Gold Fields, De Beers and Central Mining. De Beers, in particular, did not mince its words:

   You will be sorry to learn that the manufacture of fertilizers has been most disappointing . . . [We] look to the Government to protect us against dumping from outside countries . . . Well, superphosphates from overseas have been sold in South Africa at lower prices than ever before; the Government was approached and . . . a dumping duty of 5/- per ton was imposed; but this is wholly inadequate, and we are faced with an almost certain loss on the manufacture of superphosphates under present conditions. (De Beers Cons. Mines, *Thirty-fifth Annual Report* for the year ended 30 June 1923, p. 31)

   See also Cons. Gold Fields of SA, *Report of the Directors*, 30 June 1922, p. 23; and Central Mining and Investment Corp., *Report of the Directors*, 31 December 1923, p. 15.
19. Hobsbawm (1972, p. 223) writes:

   Nevertheless, when all reservations have been made, the record of British industry between the wars was not unimpressive . . . Naturally, this was achieved mainly by the new growth industries. The output of electrical goods almost doubled between 1924 and 1935, that of motor-cars more than doubled, as did the supply of electricity. The output of aircraft and silk and rayon (mainly the latter) multiplied five times over in the same brief period. In 1907 the 'growth industries' had produced a mere 6.5 per cent of total output; in 1935 they produced almost one fifth.

   See also Dobb (1963), pp. 320–88.
20. In 1924 Phillips observed:

   We live in a world of change, and the laws of economy which may fit one set of conditions may be, and must be, unfitted to another . . . The extreme Free Trader would admit all commodities free of duty. He stands for cheapness and argues that money saved by importing commodities cheaper than home industries can supply them releases money to be spent otherwise. It is obvious that no country could sustain its people and find work for them if all its commodities were imported.

   Phillips then goes on to argue that his own experience in South Africa: 'has led me to the conclusion that anything produced from the ground in one's own country is infinitely more valuable than what is commonly regarded as wealth produced in any other way. Production from the surface of the soil, or below it, has a value to the country transcendently greater than its market price.' (Central Mining and Investment Corp., Report of the Proceedings at the Nineteenth Ordinary General Meeting, 21 May 1924, p. 6.)
21. De Beers Cons. Mines, *Thirty-sixth Annual Report* for the year ending 30 June 1924, p. 3.
22. In terms of the agreement De Beers acquired half of the capital of AE & I and ICI the other half, that is, £1 100 000 each. Each company had four seats on the board of the new company with the De Beers chairman acting as chairman 'with a casting vote'. According to De Beers: 'From the foregoing, you will see that neither company has swallowed the other, but they are equal partners, and must continue so

long as they retain their respective shareholdings, and on that point you may be sure the agreements are not entirely silent.' (De Beers Cons. Mines, Chairman's Report, Minutes of the Twenty-sixth Ordinary General Meeting, 30 June 1924, p. 36.) Despite these formal arrangements, ICI undoubtedly held technological superiority with all that that implies for the exercise of power in a partnership of this kind.

23. De Beers Cons. Mines, Minutes of the Twenty-sixth Ordinary General Meeting, 30 June 1924, p. 36; and Cons. Gold Fields of SA, *Report of the Directors*, 30 June 1924.

24. The unemployment rate among white workers was particularly high at the time; trade union membership among whites fell from 108 242 before the strike to 81 861 immediately afterwards; and strike action declined markedly from 37 strikes between 1919 and 1922 to a mere 6 between 1923 and 1929. (Lewis, 1978, pp. 121–2.)

25. Between 1915–16 and 1929–30 the number of white male workers employed in secondary industry rose by only 22 per cent, compared with a 65 per cent increase in the number of white females employed and a 49 per cent increase in the number of black males. (Calculated from figures in Lewis, 1978, p. 124.)

26. Eddie Roux, a prominent activist at the time, had this to say about organizing African workers in industry:

> It was found that the African workers in the so-called 'secondary' industries were easiest to organize. Though often classed as unskilled, they are really quite skilled and it is not easy to replace them at short notice. They are usually location residents and have their wives and children with them, though they may not have severed completely their ties with the country-side. They constitute the nearest approach to a Bantu proletariat in South Africa. In contrast to the more shifting and semi-peasant miners, building labourers and railway construction workers here today and gone tomorrow, always preoccupied with cows and land, these urban workers were comparatively quick to grasp the idea of trade union organization. (Roux, 1966, pp. 207–8.)

27. Formed in 1919, the ICU was a loosely organized alliance of workers, peasants and intellectuals whose membership reached almost 100 000 in 1926–7.

28. In fact, some joint strike actions involving black and white workers did occur during this time. (Lewis, 1978, pp. 137–8.)

29. The proportion of foreign Africans on South Africa's mines rose from 43.5 per cent in 1932 to 52 per cent in 1939. (Table 3, column 8.)

30. Chamber of Mines of South Africa, *Eighty-sixth Annual Report, 1975*, p. 59.

31. Union of SA, *Official Year Book of the Union of SA*, no. 17, 1934–5, pp. 505–16; no. 20, 1939, pp. 827–36; and no. 22, 1941, pp. 786–95.

32. A limit of £6m was applied in the first year, £7.4m in the second and a maximum of 50 per cent of excess profits for the three remaining years. (Kaplan, 1976a, p. 154.)

33. Kaplan (1976a) develops a different argument according to which the state supported 'national capital' (read agriculture and manufacturing) in its 'class struggle' to expand at the expense of 'foreign capital' (read mining). (See especially pp. 149–56.)

34. Board of Trade and Industries, Report no. 282, p. 127.

35. Board of Trade and Industries, Report no. 282, p. 127.

36. *Commerce and Industry*, vol. III, no. 7, January 1941, p. 151.

37. SA Bureau of Census and Statistics, *Union Statistics for Fifty Years* (1960).

38. In 1928 Anglo was the third largest producer in the industry, accounting for 9.8 per cent of the total and well behind the two leaders, Central Mining (43.2 per cent) and JCI (27.6 per cent). In 1958 Anglo accounted for 27.6 per cent of the total, Central Mining 19.8 per cent and JCI a mere 2.8 per cent (Table 5, column 4).

39. Union of SA, *Official Year Book of the Union of SA*, no. 13, 1930–1, pp. 426–35; no. 17, 1934–35, pp. 505–16; no. 20, 1939, pp. 827–36; and no. 22, 1941, pp. 786–95.

40. These included a 20 per cent share in West Wits. Anglo acquired its 50 000 shares in

West Wits at less than £2 each. According to Hagart (1967, p. 107) within a few months they were worth £10 each.

41. The Anglo American Corp. alone spent at least £3m on drilling 466 different boreholes covering a total footage of over 1 900 000 feet (or 360 miles/580 km) in an effort to 'prove' the Orange Free State gold field. (Gregory, 1962, p. 532.)

42. R. B. Hagart, Anglo American's deputy chairman, was appointed chairman of SA Townships and two other Anglo American representatives joined him on the board, giving Anglo American three members on a six-man board, one of whom (the chairman) had a casting vote. In addition, Anglo American became secretaries and consulting engineers to SA Townships, whose assets were valued at over £2m, including gold and coal mining interests. (Gregory, 1962, pp. 550–2.) One irritant for Anglo was the fact that, prior to take-over, SA Townships had awarded technical control over the first gold mine to be opened on her Orange Free State properties (St Helena) to the Union Corp.

43. The Anglo American Corp. also took over technical control of African and European and changed the name of Lewis and Marks Ltd to Free State Mines Selection.

44. The St Helena Mine, developed on Anglo's property, was controlled by Union Corp. In addition, Anglo held minority interests in mines developed in the Free State by Anglo-Transvaal, Central Mining, Gold Fields and JCI (Table 7).

45. Anglo American's major copper interests were in what was then Northern Rhodesia. In 1924 Anglo had acquired its first interest there through an 8 per cent stake in the Bwana M'Kubwa Mine. By 1928, in the face of considerable American competition, the Group had formed the Rhodesian Anglo American Corp. (RHOAM) to hold its expanding copper interests. By 1931 RHOAM's authorized capital had reached £6.5m. As a result of a series of amalgamations carried through during the 1930s control over the Northern Rhodesian industry came to be divided between the Rhodesian Selection Trust (RST) and RHOAM (incorporating *inter alia* the Rhokana Corp. and the Broken Hill Co.). By 1939 RHOAM was responsible for 39 per cent of the total copper output of Northern Rhodesia (232 000 long tons) and by the end of the war the company's contribution had reached approximately 50 per cent. (See Gregory, 1962.)

46. The diamond industry recovered remarkably quickly in the mid-1930s: in one year sales of the Anglo-controlled Diamond Corp. jumped by 163 per cent (from £3.26m in 1935 to £8.5m in 1936). Between 1936 and 1937 the corporation earned £17 724 000 on diamond sales alone. (Gregory, 1962, pp. 248, 311.)

CHAPTER 6

Postwar Expansion in Gold: Anglo Takes Control

The actual development of the Orange Free State gold field proved to be as decisive a phase in Anglo American's history as the preceding phase had been. In the immediate postwar period Anglo embarked upon a programme of development, whose scale was so large that it transformed the Group into by far the largest gold mining concern in the world. However, this phase in the Group's evolution cannot be considered in isolation from the important social changes which were taking place in South Africa at this time.

THE 1946 STRIKE AND ITS AFTERMATH

During the Second World War capitalists in the gold mining industry were again confronted by declining profitability: working profits plunged by 26.5 per cent between 1940 and 1945 (from R1.62 per ton to R1.19 per ton). (Table 6, column 3.) The main causes of this were the rise in working costs—up by 14.9 per cent over the same period (from R2.28 per ton to R2.62 per ton) (Table 6, column 2)—and the shortages of labour (the total labour force employed on the gold mines fell by 4.9 per cent between 1939 and 1945: from 393 677 to 374 533).[1] These conditions were both brought about by the war: shortages and inflationary prices forced up the cost of stores, while wages rose as workers sought to keep pace with inflation under conditions of increasing labour scarcity.[2] In addition, the mine-owners' profits were hit when the state imposed a Special War Contribution Tax on the gold industry (by 1942 the state was taking almost 71 per cent of the taxable profits of the mines).[3] However, these statistics do not adequately convey the full force of the dangers capitalists faced as the war dragged on. To understand these we must examine the growing intensity of the class struggle in the industry and within South Africa as a whole.

The system of migrant labour secured labour-power at a cheap rate by allowing only the male labourer into the areas of capitalist production, thus forcing his family to remain in the rural reserve areas, eking out a subsistence existence from the land. However, by the late 1930s the contradictory nature of this form of proletarianization—which relied on undermining reserve production so as to force labour out at the same time as attempting to preserve a subsistence base for the family of the labourer—had broken the productive power of the reserves.[4] As a result ever larger numbers of African migrants were forced by the objective conditions of their existence to demand wage increases to stave off starvation for themselves and their families. The increasing urgency of these demands was accompanied by a resurgence of militancy among the black working class. Substantial advances in black trade union membership were recorded during the war and there was a marked increase in black strike activity.[5] The state responded to these developments by introducing War Measure 145 of December 1942 which outlawed strikes and imposed severe sanctions against strikers. However, black workers continued to press forward against a state weakened by the pressures of the war: over the next two years some 60 illegal strikes were recorded and by the end of 1944 it was clear, as a state functionary noted, that 'Natives seem to be ignoring War Measure 145'.

This forward movement of black industrial workers brought important victories: their real earnings, which had risen by only 9.8 per cent between 1930–1 and 1939–40, rose by 51.8 per cent between 1939–40 and 1945–6 (O'Meara, 1975a; see also Stein, 1979). Nor was this movement confined solely to black *industrial* workers. One of the most significant developments of the war years was the mass organization of African *mine*-workers, culminating in 1946 in the largest strike in South Africa's history.[6] Both this strike and the organization that preceded it were integrally related to the general social conditions described above. Real wages for black mine-workers had begun to decline at precisely the time the Lansdown Commission was reporting reserve production to be 'a myth' (F. Wilson, 1972, p. 46). According to the Commission's own calculations, African mine-workers could no longer survive on their existing incomes.[7] Drawn by the higher wages paid in manufacturing, an increasing proportion of black workers began to move away from the mines, while those who remained began organizing themselves.

In August 1946 the African Mine Workers' Union officially launched a strike around the central demand of a minimum wage of 10s. per day.[8] Almost 100 000 black mine-workers responded to the call and the following day the Transvaal Council of Non-European Trade Unions (CNETU) called for a general strike in support of the mine-workers. The state's response was both swift and violent: police reinforcements were rushed to the Rand; strikers were fired upon, beaten up and literally driven down the mines by armed police; meetings and marches were broken up and numerous people arrested. Within six days the strike was over with not a single concession having been won from the Chamber of Mines.

The state's harsh response to the mine-workers' strike (compared especially with its more tolerant approach to black industrial workers) was to a large extent dictated by the key role which gold mining played within the postwar capitalist economy. Though the war had stimulated industrial production in South Africa to a considerable extent (so that by 1946 its contribution to the GDP was greater than that of mining), this in no way undermined gold mining's strategic importance. The expanded reproduction of the gold sector was crucial to the whole economy, since it provided both a source of surplus value which the state could use to promote production in other sectors and also because it was the most important source of foreign exchange earnings (through which, in turn, it became possible for agriculture and especially manufacturing industry to import machinery and equipment).[9] Thus in order to defend and expand South African capitalist production in general, the profitable base of the gold mining industry had to be defended. Yet during the war the very reverse had occurred: profitability in gold mining had actually fallen. Furthermore, this decline was occurring at precisely the time when capitalists were attempting to open up a major new gold field and, hence, when the need for revenue for reinvestment was at a premium. Consequently, capitalists could ill afford to pay out higher wages to black workers; on the contrary, what they wanted was the greater exploitation of labour-power so as to reverse the downward trend in the rate of profit.

It is these conditions—conditions which affected all sectors of the economy—which are crucial in assessing the state's action in 1946. Having smashed the organized resistance of black mine-workers, it was possible for the state to further restructure the forms of labour supply and control in the industry (to cope with the new demand) and for the groups, while holding black wages down, to reorganize production on a more mechanized basis. Through the successful application of this strategy, the productivity of labour in the industry could be increased and a new era of prosperity opened up.

The smashing of the strike thus signalled the beginning of a new phase of restructuring through which the state sought to accommodate the changes in production which had occurred during the war. Basically, the state had to try and reconcile a new phase of expansion in manufacturing with the necessary expansion of the primary sectors (especially gold) on the basis of a sufficient supply of cheap labour-power. The way in which it did this was by building on the relations already established during the 1930s: that is, by intensifying its controls over the labour supply in the rural areas so as to tie black labour down even more rigorously on the farms; by increasing the flow of *indigenous* black workers from the mines to the urban areas where they were to be subjected to even more controls; and by increasing the recruitment of *foreign* black labour for the mines.

As far as farm labour was concerned, the state both tightened up the system of influx controls (through administrative proclamation and the provision that no African worker could alter employment without first having his pass or reference book signed by his employer) and established a new system of labour bureaux. This latter system sought to prevent any African from leaving a particular rural district until the local labour bureau was satisfied that all labour requirements in the district had been met. Regarding the supply of labour for manufacturing, a quota system seems to have been introduced for the number of black *South African* workers who could be employed on the mines, forcing some of these workers into manufacturing employment.[10] At the same time black urban workers were subjected to further labour controls: through the Native Labour (Settlement of Disputes) Act of 1953 they were barred from belonging to legally registered trade unions, excluded from participating in the formal channels of wage negotiation and denied the legal right to strike. As far as the mines were concerned, measures agreed by the South African state and the British colonial regimes in the region enlarged the northern catchment area from which *foreign* African labour was drawn to South Africa.[11] As a result, between 1946 and 1960 not only did the size of the total black labour force on the mines rise by 30 per cent, but the proportion of foreign African workers rose from 58.7 per cent to 63.3 per cent. (The major increase of 156 per cent was of workers from Northern and Southern Rhodesia, Nyasaland and other central African States) (Table 3).

Through these various oppressive measures the state facilitated the provision of black labour-power to the major sectors of capitalist production. In so doing it laid another major plank in the construction of one of the most oppressive capitalist systems yet devised—apartheid. During the remainder of this chapter we will examine the implications of these political developments for expansion in gold production and in the following chapter will examine their effects on the manufacturing sector.

FINANCING THE NEW GOLD FIELDS

Although assured of state support for the provision and control of labour, the groups none the less faced a daunting task in having to develop a large new gold field at a time when there was a relative shortage of labour.[12] One means of resolving this problem was to increase the absolute supply of labour to the mines, but another and equally important approach was to reduce the demand for labour on the new mines. The most important means of achieving this was through mechanization of the labour process, since this would reduce the number of workers needed per mine. However, to do this effectively would involve a considerable capital outlay for expenditure on machinery and equipment.

Bound up with the question of mechanization were other reasons why capital expenditure on the new field was likely to be high. Especially important in this regard was the fact that in the Orange Free State mining had to be carried out on a substantially deeper level than ever before. Unlike the Main Reef on the Witwatersrand, which 'outcropped' (or emerged) at several places on the surface, the reef in the Orange Free State lay at least 300m (1000 ft) under the surface and was covered by thick layers of lava. Furthermore, the Free State field suffered from severe 'faulting'—that is, uneven and broken reef—which necessitated a considerably greater amount of underground development work than was customary on the Witwatersrand where the Main Reef Series exhibited an unprecedented uniformity and consistency (MacConachie, 1967, pp. 130–7). These geological conditions not only posed new technical problems but also increased both the cost level and the amount of time needed to bring a gold mine to the production stage. Given the inflationary conditions within capitalism in the immediate postwar period, the inevitable result was the rocketing cost of developing a gold mine; whereas the average cost of developing a Witwatersrand gold mine immediately prior to the outbreak of war had been about £3m, in 1950 the cost of developing a gold mine in the Orange Free State was estimated at between £7m and £8m (Oppenheimer, 1950, p. 150) and by 1959 at above £15m (Mennell, 1961, p. 97).[13]

These increases, as well as the considerably longer time lag involved,[14] militated against attracting sufficient investment on the large scale required from the industry's 'traditional' source of speculative investors. In addition to these difficulties was the fact that the gold field was located in a remote and arid semi-desert area which meant that, before the field could be exploited, a complete network of infrastructure (like water, power, transport, housing, schools, shops and in fact whole towns) had to be built from scratch. In response to these conditions the groups began to evolve new approaches to the question of attracting finance to open up the new fields.

These approaches may broadly be classified under four headings: the issue of loan-stock to capture institutional investors in Britain; tapping new sources of foreign investment; utilizing local sources of investment; and the use of 'internal' financing (by which is meant the utilization of financial resources held within the groups themselves). All of these approaches had been used *on occasions* in the past, but the significance of the postwar phase of investment was that it was *based on* these four approaches and as such represented a major transformation in the nature of the mining finance system in South Africa. As we shall see, the key to the successful utilization of each approach was the greater financial strength of the groups themselves.

The first approach involved adopting a new means of attracting British investment to the industry. Previously British investment had flowed largely through direct ownership of mining shares by private investors willing to take risks. However, the Labour government which came to power after the war imposed heavy taxes on this group, encouraging many to channel their funds into areas where tax relief was afforded, such as financial institutions. As a result of major transformations in the British economy during the interwar years, these institutions had emerged as the dominant institutional form of finance (monopoly) capital in the country[15]—and it was their resources which the groups now sought to tap. However, to do so meant that the risk element in gold mining investment had to be considerably reduced, since the institutions tended to be conservative in their investment policy.[16] The groups' decision to issue convertible debentures or loan-stock on an unprecedentedly large scale was intended to overcome this problem, since this form of investment would enable institutions to receive some yield on their investments from the beginning and, most important, would provide a greater degree of security than ordinary shareholdings.[17]

However, this new form of investment could only win wide support among the institutions in Britain if, in Harry Oppenheimer's words: 'Someone stands behind with the faith and the resources to subscribe for the equity capital which must bear the greater part of the risk at a time when others are not prepared to do so. This has been and remains the function of the controlling houses' (Oppenheimer, 1954). Thus the success of this form of investment rested entirely on the capacity of the groups to bear both the major part of the risk themselves as well as a large portion of the financial burden. Without the enormous financial strength of the groups this form of investment therefore would never have succeeded. And succeed it did: 27 per cent (£100m) of the total (£370m) raised between 1946 and 1960 for investment in the South African gold mining industry came from Britain through this method.[18]

The next approach involved tapping sources of investment finance in developed countries other than Britain. Although there had been occasions in the past when certain groups had made use of these sources of investment (for example, when the Anglo American Group tapped American financial resources in order to open up the Far East Rand), these had neither been as intensive nor as long-term as was envisaged in the immediate postwar period. To encourage new investment from these quarters large financial institutions, known as investment trusts, were launched in Europe and America after the war: the South African

Trust Fund was set up in 1948 to attract Swiss capital and, a decade later, the American–South African Investment Trust was floated (Jann, 1954, p. 4; Mennell, 1961, p. 127; and Coombs, 1957). These financial institutions played an important role in developing the new gold mines: by 1954 the South African Trust Fund was 'the largest Swiss— probably the largest Continental—investor in South African securities' with about 70 per cent of its interests in gold shares; while by 1959 93 per cent of the capital of the American–SA Investment Trust ($30m) was invested in gold mining. In general, the groups devoted far more of their energies to fund-raising in these quarters, often with considerable success. [19] In all about 23 per cent (£85m) of the total invested in the industry between 1945 and 1960 was raised in the United States and on the Continent. [20]

Nor were these overseas capital markets the only sources which the groups sought to utilize. Although the scale of the South African capital market could not compare with those of Europe and the United States, none the less in the period after the war the local market entered a phase of unprecedented expansion. Between 1948 and 1958 Personal and Corporate Savings in South Africa rose by 1654 per cent (from £13m to £215m) while the Current Surplus of Public Authorities rose by 125 per cent (from £28m to £63m); the total gross capital formation increased by 102 per cent over the same period (from £280m to £565m); by 1958 the share capital and deposits of permanent building societies alone amounted to £512m, while in that year the combined assets of the four financial institutions which between them controlled the country's life insurance business had reached £223m (Mennell, 1961, pp. 131–2). The sudden acceleration of corporate savings in South Africa and the emergence of large blocks of finance under the control of financial institutions provided a potentially useful source of investment which the groups sought to capture. (We shall discuss in the next chapter how this capital market arose.) The state played a key role in this regard when in 1949 it established the National Finance Corporation (NFC) to receive demand deposits from the 'public' (in amounts of not less than £50 000 at one time) which were then invested and on which interest was paid. [21] By 1958 this corporation controlled deposits valued at £58m, a large proportion of which found its way into the new gold mines either in the form of direct shareholdings or as unsecured loans. At least 7 per cent (£26m) of the £370m raised for development of the new gold fields came from *non-mining* sources within South Africa itself.

The bulk of this development finance originated within the groups themselves. Although this method of 'internal' financing had been employed to develop new mines in the past, the scale on which it was used increased substantially in the postwar period. Whereas in the whole period between the industry's inception and 1945 approximately

31 per cent of total investment came from 'internal' financing (£75m out of £240m), in the fifteen years from 1945 to 1960 this method accounted for 43 per cent of the total (£160m out of £370m) (calculated from Mennell, 1961, p. 104). This increase testifies not only to the greater financial strength of the groups, but also to their crucial role in generating vast blocks of finance themselves and directing these to new growth points in the economy. An examination of Anglo American's role in financing the new mines will help illuminate this phenomenon.

During the 1930s the Diamond Corporation had gradually begun to off-load the large stock of diamonds which it had accumulated during the Depression. Since these diamonds had been bought at abnormally low prices and were subsequently sold on a consistently improving market, De Beers (which controlled the Diamond Corporation) received unusually high profits from these transactions. The fact that these 'windfall profits' (valued at £50m) were accumulating in one sphere of Anglo American Group activity at a time when in another sphere, that of gold, there was a marked shortage of investment finance prompted the Group to channel these resources into gold production. By 1954 a total of £23 091 867 had been moved by means of loans or shareholdings from De Beers into the gold mining industry via a company, the De Beers Investment Trust, formed in 1952 specifically for this purpose.[22] This direct injection of capital accounted for 6.2 per cent of the total invested in gold mining between 1945 and 1960. Furthermore, by 1954 De Beers had deposited £20 849 000 with the National Finance Corporation from where much of it found its way into gold mining.[23]

We have already seen that Anglo was active in raising loans in Switzerland and Germany, but this was only the tip of the iceberg as far as its overseas activity was concerned. Between 1946 and 1953 alone the Group raised a total of £48 263 000 in London and on the Continent, £32m of which was used to develop its mining interests in South Africa and the remaining £16m to develop its Rhodesian interests.[24] In just fifteen months (between March 1953 and June 1954) the Anglo American Corporation prepared 12 major financial schemes for companies in the Group, undertook underwriting commitments on 15 issues of shares, debentures and notes for companies in other groups, as well as subscribing for large blocks of shares in 18 companies and making loans to 32 companies. Together with the capital injected by De Beers, this adds up to by far the largest contribution of any group to the postwar development work and accounts for almost as much as was raised through the combined efforts of the rest of the groups: for instance, Anglo alone supplied, both directly and indirectly, 42.3 per cent (£110m) of the total raised for development of the Orange Free State field (£260m).

Overall, the postwar financing of the new gold fields was the largest and most spectacular financial undertaking ever conducted in South Africa. The amount raised in the fifteen years after the war (£370m) was 1.54 times larger than the total amount raised since the industry's inception in 1886 (£240m).[25] Of that postwar total, 27 per cent was raised in Britain, 23 per cent in the United States and on the Continent, 7 per cent in South Africa and a massive 43 per cent through 'internal' financing by the groups.[26]

But the real significance of this phase of financing goes beyond just its phenomenal scale and the important contribution made by Anglo. In particular, the shift from using private sources of investment to the large-scale use of institutional sources—whether in Britain, South Africa or through Trust Funds—points to significant changes in the international form of organization of finance capital. Classical Marxist theorists have defined finance capital as the merging of bank capital with industrial capital (see Introduction). However, the strengthening of monopoly relations in production which took place among the imperialist powers between the wars and immediately after the Second World War was accompanied by a new form of financial domination in the world. This included *inter alia* a new monetary system, the rise of the multinational corporation and, most important from our present point of view, the rise of a wide range of financial institutions fulfilling the role previously dominated by banks of providing the link between money capital and capital in production. This new system of international finance was thus the institutional expression of a stronger and more developed form of finance capital and as such had important implications for the South African mining groups. By adapting and reorganizing their methods of fund-raising to meet the requirements of the new system the groups participated directly in the process of restructuring the financial relations of international monopoly capitalism. As we shall see, in the end the groups—and especially Anglo American—were to gain from these developments both important new powers in production and also a far more influential position in international finance.

MECHANIZATION OF THE GOLD MINES

One of the distinguishing features of the Orange Free State gold mines was their greater mechanization compared with the mines on the Rand. As we saw earlier in this chapter, mechanization of the new mines provided the most effective means through which the groups could overcome the dual problems of labour shortages and harsh geological conditions.[27] With their efforts to raise investment finance for the industry achieving spectacular successes after the war, the groups were able to press ahead with their programme for mechanization. The result was a technical revolution which transformed several branches of the labour process both underground and in surface work. New techniques were devised in virtually every sphere of underground development and stoping (shaft-sinking, rock drilling, ventilation, tunnelling, clearing and hoisting)—all based on mechanical improvements to existing technologies. Furthermore, diesel-powered locomotives (which had been first introduced in 1939) were now used extensively underground, while steam power was finally replaced by electric power as the motivating force for machinery. At the same time pneumatically operated mechanical devices, such as cleaning devices and shovel loaders, were brought in to replace simple hand tools. The effect of these innovations was a substantial increase in the mass of machinery employed on the mines, especially underground.[28]

These changes had important consequences for labour utilization. First they increased the skill differential within the labour force. As hand tools gave way to machinery, as small machines gave way to larger ones and as simple systems were replaced by more complex ones, so the demand for semi-skilled forms of labour increased. As a result the Chamber commissioned the Council for Scientific and Industrial Research to investigate techniques for labour training on the mines.[29] A two-stage training scheme was subsequently introduced for unskilled African workers involving both a system of 'aptitude testing' (designed to classify them into one of the six broad categories into which their jobs were divided) and a phase of more specialized training in one of the 60 jobs to be performed (involving both lectures and demonstrations in 'training schools' and 'practical application' underground). While too much emphasis should not be placed on the degree of training provided through these methods, none the less the fact that the groups chose *this period* to introduce them is an expression of their need to raise the general skill level of the labour force in accordance with the greater degree of mechanization.

Secondly, these changes led the groups to try and reduce labour turnover, especially among the more highly trained section of the African labour force. One method developed was to extend the length of service of contract workers on the mines by extending the length of their contracts, while another was to attempt to breach the migrant labour system as far as the most skilled African workers were concerned, allowing them and their families to live permanently on the mines. However, attempts to develop this latter scheme were frustrated by the state and in the end only a very tiny group was permanently housed on the Orange Free State mines.[30] The stabilization that did occur was thus primarily achieved through the first method—that is, within the existing institutional framework of the migrant labour system—and did not in any sense breach that system.

Thirdly, most of the mechanical innovations involved a substantial degree of labour-saving, which helped the Chamber to contain the demand for labour.[31] Between 1945 and 1951 the total number of African workers employed on the mines actually fell by 4.4 per cent (from 320 147 to 306 100) (Table 3, column 7). Although (as is to be expected at a time when new mines were being opened) the numbers began to rise thereafter, the new mines were considerably *less* labour-intensive than their predecessors. In 1961 the average number of workers (both black and white) employed per gold mine was 12.3 per cent lower than the corresponding figure in 1936 (9908 and 11 296 respectively).[32] If we examine the employment differential among *black* workers on large and small mines over time this trend becomes even more marked. Although on small mines there were an average of only 11 per cent fewer African workers employed in 1969 than in 1936 (1001 and 1130 respectively), on large mines the average decrease was 44 per cent or 11 174 fewer black workers (13 980 and 25 154 respectively) (F. Wilson, 1972, p. 157). Since most of the mines developed in the Orange Free State were considerably larger than their predecessors on the Rand, these figures suggest that it was mechanization of these Free State mines which brought the greatest labour-saving to the groups.

Finally, the mechanical changes were accompanied by substantial productivity improvements. These occurred in almost every branch of underground activity, sometimes reaching spectacular proportions.[33] While in 1969 a gold mine employed on average 14 per cent *fewer* black workers than in 1936 (7435 and 8636 respectively), it produced on average 109 per cent *more* gold in the later year than in the former (684 000 fine ounces and 327 000 fine ounces respectively) (F. Wilson, 1972, p. 157). If we examine a narrower time-span the take-off point becomes clearly demarcated. Whereas prior to 1951 there was hardly any recorded improvement in mining productivity, from that date until 1959 output per man (black and white) rose by 43.3 per cent or 13.5 ounces of gold per worker (Table 4, column 5). While mechanical changes *underground* made an important contribution to this improvement, technical improvements carried out at this time in *surface* work—in particular the electrification of metallurgical practices—played a major part as well.[34] Thus since it was during this period that the new gold mines of the Orange Free State and Far West Rand commenced production,[35] it seems as if their greater mechanization played a major part in producing these sudden productivity improvements—the largest in the industry's history.[36] Of course improvements in productivity are not just achieved through mechanization, but can also be brought about by *rationalization* of the existing labour process—that is, without the introduction of new mechanical equipment. There are clear indications that the groups did introduce certain measures at this time designed to increase productivity through this means (such as the use of African 'boss boys' to intensify the supervision of African workers), but the effect of these measures would seem to be slight when compared with those produced by the mechanical changes referred to.

The greater mechanization of the mines is also reflected in the rise in the level of expenditure on stores in relation to wages.[37] Between 1945 and 1960 the value of stores as a proportion of total costs (stores plus wages) rose by 12.3 per cent (from 47.1 per cent to 59.4 per cent).[38] This increase must be compared with the decline which occurred in the proportional contribution of stores in the preceding period. The decade 1935–45 saw the proportion of stores in the total fall by 4.5 per cent (from 52.6 per cent to 47.1 per cent), while the subsequent decade (1945–55) saw a sudden rise of 11.6 per cent (to 58.7 per cent). Furthermore, in 1966 the proportion of stores in total costs was higher in the Orange Free State, where all the mines were new, than in the Transvaal, which had both old and new mines (62 per cent as compared with 57 per cent),[39] suggesting again that the major thrust in mechanization was on the new postwar mines.

As a general category, mining 'stores' are constituted by those items, such as fixed capital goods and equipment (see Note 37), which together form the technical component of capital (part of the means of production). Consequently, a higher expenditure on stores (or dead labour) as opposed to living labour (expressed in wages) broadly reflects a rise in the technical composition of capital and may be referred to as an 'increase of the constant constituent of capital at the expense of its variable constituent' or as a rise in the organic composition of capital (Marx, 1974, vol. I, p. 583; see also p. 574). Overall, then, we can conclude that the more mechanized form of development of the postwar gold mines, which arose out of the necessity to reduce the demand for labour *and* to overcome new technical problems, produced a rise in both the technical and organic compositions of capital in the industry. This rise enabled mining capitalists to keep the demand for labour within manageable proportions (especially by reducing the numbers required per mine) and to achieve major productivity improvements. As far as black mine-workers were concerned, the changes meant primarily a greater level of exploitation (in the technical sense) since they were brought into more skilled work without being compensated through corresponding wage increases. The result was not only a major rise in the value of mining output, but also a sudden rise in the mass of surplus-value produced.

The *volume* of output in the industry had declined by 20 per cent in the period during and immediately after the war (from 448 128 kg to 358 202 kg between 1941 and 1951) (Table 2, column 2). However, over the following decade—the period when the Orange Free State mines and most of the new Far West Rand mines were coming into production—this trend was suddenly reversed and output soared by 99 per cent (reaching 713 562 kg in 1961) (Table 2). A similar trend occurred in the *value* of output, though here the issue is complicated by the 1949 rise in the price of gold.[40] Using the 1948 price, the value of mining output (having declined earlier) rose by 74.2 per cent between 1951 and 1959 (from £99.3m to £173.1m).[41] However, if we add the value of the price rise, then the increase between 1948 and 1961 was substantially larger: 188 per cent (to £287.5m; converted from £1 = R2) (Table 2, column 3). Thus the phase of mechanized development produced a considerable increase in the value of the industry's output which was further improved by the 1949 price rise.

Similar increases occurred in the mass of *surplus-value* produced in the industry. Surplus-value is appropriated by capital in a number of different forms, one of which is dividend payments to shareholders. These had fallen by 40 per cent during the profitability crisis between 1940 and 1947 (from £21.2m to £12.8m).[42] However, the gold price rise brought a 107 per cent increase in the value of dividends (to £26.5m in 1950) and, although over the next few years (while development work was at its peak) they fell back slightly, between 1953 and 1960 dividends rose by 153 per cent (to £51.0m).[43] In this latter year dividends were 298 per cent higher than they had been in 1947, reflecting the tremendous advantages which the gold price rise and the postwar development work brought to shareholders in this form alone.

A proportion of surplus-value is, of course, also appropriated by the state through taxation and other means and here a similar trend is apparent. State revenue from the gold mines fell by 69 per cent between 1945 and 1948 (from a high of £20.1m to a low of £6.3m) (all data from Table 8). However, in 1952 revenue from the mines rose by 63.5 per cent (to £22.9m) as the state took its share from the gold price rise. Revenue from mining fell again to £14.7m in 1955 (to allow development work to proceed), but between 1955 and 1960 a consistent rise of 83 per cent was recorded (from £14.7m to £26.9m). Thus between 1948 and 1960 state revenue from gold mining rose by a phenomenal 327 per cent, providing some idea of the extent to which the new gold fields were financing the apartheid state.

These various statistics provide indices by which we can gauge some of the implications for the South African capitalist class of the mechanized development of the new gold fields. The advances made at this time secured for this class a major new base in production which was to raise South Africa to a position of undisputed control over the vast majority of the world's known gold resources: by 1966, when the Orange Free State accounted for 32.6 per cent of South Africa's gold supply, the country was producing three-quarters of the world's total (excluding the Soviet Union).[44] As we shall see in Chapter 7, the benefits which these developments brought to South Africa's balance of payments were to have important consequences for the manufacturing sector. But it was not just in these terms that the capitalist class benefited from this phase of economic activity. The huge rise in the mass of surplus-value accruing in the industry provided a major new source of wealth and financial power to both mining capitalists and, through the state, to other sections of the capitalist class. However, the relations of control which had been established in the industry in the preceding years were to ensure that one capitalist group alone was to reap the lion's share of these rewards.

ANGLO AMERICAN AND THE CONCENTRATION OF POWER

The mass of surplus-value which accrued to mining capitalists would of course be apportioned among the groups on the basis of their access to the sources of expanded surplus-value. During the 1950s the bulk of the industry's gross profits—that is, 70 per cent of the total—were coming from the new mines of the Far West Rand and Orange Free State.[45] These were the fields in which the Anglo American Group was most prominent: in 1959 the chairman disclosed that about 90 per cent of the Group's gold mining interests were now held in the Orange Free State, Far West Rand and Klerksdorp fields, giving the Group direct access to the most important sources of surplus-value in the industry (Graham, 1964).[46]

Table 5, column 2 reveals how Anglo American's access to the most lucrative producers in the industry (the rich mines) was improved by the postwar development phase. From having no rich mines and only 3 average mines in 1936 (behind both Consolidated Gold Fields, with 1 rich and 2 average mines, and Central Mining, with 4 average mines), by 1961 Anglo American had moved to a position of control over 3 rich mines (putting her well ahead of her nearest rivals, Central Mining and Gold Fields, with 1 rich mine apiece). In addition, in this latter year Anglo American controlled 12 gold mines, which was more than any other group. (Gold Fields had 11, Central Mining 8, Union Corporation 7, Anglo-Transvaal 4, General Mining 3 and JCI 2) (Table 5). It was this shift in Anglo's productive base which lay behind the Group becoming the industry's largest producer in 1958 (Table 5, column 4).

However, the above data concern only the question of *access* to the lucrative resources of the new gold fields and do not cover the issue of their form of *exploitation*. Here again, important differences emerge between Anglo American and the other groups. Table 9 provides a detailed breakdown of profitability in the industry in 1966, comparing Anglo American's mines (Part I) with those controlled by the other groups (Part 2).[47] The first striking point about the data is the difference in the levels of capital expenditure on mines developed before and after the war: the average capital expenditure on postwar mines was 4.65 times higher than the corresponding average on prewar mines

(R45 153 154 and R9 704 194 respectively) (column 5). This difference reflects the higher costs involved in postwar development work as a result of both the transition to more mechanized methods of production and inflationary factors. But what is more interesting for our present purposes is the fact that in both the pre- and postwar periods average capital expenditure on Anglo American Group mines (Part 1) is higher than the corresponding average for mines outside Anglo's control (Part 2): 1.2 times higher in the prewar period (R11 967 454 and R9 057 143 respectively) and 1.3 times higher in the postwar period (R52 275 429 and R40 963 581). Since the inflation factor is not relevant to these comparisons, these figures point to a higher technical composition of capital on Anglo's mines than on those of the other groups in both periods. This suggests that, especially as far as the postwar mines are concerned, on average Anglo's mines were more productive than those of its competitors.

These two factors (the higher technical composition of Anglo's capital and its access to the richest resources in the industry) are probably together responsible for the fact that during the postwar period average profitability on Anglo mines was 1.3 times larger than the average for the rest of the industry (R6.23 per ton and R4.86 per ton respectively) (column 3).[48] These results, when translated into total profits, are extraordinary: in 1966 nine of Anglo's postwar mines earned a combined profit (R140 100 735)—which was almost as great as the combined total profits of the seventeen mines developed in the same period in the rest of the industry (R149 490 288) (column 4).

These statistics give some idea of the extent to which Anglo American's new position in production had strengthened the Group financially against its competitors. By the time the bulk of the development work had been completed Anglo had become the dominant financial power and undisputed leader in the industry. In just six years (between 1954–5 and 1960–1) the corporation's principal sources of income (investment and management services) rose by 167 per cent (from £5.1m to £13.6m) and its income from dividends by 212 per cent (from £2.6m to £8.1m). Over the longer period from 1958 to 1968 the market value of the corporation's investments rose by a phenomenal 619 per cent (from £66.5m to £478m).[49] By 1960–1 the market capitalization value of the Anglo American Corporation's issued ordinary share capital (£87.3m) was fully two-thirds of the combined market capitalization value of the rest of the groups together (£130.8m) and was equal to 40 per cent of the market capitalization value of the whole industry (£218.2m).[50] Anglo's market capitalization value was in fact 2.6 times greater than that of its closest competitor, Gold Fields (£33.7m), and a massive 15.3 times greater than that of the smallest group, Anglo-Transvaal (£5.7m), giving a rough idea of the extent to which Anglo had outstripped its competitors.

Thus by the early 1960s the relations of financial power among the groups had been so radically altered that leadership in the industry had passed from Central Mining (which had held that position since the 1890s) to Anglo American (with Gold Fields in second position). C. S. Mennell, who is today Deputy Chairman of the Anglo-Transvaal Group, summed up the situation thus:

> . . . one mining finance house, Anglo American, has, since the end of the War, become not only the predominant Group but, in many ways, the leader of the industry. Its great financial strength has enabled it either to control most new ventures as they emerge or to acquire very considerable interests in such ventures (which would give them 'legal control' in other than the oligopolistic conditions prevailing). Anglo American is represented on the boards of 21 of the 23 gold mining companies floated since the War . . . In addition this Group has its representatives on the Boards of no less than three of the other seven Mining Groups. (1961, p. 47)

Mennell then went on to argue that: 'Not only has Anglo American become the undisputed leader of the industry but it has also become to a considerable extent, the banker to the industry. This Group has played an essential role in the initial financing of all but two or three of the 23 mining companies since the war' (p. 137). Thus at the same time as the monopoly tendency towards centralization of capital manifested itself in the form of Anglo American's undisputed domination in the industry, the Group itself became transformed into one of the great financial institutions of the era: the producer became a banker as well.

CONCLUSION

In concluding this analysis of Anglo's rise to power in the gold industry we should not lose sight of the Group's considerable power in other branches of mining as well. For instance, as early as 1952, in addition to producing 25 per cent of South Africa's total gold output, Anglo also produced 24 per cent of South Africa's uranium, 43 per cent of southern Africa's combined coal output, 51 per cent of Northern Rhodesia's copper and a massive 41 per cent of the world's total sales of industrial and gem diamonds (Hagart, 1952, p. 6). However, it was the control which Anglo acquired during the 1950s in gold, reinforced by its position in diamonds, which was mainly responsible for the Group's acceding to the leadership position in South Africa's mining industry. Over the years since then, Anglo American has consolidated that position. In particular, the opening of the Western Deep Levels Mine during the 1960s (at that time the largest and deepest gold mine in the world) brought a major new producer into the Anglo stable, thereby further entrenching the Group's position.[51] By 1968 the total value of output from Anglo American's twelve gold mines represented more than 3 per cent of South Africa's GNP.[52]

At the same time as expanding its base in production, Anglo also began to cement the industry's power relations. In 1958 one of the other groups (probably Gold Fields) tried to gain control of Central Mining (which also controlled Rand Mines). The transfer of the assets of this large group to that of a competitor would have posed a serious threat to Anglo's dominant position. Consequently, in conjunction with Engelhard interests in the United States, Anglo took a controlling interest in Central Mining. A process of rationalization within the control structure of the enlarged group then followed. Anglo hived Central Mining off from its partner (Rand Mines) and merged it with two other British-based companies under Anglo control—the old Chartered Co. (the British South Africa Co.) and Consolidated Mines Selection (the original parent company in the Anglo American Group)—to form Charter Consolidated based in Britain.[53] With Central Mining thus integrated into Anglo's expanding overseas section, Rand Mines was brought under the wing of the Rand Selection Corporation, a major Anglo holding company operating within South Africa.

The next group to fall under Anglo control was JCI. During the 1960s Afrikaner financial interests, which had long been looking for a foothold in gold mining, sought to gain control of JCI. But before they could they were blocked by Anglo which, through Rand Selection, acquired a 50 per cent stake in the group. The JCI take-over is important because it raises the question of Anglo's relation to Afrikaner capitalist groups in the country. What makes the take-over all the more interesting is that it did not prevent Afrikaner interests from subsequently acquiring another gold mining group, General Mining—but this time with Anglo's consent. The question is: why should Anglo block Afrikaner interests in their take-over bid for JCI and then willingly hand General Mining over to them? The answer may be summed up in one word: diamonds. The Oppenheimers clearly understood the political importance of allowing Afrikaner interests a share of the gold mining cake in South Africa. The Nationalist government and its Afrikaner propagandists had long raged against the 'Hoggenheimer' control over South Africa's mineral resources and in 1964 had gone so far as to set up a Commission of Inquiry into Anglo's affairs. Participation for Afrikaner interests in one of the main gold mining groups was a way in which these criticisms might be muted. However, the problem with JCI was that it was not solely a gold mining concern (in 1960 only 13 per cent of its interests were in gold mines). Much more important were its substantial interests in the diamond industry (35 per cent of the Group's total interests were tied up in diamonds, mainly through its large holdings in De Beers and the Diamond Producers' Association).[54] Control over JCI would have given Afrikaner capitalists access not only to gold mining but, more especially, to a substantial stake in De Beers and the world of diamonds. Furthermore, through these latter interests they would have acquired access to the Anglo American Group itself—with all the political dangers that involved for Anglo. Far better from Anglo's point of view to hand over formal control of a group like General Mining, which at that time was even smaller than JCI, had no real involvement in diamonds and was not closely integrated with Anglo's internal operations.[55]

The decade of the 1960s was thus a phase of further centralization for monopoly capital in the industry as Anglo consolidated its power, bringing previously independent groups like Central Mining, Rand Mines and JCI under its control. By the end of the decade Anglo also held minority interests in three of the remaining four groups (Consolidated Gold Fields, General Mining and Union Corporation) and it was only Anglo-Transvaal, the smallest of all, which remained beyond Anglo's formal sphere of influence. Although there have been important changes during the 1970s—as the groups have concentrated new gold and other mineral resources under their control and further centralized their power relations—these have not threatened to dislodge Anglo from its leadership position. On the contrary, these developments have strengthened that position.

A survey of the gold mining interests of the various groups in 1975 and 1976 (Table 10, Parts 1 and 2) reveals that Anglo American was in control of almost a third of the operating gold mines in South Africa (12 out of 39). Anglo's nearest competitors were Gold Fields and Union Corporation (with 7 apiece), with the rest trailing well behind (Barlow Rand 5; General Mining 4; and Anglo-Transvaal and JCI 2 each). Furthermore, 9 of Anglo American's mines had long life expectancies (compared with 5 of Gold Fields' and 4 of Union's), while included among Anglo's mines were the richest and largest producers in the industry.[56] Nor does Anglo's power in gold production end there, for the unprecedented rise in the gold price throughout the 1970s has ushered in a major new phase of gold mining development in South Africa.[57] Old mines have been reopened as it became profitable to mine previously discarded deposits, and new mines opened up. Anglo has been particularly active in both these areas, in general using the most advanced mining technologies yet devised in developing its new mines. Some of these, like Anglo's directly controlled Elandsrand Mine and JCI's Randfontein Mine, have set new standards in mechanized development which could revolutionize mining practice in South Africa.

These developments have occurred together with further shifts in the concentration of power in the industry. As early as 1971, Anglo swapped its controlling interest in Rand Mines for a substantial minority stake in the industrial conglomerate, Thos. Barlow and Sons.

Through this transfer, which resulted in the formation of the new Barlow Rand Group (in which Anglo was the second largest single shareholder), Anglo opened up new institutional links between mining and industry in South Africa (see Chapter 8). However, the resurgence of gold mining activity which followed the price rises led to new alignments being forged in mining. In 1974 Gold Fields, still Anglo's major competitor, sought to gain control of Union Corporation. A counter-bid by General Mining successfully out-manoeuvred Gold Fields and produced the new General Mining–Union Corporation combination in which Anglo holds a large minority share. In 1980 Anglo finally put an end to Gold Fields' position of independence when it acquired a 28.9 per cent stake in the Group. Thus Anglo American has entered the 1980s in formal control of JCI and with a large minority stake in three of the remaining four Groups (Barlow Rand, General Mining–Union Corporation and Gold Fields). Only the smallest Group, Anglo-Transvaal, is still outside its formal influence.

The process of centralization among gold mining capitalists has thus secured for Anglo a virtually unassailable position in the industry both now and in the foreseeable future.[58] Taken together with its hold over the diamond industry—it controls between 80 and 85 per cent of total world production[59]—the Group ranks among the greatest mining monopolies in the world today. The origins of this immense power cannot easily be located in a group as diverse as Anglo American. Yet undoubtedly the transactions of the 1940s and 1950s, when Anglo gained access to and began development of the newly proclaimed gold fields, must count among the most important in its history. As we have seen, it was this phase which brought with it the changes that enabled Anglo to take control over the industry as a whole. However, this phase was accompanied by other changes in Anglo's position as new tendencies became apparent within the Group. One of the most important of these was the tendency towards financial and industrial diversification. As we shall see in the following chapters, the mining industry's leading producer was about to become a financier and industrialist as well.

NOTES

1. The African section of the labour force fell by 5.5 per cent over this period: from 323 000 to 305 400 (Table 3). In August 1943 the number of Africans employed on the Rand gold mines was only '84 per cent of the full complement of Natives that could be profitably employed.' (Union of South Africa, *Report of the Witwatersrand Mine Native Wages Commission*, Pretoria, 1944, para. 65.)
2. The value of stores consumed in the industry rose from £31.9m in 1939 to £37.6m in 1946, while the value of wages rose from £30.6m to £37.8m over this period. (Union

of SA, *Official Year Book of the Union of SA*, no. 22, 1941, pp. 786–95; and no. 23, 1946, pp. 12–19.)

3. Transvaal Chamber of Mines, *Fifty-third Annual Report*, 1942, p. 52.

4. The Lansdown Commission, which investigated the conditions of black mine-workers during the war, reported on the rapidly declining productive capacity of the reserves and on the corresponding rise in the level of impoverishment, landlessness and malnutrition of the people living there. The commissioners concluded that for the majority of black migrant labourers, 'Reserve production is but a myth'. (Report of the Witwatersrand Mine Native Wages Commission, 1944, paras. 114–283.) A further indication of the desperate condition of black people in the reserves is provided by the census returns: between 1936 and 1946 the number of peasants in the reserves fell from 2 433 028 to 832 748, suggesting a rapid spread of landlessness among the mass of the population at this time. (O'Meara, 1975a.)

5. By 1945 the Council of Non-European Trade Unions (CNETU) was claiming a total membership of 158 000. Although this figure may well be inflated, there is no denying the increasing militancy of black workers at this time. The number of man-days lost through 'non-white' strike action rose by 209.8 per cent between the period 1930 and 1939 on the one hand and the period 1940 and 1945 on the other (71 078 and 220 205 respectively), while the number of 'non-white' strikers rose from 26 254 to 52 394 over this same time-span.

6. The African Mine Workers' Union (AMWU) was formed in 1941 and by 1944 had a membership of 44 000.

7. *Report of the Witwatersrand Mine Native Wages Commission*, 1944, Table XXVII, p. 19.

8. Other demands included: family housing; two weeks' paid annual leave; a £100 gratuity after fifteen years' service; payment of repatriation fares; and the withdrawal of War Measure 1425, which prohibited gatherings of more than twenty persons on mining ground.

9. Between 1947 and 1954 gold's share of total South African exports averaged 37.3 per cent per annum. (Innes, 1975, Table 22, p. 191.)

10. The Froneman Commission reported that black South Africans approaching the mines for employment on their own initiative were being turned away and con-cluded that a quota was placed on the number of indigenous black recruits to the mines. (Froneman Report, Pretoria, 1962, p. 12.) The number of black South Afri-cans working on the mines fell by 44.8 per cent between 1945 and 1956 (from 210 485 to 116 100) (Table 3, column 1).

11. The WNLA was given recruiting facilities in the two Rhodesias and Nyasaland following a conference with the governors of these colonies in 1938. In 1959 similar facilities were granted in the British colony of Tanganyika.

12. In fact four new gold fields were opened up in South Africa between 1935 and 1955, accounting between them for 55.6 per cent of South Africa's total output in 1958. Of these new fields, the Orange Free State alone accounted for 24 per cent of the total in that year, the Far West Rand about 17 per cent, Klerksdorp about 14 per cent and Bethal about 1 per cent. (Graham, 1964.)

13. See also Anglo American Corp. of SA, *The Orange Free State Gold Field*, 1959, pp. 24–5.

14. Largely because of the greater technical problems involved in the deeper new mines the length of time required to bring a new gold mine to the production stage in the postwar period was at least six years, compared with a period of approximately two years in the prewar period. (Hagart, 1952, pp. 1–5.)

15. These financial institutions have been defined as: 'any impersonal investor, anyone acting in a fiduciary or comparable capacity on behalf of other investors or savers'. This definition thus includes: insurance companies, banks, pension funds, invest-ment and unit trusts, the Church Commissioners, the Public Trustee, the Charity Commissioners, the building societies, the Post Office, the Trustee Savings Bank, as

well as smaller investing institutions such as universities, colleges, public schools and trade unions. S. P. Chambers, at one time the Finance Director and later Chairman of ICI in Britain, has pointed out that: 'The rapid growth of these financial institutions is one of the outstanding phenomena of the last twenty or thirty years.' In March 1956 financial institutions held over 50 per cent of all stock exchange securities in Britain (valued at £33 633 000 000). (See Chambers, 1952, and Wincott, 1957.)

16. Chambers (1952) noted:

> Insurance companies and pension funds tend to play safe and to put their money very largely into debentures and fixed-dividend preference shares. Insofar as they invest in ordinary shares, they tend to go for the safer and older companies. Because of their position as trustees for pensioners and policy-holders, institutions are less inclined to put money into new enterprise and into ventures of a more forward-looking and speculative character.

See also Hagart, 1952.

17. The terms 'convertible debentures' (which are the equivalent of 'bonds') and 'loan-stock' are used interchangeably. (Other variations of this general form of investment which were used at this time include the raising of unsecured loans and the issuing of new debentures.)

18. Anglo American Corp. of SA, *The Orange Free State Gold Field*, p. 10.

19. In 1950 and 1952 Anglo American raised two loans in Switzerland totalling £5.7m (£3.8m went to the Orange Free State); in 1958 it succeeded with the issue of a £4.6m loan on the West German market (through the Deutsche Bank); and it succeeded in raising American capital for its Klerksdorp mining interests. Anglo-Transvaal secured $50m in loans and stock from the US-based Kennecott Copper Corp. for development of its Orange Free State gold mines. And in 1957 the Engelhard Group in America bought a substantial interest in the Central Mining Group. (Jann, 1954, and Mennell, 1961).

20. Approximately £20m was raised in the United States for development of the Orange Free State mines. (Graham, 1964.)

21. Ernest Oppenheimer was actively involved in the establishment of the NFC. (Hagart, 1967, p. 110.)

22. Not that this action was necessarily popular with all of De Beers's shareholders, some of whom would have preferred larger dividends to take home. In an article entitled 'King of Diamonds' *The Economist* of 19 June 1954 gives us an insight into the way decision-making worked within the Anglo American Group:

> De Beers Investment Trust has recently pumped large sums into the expanding economy of South Africa and Rhodesia mainly by way of short-term loans often carrying conversion options into ordinary shares . . . The decision to apply diamond profits to develop gold, coal, and other resources . . . attracted much comment in Britain. It was argued that shareholders might have been allowed to decide for themselves whether to invest their money in the speculative ventures of the Orange Free State but Sir Ernest would have none of it. He saw that to bring the Orange Free State mines into production . . . would be no light task. He was the mining financier with large cash resources at his disposal and he claimed he was 'reviving the tradition of Cecil John Rhodes, the De Beers Chairman of 54 years ago'. So shareholders . . . have followed Sir Ernest pioneering with the mantle of Rhodes around his shoulders whether they liked it or not. (pp. 991–3)

Of the total invested in gold mining by the De Beers Investment Trust, £16 291 364 went into the Orange Free State, £5 057 875 into the Far West Rand and £1 742 628 into the mining finance houses. A further £490 365 was invested in Rhodesian coal mining, £245 000 in Rhodesian copper mining and £5 060 977 in South Africa's chemical industry. (Anglo American Corp. of SA, Chairman's Report to Shareholders, *Annual Report, 1954*, p. 12.)

23. ibid., p. 12. This figure represented 36 per cent of the total value of deposits held by the NFC in 1958 and suggests that the Anglo American Group exerted a powerful influence over this corporation.

24. Of the £32m spent in South Africa, London contributed £23.25m and the Continent £8.75m. (Anglo American Corp. of SA, Chairman's Review, 'Mining Finance in South Africa', *Annual Report, 1954*.)

25. Anglo American Corp. of SA, *The Orange Free State Gold Field*, p. 9.

26. 70.3 per cent (£260m) of the total was spent on development of the Orange Free State gold field (ibid., p. 10).

27. In addition to the geological differences already mentioned between the Orange Free State field and the Rand, there were others such as: the difference in the 'geothermic gradient' (the relationship between rock temperature and depth), with the rock temperature in the Orange Free State rising by 6.5°F every 1000 ft compared with 5°F every 1000 ft on the Witwatersrand; the dangers of underground water fissures were more prominent on the Free State, interfering with shaft-sinking operations and causing underground flooding; and methane gas was present in large quantities underground in the Free State, increasing the dangers of fire hazards. (Black, 1960; and Anglo American Corp. of SA, *The Orange Free State Gold Field*, p. 22.)

28. Perhaps nowhere is this better illustrated than in the 614 per cent rise in the number of scrapers, haulages, loaders and winches purchased annually in the industry between 1947 and 1956 (up from 567 to 4047). (Black, 1958, p. 4.)

29. Writing in 1967 Anglo American's consulting engineer noted that:

> Many years ago such training [for Africans] as took place was usually of a desultory nature, and was done by placing the new recruit alongside an experienced African and allowing him to assimilate the required skill in this haphazard way. Under modern conditions and with ever-increasing costs this could no longer be accepted practice and, during the last twenty years, short and rapid training methods have been devised. (MacConachie, 1967, p. 138.)

30. According to Harry Oppenheimer (1967): '. . . it had been intended to house a substantial number of African employees [about 10 per cent of the total] with their wives in villages on the mine properties, but the government, for reasons of policy, drastically reduced the scope of these plans' (p. 103).

An Anglo American press release at the time stated:

> While the hostels accommodate natives who are either single or have left their wives and families in the Reserves, the Corporation has undertaken a housing scheme at its Orange Free State mines for married native mine workers, reserved for men in the more essential and semi-skilled jobs. As the mines are more highly mechanized than the other gold mines on the Witwatersrand, the need has increased for responsible natives capable of supervision and of handling mechanical equipment. These positions are filled, where possible, with settled married workers living with their families in the mine villages. The scheme is restricted to Union natives and only a very small proportion of the total labour force is housed in the villages. (Anglo American Corp. of SA, press release, Free State Geduld, Welkom, Orange Free State, 6 January 1956)

31. Particularly important in this regard were the introduction in 1946 of pneumatically driven shovel loaders to clear the underground tunnels and the introduction in 1949 of mechanical cleaning devices to remove the broken rock from the shaft. Both these tasks had previously been performed by large numbers of unskilled Africans using picks and shovels. (MacConachie, 1967, p. 134.)

32. Union of SA, *Official Year Book of the Union of SA*, no. 20, 1939, pp. 827–36; and South African Bureau of Statistics, *Statistical Year Book, 1964*, L.1–11 and H.1–80.

33. The rate of shaft-sinking increased from 400 ft (120m) per month in 1940 to over 700 ft (210m) in 1960 (the record for one month in this latter year was 1251 ft/380m).

During the 1950s tunnels were advanced by over 2000 ft (600m) per month compared with 400 and 500 ft (120m and 150m) during the 1930s. Other major
improvements were recorded in rock-drilling (as the hand-operated jack-hammer
drill was superseded by the Air Feed rock drill) and hoisting (as miners reached
depths of 5000 ft./1500m and more). (MacConachie, 1967, pp. 135–6, and Black,
1958, p. 5.)

34. New electric furnaces were introduced after the war to carry through the
electrification of various aspects of metallurgical practice, such as assaying, calcining
and smelting. In addition, submerged arc electric furnaces were introduced on the
larger mines of the Orange Free State and Far West Rand to cope with the larger
number of gold bars needing to be melted. (MacConachie, 1967, p. 137.)

35. In the Transvaal, Blyvooruitzicht and Vlakfontein commenced production in 1942;
Libanon in 1949; Stilfontein in 1952; West Driefontein and Doornfontein in 1953;
Hartebeesfontein in 1955; Vaal Reefs and Merriespruit in 1956; Buffelsfontein in
1957; and Winkelhaak in 1958. In the Orange Free State, St Helena began produc-
ing in 1951 followed by Welkom in the same year; Western Holdings, Freddies
North and Freddies South in 1953; Harmony, Virginia, President Brand and Presi-
dent Steyn in 1954; Loraine in 1955; and Free State Geduld in 1956. (SA Dept of
Mines, *Mining Statistics*, 1966, pp. 45–6.)

36. This is confirmed by a comparison of the productivity levels on Transvaal mines
(which includes old and new mines) and those on the Free State mines (which were
all new) between 1956 and 1960: the average annual productivity per man in the
Orange Free State was 1.5 times higher than the average in the Transvaal (60.78
ounces compared with 39.80 ounces respectively). (SA Dept of Mines, *Mining
Statistics*, 1966, p. 17; and South African Bureau of Statistics, *Statistical Year Book*,
1964.)

37. Subsumed under the general category of 'stores' are items such as machinery and
plant, electrical machinery and plant, iron and steel, electrical equipment, pipings
and tubings, buildings, electrical power, tools, explosives, cement and concrete,
and timber. (SA Dept of Mines, *Mining Statistics*, 1972.)

38. The increases were as shown in Table E.

Table E   Value of Stores as a Proportion of Total Costs

Date	Value of stores (£)	Value of wages (£)	Stores as % of total
1935	25 631 000	23 091 000	52.6
1945	32 014 000	35 968 000	47.1
1950	58 803 000	50 854 000	53.6
1955	102 550 000	72 304 000	58.7
1960	132 919 000	90 919 000	59.4

Source Union of SA, *Official Year Book of the Union of SA*, no. 20, 1939, pp. 827–36;
and Bureau of Statistics, *Statistical Year Book*, 1964, L.1–11 and H.1–80.

39. Compiled from SA Dept of Mines, *Mining Statistics*, 1966, p. 13; and SA Dept of
Statistics, *South African Statistics*, 1974, pp. 7, 38.

40. Following the devaluation of sterling the gold price rose by 44 per cent (from £8.625
per fine ounce to £12.413).

41. Compiled from SA Bureau of Census and Statistics, *Union Statistics for Fifty Years*,
1910–1960, p. K–4.

42. Working profits in the industry fell by 20 per cent between 1945 and 1948 (Table 6).

43. Union of SA, *Official Year Book of the Union of SA*, no. 27, 1952–3, pp. 918–27; and
Bureau of Statistics, *Statistical Year Book*, 1964, L.1–11, H.1–80.

44. SA Dept of Mines, *SA Mining Statistics*, 1972 and Chamber of Mines of SA, Eighty-
sixth Annual Report, 1975, p. 61.

45. *The Mining Journal, Annual Review*, 1960, p. 282.
46. The only new gold field in which the Group was not an important influence was the relatively small Bethal field, which was dominated by the Union Corp.
47. The year 1966 has been chosen since by this time all the gold mines developed after the war had reached full production.
48. The marked difference between average profitability on pre- and postwar mines needs to be emphasized as well. Average profitability on prewar mines was R0.98 per ton and on postwar mines R5.37 per ton (Anglo: R6.23 per ton). (Table 9, column 3.)
49. *Financial Mail*, Special Survey, 'Inside the Anglo Power House', p. 7.
50. The market capitalization value of the issued ordinary share capital of the various groups at the end of 1960 was as follows:

Gold Fields	£33 704 000
JCI	£15 108 000
Rand Mines	£12 740 000
Central Mining	£15 500 000
General Mining	£15 319 000
Union Corp.	£32 750 000
Anglo American	£87 343 000
Anglo-Vaal	£5 715 000

(From Graham, 1964.)

51. This mine began working at depths of 2½ miles (4 km) below the surface. (See Anglo American Corp. of SA, *Western Deep Levels: Deepest Mine of the Future*, and *Western Deep Levels Ltd: The Story of a Great New Gold Mine.*)
52. Over R300m worth of gold or about 40 per cent of the total produced in the industry in that year. (*Financial Mail*, Special Survey, 'Inside the Anglo Power House', p. 41.)
53. This move, which established Charter Cons. as a powerful London-based mining company, was linked to Anglo's successful attempt to take a controlling interest in the Hudson Bay Mining and Smelting Co. in Canada, whose assets (involving interests in copper, zinc, gold and silver mining) were valued in 1962 at over $40m. (*Financial Mail*, 23 February 1962, p. 239.)
54. JCI also had important copper and platinum interests, controlling *inter alia* the world's largest platinum mine at Rustenberg. (Mennell, 1961, p. 50.)
55. In 1965 South Africa's second largest coal producer, Federale Mynbou (a company controlled by Afrikaner interests), acquired a 46 per cent direct interest in General Mining and, through a 51 per cent holding in a third company, Hollard Straat Ses Beleggings, an indirect holding of 15.7 per cent. However, Federale Mynbou's minority partner in the Hollard Straat Co. was Anglo American (with a 49 per cent holding) ensuring Anglo was well placed to keep a watchful eye over developments within General Mining. (*SA Mining and Engineering Journal*, 30 December 1970, pp. 81–7; and *Financial Mail*, Special Survey, 'Inside the Anglo Power House', p. 23.)
56. In terms of average grade of ore Anglo had 6 rich gold mines compared with 3 for Gold Fields and one each for the rest of the groups, excluding General Mining which had none. (Table 10.)
57. In 1973 the dollar price of gold rose from $35 an ounce to $42.22. By August 1978 the price had reached $200 an ounce; by mid-1979 $300; and in January 1980 it reached the phenomenal level of $850 per ounce. Though it has fallen back since then, it is still well above the 1978–9 levels. (Innes, 1981a, pp. 27–9.)
58. As an Anglo American advertisement puts it: 'Wherever you find gold, the chances are that we had something to do with it.' (*Financial Mail*, Supplement, 'Gold'.)
59. Martin and Co. (Stock and Share Brokers), 'De Beers Consolidated Mines—a comprehensive review of the world's leading diamond producer', (1971), p. 7.

CHAPTER 7

Postwar Industry and Finance:
The Role of the Groups

INDUSTRIAL EXPANSION DURING THE WAR

As in the case of the First World War, the disruptions brought about by the Second World War afforded new opportunities for South African capitalists to expand the country's manufacturing industry. However, this time the state was ready to play a direct role in promoting this process. In a speech ('Greater South Africa') delivered in Johannesburg in 1940, the prime minister, General J. C. Smuts, argued:

> It is generally recognized that a great opportunity has arrived for us to push forward industrial development in this country. The great world crisis now upon us may prove a unique opportunity for forwarding our industrial development. The war must inevitably throw us back on our own resources. Much that has been imported will now have to be manufactured locally. Much that has been exported will now, with restricted sea transport, have to be worked up and processed and consumed in this country. It is an ill wind that blows nobody any good, and this world blizzard may mean much for the economic progress of South Africa. It is for this reason that the Government have decided to ask Parliament to establish an Industrial Development Corporation which will be able to help to finance and guide our industrial development and prove for industry the sort of boon that the Land Bank has proved for agriculture.

The state's role in fact went far beyond simply the establishment of the IDC in 1942. During the war the state also embarked on an important expansion programme for ISCOR; built and financed annexe factories under the control of private companies; assisted in the organization and provision of a market for a number of industries; and through a change in the administration of tariff policy effectively increased protection for industry.[1] Much of the finance for these ventures came from the war taxes which were imposed on the gold mining industry after 1940 (see Chapter 6). Thus while during the war state policy was geared to the promotion of the manufacturing sector, it was in fact the gold mining industry which provided much of the financial backing for this policy.

However, the state did not limit itself only to *financial* support for industry. The growing urban working class had to be controlled if industry was to benefit from its labour. As we have seen, the early years of the war brought with them rapid inflation and a corresponding intensification of black workers' demands for wage increases. Through a combination of concessions and repression the state sought to contain these demands and restrict the rise of militancy among black workers.[2] The growth of black trade unions and the strike waves of 1942 and 1944 testify to the fact that the state was only partially successful in this regard. However, wage demands were largely contained and, overall, South Africa's manufacturing sector was able to make considerable advances during the war. Virtually every industrial group within the manufacturing sector expanded, based especially on the greater employment of black labour. While the number of white workers in the sector rose by only 20.6 per cent between 1938–9 and 1944–5 (from 93 054 to 112 219), the number of black workers rose by 74 per cent (from 143 069 to 248 785). The gross value of industrial output rose by 116 percent (from £141m in 1939 to £304m in 1945),[3] so that by 1946 the manufacturing sector had comfortably surpassed both mining and agriculture to become the largest single component in the GDP (17 per cent of the total compared with 11.9 per cent and 13 per cent for mining and agriculture respectively) (Table 11).

In summing up this important phase of South Africa's industrial history two points should be made about the character of the growth that occurred. The first is that much of it was aimed at meeting the war needs of South Africa and its allies. The money channelled into ISCOR and the existence of a small engineering industry linked to the mines enabled South African industry to produce a wide range of weaponry, ammunition and vehicles.[4] Though as a result new skills and techniques were developed, this market was of course only transient and would cease when the war ended. Secondly, cut off from imports of machinery and equipment, this phase of industrial growth was of necessity highly labour-intensive.[5] Thus, although the manufacturing sector reached new heights during the war, it faced the postwar period not only with its black labour force as yet unsubdued, but also with a relatively backward labour process and the certain prospect of losing its important market for war materials.

CLASS STRUGGLE AND INDUSTRIAL INSTABILITY DURING THE 1950s

One of the crucial questions the South African state faced after the war was that of finding a way, under the new and less favourable conditions that prevailed, of building on the advances manufacturing had made during the war. The dangers posed by the more militant black working class were amplified by the 1946 mine-workers' strike. Although this strike was suppressed and attempts by CNETU to build support for it among urban workers failed, the state still needed to find a long-term solution to the problem of African labour control. Similarly, the dangers posed by the resumption of industrial production in the capitalist centres abroad was emphasized by the rising import bill and subsequent balance of payments crisis which hit South Africa in 1948–9. Although the introduction of a new range of import controls and devaluation of the South African pound overcame the immediate crisis, the problem of reconciling the country's industrial growth with renewed overseas competition remained.

As we saw in the preceding chapter, the state at this time attempted to resolve the labour question through a protracted and elaborate process of restructuring which further extended the repressive controls over black labour. At first sight such an extension of control seems to contradict the requirements of a 'modernizing' industrial economy which, according to most growth models, requires a *free* labour market in order to develop. Adopting this line of argument, many writers have claimed that the state's new labour controls, and the overall political policy of apartheid which accompanied them, were in fact antagonistic to the needs of manufacturing and seriously impeded its progress. Usually these writers explain state policy in terms of the National Party government's need to defend the interests of its major constituents, white rural-based Afrikaners, who were so 'backward' in their culture and thinking that they could not adapt to the demands of a modern industrial economy. A neo-Marxist version which has certain similarities with the above argues that the state was under the hegemony of the agricultural 'fraction' of capital and therefore supported their interests against those of the manufacturing 'fraction'. (For examples of the former approach see *inter alia* Lipton, 1974a, 1974b, and Leftwich, 1974; for an illustration of the later approach see Davies, Kaplan *et al.*, 1976.) Whichever of these approaches one takes, they both have certain arguments in common: first, that on the labour question the interests of the primary sectors, like mining and agriculture, are incompatible with those of the secondary sector, manufacturing; and, secondly, that state labour policy at the time was intended to support the former against the latter.

In our view both these arguments are short-sighted in that their view of the 'needs' of South Africa's manufacturing industry during the 1950s is influenced by theoretical models derived from the experiences of European and American industrial growth (this seems to be as true of those within the Marxist camp as of the liberals) (see especially Marx, 1974, vol. I, Chapter 25; and Rostow, 1960). In general, these models argue that manufacturing industry requires a labour force which is free to sell its labour-power to the highest bidder and therefore must be mobile. Secondly, because manufacturing requires more skilled labour than, say, agriculture its labour force should have opportunities for education and training and should be permanently urban-based so as to encourage stability and discourage rapid turnover. The apartheid labour system—with its rural-based migrant workers, its strict controls preventing African mobility, its Job Reservation legislation and lack of educational and training facilities for African workers—clearly fulfills none of these criteria. Furthermore, it is argued that the free bargaining system associated with most industrial experiences leads to relatively higher wages which in turn promote the growth of an internal market so necessary to manufacturing expansion. In South Africa the emphasis on cheap black labour thus denied manufacturing this crucial local market. Many of these arguments are undoubtedly accurate: the restriction of the internal market *is* an impediment to manufacturing, especially because of the difficulties involved in competing on foreign markets; the lack of educational and training facilities and the laws which prohibit African job advancement all lead to the occurrence of bottlenecks in skilled labour; while the high rate of turnover in black labour does create instability. But before these contradictions can be taken to imply an *anti-manufacturing* policy on the part of the state one should examine more closely the conditions of South African manufacturing production during the 1950s.

Despite its large contribution to the GDP (averaging 20 per cent of the total between 1950 and 1960) (Table 11), the manufacturing sector was at that time in a state of relative backwardness. As we saw, the growth which had occurred during the war had been largely labour-intensive in character as small entrepreneurs emerged to fill the space created by the withdrawal of imported commodities. Even during the 1950s the vast majority of industrial establishments in South Africa were very small concerns employing only a few workers: in 1953–4, for instance, 65 per cent of all industrial establishments employed fewer than nine workers, while 92 per cent employed fewer than forty-nine.[6] A higher wage policy for black industrial workers, while facilitating the expansion of the internal market, would have imposed an intolerable burden on these small capitalists.[7] What they required was a labour policy which kept black wage rates as low as possible, thus enabling them to expand the absolute size of their labour force. Secondly, being highly labour-intensive, these firms were not seriously affected by problems of skill shortages. Overall, what they required was what the state sought to supply: a system of strict labour control which prevented African wage rates from rising at the same time as it provided a sufficient labour supply.

However, just as it would be wrong to argue that state policy favoured the primary sectors at the expense of manufacturing, it would be equally wrong to argue that state policy was perfectly rational and able to meet all the needs of all sectors (for examples of this approach, see especially Wolpe, 1972, and Johnstone, 1970b). Certainly the policy was not directly favourable to the requirements of larger and more mechanized industrial firms which did require a stable urban-based black proletariat with access to training and education. But even here state policy can be seen to have brought these firms indirect advantages. The key to securing their future lay in more rapid mechanization and here the mining industry had an important role to play both in terms of generating surplus-value which could be used to help finance mechanization and also in terms of earning the foreign exchange with which to import the necessary machinery and equipment. By looking after the labour needs of the mining sector the state protected the financial position of that sector whose expansion was the *sine qua non* of capital-intensive growth in manufacturing.

Thus what state policy in effect did was not to restrict industrial growth, but rather to encourage a particular form of industrialization based largely on labour-intensive methods of production. The immediate result was the expansion of the labour-intensive light industries rather than the more mechanized capital goods sector. For instance, during the early 1950s it was industries like food, beverages, paper and textiles which expanded (together with the more labour-intensive mineral processing group of industries), while in the late 1950s, when there was little growth, the trend to labour-intensity became even more marked.[8] Not that the state was unaware of the importance of mechanization to industry's future. The Board of Trade and Industries had specifically pointed to the advantages which mechanization would bring under conditions of cheap black labour.[9] But here state policy was limited to a large extent by the contradictions arising out of South Africa's position in the international capitalist system.

The state's attempts to resolve the 1948–9 balance of payments crisis had not prevented imports from continuing to expand. It was machinery and equipment for mining, industry and, to a lesser extent, agriculture which bore the major responsibility for this increase (rising as a proportion of total imports from 26 per cent in 1947 to 34 per cent in 1957).[10] By 1953–4 the economy had once again been plunged into a balance of payments crisis. The fiscal and monetary restraints subsequently imposed by the state immediately hit industry, restricting in particular investment in new machinery and equipment. These balance of payments pressures thus severely hindered the process of industrial mechanization.

South African industry was here caught in the vicious circle imposed by the new form of imperialism. As we saw in Chapter 4, the interwar growth of heavy industry and capital goods production in the developed capitalist states had corresponded with the evolution of an imperialist system which promoted the export of the products of these industries. Control over the technological means of production of industry was thus located in the developed capitalist states. In their efforts to gain access to these technologies (largely in the form of capital goods) South African industrialists found themselves thwarted by the economy's incapacity to earn sufficient foreign exchange to pay for them. The only way in which they could break free of this cycle was through production of their own capital goods. Yet here again they found themselves trapped in the web of imperialism, since research and development work as well as scientific and technical apparatuses required for technological development were all concentrated in the developed states. Despite efforts to promote capital goods substitution in South Africa, in the 30 years between 1926–7 and 1956–7 only 17 per cent (R198m) of the net value of all substitution of imported goods involved capital goods.[11]

Thus under the combined impact of this international system of imperialism and a local labour system which reproduced a cheap and low-skilled black labour force, South Africa's manufacturing industries were pushed relentlessly into labour-intensive lines of development. Yet here again they ran into serious obstacles as both the problem of their lack of competitiveness with imported commodities and the question of how to implement a policy of strict labour controls over an increasingly militant labour force reasserted themselves. While the state sought to deal with the former problem largely through the system of import controls and tariff barriers, the solution to the latter question was to be both more complex and ultimately far more violent.

The major problem for manufacturing was that it was being pushed into greater reliance on black labour at precisely the time that black workers were responding with increasing hostility to the state's efforts to tighten controls over them. State policy in this respect was two-fold. On the one hand, it sought to impose an even tougher discipline over black industrial workers through an extension of administrative controls. In this respect the Viljoen Commission of Inquiry, which reported in 1958, is important since it was expressly concerned with 'the importance of labour cost as a constituent element in the cost structure of secondary industry and the desirability of building up a contented and efficient labour force'.[12] According to the commission, the tightening of administrative controls was necessary to achieve both efficiency and flexibility in the administration of black industrial workers. In this way—and in particular through the notion of administrative flexibility—the commission hoped to be able to reconcile the existing labour system with the differing labour requirements of small and large industrialists. On the other hand, the state was equally concerned with finding a solution to the serious social problems which accompanied industrialization. Of prime importance in this regard was the danger posed by the concentration of masses of African workers and work-seekers in and around the urban areas. This problem had been causing concern since the boom of the war years. As early as 1945 the Board of Trade had argued:

> Racial and class differences will make a homogenous Native proletariat which will eventually lose all contact with its former communal rural relations which had previously given their lives a content and meaning.

> The detribalization of large numbers of Natives congregated in amorphous masses in large industrial centres is a matter which no government can view with equanimity. Unless handled with great foresight and skill these masses of detribalized Natives can very easily develop into a menace rather than a constructive factor in industry.[13]

The state's response to this potentially serious threat was to try and develop a system of social control which permanently located the urban proletariat in the rural areas in terms of family, cultural and political ties, while continuing to reproduce its economic dependence on urban wage labour. The apartheid system—with its policy of restructuring the original reserves into self-governing Bantustans—provided the institutional framework through which such a policy could not only be implemented, but also rationalized.[14]

Thus state policy at the time was not just confined to seeking to extend administrative controls over black industrial workers; it also involved a process of massive social restructuring which, in its political form of apartheid, affected all black people as citizens of South Africa—and therefore affected every black worker *as a citizen* as well. Precisely because of this, black workers' resistance to the labour controls was quite easily swept up in the tide of resistance which was mounting among all sections of the black population against apartheid. The black workers' struggle had thus entered a new phase in which the struggle for labour rights was incorporated in—and, one might argue, subsumed under—the popular struggle against the apartheid policy of the state.[15] Probably the clearest expression of this tendency lies in the extremely close links forged in the late 1950s between the South African Congress of Trade Unions (SACTU), representing mostly African workers, and the African National Congress of South Africa (ANC). This latter organization included within its growing ranks not only militants from within the black labour movement, but also those from within other classes among the black population, such as the peasantry and petty-bourgeoisie. As such, it clearly expressed at an institutional level the class alliance which was being forged among black workers, peasants and the petty-bourgeoisie in response to the intensification of black oppression under apartheid.

The threat which this newly forged alliance posed to the capitalist class and the state in South Africa should not be underestimated. Although the political programme of the ANC (as specified in the Freedom Charter of 1955) was not anti-capitalist in orientation, it did demand that the apartheid form of state (based on a denial of meaningful political rights to blacks) be replaced by a democratic form of state (based on universal franchise) and that the current white owners of the mines, major banks and industries be expropriated. These and other radical populist demands in the programme (particularly those relating to black land ownership and legal rights) were aimed specifically at dismantling the network of racial controls which supported the existing form of the capitalist system and, if implemented, spelt an end to the concentration of wealth and power in the hands of *white* capitalists. Equally—if not more—threatening to the future of this class was the new strategy through which the ANC sought to secure its goals. Prior to 1949 the ANC's strategy had been to seek reforms through negotiation and persuasion, but during the 1950s it adopted a strategy of direct mass action, which incorporated tactics such as boycotts, civil disobedience campaigns, mass rallies, marches and general strikes (the so-called 'stay-at-homes'). As a result mass protest activity rose to a crescendo towards the end of the decade, provoking the Minister of Justice to claim that the ANC was conducting 'a reign of terror' designed 'to bring to its knees any white government in South Africa which stands for white supremacy and white leadership . . . What they want is our country' (cited in Lambert, 1978, p. 135).[16]

Nor could the South African economy escape from the force of this resistance. Even though the political form of the struggle had shifted the focus of protests away from the factory floor, many of the mass actions, such as the stay-at-homes and bus boycotts, hit productivity directly. But most important from manufacturing's point of view was the overall destabilization caused by a black workforce which refused to accept the discipline so necessary to sustain growth at this time. Swamped by cheap imports (despite the state's efforts dumping remained a problem) and denied the docile and pliable labour force necessary to enable it to reorganize itself, manufacturing lurched from instability in the early 1950s into decline and, ultimately, crisis. Industrial output, which had grown by 7.2 per cent in 1954, grew by 4.4 per cent in 1955, 3.4 per cent in 1956, 2.3 per cent in 1957 and only 1.7 per cent in 1958. In 1959 minus growth of − 1.4 per cent was recorded.[17] Every industry within manufacturing declined at this time and almost two-thirds of them recorded slumps of virtual crisis proportions.[18] With the state manifestly unable to put a decisive end to black resistance capital began to take flight from the country: after a net capital inflow of R134m in 1958, a net outflow of − R61m was recorded in 1959 and − R180m in 1960.[19] Between January 1960 and May 1961 gold and foreign exchange reserves plummeted by 51 per cent (from R312m to R153m). By the end of 1960 the deficit on the balance of payments stood at R143m and 'South Africa faced a balance-of-payments crisis more severe than any experienced since 1932' (Houghton, 1973, p. 184).

In the face of this the state moved decisively to check the deficit on the balance of payments. Import controls were intensified, the bank rate was raised, foreign exchange facilities reduced, restrictions placed on the commercial banks' stock exchange dealings and, most important of all, in June 1961 the 'Blocked Rand' system came into being (placing restrictions both on the repatriation of capital by non-South African residents and on the remittance of funds abroad by South African residents). The effect of these combined measures was that by the end of 1961 a favourable balance of payments position (of R86m) had been achieved and by February 1962 the foreign exchange and gold reserves had recovered to over R316m.[20]

However, these measures were only one aspect of the state's overall strategy to bring about a return to economic and political stability in the country and, important though they were, they dealt only with the symptoms and not the cause of the malaise. As long as the African masses remained in open revolt the malaise would continue.[21] In 1960 the state launched a campaign of concerted violence designed to quell the revolt. The Sharpeville massacre of 21 March 1960 was followed by the banning of both the ANC and a break-away group, the Pan African-ist Congress (PAC). In the same year the government declared a state of emergency, thereby assuming wide powers to arrest and detain any person suspected of anti-government activity. Nationwide arrests of African leaders were carried out while police moved into African town-ships beating up the inhabitants indiscriminately. On this occasion, however, the black working class was not so easily cowed: the Sharpe-ville massacre had set in motion a train of spontaneous strikes which rapidly escalated over the next few weeks into riots, industrial sabo-tage, mass marches and mass demonstrations against the Pass Laws. The fury unleashed by these events was, however, never to be har-nessed by the leadership. Instead, the banned Communist Party, fol-lowed shortly after by the ANC, launched the Sabotage Campaign as the first step in a programme of guerrilla warfare. Whatever the argu-ments in favour of this form of action (in terms, for instance, of meeting armed force with armed force), its immediate effect was to leave the mass of black workers leaderless and confused. When in 1963 the ANC's secret headquarters were raided and its internal organization annihilated, a phase of demoralization ensued among black workers which resulted shortly afterwards in the collapse of the ANC's trade union wing, SACTU. By 1964 the resistance movement had been de-feated and black workers forced into submission.

This political defeat paved the way for the greatest economic boom in South Africa since the war. It was thus a crucial watershed in South Africa's economic and political history and one in which mining capital-ists—and in particular the Anglo American Group—played a not insignificant role. Of major importance here was their role in stemming the dangerous flight of capital from the country through local reinvest-ment (primarily through buying up a wide range of industrial and financial shares on the Johannesburg stock exchange). More than any-thing, this move represented an ostentatious display of confidence in the state's capacity to defend South African capitalism and as such played a key role in restoring international confidence in the country's investment potential.[22] However, this dramatic plunge by the mining groups into non-mining investments was not an entirely new phenomenon (not that its political impact was therefore any less important). In the following pages we shall trace some of the most important aspects of the groups' non-mining activity during the period under review.

MINING INVESTMENT IN INDUSTRY AND FINANCE DURING THE 1950s

During the late 1940s and 1950s most of the resources of the gold mining groups was spent on developing the new gold fields. However, despite this preoccupation, there is also evidence at this time of their growing involvement in South African industry and finance. This trend was to become so pronounced that by the end of the decade it was to assume major importance for the future course of the country's economic development.

One of the groups whose investments played an influential role in industry was Anglo American. The largest industrial concerns under its control at this time were AE & CI, Boart and Hard Metals, the Union Steel Corporation and Vereeniging Refractories. Most of these companies had been acquired by Anglo during take-overs of mining conglomerates. AE & CI, for instance, came in 1929 with De Beers, while Vereeniging Refractories (formerly Vereeniging Brick and Tile) and Union Steel came in 1945 with the Lewis and Marks take-over. Only Boart and Hard Metals had actually been founded by Anglo in 1936 (as Boart Products South Africa). As we shall see, two of these companies (AE & CI and Boart and Hard Metals) were to play a particularly prominent part in South Africa's industrial history.

As we saw earlier, when AE & CI was formed out of a merger in 1924 (as AE & I), it immediately became the largest explosives and fertilizer producer in South Africa. In 1930 the company embarked upon a significant new phase of development when, using a German process, it began production of nitrate acid from locally synthesized ammonia. Initially, the new plant brought important benefits to mining since it reduced the costs of explosives by putting an end to expensive imports of sodium nitrate from Chile. When the company subsequently expanded its ammonia capacity to produce ammonium nitrate (as a replacement for nitroglycerine) blasting costs on the mines were further reduced (coming during the post-Depression phase of gold mining development this innovation was particularly important) (Cartwright, 1964). However, it was not until the period after the war that AE & CI really began to make its mark.

This phase of expansion was ushered in by a change in the formal relations of company control: in 1944 De Beers Consolidated formed the De Beers Industrial Corporation (in which the parent company held a 58.5 per cent interest) to hold its industrial interests, of which the most important was its 42.5 per cent stake in AE & CI.[23] Initially, postwar expansion remained linked to mining: in 1946 the company opened a new factory to supply calcium cyanide (used in gold extraction) to the mines and it was not long before half of the mines' requirements came from this source. However, AE & CI rapidly began to diversify its activities, seeking in particular to supply the expanding markets in agriculture and manufacturing. During the mid-1950s it extended its ammonia capacity still further through the production of urea, which is a concentrated form of nitrogenous (ammoniated) fertilizer as well as a base for industrial resins.[24] In 1952 the company produced the first locally made raw materials for conversion into plastic end-products and followed this in 1955 with the opening up of a polyvinyl chloride (PVC) plant.[25] Nor was AE & CI's expansion confined to South Africa. Since the 1930s the company had operated a mixing and bagging plant in Rhodesia and this was followed by the erection during the 1950s of superphosphate and phosphoric acid plants in that country. Out of these developments a new holding company (AE & CI Rhodesia) was to emerge. By the late 1950s the diversified AE & CI group was the largest and fastest-growing industrial concern within the Anglo American Group and was one of the leading industrial concerns in South Africa.

The other industrial company within Anglo which also grew rapidly at this time was Boart and Hard Metals. Anglo had established this company in 1936 to investigate uses and markets for industrial diamonds. Initially it had serviced South Africa's mining industry, assisting especially with the development of new techniques for drilling (Beckingham, 1972, pp. 131–2). During the postwar period, however, the company branched into the related fields of carbide cutting tools and abrasives, developing a wide range of diamond and carbide drilling, grinding and cutting equipment. Gradually during this period the company began to build up an international reputation for itself in the sphere of abrasive tools in particular.[26]

The history of these two companies, both of which are leading industrial concerns in South Africa today, provides an important insight into the way in which industrialization developed in South Africa. As the fastest growing industrial concerns within the Anglo American Group, it was no coincidence that both companies developed initially as service industries to mining. As such, they provide useful illustrations of the way in which, given certain economic and political conditions, development of a major primary industry can set in motion a number of industries which are initially totally dependent on it but which subsequently branch out into other fields and become relatively more independent. However, as these cases suggest, it is the existence of the primary industry which is the *sine qua non* of industrial growth. Furthermore, as the history of Boart and Hard Metals suggests, the fact that the primary industry is under *monopoly* control can be an important factor in stimulating industrial growth. As a monopoly combine straddling both gold and diamond production during the 1930s, Anglo American was faced with two seemingly unrelated problems: on the one hand, how to dispose of large quantities of low-grade industrial diamonds which at the time were 'virtually unsaleable'; and, on the other, the need to develop new equipment to cope with serious drilling problems in gold mining (Beckingham, 1972, p. 132). The formation of the Boart company expressed institutionally the monopoly Group's capacity to resolve these dilemmas within itself by linking them together: that is, by developing techniques through which the industrial diamonds could be used to develop new drilling equipment for gold mining. Thus a new branch of manufacturing was evolved which eventually developed an independent momentum of its own.

In addition to the industrial activities outlined above, Anglo also made a potentially important acquisition in the late 1950s when it took over a relatively small company, Transvaal Vanadium, which was the only producer of vanadium pentoxide in South Africa (Beckingham, 1972, pp. 131, 136). As we shall see, this company was subsequently to give rise to one of the giants of South African industry, the Highveld Steel and Vanadium Corporation. By 1960 the total value of the industrial interests of the Anglo American Corporation alone—that is, excluding those of other Group holding companies, such as De Beers— was reckoned at almost R50m.[27] Nor was Anglo the only mining group to have a presence in industry at this time. For instance, in that same year 17 per cent of Anglo-Transvaal's interests and 5 per cent of JCI's were tied up in industry, while 22 per cent of Central Mining's interests were in industry and commerce (Mennell, 1961, p. 50). Most of the industrial investments of these other groups in fact followed the pattern outlined above for Anglo American: that is, they occurred in sectors of industry closely allied to mining and began to expand their activities during the 1950s.

Within the Central Mining Group, Rand Mines' most important industrial interests included: Hume Ltd, manufacturers of concrete and clay pipes and products, steel pipes and fittings, railway sleepers and bricks and tiles; RMB Alloys which manufactured ferro-alloys; Southern Cross Steel which made special steels, including stainless steel; and Pretoria Portland Cement.[28] The history of this latter company provides a particularly useful illustration of the close association between the groups' industrial interests and the needs of the mining industry. Establish by the Group in 1890 this company had soon expanded geographically from its base of supplying cement exclusively to the Transvaal gold mines. In 1921 it spawned the Cape Portland Cement Company and in 1927 both the Eastern Province Cement Company and the Premier Portland Cement Company (Rhodesia). The post-Depression gold boom brought the company a phase of further expansion: in 1934 it built what was then the most up-to-date cement factory in South Africa to serve the gold fields of the East and West Rand. By the end of the war the company was well placed to benefit from the 'cement explosion' which occurred as the newly developing gold mines became the biggest consumers of cement in the country. Following this phase of rapid growth the company began reorganizing its plants to meet the needs of more diversified expansion and to this end spent £11.5m between 1957 and 1968 in modernizing and increasing its plant capacity.[29] Thus, closely linked since its inception to the gold mining market, this company has none the less diversified over time into a range of other markets.

Similarly, a number of mining-oriented companies are to be found among JCI's industrial interests. These include Lenning Holdings, a group which had been formed after the war to manufacture mining, industrial and railway equipment and which came under JCI's control in 1953.[30] Two engineering concerns within the group, JCI General Engineering and Barberton Engineering, both began by providing 'repair and maintenance' services to the gold mines (the former, which had been established in 1946 to service the Orange Free State mines, subsequently became the largest engineering works in that province). Again, Louw's Creek was a large timber plantation owned by the group and supplying the mines with timber for props and mat packs used underground. Outside these companies which serviced the mines directly JCI held other industrial interests whose origins were linked to the early years of mining, such as its substantial holdings in South African Breweries and the Argus Printing and Publishing Company.[31]

Two other groups whose industrial interests conformed closely to the above pattern are General Mining and Union Corporation. Mostly concentrated in engineering, General Mining's interests included the control it acquired in 1953 in Hall, Longmore and Co., which manufactured high quality welded steel pipes.[32] Union Corporation's interests included Eclipse Engineering, a company founded in 1927 and manufacturing a wide range of light and heavy steel castings for mining and industrial use. In 1951 this company embarked upon a new phase of expansion when it moved into the Orange Free State where it was in close proximity to the new mines. During the 1950s the group also bought up Aerflo (Pty) Ltd, a company specializing in the design and manufacture of ventilation fans of all sizes and dust extraction machinery, so as to meet the demands of the new mines.[33] Other Group interests in this broad field included Permanent Alloy Castings, Project Engineering and African Wire Ropes, while outside this field and not directly related to mining was the Group's major holding in South African Pulp and Paper Industries (SAPPI). Established in 1936, this latter company expanded into 'a vast complex of companies producing sufficient pulp and paper for nearly all South Africa's requirements'.[34]

There was only one mining group whose industrial interests did not at this time conform quite so closely to the normal group pattern of heavy concentration in mine servicing industries—and that was Anglo-Transvaal. Although its interests did include some (like Anglo-Alpha Cement and National Bolts and Rivets) which were close to mining, its main industrial interests were concentrated around the fishing industry: through the South Atlantic Corporation it controlled Irvin and Johnson (a fish trawling, processing and distribution concern) as well as Globe Engineering and its subsidiary, James Brown and Hamer (which were involved in structural, mechanical and marine engineering, as well as steel and wooden ship-building.)[35]

Thus the postwar phase of development work on the new gold fields brought with it a spate of industrial activity from the mining groups. However, this activity needs to be located in the context of the backwardness of South African industry at that time. Following the demise of the war market, development of the postwar gold mines afforded South Africa's manufacturing industry a unique opportunity for expansion, particularly as the state's import policy provided local industry with a large measure of protection from foreign competition. However, the very nature of the new market in fact put large sections of it beyond the reach of most local industrialists. What the mines mostly required were high-quality heavy industry goods (such as precision drilling equipment, various kinds of reinforced steels, iron and steel castings and pipes, ventilation and railway equipment) as well as bulk orders of commodities like reinforced timber and cement. In general, the technical capacities and financial resources of South African industrialists were far too weak to meet these requirements. Yet the state's import policy raised the cost of importing these commodities at precisely the time the groups sought to keep their cost structure down. As a result the groups themselves began to undertake the task of supplying these goods by embarking on new areas of industrial production (either through opening new plants or through expanding existing facilities).

The groups were in fact far better placed to produce these commodities than most local industrialists, since not only did they have the financial resources to embark upon large-scale production, but they also had at their disposal the means to meet the complex technical needs of the mines. As large institutions with a network of international connections, the groups were able to gain access to and benefit from the technical advances being made in the developed centres of capitalist production. Consequently, most of the industrial concerns under group control entered into technical agreements of one kind or another with important overseas industrial concerns in order to apply that expertise to South African conditions.[36]

This phase of gold mining development thus did provide a powerful stimulus to industrial production in South Africa with the groups themselves playing an influential role by promoting a number of service industries. Not only did this expand the scope of local industrial activity, but it also improved it *qualitatively* as modern foreign-controlled technologies were put to local use. At a theoretical level these developments provide a useful illustration of the way in which different monopoly tendencies can occur concurrently with—and constantly reinforce—one another. The rapid advance of the tendencies of concentration and centralization of capital which accompanied the development of the new mines (and which we analysed earlier) also involved a faster trend in the diversification of capital as the groups began to shift into industrial production. Thus this phase of monopoly evolution in mining was one of combined development in which, as the concentration and centralization of capital proceeded apace, so it generated demands for service industries which the groups themselves met, thus promoting the tendency of diversification of capital. As far as the South African economy was concerned, this phase produced an industrial and infrastructural base, located especially in engineering, which was to prove indispensable to the future of manufacturing production.

However, while the above developments were undoubtedly important to the future of industry, it was in the sphere of the financial sector that the most significant developments were taking place. Writing in 1962 one commentator noted:

> Through these past two years of political stress and constitutional change, the trend of South Africa's evolving money market has been in marked contrast to the broad trend of South Africa's economy as a whole. Whilst the rate of growth in industry has been falling off, the already vigorous growth of the money market institutions has been very sharply accelerated, with the result that the market has now reached substantial proportions. Little more than a dozen years have passed since the first moves were made to provide specialized services in this sphere in South Africa, and less than seven years since the first privately organized concern came upon the scene . . . Yet in some significant ways this young money market has come to play in the financial mechanism of South Africa a role comparable to that played by the old-established London money market in the financial mechanism of Great Britain. Measured by some purely quantitative tests, indeed, the role of the South African money market can actually be shown to be, relative to the size of the economy, the larger of the two. (King, 1962, p. 161)

The very rapid development of South Africa's money market at this time is closely related to the events already discussed.[37] We saw earlier how the postwar development of the gold fields was financed largely by a massive influx of foreign capital and by the groups themselves. As the bulk of these mines reached the production stage during the mid-1950s so revenue began to accrue locally both to the foreign investors and to the groups. With the capital demands of the mines now receding, this growing stock of finance seemed bound to be exported overseas. However, it was precisely at this time that manufacturing industry was desperately in need of finance to help 'modernize' its methods of production and increase its capacity. Clearly, as far as the capitalist class in South Africa was concerned, a way needed to be found to channel these funds into local manufacturing. The development of a local money market was to be the main means to this end.

However, to carry this through not only did investors need to be satisfied that South Africa's manufacturing industry offered a safe and good return on their capital, they also needed to be convinced that their money would be skilfully and carefully handled. As we saw, the state played a key role in easing the former fear by successfully breaking the back of black resistance in the early 1960s. As far as the latter was concerned, the active involvement in the local money market of some of the leading monopoly concerns was crucial in encouraging confidence among investors. Of particular relevance was the role played by the Anglo American Group both in encouraging confidence and, more concretely, in providing the finance which was to be the foundation of the local money market.

Earlier we touched on the role played by Ernest Oppenheimer in the establishment of the state-owned National Finance Corporation (NFC) in 1949. This corporation, designed at that time specifically to hold and transfer finance destined for the gold mines, was the first institutional step taken in creating a local money market. However, in 1955 Anglo American formed its own private merchant bank, Union Acceptances Ltd (UAL), described as 'a company planning to model itself on the pattern of a London merchant bank' (King, 1962, p. 163). In embarking on this venture Anglo American had the active collaboration of the prominent London-based financial house, Lazard Brothers, and was supported by Barclays Bank. The new bank's first few years were so successful that in 1957 the portfolios and relevant borrowings of the discount department of UAL were hived off into a separate institution, the Discount House of South Africa, also under Anglo's control. This development (separating out the previously combined financial functions of accepting on the one hand and discounting on the other) was an expression of the increasing technical sophistication of the expanding financial system. By 1960 four other privately owned accepting houses had been established in South Africa, all of which were backed by major monopoly institutions.[38]

By 1961, following this explosion in private merchant banking activity, the financial resources of the NFC had been overtaken by those of the private sector.[39] Overall, in the six years between the end of 1955 and the end of 1961 the total funds employed at call or short notice in South Africa grew by a phenomenally fast 81 per cent (from £83m to

£150m), which compared with an increase over the same period of only 30 per cent for aggregate deposits at the commercial banks (from £463m to £600m). Taking call money alone, the £110m employed during 1961 amounted to over 5 per cent of South Africa's net national income in that year.[40] Nor was expansion confined to the merchant banks alone: during the 1950s the 'building society movement' expanded more rapidly than the commercial banks, so that by 1961 their total liabilities to the public exceeded those of the commercial banks.

These changes had a special significance for South Africa's evolution as a capitalist society. The substantial growth both of the internal money market and of the building societies was indicative not just of the growing sophistication of the country's financial sector but, more especially, it signified an important step forward in the gradual transformation of South African capitalism into monopoly capitalism. What the growth of the local money market represented in particular was the clearest form yet of the merging together of bank capital and productive capital—that is, of the emergence of the phase of finance capital. It was thus during the late 1950s that South African capitalism *as a whole*—and not just specific sectors of the economy—displayed the first clear signs of having entered the monopoly phase of its evolution.

As we have seen, the monopoly Anglo American Group played an important role in this transformation and it is therefore important to analyze that role. The first question to ask is why it was Anglo which played this role rather than one of the other monopolies? The answer lies in the fact that by the early 1950s Anglo American had emerged as the most powerful group in the mining industry and was rapidly becoming one of the leading monopoly concerns in the country. With the vast wealth of its new gold mines translating itself with ever-increasing speed into a massive stock of revenue, Anglo—more than any other group—found itself under strong pressure to find profitable outlets for its accumulating funds. Consequently, as a mining-finance house with considerable expertise in the realm of investment finance, Anglo began to move into the new growth area for investment.

However, it is worth noting how cautiously the Group approached the matter initially. First, the state was prevailed upon to make the early running through the NFC (as it were, to test out the market) and only when that venture had proved successful did the Group itself enter the field through UAL. Furthermore, in embarking on the UAL project Oppenheimer was careful to solicit not only the technical skills of Lazard Brothers, but also the support of one of the two major commercial banks in the country, Barclays. This latter move is significant since the support of at least one of these banks (the two most powerful financial institutions in the country) was crucial in securing the success of the whole project.[41] (Sir Ernest was ideally placed to win the support of Barclays since he had been a director of Barclays Bank DCO from 1929 until 1949, when he was replaced by his son, Harry.) With Barclays' support behind him, Oppenheimer went ahead with launching UAL, which over the next few years rapidly acquired for itself the lion's share of the money market.

These developments thus represent a major first step in the process of large-scale diversification of Group capital out of mining. By the time the politically motivated flight of capital occurred in 1959 and 1960, the institutional apparatus already existed for Anglo American to lead the way in championing the cause of the South African state by buying up shares on the local stock exchange. Of course, it is true that the state's introduction in 1961 of the 'Blocked Rand' system (which impeded the export of revenue from South Africa) exerted a strong pressure on groups like Anglo to invest locally. But it would be quite wrong to argue that this pressure was decisive in retaining this stock of investment finance in the country against the will of those who controlled it. For a start, the 'Blocked Rand' system, significantly, did not prevent repatriation of *dividends* abroad (Houghton, 1973, p. 184) and secondly, this argument does not take account of the large scale of voluntary investment in local finance and industry which had already occurred during the 1950s. Without this immediate pressure from the state, the scale and rate of subsequent (that is, post-1961) diversification of mining capital might well have been smaller and slower, but it would undoubtedly have occurred.

The 1950s—and in particular the latter part of the decade—were thus crucial years in the history of capital accumulation and economic growth in South Africa. In the first place, they brought with them a phase of enormous expansion in gold mining, which was to prove so important in sustaining economic growth through the years ahead. Secondly, clustered around the mining industry and often under the control of the groups, a range of new industrial enterprises sprang up and began diversifying into other areas of activity. Corresponding with these developments was the very rapid growth of South Africa's financial sector. The period was thus one in which the country's economy, though still largely dependent on primary production, showed clear signs of developing a more diversified industrial base at the same time as it exhibited signs of increasing monopolization—both through the monopoly groups' penetration of industry and through the emergence of new financial forms and institutions under monopoly control.

Yet the period did not produce any great economic boom. On the contrary, some sectors like industry experienced a relative decline over the latter part of the decade. Both the serious political and social upheavals in the country and its economic position on the periphery of the world capitalist system were largely responsible for this. However, by the early 1960s the state had moved decisively to rectify this position. Thus with the working class more or less subdued and an indus-

184 Anglo American

trial and financial base already laid South Africa seemed well placed to embark upon a new era of economic expansion.

The 1950s were also decisive in the evolution of the Anglo American Group as the years in which it established its leadership position in the gold mining industry. Furthermore, it was at this time that the Group became active in developing the local money market and in developing its industrial interests. As the potential for expansion in these latter areas opened up during the early 1960s and under pressure from revenue generated by its new gold mines, Anglo began to play an even more significant role in the development of South African finance and industry. As a senior member of the Group has argued:

> It was not until the beginning of the 1960s that the Corporation was really in a position to embark upon a policy of industrial diversification to a meaningful extent. Until then our technical and financial resources had been largely absorbed in developing the new gold mines in the Orange Free State. Most of these ventures had proved remarkably successful, justifying major increases in productive capacity that in turn required major appropriations from profits. But as the gold mines became somewhat less capital hungry, our investment in industry gathered pace. (Beckingham, 1972, p. 132)

In the pages that follow we shall trace the course of these industrial investments and examine their impact on the structure and form of industrialization in South Africa.

NOTES

1. Board of Trade and Industries, Report no. 282, p. 42, paras. 113–15.
2. The Wage Board Investigation into Unskilled Labour in the Witwatersrand and Pretoria area, set up by the state, was followed by Wage Determination 105 which fixed the minimum wage at 25s. per week rising to 27s. over two years. This was almost double the average wage on the gold mines and was considerably higher than that in agriculture. However, the Smit Report of 1942 calculated the Poverty Datum Line for an average urban African family at 37s. 6d. per week. Relaxations in administration of the Pass Laws and influx control were accompanied in December 1942 by the draconian War Measure 145 which *inter alia* outlawed strikes. (See Chapter 6 and Stein, 1979, pp. 2–6.)
3. SA Department of Statistics, *Union Statistics for Fifty Years 1910–1960*, L-30, L-3.
4. During the war South Africa supplied to its own forces and those of its allies *inter alia* the following materials: 8 053 415 shell castings; 2 568 652 complete mortar shells; 4 970 502 complete shells; 5770 armoured cars; over 2 000 000 steel helmets; 400 2- and 6-pounder anti-tank guns; 19 605 bayonets; 466 938 complete land mines; 14 000 3- and 5-tonner trucks; 1000 ambulance cars; 560 staff cars; 200 mobile workshops; 2200 water tank trailers; and 1369 light delivery trucks. (SA Bureau of Statistics, *State of South Africa, Economic, Financial and Statistical Year-Book for the Republic of South Africa, 1973.*)

5. Board of Trade and Industries, Report no. 282, Table XIV, p. 19. Commenting on the trends during the war, Houghton (1973, p. 123) writes:

> The period from 1939 to 1945 presented a great challenge to South African manufacturing industry . . . throughout industry many skilled workers were drawn into the army, although attempts were made to keep key men at their civilian jobs. The shortage of skilled men was acute and industrial output was enabled to expand only by the increased employment of non-white workers in semi-skilled and skilled jobs. There were also other difficulties on the supply side, because importation of tools, machine parts and semi-processed components was often impossible, and great ingenuity was displayed in the engineering industry in overcoming these bottlenecks. On the demand side there was a great increase in the consumption of the products of South African factories. Not only was the normal civilian demand cut off from overseas sources of supply, but South African industry also made a substantial contribution to the allied war effort in ship-repair work, manufacture of munitions and the production of armoured cars. This was possible only because of the increased output of high-grade steel from ISCOR . . . The Second World War found South African industry much better equipped to meet the challenge of temporary isolation than it was in 1914, and the rapid expansion to meet wartime demand was proof that it was more broadly based and more mature.

6. *Report of the Commission of Enquiry into the Export Trade of the Republic of South Africa*, Pretoria, 1972, RP 69/72, Table 9/8.
7. Like most manufacturing capitalists, South African industrialists not only wanted a larger internal market; they also wanted other capitalists to pay the higher wages that would create it.
8. The only exception was the newly established capital-intensive machinery industry which grew rapidly during the early 1950s. However, along with other capital-intensive industries, it declined during the latter part of the decade. (SA Bureau of Census and Statistics, *Union Statistics for Fifty Years*; and SA Department of Statistics, *South African Statistics, 1965*, Pretoria.)
9. According to Report no. 282 of the Board of Trade and Industries, 'The extension of manufacturing can be stimulated through increased mechanization so as to derive the full benefit of the large resources of comparatively low-paid non-European labour' (p. 45, para. 132).
10. Volkskas, *Finance and Trade Review*, December 1969.
11. On the other hand, significant advances occurred over this period in the net substitution of consumer and intermediate goods which accounted, respectively, for 48 per cent (R563m) and 35 per cent (R411m) of the total (ibid.).
12. *Report of the Commission of Enquiry into Policy Relating to the Protection of Industries*, p. 32, para. 263.
13. Board of Trade and Industries, Report no. 282, p. 46, para. 135.
14. The Board of Trade Report argued for a long-term political strategy which encompassed many of the features of modern-day apartheid:

> As the Board believes that the future development of industry in the Union is inseparably wrapped up with the Native the whole problem calls for vision and statesmanlike guidance. It is possible that it will involve a policy of regional planning and development in order to bring about a greater measure of decentralization of industry, the transfer and development of some of the industries making cheap standardized wares for Native consumption to Reserves, as well as for a policy of residential separation and racial parting in factories, and even for a large measure of territorial segregation. (ibid., p. 46, para. 135)

15. As the campaign against the apartheid state gathered momentum so the level of strike action around specific factory issues declined: there were 113 such strikes

involving 8970 black workers in 1957; 67 involving 7529 in 1958; 43 involving 3604 in 1959; and 36 involving 5266 in 1960. (Lambert, 1978, pp. 117–18.)

16. The first outburst of mass action took place on 1 May 1950 in response to the introduction of the Suppression of Communism Bill which both outlawed the Communist Party and increased the repressive powers of the state. A one-day work-stoppage was called which received wide support from African workers but which ended in the massacre by police of nineteen Africans. A national day of protest was called for 26 June (which became known as 'Freedom Day') in which the ANC proclaimed that 'the African people should refrain from going to work, and regard this as a day of mourning for all those Africans who lost their lives in the struggle for national liberation'. In 1952 the Defiance Campaign of civil disobedience was launched and in 1955 the Congress of the People was held at Kliptown to ratify the Freedom Charter. In the same year the multiracial South African Congress of Trade Unions was formed which worked closely with the ANC. In addition, campaigns were launched covering many different aspects of the lives of Africans: such as the campaigns against mass removals of Africans in Johannesburg; against the low wages of black agricultural workers; against Bantu education; and in 1956 against the extension of the Pass system to African women. A day of 'protest, prayer and dedication' was called by the Congress Alliance for Freedom Day, 1957, and in the same year a massive bus boycott was declared with tens of thousands of Africans walking up to twenty miles per day to and from work over a three-month period rather than pay a one penny fare increase. During 1959 a campaign was launched against the Pass Laws, during the course of which police opened fire on demonstrators at Sharpeville killing at least 67 and wounding 186 people.

17. Standard Bank of SA, *National Income and Production Indices, 1946–1959*, pp. 1–2.
18. SA Bureau of Census and Statistics, *Union Statistics for Fifty Years*, and SA Department of Statistics, *South African Statistics, 1965*.
19. SA Reserve Bank, *A Statistical Presentation* (1971), p. 9.
20. ibid.
21. Despite the restrictions on capital flows abroad, capital continued deserting the country after 1960: the net outflow of − R129m in 1961 was followed by a net outflow of − R88m in 1962, − R80m in 1963 and − R41m in 1964. The trend was only reversed, spectacularly, with a net inflow of R255m the following year (ibid., pp. 9–10).
22. By the mid-1960s capital was flowing into South Africa faster than ever before: the net inflow of R255m in 1965 was followed by further net inflows of R141m in 1966, R162m in 1967, R459m in 1968, R197m in 1969 and R501m in 1970. (SA Reserve Bank, *A Statistical Presentation*, p. 10.)
23. Financial Mail, Special Survey, 'Inside the Anglo Power House', p. 31.
24. AE & CI, *Anniversary Report, 1973*, pp. 15–16.
25. Polyvinyl chloride is today the base for a wide range of commodities: it is used to contain and package chemicals, for garden hoses, for piping in buildings and in agriculture, for footwear and floor tiles, as well as for dam linings, making dolls, inflatable toys and gramophone records.
26. *Financial Mail*, Special Survey, 'Inside the Anglo Power House', pp. 5, 33.
27. ibid., p. 31.
28. *Financial Mail*, Special Survey, '1961–1966: The Fabulous Years', pp. 99, 121.
29. *SA Mining and Engineering Journal*, 29 September 1969, pp. 131–5.
30. ibid., p. 123; and *Financial Mail*, Special Survey, '1961–1966: The Fabulous Years', p. 119.
31. *SA Mining and Engineering Journal*, 29 September 1969, pp. 44, 111–15. See also *Financial Mail*, Special Survey, 'Gauging JCI's Mettle', pp. 55, 59 for further details.
32. *SA Mining and Engineering Journal*, 30 December 1970, p. 163.
33. *SA Mining and Engineering Journal*, 29 September 1969, p. 139.
34. Union Corp., *Union Corporation Ltd: Group and Associated Companies*, pp. 13–14.

35. *Financial Mail*, Special Survey, '1961–1966: The Fabulous Years', pp. 97, 111, 119, 121, 153.
36. ICI afforded 'technical assistance' to AE & CI which it owned jointly with De Beers; Southern Cross Steel was jointly owned by Rand Mines and the Eastern Stainless Steel Corp. of America; JCI's Lenning Holdings and General Mining's Hall, Longmore and Co. both had important German and American links; Union Corp.'s Eclipse had important British connections; and Anglo American's Boart and Hard Metals boasted that it gained access to the technical expertise of companies 'throughout the world'. (Respective sources: AE & CI, *Annual Report 1973; Financial Mail*, Special Survey, '1961–1966: The Fabulous Years', p. 121; *SA Mining and Engineering Journal*, 29 September 1969, pp. 129, 139; and *Financial Mail*, Special Survey, 'Inside the Anglo Power House', p. 33.)
37. The term money market, which relates to the centralized borrowings and lendings of the most liquid funds after cash in the financial system, is here used to denote the central pool of funds borrowed by specialized institutions that undertake to make repayment either on call or on very short notice. Consequently, the size of the market is measured by the size of the pool.
38. These included: the Central Finance and Acceptance Corp. which was backed by the Afrikaner-controlled SANLAM Group (which itself held extensive insurance and building society interests); the Accepting Bank for Industry in which the state-owned IDC held a 40 per cent share; and the Philip Hill Acceptance Co. which was a wholly owned subsidiary of Phillip Hill, Higginson, Erlangers of London.
39. At the end of 1961 the call borrowings of the private money market institutions stood at over £71m while those of the NFC totalled £69m. (King, 1962.)
40. This figure of 5 per cent was higher than the corresponding 3.75 per cent of the UK national income which was contributed by the London discount houses, though the absolute amount in the latter country (£910m) was well in excess of the South African figure. An even wider disparity emerges between South Africa and the UK if we compare the volume of call money with that of bank deposits: during 1961 the call loan fund was almost 20 per cent of all commercial bank deposits in South Africa while in Britain the corresponding proportion was under 10 per cent. (King, 1962, pp. 161–70.)
41. Barclays and Standard Banks between them accounted for 83 per cent of all bank deposits in 1955 and, despite the emergence of seven other banks by 1962, still held 78 per cent of total deposits in that year. (King, 1962.) The support of these banks was important since they had to be convinced that the losses they would encounter over the short term would bring them advantages over the long term.

CHAPTER 8

The Anglo Monopoly
in Industry and Finance

The smashing of the black working class in the early 1960s paved the way politically for the most spectacular economic boom in South Africa's postwar history. Between 1963 and 1968 the GDP at current prices increased by an annual average rate of 9.3 per cent (compared with 5.2 per cent over the preceding five years, 1957–62).[1] This is exceptionally high by international standards and placed South Africa among the fastest growing industrial economies in the capitalist world at this time, ahead of those in western Europe and North America.[2]

This rapid rate of expansion may be primarily attributed to the performance of the manufacturing and construction sectors: between 1963 and 1968 the physical volume of output in manufacturing rose by 8.4 per cent per annum (compared with 5.4 per cent per annum in the five years 1958–63),[3] while, in relative terms, the sector's contribution to the GDP improved from 21.3 per cent of the total in 1962 to 23.4 per cent in 1970 (Table 11). Over this latter period the construction sector's contribution to the GDP rose even faster: from 2.8 per cent of the total to 4.8 per cent (Table 11). The combined increase of these two sectors in the GDP (up from 24.1 per cent of the total in 1962 to 28.2 per cent in 1970) compares with the declining contribution over the same period of mining (down from 13.3 per cent of the total to 10.5 per cent) and agriculture (down from 12.2 per cent to 9.1 per cent) (Table 11).

This remarkable advance for manufacturing was achieved in large part both through an increase in the level of employment of labour and through an improvement in productivity of labour. The number of workers employed in manufacturing increased by 63 per cent between 1960 and 1970 (from 658 026 to 1 070 033)—compared with an increase of 24 per cent between 1950 and 1960 (from 530 225)—causing manufacturing's share of the total labour force in the economy to rise from 11.9 per cent to 12.8 per cent.[4] As far as construction was concerned, an even more marked increase in employment took place: the

9 per cent increase recorded between 1950 and 1960 (from 115 432 to 125 962) was completely overshadowed by the 182 per cent increase between 1960 and 1970 (to 355 759).[5] Overall, the tendency in both these sectors at this time was towards employment of an increasing proportion of *black* workers: between 1948 and 1968 the proportion of African, coloured and Indian workers in the total rose from 60.5 per cent to 74.9 per cent in manufacturing and from 72.7 per cent to 80.9 per cent in construction.[6]

These increases in turn raise the question of labour supply. It would seem in fact that a substantial proportion of new black workers in manufacturing and construction was drawn from the mines. Between 1960 and 1970 the number of *local* African workers on the mines declined by 36 per cent (from 150 900 to 96 900). Despite this, the mines managed to slightly increase their total black labour supply (up from 396 700 in 1960 to 401 200 in 1970) by extending their recruiting facilities outside South Africa (over this period the proportion of *foreign* black workers in the total rose from 63.3 per cent to 75.8 per cent) (Table 3). A further proportion of new black workers in manufacturing and construction probably came from agriculture as mechanization in some areas resulted in a *relative* decline in black labour demand in this sector. In *absolute* terms, however, the total labour force in agriculture rose slightly (from 1.7m in 1960 to 2.2m in 1970).[7] Thus the patterns of labour supply evolved in the early postwar period were still functioning effectively during the 1960s, though the burgeoning needs of manufacturing and construction were forcing mining into a dangerous dependency on foreign sources of black labour supply.

Labour productivity in manufacturing, which had slumped during the 1950s, picked up again during the 1960s: between 1958 and 1968 the physical volume of output rose by 6.9 per cent per annum compared with a 4.7 per cent growth per annum in employment. Comparing the two periods, 1958–63 and 1963–8, a major UAL economic survey noted: 'Even allowing for overtime hours worked, growth in productivity was greater in the second period. This was probably due to the larger amount of capital equipment installed in recent years.'[8] A closer look at the capital/labour ratio in the manufacturing sector between the period 1950–60 on the one hand and 1960–70 on the other confirms this argument: while production in the early period was generally *labour-intensive* in character, the latter period exhibited a marked tendency towards *capital-intensity*.[9] Furthermore, a comparison of capital/labour ratios in small and large establishments between 1962 and 1972 reveals that in general the tendency towards capital-intensive production was more marked in large than in small establishments (Tregenna-Piggott, 1975, p. 12). To sum up, then, it would seem that the industrial boom of the 1960s was markedly capital-intensive in character, therefore contributing to productivity improvements in the sector, and that in general the increase in capital-intensity was higher in large than in small establishments.

As is often the case under capitalism, the boom of the 1960s contained within itself the seeds of its own decay. In this case, it was the contradictions arising out of South Africa's technological dependency on the developed capitalist states, manifesting itself again in the form of a balance of payments crisis, which reversed the process. While the capital-intensive character of the boom was made possible through the importation of machinery and equipment, there was no corresponding rise in the value of exports and consequently a large deficit built up on the balance of payments, which eventually forced the state to slow the economy down. Between 1961 and 1971 the share of the value of machinery and equipment (including transport equipment) rose consistently as a proportion of total imports from 36 per cent to 48 per cent. Over this period the total value of imports rose by a massive 186 per cent (from R1005m to R2878m), while the total value of exports rose by only 81 per cent (from R853m to R1541m).[10] This failure of South Africa's exports—and in particular, exports of manufactured goods—to keep up with the rising value of imports resulted in the country's trade deficit, excluding gold, widening from R152m in 1961 to R1337m in 1971.[11] Although in the early years of the boom the inclusion of export earnings from gold was sufficient to wipe out the trade deficit, by 1971 even gold exports valued at R922m (or 32 per cent of the total value of imports) were not sufficient to prevent a trade deficit of R430m. Consequently, throughout the boom South Africa was saddled with a consistently rising deficit on the balance of payments: from R48m in 1964 to R1003m in 1971.[12] Eventually, these pressures took their toll and the South African economy was forced into recession. It was thus one of the major driving forces behind the boom—the use of sophisticated machinery from abroad—which was ultimately responsible for bringing it to an end.

By the early 1970s the world capitalist system was lurching into crisis on a scale not experienced since before the war. Consequently, although during the early part of this decade South Africa was able to recover from the balance of payments crisis, the world recession, combined with a resurgence of militant trade union activity among black industrial workers, kept the local economy in a depressed state through much of the decade. It should be said, however, that to an extent South Africa's role as a major gold producer did shelter the economy from the full force of these conditions. After the introduction of the two-tier Gold System in 1969 the gold price began to rise from its fixed level of $35 an ounce. (See Note 57, Chapter 6.) The sharp increases in the gold price brought a 200 per cent rise in the value of South Africa's gold exports between 1969 and 1975: from R847m to

R2540m. Though an increase of this kind might be expected to produce a boom in the economy, in fact its impact was largely neutralized by the 479 per cent rise in the cost of South Africa's oil imports between 1973 and 1975 (up from R190m to about R1100m).[13] The subsequent explosion in the price of gold in late 1979 was to alter the situation decisively in favour of the local economy, leading to another boom in the early 1980s. However, through most of the decade of the 1970s the two price rises tended to counter-balance one another and the South African economy remained in a state of general, though not chronic, recession.

No survey of the industrial boom of the 1960s would be complete without reference to the phenomenal expansion of the financial sector which occurred at the same time. Following the introduction of new legislation in the mid-1960s to cope with the expansion that had taken place over the past decade, the financial sector entered a new era of growth. The 1969 UAL Survey noted:

> One of the most remarkable features of the past ten years has been a complete transformation of the monetary and banking scene. New institutions blossomed and the range and variety of services offered in the credit markets expanded considerably. Amended legislation in 1964 governing banks and building societies gave recognition to the new institutional structure and vigorous competitive environment that had emerged out of a somewhat staid and static past.[14]

Between 1958 and 1968 the aggregate deposits of the banking institutions more than trebled; the deposits of the commercial banks more than doubled; those of the merchant banks and hire-purchase, general and savings banks rose very much faster (though the commercial banks remained the largest single group); and the total call funds of the two discount houses grew by 1442 per cent (from R19m to R293m). In addition, the commercial banks established subsidiaries which sought to cater for medium-term capital requirements and the credit card system was introduced. By 1967 there were 58 registered banking institutions in South Africa, comprising 9 commercial banks, 4 merchant banks, 8 hire-purchase banks, 2 discount houses and 35 general and savings banks. Finally, by 1969 12 institutions had emerged on the capital market offering sophisticated services for long-term funds.[15]

Thus a substantial change in the nature of South Africa's financial sector was carried through at precisely the time South African industry was being transformed through mechanization of its methods of production. These changes therefore represent far more than simply a *quantitative* increase in the number of financial institutions operating in the country and in the number of industrial enterprises using machinery. They also express a profound *qualitative* change, as the capitalist forms of finance and industry began to change under the impact of increasing concentration of capital. Thus the postwar developments in gold mining had set in motion processes in other sectors of the economy which were radically altering the form and nature of South African society. As we shall see, these changes were also manifesting themselves in the closer relations which were being forged among the various sectors of the economy.

Earlier we saw that as monopoly relations became entrenched in the separate branches of gold and diamond mining so pressures increased for these branches to merge—a condition which expressed itself institutionally through Anglo American's take-over of De Beers. The profound developments which occurred in South Africa's industrial and financial sectors during the 1950s and 1960s meant that monopoly relations were now no longer confined to mining but were evident in these sectors as well. This in turn generated pressures for these sectors to merge together under a more centralized control. As we saw, the mining groups with their large stock of investment finance, access to technological information and financial expertise had become more active in industry and finance during the 1950s, thereby establishing new institutional links between the different sectors. Inevitably, as the dominant mining group, Anglo American had played an influential role in this process, particularly through its financial activities. As the tendency towards monopolization in industry and finance intensified during the 1960s and as the investment requirements of mining diminished, so Anglo American in particular became ever more active in diversifying out of mining—in the process bringing large blocks of industry and finance under its centralized control.

ANGLO AMERICAN AND MONOPOLY CONCENTRATION IN INDUSTRY AND FINANCE

Although we shall be confining ourselves to an analysis of Anglo American's role in the diversification of mining investment, it is important to emphasize that we understand Anglo as expressing a generalized tendency among mining monopoly capitalists. Over the years Anglo's role in diversification has tended to be far more prominent, if not spectacular, than that of the other groups, but this should not be taken to mean that the same tendency has not manifested itself (though to differing degrees) within these other groups. However, undoubtedly it was Anglo American, in control of the vast financial resources generated from the Orange Free State gold mines, which was ideally poised to benefit from the new investment opportunities which were opening up in industry as the state brought black resistance to a temporary end.

During the 1960s Anglo American embarked on a phase of massive investment in South African industry, contributing substantially to the industrial boom of that decade: between 1960 and 1968, for instance, the value of the Anglo American Corporation's industrial interests in

South Africa rose by about 470 per cent (from approximately R50m to R285m).[16] An examination of the industrial portfolio of the Anglo American Group as a whole (and not just the *corporation*) reveals that by 1969 the value of the industrial interests of the three key South African holding companies in the Group (the Anglo American Corporation, De Beers Consolidated and Rand Selection) had reached about R600m. Between 1967 and 1968 the value of the *direct* industrial investments of the Anglo American Corporation rose from R123.2m (20 per cent of the total) to R191.3m (also 20 per cent),[17] while that of Rand Selection rose from R79.2m (21 per cent of the total) to R111.6m (19 per cent). However, while these interests represented approximately one-fifth of the total investment portfolios of the two companies, the return on these investments, as a proportion of total income, was relatively poor (representing only 11 per cent and 12 per cent respectively over the two years in Anglo American's case and 12 per cent and 13 per cent respectively in Rand Selection's case).[18] As we shall see, the main reason for this lay in the nature of the Group's industrial investment strategy whose main thrust at this time was to initiate large-scale investment undertakings, often on a highly capital-intensive basis, rather than simply take over existing concerns.

We noted earlier that De Beers Consolidated had formed the De Beers Industrial Corporation (DEBINCOR) in 1944 to hold its major industrial interests. Twenty years later as Anglo's industrial diversification programme began to gather momentum, the Group floated another industrial holding company, the Anglo American Industrial Corporation (AMIC), to centralize control over the disparate industrial interests of the Anglo American Corporation and Rand Selection in particular. With the Anglo American Corporation and Rand Selection firmly in control of AMIC (with holdings of 28.5 per cent and 29.5 per cent respectively) and De Beers and AMIC in control of DEBINCOR (58.5 per cent and 26.4 per cent respectively), these two holding companies emerged as the main vehicles for the Group's industrial expansion in South Africa. However, before examining their growth during the 1960s, it should be noted that these companies do not hold all of the Group's industrial interests, but only primarily those of the three holding companies, Anglo American, Rand Selection and De Beers. Outside these, but still within the broad ambit of the Anglo American Group, there are such giants as Charter Consolidated, Rand Mines and JCI, all of whose industrial interests were expanding at this time.

Finally, a few comments are necessary to define the form of 'control' that exists within Group companies. In the early phase of Anglo's industrial diversification, the Group did not always acquire control over its investments, preferring to leave the expansion and running of the company to its existing management. Throughout this phase the

Group seems to have been familiarizing itself with conditions in industry rather than laying down a permanent basis for future control relations and it rapidly came to transcend this position during the 1960s when it began exerting a more direct influence over the affairs of its companies.[19] However, the form of control which Anglo developed in industry is somewhat different from that which it exerted in mining. As Anglo American's chairman, Harry Oppenheimer, put it: 'You can't, on the whole, provide the same technical control that you do with mines. I don't think we should try to keep our industrial companies tied *in the same centralised way* that has worked pretty well with mining operations.'[20] Thus a minority stake held by Anglo in one of its industrial concerns should not be taken to mean that the Group was not in control of this company. As Oppenheimer himself has said: 'Though when I say "control", I don't mean necessarily 51 per cent.'[21]

But this does raise the question of how precisely control is to be exercised if not through a tightly centralized form. In general terms of course there are a number of ways in which one company may exercise control over another. First, through shareholdings, such as either ownership of 51 per cent or more of the shares in a company or ownership of the largest single minority block of shares (for example, a 30 per cent holding where no other company or individual or group has a similar or greater holding); secondly, through the technology utilized or through a company's sources of supply or markets; and, finally, through financial mechanisms. As our investigation proceeds it will become clear that the Anglo American Group in fact makes use of all these various methods and, consequently, in our analysis we shall assume Anglo American to be in control of a company if any of the above criteria apply. However, only if Anglo American holds more than 50 per cent of a company's shares will we speak of that company as a subsidiary of the Group (in which case *total* control will be assumed). In all other cases we will assume relations of control to be more flexible yet still *effective*.

Anglo American's industrial subsidiaries

Among Anglo's subsidiaries are some of the Group's most important industrial ventures: for example, the Highveld Steel and Vanadium Corporation; Scaw Metals; Boart and Hard Metals; Transalloys; Forest Industries and Veneers; and Mondi Valley Paper. An analysis of the growth of some of these companies during the 1960s and 1970s will help to illustrate both the nature of Anglo's investment strategy and the extent of the Group's growing power in South Africa's manufacturing industry.

Anglo American's largest industrial undertaking during the 1960s was the establishment of the Highveld Steel and Vanadium Corporation. During the late 1950s Anglo had expressed an interest in South Africa's vast vanadium reserves (the largest in the world) and had eventually acquired the Transvaal Vanadium Company, which was the only company in South Africa engaged at that time in the production of vanadium pentoxide. In 1961 the Highveld Steel and Vanadium Corporation was formed to build a pilot plant which would seek to develop a profitable process for the recovery of not only the vanadium in the ore, but also its iron. Although this would enable production of a high quality steel, the technical problems involved were acute since the high titanium content of the ore made it difficult to treat in conventional blast furnaces. However, in 1963 after intensive research, a full-scale plant was built with a capacity that was to make the company one of the largest producers of vanadium pentoxide in the world (Beckingham, 1972, p. 136).[22] Thus Anglo American's intention from the very beginning was to enter specialized steel production on an exceptionally large scale. In order to carry this through successfully the Group sought overseas assistance in developing the necessary technologies: the American company, Newmont Chemical, was brought in as a partner and the steel works were designed by Davy United of Sheffield in Britain.[23] Furthermore, the Group also ensured a captive market for a large portion of Highveld's output by buying into companies which were important consumers of specialized steels, such as Scaw Metals, Stewarts and Lloyds, Union Carriage and Wagon, and Hall Longmore.[24]

To bring the Highveld company to the production stage a massive financial injection of R127m was required.[25] Most of this was spent on plant and equipment, since Highveld was developed along highly capital-intensive lines and utilized up-to-date technologies developed abroad. Not only does this provide a useful insight into how the balance of trade crisis emerged in South Africa, but the fact that Highveld only recorded its first annual profit a decade after it was founded helps to explain why the proportion of Anglo's revenue from industrial investment was so low at this time. When it came, however, Highveld's positive impact on both Group profits and the trade balance was impressive: in 1971 alone it produced almost 600 000 tons of steel, earned a profit of R2.1m and earned over R20m on exports (or R50m between 1969 and 1971).[26] By 1970 Highveld was the fourth largest quoted industrial concern in South Africa with total assets valued at R138.4m.[27] These included its two wholly owned subsidiaries, the Transvaal Vanadium Co. and Ironstone Minerals (which between them controlled 180 million tons of proven iron ore reserves), and the two mines which supplied its full ore requirements. Nor did the company's improvement falter through the more difficult economic climate of the

1970s: pre-tax profits rose continuously from R7.5m in 1973 to R33.1m in 1977, in which year the company had become the ninth largest profit-earner in the country.[28]

Anglo's involvement in Highveld is important from a number of viewpoints. At a general economic level, the Group seemed intent on capturing the burgeoning market for specialized steels which accompanied the boom.[29] As such it was to play a positive role in promoting a mechanized heavy industry sector which was so crucial to the future of South Africa's industrial development. However, to carry this through on a sufficiently large scale meant that initially Highveld exerted a negative influence on South Africa's trade balance. But once development was completed this influence became positive both through expanding exports and through winning sections of the local market away from imports. As we have seen, though, to carry this through successfully required considerable financial resources both for the initial investment in plant and equipment and to sustain the new company through the decade required for development. Only an extremely large group such as Anglo could carry out a task of this kind and its intervention thus became a *decisive* influence in conditioning the future form of South Africa's industrial growth. Furthermore, through its intervention Anglo promoted the process of monopolization in industry, not only by the capital-intensive nature of its investment, but also by bringing a whole branch of industrial production and marketing under a single control. This vertical integration started with the control which Anglo exercised, through its 52 per cent share in Highveld, over some of the world's largest vanadium reserves. From there it spread through the Group's mining of these reserves to its manufacturing of vanadium pentoxide out of the products of its mines and (using the product as an alloy) to its manufacturing of rolled steel. Nor did the process of vertical integration stop there. A portion of the total output was then sold (in the form either of vanadium pentoxide or rolled steel) to one or other of the specialized steel consumers in which the Group had significant interests (such as its wholly owned subsidiary, Scaw Metals). Thus not only the whole of the mining of the raw material and the whole of its basic manufacture but also a proportion of its marketing and subsequent manufacture occurs within the nexus of Group control. Having examined Anglo's role in the early part of this process, it would be useful to turn to the other end of the continuum to examine, through a study of Scaw Metals, Anglo's involvement in subsequent and more complex phases of steel manufacture.

When Scaw Metals was taken over in 1964 to become a wholly owned subsidiary of AMIC it already had a long history as a relatively successful producer of steel parts and grinding balls for the South African mining industry. As such the company's early history reproduces closely the pattern of evolution described for industrial companies in the preceding chapter. Established as the Steel Ceilings and Aluminium Works (hence the acronym Scaw) during the industrial boom of the early 1920s to manufacture a limited range of steel castings and parts for the mines, the company extended its activities during the 1930s to include the production of cast steel grinding balls. Although during the war the company opened a munitions factory, the gold mines still remained its principal market: in 1949 a steel foundry was erected and in 1951 a ball forge commissioned, enabling the company to increase its capacity for the production of rolled steel (mainly to supply the developing gold mines).[30]

In 1956, however, Scaw began to transform itself into a more diversified engineering concern when, following the conclusion of technical aid agreements with General Steel Industries of the United States and the English Steel Castings Corporation, it began to manufacture cast steel bogies and other items for the expanding railway system in southern Africa. In 1962 this area of production was further expanded when, following the conclusion of another technical agreement—this time with the Abex Corporation of America—the production of railway freight car wheels was begun. (The same licence also allowed Scaw to manufacture earth-moving and heat-resistant steel castings which were designed and produced by Abex.) It was these various areas of the company's activities which particularly attracted Anglo to Scaw, since the company was rapidly becoming a major consumer of the kinds of specialized steel which Highveld was to produce. In a sense, then, the R10m programme which Anglo initiated at Scaw in 1966 (to build a new steel rolling mill) had as much to do with establishing a market for Highveld as with boosting the productive capacity of Scaw.[31]

Under Anglo's control Scaw Metals expanded rapidly. Today the company manufactures 12.5 per cent of the total world supply of grinding balls (used by mines in the crushing of ore). Though as an unquoted company it does not qualify for inclusion in the *Financial Mail*'s Top 100 Companies Survey, with total assets of R40m in 1969 it would have ranked among the top twenty companies in South Africa in that year.[32] In 1979 the company was worth about R90m and with pre-tax earnings of R30m was among the twelve leading profit-earners in South Africa. Although the company is a relatively large employer by South African standards (with about 2000 black workers in 1979) it continues to scour the developed capitalist world for the latest and best technology and has recently introduced a new R20m rolling mill. It should be emphasized, however, that much of its work is carried out under licensing agreements with foreign concerns and royalties are paid to many of the developed capitalist countries. This arrangement enabled Scaw to become one of South Africa's leading exporters of manufactured goods: for instance, the company exports rolled steel and foundry products to more than twenty countries in the world (including undercarriages for American railway freight cars). Finally, Scaw controls an array of companies operating in related fields. Its subsidiary, Flather Bright Steels, is one of South Africa's leading producers of bright drawn and turned steel bars,[33] while a Zambian-based company under its control, Scaw Ltd, is the major supplier of grinding media and steel and iron castings to Zambia's mining industry. In addition to two other wholly owned subsidiaries, Scaw Alloys and the Scaw Metals Housing Co. (a property concern), Scaw has investments in Highveld Steel, RMB Alloys and the Raine Engineering Co.

As with some of the other industrial concerns examined earlier, the 1950s were a crucial turning-point for Scaw Metals as it diversified its activities out of the strict confines of supplying the mines. Just as in the case of these other companies, Scaw managed to achieve this diversification only through the technological support it received from foreign manufacturers. Today Scaw performs a key role in developing South Africa's heavy industrial potential and has even acquired an international reputation for certain products. While such a development *seems* to imply that the South African economy is breaking free of the shackles of imperialist dependence, it should not be forgotten that the condition of Scaw's success (like that of Highveld) remains its access to and dependence on foreign-controlled technologies.[34] Should this link be severed the company's capacity for expansion would be drastically limited. The form of South Africa's dependence on the imperialist powers has undoubtedly changed—but it has not been broken.

Yet the fact that this form has changed—the fact that Scaw has acquired the full capacity and technical refinement of a modern heavy engineering concern (even if it has not achieved this alone)—is of major importance to the future course of industrialization in South Africa. As companies like Scaw and Highveld expand so they enhance the capacity and potential of the industrial economy itself, shifting its centre of gravity away from the light industries. Through this transition South Africa's economy begins to acquire its own capacity to sustain these light industries (as well as mining and agricultural activity). To sum up, perhaps one could say that industrialization in South Africa is in the process of shifting into a higher gear—and Anglo American clearly has a mighty hand on the gear lever.

Though concentrated mainly around heavy industry, Anglo's industrial initiatives during the 1960s were by no means confined to this sector. One of its most important new undertakings through a subsidiary was in fact in the paper industry, though here again the same tendencies are apparent as emerged in relation to its involvement in heavy industry. When the Group formed the Mondi Valley Paper Co. in 1967, South Africa's paper industry was dominated by one company,

SAPPI, which was under the control of the Union Corporation mining Group. The Anglo Group's 87 per cent holding in Mondi Valley was supplemented by a 13 per cent holding from the British paper giant, the Bowater Paper Co.[35] This latter company supplied the Mondi company with technical assistance and was instrumental in setting up the company's first two factories. Costing around R50m to build, these factories (comprising a groundwood mill, a high speed paper machine and a paper finishing department) commenced operation in 1971 and 1972 with the production of newsprint and a wide assortment of other papers.[36] Since the Anglo Group also controlled South Africa's largest newspaper group, the Argus Printing and Publishing Co., Mondi would seem to have been assured of a market for its newsprint. In addition to supplying the internal market, Mondi also began producing for export and by 1973 had already supplied paper worth R7m to the Far East and South America.[37] By 1977 Mondi had acquired a subsidiary, South African Board Mills, which in addition to its interests in timber plantations also manufactured paper board for the packaging, printing and stationery industries—a field in which Anglo through its holding in the Central News Agency was well represented.

The Mondi case thus provides a further illustration of the tendencies analysed earlier: that is, capital-intensive development arising out of technological linkages with foreign specialist firms; the subsequent boost to both exports and import substitution; and strong vertical integration (from Group control over timber plantations to the manufacture of newsprint for consumption in Group-owned newspapers and the manufacture of paper board for consumption by Group stationery interests). Yet in the case of the paper industry monopoly relations are even more firmly entrenched, since today two companies—the newly renamed Mondi Paper Co. and SAPPI—between them dominate production in the industry. Since both these companies are controlled by mining groups which are themselves linked, some idea may be gained of the extent to which diversification of mining investment during the 1960s promoted both the emergence of monopoly relations in specific industries and the linkages between sectors and industries under monopoly control.

There are many other examples one can draw on to confirm these tendencies. For instance, South African Nylon Spinners, in which DEBINCOR holds a 37.5 per cent interest, was formed in 1964 with the support of the British monopoly group ICI Fibres, which holds 25 per cent. This company became South Africa's first nylon producer and today (as an AE & CI subsidiary) is the country's largest manufacturer of synthetic fibres (Beckingham, 1972, p. 135).[38] Of course, not all of Anglo's industrial undertakings have been as successful as these. Transalloys Ltd was established as an Anglo subsidiary in 1964 to develop, in conjunction with Swedish partners, a Swedish process for the production of low carbon ferro-chrome. However, the process proved unprofitable and it was only Anglo's financial support that kept the company afloat until a salvage operation could be mounted. Relief eventually came when a New York conglomerate, Air Reduction, acquired a 35 per cent stake in the company and provided technical assistance for the transition to ferro-manganese production as well as undertaking to market the commodity abroad. As a result of both Anglo's financial support and this foreign technical and marketing aid, Transalloys was eventually able to declare its first profit in 1971 (Beckingham, 1972, pp. 136, 139).[39]

Before examining the growth pattern of some of Anglo's leading industrial associates (as opposed to its subsidiaries) it is worth commenting on the fact that the heavy technological dependence which emerged between these local industrial concerns and foreign enterprises during the 1960s was accompanied by a marked shift in the local concentration of foreign investment. Between 1956 and 1966, while the concentration of foreign investment in mining declined from 37 per cent of the total to 28 per cent, the proportions concentrated in manufacturing and finance rose, respectively, from 25 per cent of the total to 29 per cent and from 18 per cent to 23 per cent (First *et al.*, 1973, p. 82). This phenomenon illustrates just how successful the South African ruling class had been, not only in stemming the outflow of capital in the wake of Sharpeville, but also in subsequently redirecting foreign capital flows into the new growth area of the economy. In terms of both technical knowledge and investment, foreign capitalists thus played a prominent role in promoting South Africa's industrial boom, often through the international channels provided by locally based conglomerates such as Anglo.

Anglo American's industrial associates

Anglo American's industrial interests of course extended far beyond the sphere of the subsidiaries examined above. Outside these, but still under Anglo's effective control, were a whole array of associated companies engaged in many different kinds of industrial activity. Foremost among these was AE & CI, a company whose activities during the 1960s became increasingly closely linked to the expanding heavy industry sector. As we shall see, this company expanded particularly fast during the boom.

In 1966 AE & CI commissioned a large petrochemical plant and followed this up in 1974 with a giant ammonia plant which cost R80m to build and which, according to a *Financial Mail* survey, 'is accepted internationally as achieving the maximum advantage from economies of scale'.[40] Originally a manufacturer of explosives, AE & CI's two South African explosives factories were, in 1974, the largest and second largest of their kind in the world.[41] All of the above plants make use of technologies which are developed abroad. As the company itself explains: 'AE & CI has access to the technical information, patents and processes of Imperial Chemical Industries Limited under terms separately negotiated.'[42]

As an industrial monopoly combine AE & CI has no equal in South Africa. It manufactures and supplies virtually the whole of the country's explosives requirements (sales to the Chamber of Mines absorb 80 per cent of total output) and about two-thirds of its nitrogenous fertilizer; it has a monopoly over the production and sale of polyethylene and PVC; and it is the country's sole supplier of a wide range of industrial chemicals. The company is highly capital-intensive with fixed costs averaging 57 per cent of total overheads and 'variable' costs comprising 'mostly materials and power'.[43] Despite this, it is one of South Africa's largest industrial employers: in both 1973 and 1974, with a total labour force of about 15 500, the company was ranked twelfth in the employment stakes.[44] Overall, it has consistently been at the top end of South Africa's industrial league table. In both 1968 and 1969 it was the largest industrial concern in the country (with total assets of R180m and R204m respectively) and, though over the following years it was forced further down the ladder to fourth and fifth positions, it continued to grow at an extremely rapid pace. Between 1969 and 1973 the company's pre-tax profits rose by 117 per cent and its sales by 94 per cent.[45] By 1978 it had a market capitalization value of R498m, which put it well ahead of its industrial rivals.[46]

AE & CI has also spawned a number of subsidiaries and associate companies. Among the most important of its subsidiaries is the wholly owned AE & CI Rhodesia, which is the parent company in a fertilizer-based group that includes Rhodesia Chemical Industries, Dorowa Minerals, the Rhodesia Fertilizer Corporation and Albatros–Fisons.[47] Another major subsidiary is Rand Carbide. Formed in 1918 by Rand Mines and Barclays Bank (with a capital of £20 000), this company was brought under AE & CI's control in 1934 as a vehicle for entering the plastics industry. (An acetylene process enables calcium carbide to be used in the production of PVC.) When AE & CI established the first PVC plant in South Africa in 1955 Rand Carbide supplied the necessary basic materials. In 1965 the group further extended its involvement in plastics when Rand Carbide acquired a 41.7 per cent share in a Dutch company, Holland Electro Chemical Industries, which was the sole producer of vinyl acetate from acetylene in South Africa. In 1962 Rand Carbide opened up a new field of activity when it began production of ferro-silicon. The manufacture of this commodity (which is used in the production of steel) linked Anglo's chemical group to the activities of its steel producers, like Highveld and Scaw, thereby spinning a further thread in the monopoly web. By the mid-1970s Rand

Carbide was South Africa's largest producer of ferro-silicon (about R3m, or 35 per cent, of which was exported) and was the country's sole producer of carbide (for both local consumption and export). This company's evolution thus provides further evidence of the tendencies discussed earlier, including monopoly control over a specific branch of production and, most important, the extension of vertical integration in particular areas of production. Recent developments illustrate just how beneficial this latter process can be to an expanding group such as this: the construction of AE & CI's massive new PVC plant immediately led Rand Carbide to begin building a new factory which was designed to expand its production of carbide.[48]

Among AE & CI's associated concerns are Resinkem, SA Peroxide, Anikem, SA Titan Products and Polyfos. Most of these ventures further underline our argument concerning South African dependence on foreign companies for technology. For instance, Resinkem was formed in 1974 as a 50–50 venture between AE & CI and the German chemical giant, BASF, to manufacture formalin and urea formaldehyde resin. SA Peroxide, which manufactures a range of peroxide chemicals that are marketed by AE & CI, is 60 per cent owned by Laporte of Britain and 40 per cent by AE & CI. Anikem is another 50–50 venture—this time between AE & CI and Nalco Chemicals of Chicago—which produces a wide range of water-treated specialty chemicals. And, finally, SA Titan Products is 60 per cent owned by British Titan and 40 per cent by AE & CI. In these and many other cases the link-up with a foreign firm enables AE & CI to gain access to foreign technologies while helping the foreign firms to slip into the South African market under import restrictions. For instance, following the imposition in 1971 of tariff barriers restricting imports of titanium dioxide pigments, SA Titan Products, which produces these commodities, reported its progress to be 'very satisfactory'.[49]

Before closing our analysis of Anglo's industrial interests mention needs to be made of one Anglo subsidiary which does not display the same tendency towards heavy dependence on foreign sources of technology. This company is Boart and Hard Metals and it heads a group which operates in a variety of ways within a highly specialized field. Its activities include the manufacture and marketing of all types of diamond and tungsten carbide tipped drilling tools; undertaking surface and underground contract drilling; providing certain ranges of mining equipment and mining services to all major mining countries; and supplying a wide range of tungsten carbide and diamond products to industry, particularly in southern Africa and Australia.[50] Since its inception in 1936 this company has gradually developed a singular expertise in the field of diamond drills and cutting equipment which has made it a world leader in this field. By 1971 it had acquired over one hundred subsidiary and associated companies located throughout the capitalist world.[51] While many of these companies were located (as is to be expected) in mining countries on the periphery of world capitalism, such as Zambia and Australia, the company has in fact made substantial inroads into the very centres of the developed capitalist world. For instance, through its wholly owned subsidiary, Boart International Luxembourg, the company owned: 100 per cent of Boart Canada which manufactures diamond drilling bits for the Canadian mining industry; 100 per cent of Boart Sweden which was established 'to expand the Group's activities in Scandinavia'; a 70 per cent interest in Vestfold Stalindusti, a Norwegian carbide drill producer; and a 90 per cent holding in Mining Developments (UK) Ltd, 'a company engaged in the development of new mining equipment and techniques'. In addition, the company held 100 per cent of Portadrill, Inc., 'a major American manufacturer of rotary blasthole, exploration and waterwell drilling equipment'; 100 per cent of Gill Enterprises, an American concern manufacturing tungsten carbide percussion drilling tools; and 100 per cent of each of the following: Boart Hardmetals (Europe), Boart Hardmetals (Canada), Canadian Longyear and the Longyear Company, USA.[52]

During 1976 and 1977 Boart undertook a thorough reconstruction of its overseas holdings, while also rationalizing its southern African interests. The result was the emergence of Boart International Ltd, a company with 76 subsidiaries operating in 26 different countries throughout the world. While pre-tax profits of R32.3m in 1977 put this company among the top ten industrial earners in South Africa, what is most significant about these profits is that approximately 56.7 per cent of the total was earned outside Africa.[53] It is thus clear that the technological expertise which this company has acquired through its long and intimate association with mining practice in South Africa has made it a world leader in this field, thereby distinguishing it from most other locally based industrial concerns.

However, the technological independence which Boart has achieved in international terms in no way contradicts our argument regarding the general level of technological dependence of the South African manufacturing industry. The point about Boart is that it has had a *unique* opportunity—that is, one which is denied to most South African companies—to develop its technological capacity. Through its position as a member of the Anglo American Group, not only does it have access to the drilling experience and know-how of a wide range of mining companies involved in different kinds of mining, but it also has access to the research facilities and technical expertise which De Beers has acquired in industrial diamonds, which are the most important materials Boart uses. These specific conditions not only set Boart well apart from other industrial concerns in South Africa, they also place it in a unique position in relation to similar concerns elsewhere in the world, giving it a marked advantage over them. Boart's spectacular success therefore affirms our argument that technological independence generally occurs in those areas in which research and development resources and expertise are concentrated.

By the early 1970s Anglo's diversification programme had developed to such an extent that the Group was active in eleven different branches of South Africa's manufacturing industry: iron, steel, vanadium and ferro-alloys; heavy engineering; food and beverages; timber, paper and board; printing and publishing; computers; fibres and textiles; motor vehicles and transport; explosives, chemicals and fertilizers; civil engineering and construction; and refractories and other structural clay products. By 1976 Anglo's various interests were held through a network of at least 152 different holding and operating companies.[54] Nor were these companies small concerns; on the contrary, some among them were giants by South African standards. In 1976, for instance, South African Breweries (in which Anglo held a 32 per cent stake) was the second largest industrial company in South Africa, while Pretoria Portland Cement (in which the Group held a 26 per cent interest) was ranked 26th.[55] Others, like LTA Ltd and the Argus Printing and Publishing Co., though not quite as big (ranked 54th and 74th respectively in that year), were none the less extremely powerful in that they controlled large sections of their respective markets. Since neither of these companies is strictly a manufacturing concern, it would be useful briefly to consider the power which they wield.

Formed by Anglo in 1965 out of a merger of three substantial companies in the building, contracting and civil engineering industry (Lewis Construction, James Thompson and Anglo American Construction), LTA is one of the two largest building and civil engineering groups in southern Africa. Together with the South African concern Murray and Roberts, it dominates the construction industry in South Africa. LTA's first major undertakings were to lead the consortia responsible for building the Orange-Fish River Tunnel in South Africa (through a 30 per cent share) and the massive Cabora Bassa Dam in Mozambique (through a 20 per cent share). Since then the company has participated *inter alia* in the construction of airports, power stations (including nuclear power stations), office blocks, tunnels, an underground pumped storage scheme in the Drakensberg mountains, major roads and bridges in South Africa and Namibia and a railway in Swaziland. Nor does LTA confine its activities to the southern African region: one of its subsidiaries, Shaft Sinkers, has won contracts throughout the world to build shafts and tunnels.[56]

The extent of monopoly power in the newspaper media in South Africa is not dissimilar from the conditions described above. Virtually since their inception the 'pro-government' Afrikaans-language papers have been subordinated to monopoly control by state and closely allied Afrikaner capitalist interests. In the more 'liberal' English-language media, however, things were rather different with the two *separate* companies, the Argus Printing and Publishing Co. and South African Associated Newspapers (SAAN), dominating the field. The former company had always been under the loose control of some mining groups, of which the most prominent was JCI. However, when Anglo took control of JCI in 1960, the combined interests of the enlarged group gave Anglo a controlling stake of about 40 per cent in the Argus company and, therefore, in the ten major papers under Argus control. From that position a campaign was subsequently launched to bring the SAAN group under Argus control. Although initially thwarted by the government, in 1971 the Argus managed to acquire a 31.25 per cent controlling interest in SAAN, which gave it indirect control over seven of the ten remaining English-language papers in South Africa. Thus with seventeen of South Africa's twenty English-language papers under Argus control (including newspapers aimed at a black audience) Anglo has clearly risen to a position from which to challenge the Afrikaans-language monopoly.[57] Harry Oppenheimer has often claimed, though, that Anglo does not 'interfere' with editorial policy. In reply one could, perhaps, argue that since he owns the papers anyway, such 'interference' is unnecessary. But it is noteworthy that the new Zimbabwean government seems not to share his views. In 1981 the government bought out the controlling interest which the Argus group had held in Zimbabwe's largest newspapers, the *Rhodesia Herald* and *Bulowayo Chronicle*.

Thus by the 1970s Anglo American's diversified interests had come to extend well beyond South Africa's manufacturing industry, reaching into construction and a key branch of the media. Overall, by 1976 the Anglo American Corporation, Rand Selection, AMIC and DEBINCOR had amassed between them R847m worth of industrial and commercial investments in South Africa. In that year AMIC alone had 70 different subsidiaries in the country and a further 69 outside South Africa.[58] Significantly, many of these investments brought with them new forms of monopoly control, giving Anglo American an important power base outside mining. Under Anglo's pervasive influence new monopolies were created in various branches of manufacturing industry, in the construction sector and in the media, extending Anglo's influence not just economically, but also politically and ideologically. But the extent of Anglo's diversification programme cannot be measured only by these interests. Outside their sphere were sectors, like finance and property, in which, as we shall see, Anglo's influence grew steadily throughout the 1960s.

Anglo American's financial and property interests

We saw earlier that Anglo played a key role in the growth of South Africa's financial sector during the late 1950s, particularly through the establishment of UAL and the Discount House of South Africa. Both these institutions benefited from the subsequent boom, with UAL, for instance, diversifying out of merchant banking into mutual funds, management consultancy and real estate development. By 1968, not only was UAL the largest merchant bank in the country (with total assets of R142m), it was also South Africa's seventh largest bank.[59] UAL's activities continued to expand during the early 1970s. Between 1967 and 1973 it raised over R1bn for the public and private sectors in South Africa (over R600m for state corporations and local authorities and almost R500m for the private sector); between 1969 and 1973 it obtained on its own over 40 per cent of the funds raised in fixed-interest securities for South Africa's private sector; while the company's investment division handled the portfolios of over 100 institutions and many more private clients.[60] In 1972 the bank opened up a new operation which was designed to promote South Africa's exports abroad when it formed a subsidiary, the UAL Export Finance Company, to assist local companies in the provision of extended credit terms to foreign buyers. The system proved remarkably successful and by 1974 UAL was handling over half of all South Africa's exports of capital goods.[61]

However, UAL's activities during the 1960s extended well beyond the field of banking. In 1962 the company formed a subsidiary, City Developments, which rapidly became a major channel for institutional investment into the field of urban property development.[62] By the late 1960s City Developments had been integrated into Anglo American's expanding property portfolio which included: South African Townships, which held a wide range of property interests; Rand Mines Properties, the third largest township developer in the country; Anmercosa Land and Estates, which owned Group-occupied office blocks; Isipingo Property Investments; La Lucia Property Investments; and a number of smaller companies.[63] Undoubtedly the most important property venture undertaken by the Anglo Group during the 1960s was the development of the massive Carlton Centre, covering 2½ hectares (6 acres) of ground in the centre of Johannesburg. This centre, which is the largest office, shopping and hotel complex in Africa, cost R88m to build.[64] By 1970 Anglo's property interests had become so large that it formed a new company, Anglo American Properties Ltd. (AMAPROP), to hold them. With total assets valued at R52m, AMAPROP immediately became South Africa's second largest property concern.[65]

Thus again we find evidence of Anglo's diversified investments bringing with them new forms of monopoly control. In the finance sector, not only had UAL managed to emerge by the 1970s as one of South Africa's leading banks, but it had also achieved a dominant position for itself in various branches of specialized financial activity, such as fixed-interest securities and export credit facilities. Similarly, Anglo's immense property stake gave the Group a commanding position in this sector. These developments closely reproduced the pattern of Anglo's investments in other economic sectors: the carve-up of South Africa's construction sector between Anglo's LTA and Murray and Roberts; the take-over of the English-language newspaper world; the creation of various monopolies in the chemical sector, such as in the production of carbide, ferro-silicon, PVC, explosives and nitrogenous fertilizer; the monopoly in the manufacture of diamond drilling equipment and cutting tools; the shared monopoly (with Union Corporation) in the production of paper; the dominance in production of synthetic fibres; and, of course, the growing influence in various aspects of steel production. These were the areas in which Anglo American made its greatest forward strides during the 1960s, usually based on extremely large initial outlays of capital, such as Highveld's R127m, Mondi's R50m, AE & CI's R80m in petrochemicals and the Carlton Centre's R88m.

Through these and other investments new areas of production were opened up (for instance, in specialized steels, ferro-manganese and ferro-silicon, synthetic fibres and carbides) and the scope of South Africa's manufacturing industry widened and deepened. Of particular relevance here was the boost given to production of heavy industry goods. By the 1970s South Africa had a vibrant manufacturing sector which, though still dependent on foreign technologies, was able to provide substitutes for an ever growing category of imports. But while the *nature* of South Africa's manufacturing production was changing, so was its *form.* The new industries and companies were more capital-intensive than their predecessors; one or a few corporations began to dominate whole branches of production, often forging tight links through various stages of production and marketing of a commodity; huge financial holding companies, like AMIC, arose wielding awesome financial power; and, closely related to these developments, were the transformations in the associated sectors of construction, finance and property. Gone was the era in which a multiplicity of tiny concerns, vying with one another for minute fractions of the local market, dominated South Africa's manufacturing sector; in its place had come the era of the monopolies. Across the face of this new era, like a colossus, strode Anglo American, concentrating ever greater areas of production and ever larger resources of capital under its single control.

ANGLO AMERICAN AND CENTRALIZATION IN INDUSTRY
AND FINANCE

The industrial boom of the 1960s did not last. As we saw earlier, around the turn of the decade the state had been forced to slow down the growth rate in order to wipe out the huge deficit which had arisen on the balance of payments. In 1971–2 the GDP grew by only 3.3 per cent in real terms compared with 7.1 per cent in 1968–9.[66] Under these conditions the manufacturing sector, together with the rest of the economy, moved into recession. Nor did the economic situation improve much over the next few years. Although the balance of payments position eased, spiralling world prices (especially for oil) created an international recession which, together with black workers' unrest in local industry, served to stifle South Africa's industrial expansion for much of the decade.[67]

Inevitably, many companies were damaged by these events. But, significantly, the recession did not prevent monopoly relations from further extending themselves in different sectors of the South African economy. On the contrary, the onset of the recession actually served to stimulate the monopoly tendency of centralization of capital. As smaller companies began to flounder under the impact of the recession and as even some larger ones began to weaken, so the tendency towards take-overs and mergers gathered pace, bringing with it ever larger and more powerful groupings of capital. Just as it was the country's largest monopoly, Anglo American, which led the way during the phase of concentration, so now the Group was in the forefront during the phase of centralization. This latter tendency became most marked in three areas: within manufacturing; between mining and manufacturing; and within finance.

Manufacturing

We shall focus here on four examples of the way in which the Anglo American Group extended its power in production and marketing selected from four separate branches of industry (steel, motor, freight and chemicals). As we shall see, in each instance it was the *worsening* of the economic climate which enabled the Group to improve its position.

Regarding steel, by 1971 it was clear that the serious slump in the steel market which had begun in the late 1960s was to be of a long-term duration.[68] In that year South Africa's two largest steel producers, the state-owned ISCOR and Anglo American, entered into an agreement with the British Steel Corporation to form International Pipe and Steel Investments South Africa (IPSA). This company in turn immediately acquired control over three of the largest steel consuming companies in South Africa: Stewarts and Lloyds of South Africa (one of the top 20 industrial concerns at the time); the Vanderbijl Engineering Corporation (one of the top 30 companies); and Dorman Long (Africa) Ltd (one of the top 40).[69] Through the merger, South Africa's major suppliers of steel were largely able to overcome the disruptive effects of competition for a shrinking market by establishing control over their major markets and working out quota arrangements among themselves.[70] Following the merger not only did IPSA immediately begin to expand (through Stewarts and Lloyds taking control of two smaller engineering concerns), but it also underwent an internal rationalization programme (when Dorman Long and Vecor were merged in 1973 to form the Dorman Long Vanderbijl Corporation).[71] The merger thus provides a classic example of a defensive alliance among monopolies to defend their interests at a time of mounting economic difficulties.

While the above serves to illustrate the way in which monopoly groups can consolidate their position in an industry during a recession, the process of centralization in the motor and freight service industries illustrates the way in which monopolies are able to use a recessionary period to expand. In 1970 Anglo American's interests in the motor industry were confined to a half share in McCarthy–Main Holdings and a minority share in McCarthy Rodway through which it participated in the *distribution* of motor vehicles, earth-moving equipment and air conditioning equipment (through the activities of Illings, Atkinson & Oates Motors, Metair Holdings and Motor Assemblies). However, as the economy lurched into recession, the motor industry was hit particularly severely.[72] In the difficult years which followed not only did the McCarthy Group develop into South Africa's largest retail motor organization (holding the sole franchise for the distribution through 80 outlets in South Africa of the products of Mercedes Benz, Peugeot, Chrysler, Toyota, Leyland, Mazda, Mack, Komatsu, Hitachi, Citroën, BMW and Datsun), but it also became involved in a computer bureau, motor insurance brokering, the financing of vehicle hire purchase and leasing transactions and property.[73] At the same time Anglo American both increased its holdings in the two leading companies in the group and intensified the control which these latter companies exercised over their subordinate concerns (for example, Atkinson Oates became a 100 per cent owned subsidiary of McCarthy Rodway). In 1974 McCarthy Rodway's name was changed to McCarthy Group and by 1976 the company was ranked among South Africa's top 50 industrial concerns.[74]

But the most significant development occurred in 1976 when Anglo merged Illings with Chrysler South Africa to form the Sigma Motor Corporation, thereby moving from the sphere of motor vehicle *retailing* into motor *production*. Anglo acquired a 75 per cent stake in the new company, and, with the remaining 25 per cent held by the

American-based Chrysler Co., was guaranteed opportunities for important technological support.[75] According to AMIC, although formed in a 'difficult year for the motor industry', Sigma's prospects were bright: 'Sigma will benefit from the merger by its ability to improve its market penetration and at the same time achieve full utilisation of its production facilities and a resultant reduction in its unit cost.'[76] Sigma's early years have indeed lived up to Group expectations: in 1979 it acquired Pacsa, a company manufacturing Peugeot and Citroën vehicles in South Africa. With total assets well in excess of R100m Sigma had become 'one of the largest motor manufacturers in the country'.[77] (Subsequently, Sigma was involved in negotiations with British Leyland for a 51 per cent share in the latter's manufacturing operations in South Africa, but the deal fell through.) The case of the motor industry therefore provides a spectacular example of the way in which monopolies like Anglo American are able to improve their position in a recessionary period. The spate of mergers and take-overs which Anglo carried through during the 1970s catapulted the Group from a minority position in the industry's retail section into becoming the largest retailer and one of the largest producers in the industry.

The freight service industry provides a further illustration of this tendency. In 1971, which was a time when this industry faced rapidly rising costs, Anglo American had a minority holding both in a road hauler and car hire group, United Transport Holdings, and in a freight, forwarding, clearing and travel agency concern, Freight Services Holdings. Continued cost difficulties, arising *inter alia* out of the imposition of import controls in November 1971 and air fare increases, led Anglo to reassess its growth strategy in the industry. It quickly sold off its interest in the United Transport Co. and increased its share in Freight Services Holdings to a controlling 55 per cent. It then launched Freight Services on the take-over path, bringing two of its major competitors, Ewing McDonald and Co. and the Dart and Howes Group, under its control in 1973 and 1974 respectively.[78]

However, conditions in the industry continued to deteriorate and in 1975 Anglo merged Freight Services with two of the industry's largest companies, Aero Marine Investments and Manica Holdings. These latter concerns were in fact members of a giant shipping group controlled by the South African Marine Corporation (Safmarine)—one of the ten largest industrial groups in South Africa. The merger meant that control over the newly enlarged Freight Services Holdings was now held jointly by Anglo and Safmarine (with 50 per cent each) through a third company, Redbury Holdings.[79] The merger had major long-term implications for the industry, creating an institution powerful enough to carry through the transformation to the highly capital-intensive field of containerized shipping:[80] during 1977 Freight

Services formed South African Container Depots Ltd to run South Africa's first full container service. At the same time Freight Services embarked upon a phase of major rationalization and expansion, in the process gaining control over the largest travel organization in South Africa, Musgrove and Watson Castle Marine. Thus through a spate of defensively inspired take-overs and mergers Anglo American emerged, together with Safmarine, in control of one of the largest and most mechanized freight groups in the country operating a range of activities that included: clearing and forwarding; buying and confirming; ships agency and the servicing of ships; as well as providing a comprehensive travel service and many other ancillary services related to the movement of people and goods on both a national and international scale.[81]

The above illustrations both confirm the manifestation of the monopoly tendency of centralization in South African industry and provide further evidence of the extension of Anglo American's industrial power. But it is to the chemical industry that we must turn for the most blatant examples of these tendencies. The first comes from the vinyl division of AE & CI's operations. Vinyl production had expanded rapidly in South Africa during the 1960s with a number of companies, and in particular two groups (AE & CI and Duropenta Industries), competing closely for a relatively small market. Despite AE & CI's successful attempts to buy up a number of its smaller competitors, its vinyl division failed to produce profits and, during the recession of 1971, the company's position worsened considerably. Clearly, stronger action was required: AE & CI responded by taking over its major local competitor, Duropenta, whose three factories it then closed down. As a result AE & CI's turnover shot up nearly 200 per cent over a two-year period and its share of the market increased from 25 per cent to 41 per cent (other local producers capturing 14 per cent and importers 45 per cent). A similar situation occurred in AE & CI's fertilizer division. There AE & CI found its dominant position in the market challenged by the rising star of Triomf Fertilizer: by 1970 Triomf had acquired 20 per cent of the market, leaving AE & CI with about 33 per cent. However, when Triomf persuaded four major co-ops to take a 40 per cent interest in Triomf, hence securing their business, the writing was on the wall for AE & CI. The latter responded by taking a 49 per cent interest in Triomf and merging the fertilizer marketing and production sections of the two companies under Triomf. With over 50 per cent of the market now under AE & CI–Triomf control, the group negotiated a market-sharing agreement with the other large producer in the industry, Fedmis, which tied up 90 per cent of the market among the three companies.[82]

But it was the rising oil price which produced the largest merger in the history of South Africa's chemical industry when in 1975 AE & CI and Sentrachem (ranked fifth and nineteenth respectively among the country's top industrial concerns in that year) announced the formation of a joint R230m plastic-from-coal undertaking called Coalplex.[83] Originally, each company had planned to produce their own PVC plant using an oil-based method (ethylene), but the oil price rise meant these plans had to be scrapped. Under prodding from the state, the companies agreed to build the giant Coalplex plant (60 per cent owned by AE & CI and 40 per cent by Sentrachem) to manufacture PVC and other chemicals, such as caustic soda. Coalplex will not only diminish South Africa's dependence on imported oil, since its production process is based on the use of locally produced raw materials (such as anthracite coal, limestone, char and salt), but it will also make South Africa independent of imported caustic soda and a net exporter of PVC.[84]

Coalplex is a massive undertaking which, perhaps more than any other, expresses the high level of technical and managerial sophistication South African industry has managed to achieve. Taken together with other major changes discussed above (especially the transition to containerization and the changes which occurred in the fields of steel and motor vehicles), these developments suggest that the 1970s have proved to be crucial in South Africa's industrial evolution. If the important phase of rapid expansion and soaring growth which had characterized the 1960s had come to an end, then it had been replaced by an equally important phase of *consolidation* in which, under pressure, industry had successfully reorganized itself. Small, uncompetitive concerns were relentlessly forced to the wall and ploughed under by the momentum of the new industrial giants, thereby completing the process of industrial restructuring which was started during the boom. Out of this phase a new era of monopoly power in industry was born. Commanding financial resources far in excess of anything industry had known before and closely linked to the capitalist centres for technology (whether through British Steel, Chrysler or ICI), these new industrial giants are poised to launch South Africa into a new phase of capital-intensive industrial growth.

Mining and manufacturing

The spate of mergers associated with Anglo American during the 1970s occurred not only within manufacturing but also between manufacturing and mining. Without doubt, the most spectacular of these was the 1971 merger between Anglo's Rand Mines and Thos. Barlow and Sons to form the huge Barlow Rand mining–industrial complex. The history of the two companies involved in the merger could not have been more different.

Formed in 1893 as part of the Corner House Group, Rand Mines had become one of the country's leading mining houses. However, with no major interests in any of the developing Far West Rand or Orange Free State gold mines, the Group underwent a period of slow decline after the war, eventually, as we saw, falling under Anglo American's control in the early 1960s. Anglo in fact did little to rejuvenate the Group and, subsequently, its gold interests ran even further down (though the Group did amalgamate some of its mining interests in order to effect economies). The only long-term solution for the Group was to open up new fields of investment and during the 1960s it surpassed all other mining houses in the extent of its industrial diversification programme.[85] However, while the proportion of the Group's industrial investments rose from 14.1 per cent (R29m) of its total portfolio in 1961 to 32.4 per cent (R82m) in 1968, in this latter year these investments contributed only 22.9 per cent to total dividend income.[86] It was thus clear by the end of the decade that neither the Group's gold nor its industrial interests (of which its large minority stakes in Middelburg Steel and Alloys and Hume Pipes were the most important) were in a healthy state.

In stark contrast was the position of Thos. Barlow and Sons, which had begun life at the turn of the century as a tiny importer of engineering supplies. By the end of the 1950s this company had become an important distributor of earth-moving equipment and electrical appliances in South Africa. During the boom Barlow's underwent a phase of phenomenal expansion: between 1961 and 1970 its turnover increased by 772.5 per cent (from R33.9m to R295.4m); its pre-tax profits by 761.7 per cent (from R2.3m to R20.2m); its net asset value by 578.1 per cent (from R12.5m to R84.5m); and its labour force by 565.2 per cent (from 2476 to 16 471). By 1970 Barlow's was the third largest industrial concern in South Africa, controlling over 70 companies whose activities ranged from the *distribution and marketing* of heavy earth-moving equipment, steel, timber, building supplies, motor vehicles and mechanical handling equipment to the *manufacture and distribution* of electrical appliances, radios, electronic equipment, electrical circuit breakers, corrugated cardboard packaging and railway wagons.[87]

The merger (through which Barlow's acquired the entire issued share capital of Rand Mines) thus brought together an ailing mining group and an expanding manufacturing conglomerate in the form of Barlow Rand Ltd. The deal, which was valued at R41m (making it at that time the largest merger in South Africa's history), catapulted Barlow Rand into the ranks of the world's largest companies, ranking it, in terms of sales, 27th in Britain, 56th in Europe and 137th in *Fortune's* top 500 companies in the United States.[88] But more important from our present point of view is the fact that through the merger Anglo American became the largest single direct shareholder in Barlow Rand. The Anglo American Corporation alone held just over 10 per cent of the total, and if indirect holdings through JCI and South African Breweries are included, its share rose to almost 25 per cent.[89] Though administration of the new company remained in the hands of the Barlow family, there can be no doubt, to put it mildly, that Anglo American is a powerful influence in the new conglomerate.

No sooner was the merger completed than Barlow Rand underwent extensive rationalization. Rand Mines was stripped of all its industrial, property and financial interests (including Rand Mines Properties, Middelburg Steel and Alloys, Hume Pipes, Pretoria Portland Cement, Northern Lime, Rand Mines Holdings and the Corner House Investment Co.) which were handed over to Barlow's for administration. This left Rand Mines with administrative responsibility for the Group's mining interests only: that is, five gold mines, four collieries and three platinum and chrome mines. At the same time the Rand Mines head office staff was reorganized, with 32 per cent (140 out of 440) of its employees being reshuffled and 16 per cent (70) declared 'surplus to the group's needs'.[90] Nor did the chairmen of the ailing industrial concerns, Middelburg Steel and Hume Pipes, escape the blizzard of reorganization: both were replaced by Barlow's appointees.[91] Following rationalization, the Barlow Rand Group underwent a phase of renewed expansion: by 1972 the Group comprised 131 major subsidiary and associate companies operating in nine different countries (92 of these companies were within South Africa). Between 1972 and 1974 Group turnover increased by 64.4 per cent (from R416m to R684m) and net profits by 141 per cent (from R22.4m to R53.9m).[92] In that latter year the Group was the largest industrial profit earner in South Africa and, with total assets valued at R564m, was the country's second largest industrial concern.[93]

Barlow Rand's success during the 1970s owes a lot to the incorporation of Rand Mines. The rising gold price gave the company's gold mines new life and by 1974, when the price was still below the $200 mark, mining and exploration was already making the largest contribution to Barlow Rand's profits (accounting for 26.9 per cent of the total). Earnings from this division therefore provided the conglomerate with a lucrative source of revenue with which to promote its industrial activities, the bulk of which were in the high cost heavy industry and durable goods sectors (earth-moving equipment and heavy vehicles; steel distribution and general engineering; and alloy and steel manufacture).[94] On the one hand the Barlow Rand case thus illustrates the way in which industrial conglomerates were able to benefit from overcoming divisions between mining and manufacturing. At the same time the link-up provided Rand Mines and those mining groups closely associated with it (like Anglo American and JCI) with an institutional means through which to penetrate new fields of industrial production and marketing. The formation of Barlow Rand not only united two distinct groups into a single institution but, more important, it expressed the growing unity between different sectors of South African production.

Finance

No analysis of the mergers of the 1970s would be complete without taking account of those that occurred in the finance sector. The sheer size of these mergers and the strength of the institutions they created expressed most decisively the greater financial power of South Africa's monopoly capitalism. As we shall see, Anglo American had a hand in virtually every one of these mergers.

As in industry, these financial mergers were set in motion by the deteriorating economic situation. In 1972 the chairman of the Anglo-controlled merchant banking group, UAL Holdings, spelt out the impact which the economic climate was having on the financial sector:

> By early last year the major South African financial institutions had largely adjusted themselves to the changed and straitened circumstances—perhaps sooner than many other companies—if only because they had been buffeted for longer. But in many ways 1971 proved to be more disordered than the year before. Institutions found it difficult to adapt further in an environment of even slower growth, greater inflation and government regulation, mounting uncertainty and finally a devaluation which left most of the economic ills untouched.[95]

In addition to these general difficulties, UAL faced the specific problem of greater competition from commercial banks (which were developing merchant banking sections) and American competitors entering the field in South Africa. In response UAL undertook a number of mergers which ended in 1974 with the emergence of a massive new banking conglomerate, Nedsual, to dominate much of South Africa's banking and other financial activities.

The first step came during 1972 when UAL Holdings brought the National Board of Executors (a national trust company with interests in real estate administration and sales) under its 100 per cent control.[96] The following year UAL Holdings merged with Syfrets Trust Co. in a deal which gave the former a 61 per cent share in the new financial combine, Syfrets and UAL Holdings.[97] The rationale for the merger was clear: both groups had closely allied banking, mutual fund, insurance, property and trust interests and a merger would enable them to rationalize these and present a united front to their competitors. The result of the merger was the emergence of a financial combine which (with total assets valued at R338m and holding clients' funds worth R1200m) immediately became South Africa's sixth largest banking group.[98] What is most important, though, is that through the merger Anglo American came to collaborate directly with yet another of South

Africa's powerful financial institutions, the Old Mutual. This latter company, which had exercised control over Syfrets Trust through a 23 per cent shareholding, now became the largest shareholder in the new combine (with a 30 per cent share), while Anglo American (which had held 65 per cent of UAL) became the second largest shareholder (with 24 per cent of the total).[99]

No sooner was this merger completed than Syfrets and UAL Holdings merged with the Dutch-owned Nedbank group (the third largest commercial bank in South Africa) to form the giant financial conglomerate, Nedbank and Syfrets–UAL Holdings (Nedsual). Nedbank's activities had diversified during the 1960s out of the strict confines of commercial banking into insurance, mutual funds, merchant banking and industrial and other finance. There was thus a good deal of overlap between its activities and those of the Syfrets–UAL group (whose expertise lay in merchant banking, property finance and the executor field) and after the merger the group spent eighteen months rationalizing its organizational structure to accommodate these disparate activities under a single control.[100] The result was a new financial giant that joined South Africa's élite British-owned banks, Barclays and Standard, at the very top of the country's big bank league. With total assets of R1830m, R1630m and R1600m respectively, Barclays, Standard and Nedsual were well ahead of South Africa's fourth largest bank, Volkskas, whose total assets were valued at R985m.[101] Although the merger resulted in Anglo American's and the Old Mutual's holdings in the new conglomerate being reduced to 8 per cent and 15 per cent respectively, their financial influence had been enormously expanded thereby.[102]

The formation of an institution the size of Nedsual clearly had important implications for existing power relations in South African finance, especially as it broke the grip previously held by the two imperialist giants, Barclays and Standard. But it would be quite wrong to construe Anglo's involvement in Nedsual as part of a campaign to undermine the position of either of these banks. As we shall see, not only did Anglo have an important minority stake in both of them, but at the same time as Anglo was helping to form Nedsual it was also increasing its stake in Barclays. However, Anglo's route to Barclays was far from straightforward and went via yet another major financial take-over.

In mid-1974 one of Anglo's principal South African holding companies, the Rand Selection Corporation, carried out a R160m take-over of the South African-based international finance house, Schlesinger Insurance and Institutional Holdings (SII). Although holding a wide spread of investments in banking and property, Schlesinger's principal sphere of activity was life insurance (accounting in 1974 for 62 per cent of SII's profits).[103] As such, the take-over brought Anglo American access to a major new branch of finance. Specifically, Anglo gained: a

75 per cent interest in South Africa's largest assurance company, the African Eagle Life Assurance Society, whose subsidiaries included two other insurance concerns (the Guarantee Life Assurance Co. and South African Eagle); a 69 per cent holding in the country's seventh largest and fastest growing bank, Western Bank; a 47 per cent interest in Sorec Ltd, the second largest property company in South Africa (specializing in developing commercial property in urban centres both locally and in Britain); and a 55 per cent holding in Schlesinger European Investments, which held the group's R200m interests in Europe.[104] The acquisition of these assets (valued at R800m) immediately raised the value of Rand Selection's total assets to R1801m and those of Anglo's three main South African-based holding companies to R4844m.[105] No sooner was the merger completed than a process of rationalization began. From our present point of view the most important aspect of this rationalization was Anglo's decision to exchange the newly acquired Western Bank for shares in Barclays National Bank. As a result of this deal Anglo's share in Barclays National was raised to 17.5 per cent of the total, making it by far the largest single South African-based shareholder in the Bank, which is 64 per cent owned by Barclays International.[106]

But if the point of Anglo's involvement in Nedsual was not to undermine Barclay's position, that still leaves open the question of the long-term implications of the manoeuvres outlined above. Perhaps here it is worth considering the challenge which had been mounting against Barclays throughout the 1960s and early 1970s. That challenge came principally from a powerful new Afrikaner financial group coalesced around the Sanlam insurance company and the Volkskas and Trust Banks. Strongly 'nationalistic' in ideological orientation this group was growing rapidly at precisely the time that Barclays was being attacked by the state for being a foreign-owned concern. In 1971, for instance, the state-appointed Franzen Commission bluntly recommended that foreign participation in locally-based banks, such as Barclays National, should be reduced to 50 per cent of the total. The Anglo Group already held a small share in Barclays National Bank and, through Charter, JCI and the Anglo American Corporation, a substantial share in the Standard Bank. By increasing their share in Barclays the locally based Anglo Group helped Barclays to counter the criticism of exclusive foreign ownership. At the same time the strong links which Anglo had with Nedsual and Standard laid the basis for an extremely powerful alliance to be formed between Anglo, Barclays, Standard, Nedsual (with its attendant Dutch connections) and the Old Mutual. Through these various developments, then, a financial wall seems to have been erected which, for the foreseeable future, must be impregnable to attack by Afrikaner financial interests (or, for that matter, any other interests).

The financial mergers which occurred during the 1970s were thus part of a continuing process of reorganization in the financial forms of South African monopoly capitalism. This involved *inter alia* bringing disparate branches of finance under centralized control (such as occurred through the creation of Nedsual) and rationalizing the organizational structure of existing financial institutions (such as occurred in merchant banking through the Nedsual deal, in trust funds through the Syfrets–UAL deal and in commercial banking through the Barclays–Western Bank deal). By the mid-1970s the evolution of this process had transformed the face of South African finance capital. Most significant in this respect was the position of dominance which three institutions—Barclays, Standard and Nedsual—had attained for themselves. As we noted, Anglo American was closely involved in all aspects of this process and, through its holdings in the above banks, had carved for itself a position of considerable influence in South African finance.

Yet Anglo's financial influence reaches beyond its *direct* involvement in South Africa's leading banks. The phase of centralization also resulted in a relatively few very large companies dividing up whole branches of industry among themselves. As we have seen, Anglo American played an important part in many of these developments (such as in steel, motor vehicles, freight handling and chemicals). As a result new combinations were formed and new alliances struck, thereby extending Anglo's industrial influence beyond the realm of its own Group network. This latter process has caused Anglo to line up with some of the most formidable companies operating in South African industry, including the British Steel Corporation and ISCOR in steel; Chrysler, Peugeot and Citroën and a host of others in the motor industry; Safmarine in freight handling; Triomf and Fedmis in fertilizers; Sentrachem in chemicals; and Barlows in engineering, construction and other industries. Nor does this new power structure in industry remain autonomous from those existing in South Africa's other major economic sectors. Their linkages and alliances with Anglo meant that the above companies formed part of an ever expanding network of relations between mining and industry, which inevitably produce further reorganizations and new combinations and linkages. Here the Barlow Rand case is instructive since through this merger the original Barlow company was able, first, to gain access to the important industrial interests held by Rand Mines and then to bring them under its control, reorganizing and revitalizing them in the process through contact with its existing industrial interests. In this way new combinations emerged, new forms of integration occurred betweeen companies and new life was injected into ailing concerns (such as Middelburg Steel and Hume Pipes).

But neither do the combinations and linkages thus established between major sectors of production exist in isolation from those that have been formed in the financial sector. And here again it is Anglo American which plays a key role, helping in particular to merge the vast productive resources of large industrialists and mine-owners with the massive financial resources of the banks and other financial institutions. Through the linkages which Anglo has established for itself in production and finance, those monopolies which are allied to it (such as Barlow Rand, South African Breweries and Safmarine in production and Barclays, Standard, Nedsual, Schlezingers and the Old Mutual in finance) gain closer access to one another and enter into working relationships. In this way the financial oligarchy consolidates its power base: drawing new strength from production; gaining new sources of finance. At the very core of the oligarchic structure stands Anglo American, always extending its own position, always welding new alliances, creating new linkages. No longer is the producer just a banker; now the producer–banker becomes the means through which a widening network of other producers and bankers can link up. Out of these developments (in which Anglo plays such a prominent role) an expanding chain of financial power has been created in South Africa which constantly reinforces and extends the realm of monopoly capitalism.

CONCLUSION

In this chapter we have sought to distinguish between two tendencies in South Africa's monopoly evolution in industry and finance: concentration and centralization. We have argued that neither can be separated from the events in the gold mining industry during the 1950s—that both are related to the diversification of mining investment which occurred during and after the development of the postwar gold fields. Although after the war tendencies were developing within manufacturing which, given time, would have facilitated of their own volition monopoly concentration and centralization in the sector, both the backward nature of the labour process and the dominance of very small concerns suggests that this would have taken an inordinately long time to materialize. In the event, monopoly relations established themselves relatively quickly. Our argument is that both mining investment and foreign investment, but principally the former, were largely responsible for the speed with which this transition occurred.

Although diversification of investment out of mining began during the 1950s the industrial investments which occurred at this time were mainly related to the needs of the developing gold mines. From the late 1950s onwards—when an internal money market was created—the position began to change. Of crucial importance here was the intervention of political factors—and in particular the struggle waged by the state against the black nationalist movement. The defeat of that movement, combining with other favourable factors, laid the basis for an unprecedented industrial boom in South Africa.

From this moment onwards diversification becomes the key to understanding the rapid evolution of monopoly relations in industry and finance. First, because diversification played a major role in altering the structure of industrial production, promoting in particular the development of new heavy, intermediate and durable goods industries. Secondly, because in general these investments, together with those in the traditional light industries, tended to be large and highly capital-intensive forms of investment. These developments not only changed the nature of South African industry, they also changed its form, since increasingly industry came to exhibit signs of monopoly influence (as, for instance, single companies came to dominate whole branches of production). Most important as far as this latter phenomenon was concerned was the increasing domination of the mining monopolies, and in particular Anglo American, over various branches of industrial production. Increasingly, throughout the boom Anglo concentrated new areas of production and capital under its control. For this reason we refer to this phase—in which monopoly forms emerged as industry expanded—as that of monopoly *concentration*, since it is one in which monopoly capitalists concentrated industrial and financial resources, which had previously been beyond their reach, under their control. It is thus a phase in which great mining monopolies like Anglo established their roots in South Africa's industrial and financial structure, thereby giving institutional expression to the closer integration being forged between South Africa's economic sectors.

However, the boom did not last. Precisely because it was based on monopoly—that is, capital-intensive—forms of investment it created contradictions which proved too strong for the peripheral economy. But the boom did not put an end to the evolution of monopoly relations, only to the form it took. The recession drove a number of smaller companies to the wall, making them easy prey for their larger adversaries, while under the more difficult economic conditions even larger competing companies turned to each other for support. Thus in this phase new mergers occurred and new monopolies were created, producing the giants of present-day industry and finance in South Africa. But this phase, precisely because it occurred in a recession and precisely because it involved primarily a reorganization of relations of control among existing companies, needs to be distinguished from the earlier phase. This was not a phase in which vast *new* areas of production and finance were opened up, but one in which *existing* areas of production and finance were brought under more centralized control. For this reason we have referred to this phase as one of monopoly *centralization*. Yet because it was mining monopolies like Anglo which were the major beneficiaries of this phase, it forms a part of the overall process of diversification: a new phase in its evolution.

The result of this process is that literally a handful of companies have come to exert a *decisive* influence over the direction of South Africa's economic life. Half a dozen groups control the mining industry, while the same number dominate the financial sector. Although not as well developed yet, the position in industry reflects the same pervasive influence. By the mid-1970s 5 per cent of manufacturing companies accounted for 63 per cent of turnover in that sector. On the distribution side the position was no different: 5 per cent of all firms in the wholesale and retail trade accounted for 69 per cent of turnover, while 5 per cent of the firms in transport accounted for 76 per cent of turnover. In the construction sector the same conditions prevailed: 5 per cent of the firms accounted for 63 per cent of turnover. [107] What makes these figures even more significant is the fact that very often it is the same firms which dominate the various sectors. Here the influence of Anglo American becomes critical.

Taking 1976 as our point of reference, we find that in that year Anglo Group companies held top positions in every one of South Africa's economic sectors except agriculture. In mining the top five mining houses were all Anglo companies (AMGOLD, ANAMINT, Rand Selection, AMCOAL and TC Lands). [108] In manufacturing Anglo either controlled or held a substantial minority share in five of the top ten industrial concerns (SA Breweries, AE & CI, Barlow Rand, AMIC and Huletts) and, to extend the list, in twelve of the top 30. [109] Furthermore, five Anglo companies were among the top ten industrial concerns in terms of turnover;[110] eight among the top fifteen industrial profit leaders;[111] and eight among the top fifteen in terms of market capitalization value. [112] Two of South Africa's top ten property companies (Sorec and AMAPROP) were Anglo's, while another associated company (Rand Mines Properties) was the country's largest township developer. [113] As far as finance was concerned, Anglo had interests in seven of the country's top twenty banks (Barclays, Standard, Nedbank, Western, Nedfin, Nefic and UAL), owned one of the top three life assurers in the country (African Eagle) and had an interest in the country's largest short-term insurer (SA Eagle). [114]

Anglo's overall financial power in the South African economy may be demonstrated through the following indices. In 1976 the Group not only controlled the country's top three market leaders (De Beers, Anglo American Corporation and AMGOLD), it actually *controlled* ten of the top fifteen (the above three plus ANAMINT, Charter, Vaal Reefs, Western Deep, AE & CI, Phalaborwa and Rand Selection) and had important minority shares in a further three (East Driefontein, West Driefontein and Barlow Rand). [115] In terms of total assets, Anglo either controlled or held important interests in eighteen of the country's top 50 companies.[116] Although this latter list was headed by Barclays Bank (with total assets of R4640m), as the *Financial Mail* pointed out: '. . . if, however, Anglo American consolidated the overall value of its investments, worth about R5,300m, it would comfortably top Barclays'.[117]

Thus, today, South Africa has reached a position in which not only do monopoly companies dominate the strategic branches of its economic sectors, but one group in particular (buoyed up by a vast network of associated and allied companies) commands a key position within this power structure.[118] With its roots firmly planted in various branches of South African production and distribution, and in control of the financial arteries which feed these sectors, Anglo American has secured for itself a vital position in South Africa's monopoly capitalist society.

NOTES

1. By 1968 the GDP at current prices had reached R10 283m (from R2178m in 1948). (UAL, *Scope for Investment: South Africa's Growing Economy*, Johannesburg, 1969, p. 14.)
2. Even over the longer period (1950–66) South Africa's real economic growth was faster than all other industrialized countries with the exception of Japan. During the 1960s South Africa even outstripped countries in North America and western Europe in terms of *per capita* growth (ibid., p. 20).
3. ibid., p. 14.
4. Calculated from SA Department of Statistics, *South African Statistics, 1976*.
5. Calculated from ibid.
6. UAL, *Scope for Investment*, p. 17.
7. Between 1960 and 1968 the number of tractors employed in agriculture rose by 24 per cent (from 119 196 to 147 844); the number of combines rose by 93.5 per cent (from 10 223 to 19 782); and the number of lorries by 22.7 per cent (from 69 376 to 85 091). *(SA Statistics, 1976.)*
8. UAL, *Scope for Investment*, p. 36.
9. Derived from *SA Statistics, 1976*.
10. SA Reserve Bank, *Quarterly Bulletin of Statistics*, December 1961–December 1962.
11. The value of manufactured goods exports (SITC code 5-9) rose from 34 per cent of the total of 49 per cent (ibid.). Despite a wide range of state-sponsored schemes to promote South Africa's exports of manufactured goods, they failed to make a significant breakthrough on the major world markets and most of the above increase came about as a result of the market which developed in Rhodesia and Zambia following the imposition by the UN of sanctions against the former. (For detailed analyses of South Africa's trade position see Innes, 1975, pp. 111–68; and Bienefeld and Innes, 1976, pp. 47–51.)
12. Commenting on this phenomenon, an economic survey by a prominent financial institution noted: 'In 1970, a massive deficit of R827 million was incurred in the balance of payments on current account; it approached three times the size of the previous record deficit of R249m that occurred in 1965. In 1971, the deficit wid-

ened still further, to R1003 million.' (The Nedbank Group, *South Africa, An Appraisal,* p. 155.)

13. ibid., pp. 206, 156.
14. UAL, *Scope for Investment,* p. 42.
15. ibid., p. 42.
16. *Financial Mail,* Special Survey, 'Inside the Anglo Power House,' pp. 19, 31.
17. *Indirect* investment in industry accounted for R93.7m, bringing the overall total to R285m. (Calculated from ibid., pp. 19, 31.)
18. ibid., p. 19.
19. On this point Harry Oppenheimer has said: 'I started very much with the idea that we didn't want control, because we were entering fields where we did not have a great deal of experience. But actually, the more I've seen of this thing, the more disillusioned I've become with taking minority participation, with so-called experts from overseas in control. I think the companies we've run ourselves have done a great deal better.' (ibid., p. 10.)
20. ibid., p. 10. (My emphasis.)
21. ibid., p. 11.
22. Also *Financial Mail,* Special Survey, 'Top Companies', 26 March 1970, p. 89. Vanadium pentoxide is the raw material used in the manufacture of ferro-vanadium. Used as an alloy, vanadium refines and strengthens the structure of steel, so that less weight of steel can take a given strain.
23. ibid., p. 91.
24. *Financial Mail,* Special Survey, 'Inside the Anglo Power House', p. 35.
25. Anglo American Corp. of SA, *Annual Report, 1971,* p. 28.
26. ibid., p. 82.
27. *Financial Mail,* Special Survey, 'Top Companies', 26 March 1970, p. 31. The following year the Highveld Corp. was the tenth largest employer in South Africa with a labour force of 13 900. ('Top Companies', 16 April 1971, p. 41.) The *Financial Mail* 'Top Companies' surveys refer only to companies quoted on the Johannesburg stock exchange and not include, for instance, foreign firms not quoted locally or unquoted subsidiaries.
28. Highveld Steel and Vanadium Corp., *Annual Report, 1977,* p. 5; and *Financial Mail,* Special Survey, 'Top Companies', 21 April 1978, p. 49.
29. South Africa's demand for steel, which had risen at an average annual rate of 6.6 per cent between 1950 and 1963, leapt by 37 per cent in 1964. During 1965 and 1966 over 887 000 tons of steel were imported as overseas suppliers sought to meet the demand. (*Financial Mail,* Special Survey, '1961–1966: The Fabulous Years', p. 43.)
30. *Scaw Metals,* published by the company, p. 2.
31. ibid.
32. *Financial Mail,* Special Survey, 'Inside the Anglo Power House', p. 35; and cf. 'Top Companies', 28 March 1969, p. 29. This is of course only a rough estimation since other unquoted companies would need to be included before an accurate assessment could be made.
33. Scaw Metals and Highveld Steel both supply this company with its raw materials in the form of 'as-rolled' steel bars. The products of the company are consumed primarily by South Africa's railways, defence force and in the automotive industry. (*Scaw Metals.*)
34. Within Scaw, as within many other industrial establishments in South Africa, technical innovations do occur and adaptations are sometimes made to foreign-controlled technologies. But this does not alter the basic relation of technological dependence.
35. Anglo American Corp. of SA, *Annual Report, 1971,* p. 83.
36. Anglo American Corp. of SA, *Annual Report, 1973,* p. 84.
37. ibid., pp. 84, 87.

38. See also De Beers Cons., *Annual Report, 1977*, p. 56.
39. See also Anglo American Corp. of SA, *Annual Report, 1971*, p. 83.
40. *Financial Mail*, Special Survey, 'AE & CI', p. 24.
41. Together these two factories produced 9 million 25 kg of blasting explosives per year. (ibid., p. 68.)
42. AE & CI, 'Document for the Private Placing of 12m Ordinary Shares', issued by Union Acceptances Ltd, p. 15.
43. *Financial Mail*, Special Survey, 'AE & CI' pp. 21, 29, 66.
44. *Financial Mail*, Special Survey, 6 June 1975, p. 85.
45. Anglo American Corp. of SA *Chairman's Statement, 1973*.
46. *Financial Mail*, Special Survey, 'Top Companies', 20 April 1979, p. 65.
47. *Financial Mail*, Special Survey, 'AE & CI', pp. 79–82.
48. ibid., pp. 74–9.
49. ibid.
50. Anglo American Corp. of SA, *Annual Report, 1976*, p. 82.
51. AMIC, *Annual Report, 1971*, p. 27.
52. Anglo American Corp. of SA, *Annual Report, 1973*, p. 83; *1972*, p. 79; *1976*, p. 82; and AMIC, *Annual Report, 1971*, p. 27.
53. The company's major sources of earnings were: the tungsten carbide division in South Africa and Zambia; the drilling operations in Zambia; the percussion rock drill manufacturing group in the United States; the Portadrill Company in the United States; the Mindrill Company in Australia; and the Longyear sub-group. (AMIC, *Annual Report, 1977*, p. 34.) The company is not listed on the Johannesburg stock exchange and the profit ranking referred to in the text is therefore an approximation.
54. Based on data compiled in Appendix 1. This figure is definitely an underestimation in that it does not include all the industrial subsidiaries of those companies under Anglo American's control. For instance, Lennings Holdings, which is cited in the Appendix, controls ten separate subsidiaries, none of which is included in the Appendix. (AMIC, *Annual Report, 1971*, p. 26.)
55. *Financial Mail*, Special Survey, 'Top Companies', 22 April 1977, p. 23. South African Breweries is the largest brewery group in South Africa and, through Zambia Breweries, monopolizes the Zambian liquor industry. It also holds over 50 industrial, commercial and property interests inside South Africa, among the most important of which are OK Bazaars (in 1976 one of the top twelve industrial concerns in the country); the large Southern Suns hotel chain; the soft drink and food ventures, Schweppes South Africa and Food Corporation, respectively; a furniture group, Afcol; and a property group, Retco. (*Financial Mail*, Special Survey, 'South African Breweries: Focus on You', pp. 1–72.)
56. Anglo American Corp. of SA, *Annual Report, 1973*, p. 33; *1976*, pp. 40–1; and *1977*, pp. 37–9.
57. The South African papers *directly* controlled by the Argus Co. are: *The Star, Cape Argus, Daily News, Friend, Diamond Fields Advertiser, Pretoria News, Sunday Tribune, Cape Herald, Ilanga* and *The Sowetan*. Those under the Argus's *indirect* control (exercised through SAAN) are: *Rand Daily Mail, Eastern Province Herald, Evening Post, Sunday Times, Sunday Express, Cape Times* and *Financial Mail*. Of the eight directors of the Argus Co. two were from JCI and two from Rand Mines. (Hepple, 1974, pp. 57–67.)
58. Anglo American Corp. of SA, *Annual Report, 1976*, p. 33; and AMIC, *Annual Report, 1976*, pp. 28–30.
59. *Financial Mail*, Special Survey, 'Top Companies', 28 March 1969, pp. 111, 113.
60. Nedsual (Nedbank and Syfreto-UAL Holdings), *Annual Report, 1973/4*, p. 6.
61. UAL press release, 24 February 1972; and Nedsual, *Annual Report, 1973/4*, p. 6.
62. *Financial Mail*, Special Survey, 'Inside the Anglo Power House', p. 37.
63. *Financial Mail*, Special Survey, 28 March 1969, p. 109.

64. *Financial Mail*, Special Survey, 'Carlton Hotel: Innkeeper International', p. 7. Originally developed as a joint venture between South African Breweries and Anglo American, Breweries' interest was subsequently taken over by Anglo whose share in the project was thereby raised to 90 per cent. (Beckingham, 1972, p. 139.)

65. *Financial Mail*, Special Survey, 'Top Companies', 14 April 1971, p. 103.

66. SA Reserve Bank, *Quarterly Review*, September 1973.

67. Harry Oppenheimer's annual chairman's statements on behalf of Anglo American are a sort of 'state of the union' address and provide *inter alia* an assessment of South Africa's economic position. Throughout the 1970s they continually refer to South Africa's serious and growing economic problems. Thus we find that: '1971 was a year of difficulty and doubt'; in 1972, 'the state of the South African economy has been giving rise to increasing concern'; and in 1974, 'the South African economy is at present going through a difficult time. It does not look as though a renewed upswing can be expected until 1976'. (See Anglo American Corp. of SA, *Chairman's Statements, 1971–9*.)

68. See Anglo American Corp. of SA, *Chairman's Statements, 1970, 1971* and *1972*.

69. Anglo American Corp. of SA, *Annual Report, 1971*, p. 29; and *Financial Mail*, Special Survey, 'Top Companies', 16 April 1971, p. 21.

70. Oppenheimer referred to the deal as 'an interesting example of co-operation between private enterprise and the agencies of the State', stating that it 'is designed to co-ordinate production and utilization in important sections of the steel industry'. (*Chairman's Statement, 1971*; p. 5.)

71. Anglo American Corp. of SA, *Annual Report, 1971* and *1973*, pp. 28 and 30, respectively.

72. In 1972 Oppenheimer reported: 'The South African motor industry continued to be adversely affected by the higher cost of the [state-imposed] increased local content requirements, continued sales taxes, and also costs flowing from currency realignments.' (Anglo American Corp. of SA, *Annual Report, 1972*, p. 34.)

73. These franchises (applicable to Namibia as well as South Africa) and other interests were achieved either through agreements with the manufacturers concerned or through take-overs, such as the Atkinson Oates take-over of the John B. Clarke Motor Company in 1974, which brought in the BMW and Datsun franchises. (Anglo American Corp. of SA, *Annual Report, 1974*, p. 34.)

74. *Financial Mail*, Special Survey, 'Top Companies', 22 April 1977, p. 21.

75. Anglo American Corp. of SA, *Annual Report, 1976*, p. 38.

76. AMIC, *Annual Report, 1976*, p. 7.

77. Anglo American Corp. of SA, *Annual Report, 1979*, p. 6. Although unquoted, these assets would have placed Sigma among the top 40 industrial companies in South Africa.

78. Anglo American Corp. of SA, *Annual Report, 1971*, pp. 31, and 33; *Annual Report, 1972*, p. 34; and *Annual Report, 1974*, p. 34.

79. Anglo American Corp. of SA, *Annual Report, 1975*, p. 34; AMIC, *Annual Report, 1977*, p. 41; and *Financial Mail*, Special Survey, 'Top Companies', 22 April 1977, p. 19.

80. According to AMIC: 'The object of the merger . . . was to create a substantial group which would more easily meet challenges facing the industry, such as the introduction of containerisation in 1977 . . . The new group is being rationalised by combining the functions of certain divisions and by effecting substantial changes in the group's organisational structure'. (AMIC, *Annual Report, 1976*, p. 7.)

81. Freight Services was identified by the Bingham Report as being the central channel for moving oil to Rhodesia between 1976 and 1978 in violation of UN sanctions.

82. *Financial Mail*, Special Survey, 'AE & CI', pp. 53, 55, 73.

83. *Financial Mail*, Special Survey, 'Top Companies', 23 April 1976, p. 37.

84. *Financial Mail*, Special Survey, 'Coalplex', pp. 15–20.

85. In 1968 the chairman of the Group stated: "The extent of the diversification policy in

regard to the Company's investments can be gauged from the fact that direct mining investments now account for a little over one-third of the portfolio as against two-thirds at the end of 1963.' (Rand Mines, *Chairman's Statement, 1968.*) The Group's diversification was not confined to industrial undertakings: in 1969 it announced that together with a US company, US Natural Resources, Inc., it was forming Soekor to undertake an off-shore oil prospecting programme in South Africa. (Rand Mines press release, 18 November 1969.)

86. Rand Mines, Scheme of Arrangement for the Proposed Merger of Thos. Barlow and Sons Limited and Rand Mines Limited, 26 April 1971, pp. 16–17.
87. ibid., p. 20; *Financial Mail*, Special Survey, 'Top Companies', 16 April 1971, p. 19; and *The Star*, 15 July 1974.
88. *Sunday Times,* 2 May 1971.
89. *Rand Daily Mail,* 5 February 1971 and 6 February 1971, based on an Anglo press statement.
90. It was estimated by the Group that these head office staff changes would save over R250 000 on salaries alone. (*Sunday Times,* 8 August 1971.)
91. *Rand Daily Mail,* 22 October 1971.
92. Barlow Rand, *Annual Report, 1972,* supplement entitled 'Barlow Rand Today', p. 3; and *Annual Financial Statement, 1974,* p. 11.
93. *Financial Mail,* Special Survey, 'Top Companies', 6 June 1975, p. 43.
94. In 1974 the sources of Barlow Rand's earnings were as follows: mining and exploration 26.9 per cent; building materials 19.9 per cent; earth-moving equipment and heavy vehicles 12.4 per cent; steel distribution and general engineering 11.1 per cent; alloy and steel manufacture 5.2 per cent; paint manufacture and distribution 4.8 per cent; property 4.5 per cent; household appliances, sound products, television and electronics 4.4 per cent; motor vehicles, agricultural equipment and transport services 3.5 per cent; mechanical handling equipment and engineering supplies 3.2 per cent; packaging and paper products 1.9 per cent; and administrative and financial services 2.2 per cent. The sources of Group earnings in geographical terms were as follows: South Africa and Namibia 91.3 per cent; rest of Africa 5.6 per cent; EEC 1.8 per cent; other 1.3 percent. (Barlow Rand, *Annual Financial Statements 1974,* p. 13.)
95. UAL Holdings, *Chairman's Statement, 1972,* p. 1.
96. UAL press release, 9 May 1972.
97. *Financial Mail,* 30 March 1973.
98. *The Star,* 4 March 1973; and *Financial Mail,* Special Survey, 'Top Companies', 24 May 1974, p. 99.
99. *The Star,* 9 January 1972; and *Financial Mail,* 30 March 1973.
100. The merger, which also involved a general bank, Nedfin (49 per cent owned by Nedbank), brought together: 1 commercial bank (Nedbank), 2 merchant banks, (UAL and Nefic Acceptances), 4 general banks (2 in Syfrual and 2 in Nedbank's Nefic and Credcor), 3 personal financial planning and portfolio investment divisions, 2 insurance broking businesses, 3 mutual funds (Syfret Intergro, UAL Mutual and Sage), 2 economic research divisions and other overlapping services. (Syfrets and UAL Holdings Ltd, Circular to Members and Notice of Extraordinary General Meeting relating to the Merger of Nedbank Ltd, Nedfin Ltd and Syfrual.)
101. *Financial Mail,* Special Survey, 'Top Companies', 24 May 1974, pp. 99, 101; and *Rand Daily Mail,* 15 November 1973.
102. *Financial Mail,* 7 December 1973.
103. Rand Selection Corp., *Annual Report, 1974,* p. 8.
104. Other important acquisitions included: a 49 per cent holding in the Metals and Minerals Investment Corp., a 100 per cent holding in the Premier Finance Corp. and a 100 per cent holding in Townsview Estates. (Rand Selection Corp., *Annual Report, 1974,* pp. 3–10; *Rand Daily Mail,* 22 March 1974; and *Financial Mail,* Special Survey, 'Top Companies', 6 June 1975, pp. 123, 129.)

The Anglo Monopoly in Industry and Finance 227

105. At the time Rand Selection controlled 151 subsidiary companies, 110 of which were in South Africa. (Rand Selection Corp., *Annual Report, 1974*, pp. 28–9; *Financial Mail*, Special Survey, 'Top Companies', 6 June 1975, p. 81; and *Rand Daily Mail*, 22 March 1974.)

106. Only one other institution has more than 1 per cent of the stock of Barclays National, giving Barclays International and Anglo a free hand in administering the bank's affairs. (*Financial Mail*, Special Survey. "The Changing Face of Barclays', p. 31.)

107. *Report of the Commission of Inquiry into the Regulation of Monopolistic Conditions Act 1955*, RP 64/1977. Furthermore, the commission found that within manufacturing the following conditions existed. In the cigarette industry 2 firms control 70 per cent of turnover and 3 firms control 98 per cent. In the blanket industry 3 firms control 78.8 per cent of turnover. In the tyres and tubes industry 3 firms control 85.8 per cent of turnover. In the sheet and plateglass industry 1 firm alone controls 70 per cent of all the goods produced and 3 firms control 96.7 per cent of the goods produced. In the instant breakfast foods industry 2 firms control 70 per cent of all goods produced and 3 firms control 90.2 per cent. In the soap and candles industry 2 firms control 70 per cent of all goods produced and 3 firms control 80.5 per cent. In the engines and turbine industry 1 firm controls 70 per cent of all goods produced and 3 firms control total production. In the electric bulb industry 2 firms control 70 per cent of all goods produced and 3 firms control 91.3 per cent.

108. *Financial Mail*, Special Survey, 'Top Companies', 22 April 1977, p. 81.

109. The above five plus OK Bazaars (through SA Breweries), Tiger Oats, Tongaat, Highveld Steel, Greatermans, Pretoria Portland Cement and Stewart and Lloyds. (ibid., p. 19.)

110. SA Breweries, Barlow Rand, OK Bazaars, AE & CI and AMIC. (ibid., p. 28.)

111. Barlow Rand, SA Breweries, AMIC, AE & CI, Huletts, Tiger Oats, Highveld Steel and OK Bazaars. (ibid., p. 47.)

112. Barlow Rand, AE & CI, AMIC, SA Breweries, Highveld Steel, DEBINCOR, Tiger Oats and OK Bazaars. (ibid., p. 54.)

113. ibid., p. 103.

114. ibid., pp. 111, 135, 142.

115. Altogether the Group either controlled or held an important stake in 31 of the country's top 50 market leaders. (ibid., pp. 35, 37.)

116. The companies and their respective positions (in parentheses) were as follows: Barclays (1), Nedbank (7), Anglo American Corp. (10), De Beers (12), Rand Selection (16), National Finance Corp. (23), SA Breweries (24), Barlow Rand (27), AMGOLD (28), JCI (31), Charter (32), AMIC (37), AE & CI (38), MINORCO (41), ANAMINT (45), Huletts (46), Rustenburg Platinum (49) and Vaal Reefs (50). (ibid., p. 66.)

117. ibid., p. 65.

118. Although we have not focused on South Africa's agricultural sector here, monopoly relations did extend to this sector as well. For instance, the giant Rembrandt group of companies (the third largest industrial concern in South Africa in 1976) had extensive agricultural interests, as did Triomf Fertilizer which was associated with AE & CI. Anglo American itself had important agricultural interests in addition to its many timber interests and its holding (through the Tongaat Group) in large sugar plantations. In 1969 Anglo formed Soetvelde Farms Ltd 'to consolidate and develop the farming interests of the Anglo American Corporation and De Beers Groups'. This company is involved *inter alia* in the growing of maize, wheat, potatoes and other dryland crops and the breeding of cattle, pigs and sheep over 'large areas' of the Transvaal, Orange Free State, Northern Cape and Zimbabwe. One of its subsidiaries, Dawn Orchards, produces tomatoes, a range of vegetables and tropical fruits in South Africa, while another wholly owned subidiary, Debsham Ranches, owns 'an extensive cattle ranching operation' in Zimbabwe.

Other agricultural interests of the Group include: Rhodes Fruit and Wine Farms, which owns 'extensive estates' in the Western Cape and grows, cans and markets deciduous fruits, wine and grapes and has a large livestock heard; Hippo Valley Estates which produces sugar, citrus and related products in Zimbabwe; Dewhurst Farms which mainly distributes and sells fresh farm products; Mazoe Citrus Estates in Zimbabwe; Simoona Estates in Zimbabwe; and Sunningdale Farm and Conway Farm, both controlled through JCI. In general Anglo American Group farms are among the most mechanized in southern Africa. (Anglo American Corp. of SA, *Annual Report, 1976*, p. 83; and *Financial Mail*, Special Survey, 'Top Companies', 22 April 1977, p. 19.)

CONCLUSION

Anglo American
and South African Imperialism

This study has concentrated almost exclusively on Anglo American's position in the political economy of South Africa. In so doing it has focused not only on Anglo's rise to power within the industrial economy but also on the social and political conditions which surrounded and influenced that process. Such an approach has enabled us both to locate Anglo American in relation to the fundamental forces which motivate capitalist society in South Africa and to chart the evolution of that society over time. Inevitably, there must be omissions and shortcomings in a work which attempts such an all-embracing study over a time-span of more than a hundred years. None the less, we would argue that such weaknesses do not detract from the validity of attempting this task, since the particular perspective or overview which it affords is one which no micro-study could hope to provide. However, there *are* omissions in this study and before closing this investigation some of these omissions need to be briefly dealt with. In this conclusion we will summarize those aspects of Anglo's activities which, though largely ignored so far, we feel it necessary to comment on before putting forward a final definition of the Group. These relate to the question of corporate control within the Group and to the international scope of its activities.

Throughout this study we have tended to view the interests of the Anglo American Group and those of its successive chairmen, Ernest and Harry Oppenheimer, as more or less synonymous with one another. The reason for this is obvious: since its inception the Anglo Group has been closely identified with subsequent generations of the Oppenheimer family. Anton Dunkelsbuhler, the Group's founder, was the uncle of both Ernest and Louis Oppenheimer, the two brothers who played such a crucial role in the Group's formative years. Ernest's son Harry followed his father as chairman and today Harry's son Nicholas is an important figure in the Group as is Harry's former son-in-law, Gordon Waddell. Furthermore, within the Group's structure—and yet never in the forefront of Group activity—are to be found private companies, such as Brenthurst Investment Trust (named after Harry Oppenheimer's private home) and E. Oppenheimer and Son, which tend to be dominated by members of the Oppenheimer family. This latter company, whose origins date back to the 1860s, has had a particularly close association with the Group throughout its history. The question which immediately presents itself, of course, is that of the precise nature of the association between the Oppenheimer family and the Anglo American Group. Posed in general terms, the question of the relationship between families or individuals with large holdings in giant corporations and the operations of these corporations is one which is of particular interest to social scientists at a number of levels. One of these concerns the potential for manipulation that such a relationship might open up, while another concerns the issue of the way in which control is exercised within such a corporation. As far as the Oppenheimer family and Anglo American are concerned, we do not intend to explore the former question, but we are interested in the latter: i.e., in the nature of the relationship between the family and the Group to the extent that it raises theoretical questions about corporate control. There is a broad body of literature which argues that the diffusion of ownership which has accompanied the historical rise of large public corporations has been accompanied by an inevitable dilution of corporate control. Furthermore, some versions of this thesis claim that under monopoly capitalism 'ownership' and 'control' have been separated from one another, leading to a situation in which a 'managerial class' emerges in control of company operations (see, for instance, Berle, 1954; Burnham, 1960). At first sight it seems as if there is a good deal of truth in these propositions and that there is no reason why they should not be applicable to Anglo American. The Group does indeed consist largely of public corporations in which 'the public' is free to participate. Furthermore, the ownership structure within the Group is highly decentralized, thus suggesting a dilution of owners' control. However, against this, we have the undisputed fact of the Oppenheimer family's domination of the Group over many years. The question is: how does this domination occur and what are its implications for the application of the above theories to Anglo American?

The first point to note is that the internal control structure within the Anglo American Group is highly decentralized. Four holding companies form the inner core of the Group's control structure: the Anglo American Corporation, De Beers Consolidated, the Rand Selection Corporation and Charter Consolidated. Between them there is a complex network of cross-holdings through which each company holds only a minority share in each of its partners (see Figure 6 in Appendix 2). However, *together* these minority holdings add up to a substantial majority share in each company so that, as the *Financial Mail* put it: 'Any international giant attempting [a take-over] on a share swop basis would probably end up in the uncomfortable position of having Oppenheimer as its biggest single shareholder.'[1] The importance of this from our present point of view is that it means that it is possible for the Oppenheimer family to dominate the Group as a whole through holding only a minority of the shares in each of the four leading companies. An examination of the Anglo American Corporation's share register at three-yearly intervals reveals that, in 1973, 1976 and 1979, Harry Oppenheimer and his son, Nicholas, between them owned respectively 20.4 per cent, 20.25 per cent and 16.4 per cent of the corporation's total share capital.[2] Though extremely large in absolute terms, these holdings on their own were not sufficient to exert direct control. In 1977, for instance, De Beers alone owned 33 per cent of the Anglo American Corporation. However, if the Oppenheimers' holdings in the Anglo American Corporation are combined with the family's minority shares in other Group companies (especially its stake in De Beers through Consolidated Diamond Mines of South West Africa), these holdings would seem to give the Oppenheimers an almost unassailable position in the Group.

Yet, of course, the family's position can never be totally secure. It is always possible that some outsider or some new coalition from within may appear and buy up sufficient shares to oust the Oppenheimers from their dominant position. At this point the role of a private company like E. Oppenheimer and Son seems to be important within the Group since it helps to promote a sense of *esprit de corps* among senior management and personnel. Not only does this help to discourage a possible internal coup but, in the face of a take-over threat from outside, the danger of disunity within the ranks is subverted. The way this works in practice is quite difficult to discern precisely, since E. Oppenheimer and Son is no longer a public corporation (it converted to a private concern on 1 February 1966) and therefore does not publicly divulge the kind of information which would facilitate an inquiry of this kind. However, prior to going private the company was controlled through a majority shareholding by the Oppenheimer family. In addition, the family encouraged minority participation by non-family members who were often senior Group management and personnel. In terms of the Articles of Association of the company, the terms on which this latter participation occurred were at the sole discretion of the directors who were, for instance, able to determine the price at which shares could be bought and sold.[3] In the light of this it is interesting to observe that in 1966 all the directors of the Anglo American Corporation were also shareholders in and nominees of E. Oppenheimer and Son.[4] Since most of these directors also held key positions on the boards of other Anglo Group companies, it seems reasonable to assume that the Oppenheimer family's control over E. Oppenheimer and Son gave it an effective influence over Group affairs which exceeded that which was immediately apparent from a perusal of the share registers of the companies concerned. If this is so, then it plays havoc with theoretical notions that public ownership *necessarily* leads to a dilution of corporate control. On the contrary, it suggests that public ownership might do no more than obscure the existence of a highly centralized control structure.

Arising out of the analysis we have developed here, we would argue that under monopoly capitalism ownership and control in fact remain tightly interwoven. Certainly, we would not wish to dispute the notion that the emergence of large public corporations has brought with it a diffusion of ownership; nor even would we deny that monopolies have indeed spawned a professional, bureaucratic élite which administers the day-to-day affairs of these large and cumbersome institutions. But, following our investigation of Anglo American, we would argue that power may often be expressed through more subtle forms than simply control over 51 per cent of a company's shares and that the existence of a bureaucracy still leaves open the question of who controls the bureaucrats. Consequently, we have discovered nothing in our analysis of Anglo which leads us to believe that the era of monopoly capitalism brings with it a dilution of corporate control—or, more fundamentally, an end to the control of massive resources by a few. On the contrary, the monopoly era only throws up new organizational forms, such as multinational combines, through which ever greater financial and productive resources are brought within the reach of the few, thereby increasing their power in society a thousandfold.

This leads us to the second question we wished to address: that of the international scope of Anglo American's activities. So far we have addressed the Group largely as a South African-oriented concern and have examined the extent to which its power has increased in South African society. But Anglo American's activities are not confined to South Africa: the Group is, in every sense, an international combine whose various interests reach across five continents. In concluding this analysis of the Group we need to adopt an international perspective and look, briefly, at its position within world capitalism. This will help both to locate the Group in its international context and to illuminate an often neglected aspect of South African capitalist development: its impact on international affairs. As we shall see, the world-wide network of economic relations which Anglo American is constantly forging is no freak phenomenon: it expresses the growing strength of monopoly capitalism in South Africa. And in southern Africa, where it is most heavily concentrated, this strength emerges in the political and economic form of imperialism.

An inspection of the main holdings of the four financial companies which in 1976 formed the inner core of Anglo's Group structure reflects its character as predominantly a South African-based mining-finance conglomerate (Appendix 2). But, as we saw in Chapter 6, one of these inner-core companies, Charter Consolidated, is based in London, from where it undertakes investment on a world scale. If we widen our scope to include the ten remaining companies which hold the majority of Group interests this same pattern of South African and non-South African companies emerges. Alongside companies like AMGOLD, AMCOAL, AMIC and AMAPROP (whose primary holdings, respectively, are in South African gold, coal, industry and property), we find a spread of holding companies located outside South Africa: Mineral and Resources Corporation (MINORCO), Anglo American Corporation of Rhodesia (RHOAM), Zambian Copper Investments, Anglo American Corporation of Canada (AMCAN) and Australian Anglo American (AUSTRAM). And if we go wider still and examine the 109 financial companies which hold many of the Group's more important interests we find an even wider spread of non-South African-based companies that includes: Anglo American Corporation of Botswana, Zambian Anglo American Industrial Corporation, Anglo De Beers Forest Services (Lesotho), Angloswazi Investments, Anglo American Corporation of Central Africa, Charter France, Charter Overseas NV (Curaçao), Euranglo Ltd, Societa Nazionale Svilieppo Impresse Industriale (Italy), Anglo American Corporation of South Africa (Portugal), De Beers European Holdings, Bahamas International Trust Company, Cayman International Trust Company, Anglo American International, Anglo American Corporation do Brazil Limitada, Debhold Canada, Engelhard Hanovia Inc., and Anglo American Corporation of the United States.

It is thus clear that (in addition to its South African-based companies) over the years Anglo American has established a number of companies whose specific purpose is to build up Group interests outside South Africa. However, one should not assume that these are the only channels for the Group's non-South African investments. Most of its South African-based companies also include within their portfolios a wide range of investments in companies operating outside South Africa. For instance, of the 139 subsidiaries which AMIC held in 1976, 69 were located outside South Africa: 7 in Zimbabwe; 8 in Zambia; 2 each in Swaziland and Mozambique; 1 each in Botswana and Liberia; 8 in Britain; 4 in Federal Germany; 3 in the Netherlands; 1 each in Switzerland, Norway, Portugal, Luxembourg, Ireland, Sweden, France and Italy; 5 each in the United States of America and Canada; 2 in Mexico; 1 each in Brazil, Costa Rica, Bahamas and Chile; 7 in Australia; and 1 each in New Zealand and the Philippines.[5] The spread of international investments is thus extremely large and involves companies in a range of different economic activities. In 1976 at least 11 of Anglo's 27 leading financial companies (like banks and insurance companies) were located outside South Africa, as were 45 of its 193 major industrial and agricultural companies.[6] But it is principally through mining that the Group spreads itself internationally.

In 1976 Anglo was involved in over 250 different companies which were active in mining in at least 22 different countries of the world. These interests, which included mine holding, exploration, production and marketing concerns, were spread throughout an astonishing range of minerals and included 48 gold mines (some of which were uranium producers as well), 31 prospecting companies, 29 diamond companies, 28 coal mines, 22 copper and nickel mines, 10 oil ventures (including North Sea oil), 7 platinum mines, 5 tin mines, 5 iron mines, 2 chrome mines, 2 lead mines, 2 vanadium mines and one mine each in uranium, asbestos, potash, soda, lime, scheelite, manganese and silver. The 22 countries through which these interests were spread were: South Africa, Namibia, Zimbabwe, Zambia, Botswana, Lesotho, Swaziland, Angola, Tanzania, Mauretania, Madagascar, Britain, Ireland, Sweden, France, Portugal, Canada, Australia, Brazil, Mexico, Chile and Malaysia). This vast array of companies and international operations provides the basis for Anglo to link up with some of the world's most important international mining companies, such as ALCAN, American Metal Climax, Bethlehem Steel (US), International Nickel of Canada, Rio Tinto Zinc, Kennecott Copper (US) and Newmont Mining. But Anglo's links with the world's leading multinationals go far wider than just these *mining* companies, taking in an assortment of at least 73 international *banking* and *industrial* concerns.[7] Thus the Anglo American Group forms an important link in a vast and complex chain through which a relatively few massive international combines control the bulk of the productive resources in the capitalist world.

We will not go into any detail here on the way in which Anglo American rose to such international prominence, since that is itself a major task which goes well beyond our present scope. Yet a few comments on this theme do need to be made in order to assess correctly the relationship between Anglo's international operations and its base in South Africa. Perhaps most important is to identify the precise point in time at which this international expansion commenced.

Although (like all the major South African mining groups) Anglo had originally been based in London, the decision to transfer the Group's head office to South Africa and the subsequent collapse of the London-based Consolidated Mines Selection Co. resulted in Anglo's foreign interests being largely neglected. Although during the 1920s, 1930s and 1940s these were built up again the new investments tended to be concentrated in southern Africa, especially in Namibian and Angolan diamonds and in Northern and Southern Rhodesian copper and other minerals. The 1950s were spent mainly developing the new gold fields in South Africa, but in 1958 an event occurred which was to prove crucial to Anglo's subsequent international expansion: the take-over of the Central Mining–Rand Mines Group. Carried through in conjunction with the American-based Engelhard Group, this coup gave Anglo an important foot-hold on the American continent. With a stream of revenue now pouring out of its South African gold mines, Anglo began to reorganize its scattered non-South African interests. Consolidated Mines Selection was resurrected in London to combine these interests under a centralized control at the same time as Anglo, again in conjunction with Engelhard, took control of a major Canadian mining conglomerate, the Hudson Bay Mining and Smelting Co. No sooner was this take-over completed than in 1964 Anglo merged Consolidated Mines Selection with the recently acquired Central Mining Company and with another old imperialist war-horse, the Chartered (or British South Africa) Co., to form Charter Consolidated. From that moment onwards Anglo American's international interests grew in both scope and size.

The important point here is that Anglo's growing international presence corresponds exactly with the early phase of its diversified expansion inside South Africa. At precisely the time Anglo was creating a local money market in South Africa and taking its first major steps into South African industry (such as through the Highveld Steel project) it was also making its first significant moves to carve out an international presence for itself through Charter. These very different phenomena in fact do have a common origin in the gold mines of the Orange Free State. It was the revenue being generated here which provided the stimulus and the financial means for both aspects of Group expansion, helping to establish Anglo American not only as a diversified industrial and financial conglomerate in South Africa, but also as a multinational combine.

There is, however, a further aspect of Anglo's international expansion which is of special interest—and that is the unlikely origins of MINORCO, which is Charter's most important partner in the international field. MINORCO began life as the Zambian Anglo American Corporation (ZAMANGLO), which held Anglo's interests in Zambia, consisting mainly of a half share in the country's large copper industry. Following political independence the Zambian government nationalized the copper mines, which involved *inter alia* buying up 51 per cent of ZAMANGLO. Full compensation was paid to the company's shareholders in American dollars and without any restriction being placed on their repatriation abroad. Shortly afterwards Anglo American established MINORCO in the Atlantic tax-haven of Bermuda. Fed with revenue from the Zambian copper mines (handily converted into dollars), MINORCO became a major international force during the 1970s. With Charter concentrating its investment programme on Africa, Europe and Australasia, MINORCO largely assumed responsibility for the American side, investing in Latin

America, Canada and the United States. Nor are these latter investments small-scale undertakings: by the start of the 1980s MINORCO had become the largest single foreign investor in the United States of America (with a total revenue of $26 570m). This position was held ahead of established oil giants like the Royal Dutch Shell Group (ranked second with a revenue of $19 830m) and BP (ranked third with a revenue of $11 023m).[8] It is one of the ironies of history that a struggling underdeveloped country such as Zambia should have created the original wealth which enabled a South African multinational to become subsequently the largest foreign investor in the world's most developed capitalist state.

These international developments establish beyond doubt that Anglo American can be understood in no other way than as a multinational—and one of the world's more important multinationals at that. The fact that its highly decentralized control structure prevents the Anglo Group from appearing on the list of the world's top 100 companies should not deceive anyone into believing that it does not belong in such exalted company. Individual Group companies, such as De Beers and the Anglo American Corporation itself, have on occasion reached the lower rungs of this list and, undoubtedly, were the Group's interests to be combined for these purposes it would be a permanent fixture. However, not only is the Group large by international standards, but the very way in which it conducts its international operations is an expression of its international strength. No longer does the Group simply spread itself across the world on an unco-ordinated basis: instead, it neatly divides the world up, creating Charter to take responsibility for Group expansion in one half and MINORCO to handle the other. Nor when we speak of the world in this context do we mean only the capitalist world. Recent evidence suggests that in certain spheres at least (such as diamonds, gold and platinum) collaboration takes place between Anglo American and the Soviet Union over international pricing policy.[9]

But perhaps it is through its American involvement that the Group's current international strength is most aptly expressed. The fact that Anglo should appear well ahead of such international giants as Shell, BP, ICI, Unilever and Volkswagen (to mention only a few) in the list of foreign investors in the United States suggests a major new direction in Anglo's international investment strategy. But even more startling is the fact that the Group commands sufficient financial resources to attain such a position. Such a development, of course, may have dire implications for classical theories of imperialism which assume a one-way flow of investment (export of capital) from the capitalist centre to the periphery (see, for instance, Lenin, 1973b, and Frank, 1970b). When corporations like Anglo emerge—based in the capitalist periphery and exporting capital to the centre—it seems as if these theories are turned upside down. The question that underlies this debate is that of the relationship between Anglo American and South African capitalism. If one assumes that there is no integral relationship between the two—that Anglo is simply a free-floating international institution without a 'home base' in South Africa or anywhere else—then Anglo's growing investments in the capitalist centres tell us absolutely nothing about centre–periphery relations under capitalism. If, on the other hand, we argue that Anglo's massive presence in South Africa locates it as a specifically *South African* institution, then its growing involvement in the capitalist centres *does* have implications for centre–periphery theories of imperialism. In particular, it poses serious problems for those theories which assume that imperialism promotes growth in the centre at the inevitable expense of the chronic underdevelopment of the periphery.

In this work we have adopted the perspective that Anglo American can only be understood as a South African-based multinational combine. It is the monopoly control which the Group came to exert primarily in South African gold and diamond mining which has been the key to its subsequent success both in South Africa and abroad. Furthermore, we have argued that, primarily because of its position as a major producer of strategic minerals, South African capitalism has undergone important economic transformations, breaking free of chronic patterns of under-development and establishing a relatively strong industrial base (though still retaining a dependency relation with the capitalist centres). Similarly, we have argued that these changes in the nature of South African capitalism were accompanied by changes in its form, as monopoly relations permeated first mining and then the industrial and financial sectors of the economy, ultimately giving rise to monopoly capitalism. At every stage of this process we have seen that Anglo American played a decisive role. Of crucial significance here is the way in which these various processes coalesced in the late 1950s and 1960s. It was during this period that Anglo American, benefiting especially from its postwar investments in gold, began to diversify into local industry, finance and property, and to take its first major steps on the road to international expansion. Equally, it was during this period that South Africa's economy developed along monopoly lines. Thus Anglo's international 'take-off' occurs at precisely the time South African capitalism begins to transform itself into monopoly capitalism. The question is whether these changes are coincidental or whether they express another transition: that of the evolution of South African imperialism.

To answer this question one has to go far wider than simply recording South Africa's growing economic links internationally. In addition, one has to look at the nature of these links, their effect on the host economies, the political relations which accompany them and, most important, the impact on the social classes in the host country. These questions clearly take us well beyond our present scope and, in any event, we would be foolish to try and argue that Anglo's involvement in the United States of America or Britain implies that these states are being colonized by South African capitalism. But what of smaller and weaker states which would be more susceptible to South Africa's economic and political influence? Does the transition to monopoly capitalism in South Africa have implications for these states and, if so, what are they?

There is in fact considerable evidence that South Africa's relations with African states, and in particular those in southern Africa, have undergone a profound change in the post-Second World War period in which monopoly capitalism established itself in South Africa. Namibia provides probably the most clear-cut example of this. Although administered by South Africa since 1919, the relationship between South Africa and Namibia changed dramatically after the Second World War. Between 1920 and 1942 Namibia's GDP did not grow at all and by 1945 was only 52 per cent higher than it had been in 1920. Between 1946 and 1962, however, the GDP grew by a massive 573 per cent and, between 1962 and 1973, by a further 320 per cent.[10] This high rate of postwar expansion is exceptional by international standards and reflects a new direction in South African economic policy in Namibia. Prior to the war South Africa had done virtually nothing to develop Namibia's economic resources: state aid had been largely confined to resettling a relatively small number of white farmers and Anglo American had actually reduced the productive capacity of its diamond mines in order to protect its other diamond interests. After the war, however, the South African state and individual capitalists were instrumental in initiating Namibia's economic recovery. Anglo rejuvenated the diamond industry and, together with other South African and international monopolies, participated in a range of other mining ventures. In 1964 the South African-appointed Odendaal Commission recommended 'a broad programme of capital expenditure' in Namibia and, following this, the South African state began pumping money into the Namibian economy (at least R150m was injected between 1964 and 1969).[11] The question is: what was it that produced this *volte face* in South Africa's economic policy?

Undoubtedly, social and political factors, like the growth of a Namibian resistance movement committed to securing political independence from South Africa and the United Nation's decision to put an end to South Africa's administration, were important influences in this respect. But it is revealing that this policy change begins at the same time as the South African economy begins to transform itself along monopoly lines—that is, during the 1950s—and that the restructuring of Namibia's political economy, which the Odendaal Commission initiates, is carried through at precisely the time that the process of monopoly transformation in South Africa reaches new heights—that is, during the 1960s and 1970s. It is thus possible that the transition to monopoly capitalism in South Africa also produced the phenomenon of South African imperialism. This view is in fact confirmed by an inspection of the nature of the links forged over this period between South Africa and Namibia and of their effects on Namibia's political and economic independence. In general, these links have tended to tie Namibia into a position of increasingly strong dependence on South African capitalism which denies its political independence, distorts its economy and undermines its society as a whole.[12]

What seems to have happened is that in the pre-Second World War period, despite the fact that South Africa was in political control of Namibia, South African capitalism was too weak to gain any major economic advantage from this relationship. As we saw, during that period South African capitalism was itself restrained by its relationship to the European imperialist powers. However, the gradual shift in the form of that relationship during the 1930s and after, coupled with the important developments in South African mining and industry after the war, greatly strengthened South African capitalism, giving it the capacity from then on to exploit Namibia's economic potential. As the process of monopolization intensified in South Africa, so that country's political, economic and military stranglehold over Namibia has tightened. Whatever the formal legal relation between the two countries, Smuts's words spoken immediately after the war—that Namibia's relationship to South Africa 'more nearly approximated to that of a colonial possession than anything else'—have undoubtedly been proved correct by history (cited in Wellington, 1967, p. 329).

But it is not just in South Africa's relationship with Namibia that the former's imperialistic tendencies have manifested themselves since the war. The extremely close economic ties which South Africa has forged with the former High Commission Territories over the last few decades have inevitably undermined the political independence of these states as well. In 1965 South Africa's Prime Minister, Dr Verwoerd, stated: 'I believe that the one thing which really counts in international relationships is common economic interests. So far as these Governments [of Botswana, Lesotho and Swaziland] are concerned, their political interests will be dominated by their economic interests' (cited in Maryse-Cockram, 1970). Nor was this just bombastic rhetoric. Botswana's first President, Seretse Khama, openly acknowledged the strength of Verwoerd's position when he said:

> We fully appreciate that it is wholly in our interests to preserve as friendly and neighbourly relations with the Republic of South Africa as possible. Our economic links with the Republic are virtually indissoluble. Economically we are directly tied to the Republic for communica-

tions, for markets, for our beef exports, for labour on the mines, and in many other respects.[13]

The economic and political strength which South African capitalism acquired through its monopoly transformation enabled the state to spread its influence throughout the whole southern African region during the 1960s and 1970s, extending into Mozambique, Angola, Malawi, Zambia and (as it then was) Rhodesia. Nor has this influence been confined to southern Africa. The South African state's 'outward' policy of the 1960s, its 'dialogue' policy of the early 1970s and its 'detente' policy of the late 1970s were all intended to promote South Africa's influence throughout the African continent. And even today, though revolutions in Angola, Mozambique and Zimbabwe have forced the South African state to change tack and adopt a more militaristic policy, the fundamental drive towards outward expansion—towards imperialist domination—is stronger than ever.

It is not our purpose here to analyse whether or not this expansionist policy will be successful, nor even to analyse the social and political forces which are building up in opposition. All we are concerned to do is to establish that South Africa's transition to monopoly capitalism has been accompanied by a corresponding drive towards imperialism. If this is in fact the case then it means that, even though its influence is as yet largely confined only to southern Africa, South Africa has become an active participant in forging the international network of economic and political relations which constitutes the modern system of imperialism. As such South Africa can no longer be classified as simply an underdeveloped Third World country, but rather must be ranked as an imperialist power located on the periphery of world capitalism. Certainly, because of its historical location, South Africa is considerably weaker than those 'more traditional' imperialist powers which are located in the capitalist centres. Yet it would be quite wrong to assume that this means that therefore these powers will willingly exert pressure to force South Africa to abandon policies of which they might disapprove. Though the South African economy remains technologically dependent on the major imperialist powers, the links between South Africa and these powers, especially through monopoly investments, trade and finance, are so firmly integrated that it would be almost unthinkable that these imperialist powers would be willing to use this technological dependence as a weapon against South Africa.

The position which South African capitalism has achieved for itself is therefore one which makes a nonsense of any imperialist theory which argues that perpetual underdevelopment and economic backwardness are inevitable consequences for countries on the capitalist periphery. Clearly, the case of South Africa (as well as of others like Brazil) poses serious problems for theories which base themselves either on the historical experiences of the early twentieth century or on the current experiences of countries which do not possess commodities for which there is a large export demand. Without abandoning an historical approach, we need to evolve a theory of imperialism which draws on the current experiences of countries like South Africa as much as those of Tanzania, Upper Volta and Paraguay. Such a theory should not only be sharply critical of traditional notions of 'development' and 'underdevelopment', but should also question whether historical notions of 'centre' and 'periphery' still have the same meaning today as before. Does it in fact make sense to argue, as we have done in the preceding paragraph, that South Africa is still located on the periphery of world capitalism or is such an approach not too 'geographically' determined? Should we not rather speak of South Africa as being today a part of a wider capitalist centre, but if so, how then do we distinguish it from the position of the older imperialist powers? And what, too, of the changing relations among these latter powers and, especially, of the implications of Britain's current industrial decline? Today the processes of economic and political change are developing more rapidly than ever before and theories of imperialism which remain locked in the events and conditions of the early years of this century are hopelessly inadequate as explanations of these modern developments. There is an urgent necessity to produce a theory of imperialism which can satisfactorily answer the kinds of questions which this study of South Africa has raised.

Thus to conclude we would briefly sum up our findings on the nature of Anglo American and its relationship to South African capitalism today as follows. The Anglo American Group has evolved into a multinational combine which is engaged on a world scale in a wide range of economic activities of which mining is the most important. These interests—and therefore the Group's influence—reach out from a power base which is firmly rooted in South African society. That society itself is far from static. Over the past one hundred years it has transformed itself from an underdeveloped chattel of imperialism into an aggressive imperialist power which exhibits many of the characteristics of a monopoly capitalist society. Foremost among these is the decisive power which monopoly groups like Anglo American wield within that society. Yet if over the past century Anglo American and South African capitalism have achieved an awesome degree of power it is as well to remember that in the process they have also created a countervailing force which may well have the potential to wrest that power from them. The capitalist class which developed the world's largest gold fields has also produced the largest proletariat in Africa.

NOTES

1. *Financial Mail*, Special Survey, 'Inside the Anglo Power House', p. 17.
2. These holdings, which were split equally between the two, involved 13.25 million shares apiece in 1973; 13.34 million apiece in 1976; and 18.33 million apiece in 1979. (Anglo American Corp. of SA, *Annual Report, 1973, 1976* and *1979*.)
3. Para. 166(c)(i) of the company's Articles of Association stated: 'The shares shall be under the control of the Directors, who may allot issue or otherwise dispose of the same to such person or persons at such times and with such rights and privileges and generally on such terms and conditions and either at a premium or otherwise as the Directors may think fit.' See also para. 166(c)(ii).
4. Letter to Mr. H. Oppenheimer from H. B. Samuel, dated 2 September 1966.
5. AMIC, *Annual Report, 1976*, pp. 28–30.
6. Among Anglo's more important financial interests outside South Africa were: British and Rhodesian Discount House, Southampton Assurance Co. of Rhodesia, Rhodesian Acceptances, Merchant Bank (Zambia) Ltd, Standard Bank of Angola, Standard Bank of Mozambique, Standard Charter Bank Group, Compagnie Financière de Paris et des Pays-Bas, and International Pacific Corp. (Australia) Ltd.

   Among Anglo's more important industrial interests outside South Africa were: Chilanga Cement, Durham Industries of Canada, Dunlop (Zambia), Duncan Gilbey and Matheson (Zambia), Explosives (Zambia), Engelhard Industries, Industriade Caju Mocita (Mozambique), Kenya Fertilizers, Mozambique Fisheries, Metal Fabricators of Zambia, National Milling Company (Zambia), Zambia Breweries, Rhodesian Diamond and Carbide, Rhodesian Iron and Steel Corp., Rhodesian Alloys, South Wales Group, Scandiamant Aktiebolag, Terra Chemicals International, Rhodesian Milling Co., Unitor (Zambia), Werff Brothers, White Pass and Yukon, Wendt GMBH, Zinc Oxides of Canada, Zambia Clay Industries, Ultra High Pressure Units (Ireland), De Beers Industrial Diamond Division (Ireland), Industrias de Caju, Antenes SARL, Gerencia Industrial Limitada, and Christensen and Boart Oilfield Products. (See Appendix 2.)
7. These include: Banca Commerciale Italiane, Banque de Paris et des Pays-Bas, Crédit Foncier Franco-Canadien, Barclays Bank, Bowater Paper, Cayzer Group, British Steel Corp., Rheem International, Computer Sciences Corp., Cory Mann George, Deutsche Bank, Dunlop, Eastern Stainless Steel, First National City Bank of New York, ICI, IMI Japan, Johnson Matthey, Kleinwort Benson, Klöchner and Co., KZO, Volvo, Mazda, Lazard Brothers, Manbré and Gartons, Mitsubishi, Mitsui, Morgan Grenfell, Morgan Guaranty Trust, Nalco Chemicals, P. & O. Shipping Group, Petrofina, Rothschilds, Royal Dutch Shell, Selection Trust, Société Generale Belge, Société Nationale des Pétroles d'Aquitaine, Somic, Standard Chartered Bank, Standard Oil of Indiana, Titan Products, Union Bank of Switzerland, US Natural Oil, United Transport, Metropolitan Vickers, and Weyerhauser. In addition the Group is linked in one way or another in productive ventures with at least eight different governments: those of South Africa, Chile, Iran, Swaziland, Botswana, Tanzania, the United Kingdom and Zambia. (See Appendix 3.)
8. *Forbes*, Special Report: Spotlight on International Business, 6 July 1981, pp. 83–91.
9. 'Gold and Diamonds: The Kremlin Connection', BBC1 *Panorama* programme, 6 April 1981.
10. The figures for the GDP were as follows: 1920—R13.0m; 1942—R12.2m; 1945—R19.8m; 1946—R21.8m; 1962—R146.7m; and 1973—R615.6m. (Report of the Commission of Inquiry into South West African Affairs, 1962–3, RP no. 12/1964, p. 319; and SA Department of Statistics, *South West Africa Survey 1974*, p. 33.)
11. For details of these various economic changes and for an assessment of South African state policy see Innes (1981b, also 1978).
12. For details see the articles cited above.
13. Cited in South African Institute of Race Relations, *A Survey of Race Relations in South Africa 1966* (1967).

APPENDICES

APPENDIX 1

Tables and Figures

Table 1   South African Diamond Production and Sales 1867–1972

Year	Quantity (carats)[a]	Value (£)	Year	Quantity (carats)[a]	Value (£)
1867		500	1913	5 163 547	11 389 807
1868		450	1914	2 801 017	5 487 194
1869		24 813	1915	103 386	399 810
1870		153 460	1916	2 346 330	5 728 391
1871		403 349	1917	2 902 417	7 713 810
1872		1 618 076	1918	2 537 360	7 114 867
1873		1 648 451	1919	2 588 017	11 734 495
1874		1 313 334	1920	2 545 017	14 762 899
1875		1 548 634	1921	806 643	3 103 448
1876		1 513 107	1922	669 559[b]	2 266 631
1877		1 723 145	1923	2 053 094	6 038 207
1878		2 159 298	1924	2 440 398	8 033 406
1879		2 579 859	1925	2 430 129	8 198 128
1880		3 367 897	1926	3 217 966	10 683 597
1881		4 176 202	1927	4 708 038	12 392 308
1882		3 992 002	1928	4 372 857	16 677 772
1883	2 312 248	2 359 466	1929	3 661 212	10 590 113
1884	2 204 786	2 562 623	1930	3 163 591	8 340 719
1885	2 287 263	2 228 680	1931	2 119 156	4 182 523
1886	3 047 639	3 261 574	1932	798 382	1 679 600
1887	3 598 930	4 251 670	1933	506 553	1 560 404
1888	3 565 780	3 608 218	1934	440 313	1 437 591
1889	2 962 004	4 325 187	1935	676 722	2 171 267
1890	2 443 777	3 837 276	1936	623 923	2 125 216
1891	2 880 308	3 556 603	1937	1 030 434	3 444 678
1892	2 968 375	3 799 026	1938	1 238 608	3 496 243
1893	2 899 475	4 041 255	1939	1 249 828	2 604 172
1894	2 809 078	3 510 152	1940	543 463	1 620 467
1895	3 105 132	3 983 010	1941	158 422	946 095
1896	3 212 392	4 034 035	1942	118 821	701 964
1897	3 052 640	3 821 771	1943	302 329	1 812 175
1898	3 270 917	4 128 321	1944	933 682	5 846 179
1899	2 507 647	3 826 631	1945	1 222 945	6 425 096
1900	1 844 341	3 365 994	1946	1 349 099	9 041 762
1901	2 781 385	5 387 955	1947	1 242 423	7 166 528
1902	2 486 327	4 949 808	1948	1 382 327	8 719 356
1903	2 463 692	4 833 040	1949	1 264 794	7 646 727
1904	3 683 157	7 208 645	1950	1 731 510	10 854 496
1905	3 368 789	6 204 547	1951	2 229 000[c]	14 043 000
1906	4 136 236	9 596 643	1952	2 383 000	14 014 000
1907	5 170 812	9 985 926	1953	2 718 000	13 914 000
1908	4 091 121	5 406 581	1954	2 858 000	13 398 000
1909	5 169 871	7 199 359	1955	2 629 000	13 186 000
1910	5 456 558	8 189 197	1956	2 586 000	13 420 000
1911	4 891 999	8 746 724	1957	2 552 409	14 459 754
1912	5 071 882	10 061 489	1958	2 747 414	15 553 620

效>8

1959	2 843 148	15 658 293	1967	6 625 728	R59 308 388
1960	2 997 861	16 926 094	1968	6 941 581	R75 575 294
1961	3 788 000	19 185 000	1969	7 677 005	R103 919 149
1962	3 996 858	R36 482 578[d]	1970	7 198 457	R75 524 142
1963	4 274 767	R36 367 689	1971	6 794 782	R64 684 517
1964	4 451 065	R44 203 470	1972	7 187 741	R90 028 778
1965	4 845 049	R49 601 476	Total		*£1 820 418 550*
1966	5 732 289	R61 595 248			

[a] Figures for quantity not available prior to 1883.
[b] From 1922 onwards quantity is measured by *metric* carats.
[c] Figures for 1951–6 inclusive and for 1961 are rounded off in thousands.
[d] From 1962 onwards all values are expressed in Rands. Conversion rate: £1 = R2.

Sources   The table has been constructed from the following sources: Figures for 1867–82 are taken from Houghton and Dagut (1972), vol. 1 (1860–99), pp. 272–3; figures for 1883–1917 are taken from Union of SA, *Official Year Book of the Union of SA*, no. 2, 1918, p. 494; figures for 1918–27 are taken from Union of SA, *Official Year Book of the Union and of Basutoland, Bechuanaland Protectorate and Swaziland*, no. 10, 1927–8 p. 517; figures for 1928–36 are from Union of SA, *Official Year Book of the Union of SA*, no. 18, 1937, p. 875; figures for 1937–40 are from ibid., no. 22, 1941, p. 826.; figures for 1941–50 are from ibid., no. 26, 1950, p. 998; figures for 1951–4 are from ibid., no. 29, 1956–7, pp. 628–9; figures for 1955, 1956 and 1961 are from SA Bureau of Statistics: *Statistical Year Book 1965*, p. L7; figures for 1957–72 (excluding 1961) are from SA Department of Statistics, *South African Statistics, 1978*, p. 11.2.

Table 2 *South African Gold Output, 1884–1975*[a]

Year	Tons treated metric tons '000[b]	Fine gold kg	Realized value R'000	Year	Tons treated metric tons '000	Fine gold kg	Realized value R'000
1884		74[d]	20[d]	1930	29 232	333 316	91 040
1885		44	12	1931	30 098	338 337	92 412
1886		254	69	1932	32 409	359 511	98 195
1887		1240	339	1933	34 317	342 565	137 373
1888		7084	1935	1934	37 100	325 960	144 622
1889		10 915	2981	1935	41 529	335 109	153 066
1890		13 690	3739	1936	45 398	352 596	158 990
1891		21 413	5849	1937	48 183	364 986	165 113
1892		33 251	9082	1938	51 347	378 262	173 339
1893	2010[c]	40 130	10 961	1939	55 523	398 793	197 886
1894	2568	56 142	15 334	1940	61 356	436 895	235 981
1895	3136	62 758	17 141	1941	63 899	448 128	242 049
1896	3639	63 005	17 209	1942	63 636	439 394	237 331
1897	4831	85 336	23 308	1943	57 003	398 261	215 114
1898	6651	118 923	32 482	1944	55 333	381 939	206 298
1899	6023	113 151	30 906	1945	55 582	380 229	210 569
1900		10 852	2964[e]	1946	53 784	370 976	205 744
1901	374	8041	2196	1947	51 115	348 368	193 205
1902	3100	53 437	14 596	1948	52 466	360 329	199 839
1903	5538	92 422	25 244	1949	53 906	364 068	229 730
1904	7310	117 291	32 036	1950	56 459	361 849	289 552
1905	10 125	152 665	41 698	1951	55 890	358 202	285 896
1906	12 312	180 187	49 216	1952	56 922	367 602	294 261
1907	14 082	200 685	54 814	1953	55 639	371 395	295 130
1908	16 508	219 500	59 953	1954	59 284	411 720	329 351

1909	18 637	226 957	1955	61 990	62 366	454 154	365 491
1910	19 713	234 252	1956	63 983	63 730	494 442	396 999
1911	22 606	256 642	1957	70 098	62 550	529 715	425 170
1912	24 150	283 315	1958	77 383	62 295	549 177	440 049
1913	24 219	273 671	1959	74 749	66 190	624 107	500 272
1914	24 226	261 147	1960	71 328	66 988	665 086	536 019
1915	26 570	282 930	1961	77 276	68 547	713 562	574 900
1916	26 759	289 168	1962	78 982	71 995	792 890	636 582
1917	25 593	280 503	1963	76 615	74 087	853 229	686 312
1918	23 142	261 841	1964	71 500	75 351	905 470	730 490
1919	22 358	259 143	1965	70 781	75 396	950 332	766 549
1920	22 400	253 756	1966	91 212	74 964	960 466	776 197
1921	21 722	252 831	1967	86 164	74 038	949 679	768 098
1922	18 264	218 031	1968	64 687	73 751	967 146	784 859[f]
1923	24 893	284 568	1969	83 150	76 280	972 956	840 504
1924	26 522	297 817	1970	89 479	79 965	1 000 417	831 223
1925	26 628	298 519	1971	81 536	78 659	976 297	899 006
1926	27 658	309 628	1972	84 570	73 245	909 631	1 159 916
1927	27 429	314 845	1973	85 995	76 018	855 179	1 789 290
1928	28 206	322 054	1974	87 964	76 000	758 559	2 619 813
1929	28 679	323 860	1975	88 457	75 126	713 447	2 560 395
			Totals		3 373 532	33 372 699	26 262 203

a Includes non-members of the Chamber of Mines.
b Information not available 1884–92.
c Tons milled prior to 1910—in respect of Witwatersrand only.
d From 1884 to 1894 an additional 177 kg of gold, valued at R48 450, was produced in the Cape Province and Natal.
e 1900–2: South African War period.
f 1968–71: revenue received (from Chamber sources).
Source Chamber of Mines of SA, *Eighty-sixth Annual Report, 1975*, p. 58.

Table 3 Composition of the Black Labour Force in the South African Gold Mines, 1904–76

Year	South Africa	Basutoland (Lesotho)	Bechuanaland (Botswana)	Swaziland	Mozambique	N & S Rhodesia + Nyasaland	Total	Foreign workers as % of total
1904	18 057	2240	531	492	50 997	4550	77 000	76.4
1905	11 842	1571	591	639	59 284	7005	81 000	85.4
1908	58 303	4604	1221	1509	81 920	1266	149 000	60.8
1909	61 135	3895	1020	1413	85 282	4160	157 000	61.0
1912	64 710	9970	1146	3705	91 546	2941	191 000	57.2
1913	58 497	8804	1800	2892	80 832	2077	155 000	62.2
1915	93 396	12 355	2950	4910	83 338	1148	198 000	52.8
1918	59 534	10 349	1817	4123	81 306	805	158 000	62.3
1920	59 269	12 680	1435	2802	96 188	605	173 000	65.7
1922	78 983	14 475	2690	5472	80 959	403	183 000	56.8
1927	84 495	17 264	1483	3655	107 672	430	215 000	60.7
1929	79 950	21 586	2337	3977	96 657	389	205 000	61.0
1931	112 548	30 781	3367	5062	73 924	316	226 000	50.2
1932	131 692	31 711	4963	5872	58 483	280	233 000	43.5
1936	165 933	45 982	7155	7027	88 499	3402	318 000	47.8
1939	155 398	48 385	8785	6686	81 335	1941	323 000	51.9
1942	214 243	—	—	—	74 507	21 656	310 406	31.0
1943	207 379	—	—	—	84 478	23 213	315 071	34.2

Year								
1944	185 658	—	—	—	78 950	26 770	291 378	36.3
1945	210 485	—	—	—	78 806	30 856	320 147	34.3
1946	126 000	38 200	7000	5500	96 300	32 400	305 400	58.7
1951	108 000	35 700	9100	5600	106 500	41 200	306 100	64.7
1956	116 100	39 900	10 400	5400	102 900	59 800	334 500	65.3
1960	150 900	51 400	16 000	5600	95 500	82 800	396 700	63.3
1961	150 900	53 900	13 200	6500	100 200	89 100	413 900	63.5
1963	153 800	56 500	15 300	5800	88 700	74 200	394 300	60.9
1964	139 400	58 500	16 000	5500	97 500	71 800	388 800	64.1
1966	130 500	64 300	19 000	4300	109 000	56 300	383 000	65.9
1969	116 500	65 000	14 800	5000	99 800	69 900	371 100	68.8
1970	96 900	71 100	16 300	5400	113 300	98 200	401 200	75.8
1971	86 500	68 700	16 000	4800	102 400	107 800	386 000	77.6
1972	87 200	78 500	17 500	4300	97 700	129 200	414 300	78.9
1973	86 200	87 200	16 800	4500	99 400	128 000	422 200	79.5
1974	90 100	78 300	14 700	5500	101 800	73 100	363 500	75.2
1975	121 800	85 500	16 600	7200	118 000	15 500	364 700	66.6
1976	170 000	85 500	26 000	13 000	79 000	20 882	393 800	56.8

Sources 1904–39 figures from van der Horst (1942), pp. 216–17; 1940–5 figures from Chamber of Mines of South Africa, *Annual Reports, 1942, 1943, 1944 and 1945*; 1946–75 figures from F. Wilson (1976), p. 9; 1976 figure from D. Clarke (1977), Table 7, p. 22.

Table 4   Overall Productivity in Gold Mining, 1910–59

Date	Gold produced (fine oz)	Total labour employed	White workers	Black workers	Output per man (fine oz)
1910	7 531 000	224 347	25 634	198 713	33.57
1911	8 251 000	228 875	25 882	202 993	36.05
1912	9 109 000	231 355	24 981	206 374	39.37
1913	8 799 000	221 183	24 221	196 962	39.78
1914	8 396 000	202 385	22 025	180 360	41.49
1915	9 096 000	229 255	22 901	206 354	39.68
1916	9 297 000	238 054	23 086	214 968	39.05
1917	9 018 000	216 742	23 180	193 562	41.61
1918	8 414 000	211 773	23 397	188 376	39.73
1919	8 332 000	203 610	23 803	179 807	40.92
1920	8 158 000	207 808	22 837	184 971	39.26
1921	8 129 000	202 930	21 607	181 323	40.06
1922	7 010 000	186 339	14 681	171 658	37.62
1923	9 149 000	208 502	18 613	189 889	43.88
1924	9 575 000	210 986	19 448	191 538	45.38
1925	9 598 000	208 236	20 264	187 972	46.09
1926	9 955 000	215 747	20 685	195 062	46.14
1927	10 122 000	221 468	21 694	199 774	45.70
1928	10 354 000	231 190	22 532	208 658	44.79
1929	10 412 000	227 847	22 805	205 042	45.70
1930	10 716 000	236 305	22 895	213 410	45.35
1931	10 878 000	244 987	23 476	221 511	44.40
1932	11 559 000	253 274	24 335	228 939	45.64
1933	11 014 000	270 347	26 429	243 918	40.74
1934	10 480 000	299 954	30 235	269 719	34.94
1935	10 774 000	333 650	34 475	299 175	32.29
1936	11 336 000	361 459	37 844	323 615	31.36
1937	11 735 000	369 489	40 661	328 828	31.76
1938	12 161 000	386 607	43 087	343 520	31.46
1939	12 822 000	393 677	45 491	348 186	32.57
1940	14 047 000	428 051	47 698	380 353	32.82
1941	14 408 000	446 159	48 731	397 428	32.30
1942	14 127 000	434 284	48 536	385 748	32.53
1943	12 804 000	380 021	47 041	332 980	33.69
1944	12 280 000	366 928	45 153	321 775	33.47
1945	12 225 000	374 533	43 425	331 108	32.64
1946	11 927 000	370 959	42 624	328 335	32.15
1947	11 200 000	359 777	41 010	318 767	31.13
1948	11 585 000	341 324	41 023	300 301	33.94
1949	11 705 000	357 038	41 520	315 518	32.78
1950	11 664 000	373 888	45 387	328 501	31.20
1951	11 516 000	369 515	46 623	322 892	31.17
1952	11 819 000	367 689	47 094	320 595	32.14
1953	11 941 000	359 577	48 174	311 403	33.21
1954	13 237 000	385 280	49 888	335 392	34.36
1955	14 601 000	398 276	51 138	347 138	36.66

Date	Gold produced (fine oz)	Total labour employed	White workers	Black workers	Output per man (fine oz)
1956	15 897 000	405 870	51 252	354 618	39.17
1957	17 031 000	403 577	49 732	353 845	42.20
1958	17 656 000	407 274	49 201	358 073	43.35
1959	20 066 000	449 194	51 110	398 084	44.67

Sources   SA Dept of Mines, *Mining Statistics*, 1966, p. 17; SA Bureau of Statistics, *Statistical Year Book, 1964*.

Table 5   The Relative Positions of the Mining Houses in the Industry

Group	Column 1 No. of mines					Column 1936		
	1928	1938	1948	1958	1961	Rich	Average	Poor
Anglo American Corp.	3	5	7	12	12	—	3	1
Anglo-Transvaal	—	1	1	4	4	—	—	1
Central Mining	16	12	14	11	8	—	4	7
Cons. Gold Fields	3	6	10	12	11	1	2	2
General Mining	3	1	1	4	3	—	1	1
JCI	7	8	4	4	2	—	2	5
Union Corp.	2	4	5	7	7	—	2	—
Sundry cos. & miscellaneous producers	3	3	2	1	—	NA	NA	NA
TOTAL	37	40	44	55	47	1	14	17

2			Column 3 (% of total) tons milled				Column 4 (% of total) fine oz of gold produced			
1961										
Rich	Average	Poor	1928	1938	1948	1958	1928	1938	1948	1958
3	3	6	8.3	12.1	15.0	23.7	9.8	14.4	15.4	27.6
—	1	3	—	2.8	4.3	7.9	—	2.5	3.4	7.7
1	1	6	44.3	36.5	30.0	23.3	43.2	33.6	29.0	19.8
1	2	8	7.0	9.7	15.9	16.7	7.2	12.7	17.3	18.7
—	2	1	4.3	3.9	4.6	8.6	3.4	3.5	3.6	8.5
—	—	2	26.6	24.5	14.8	5.7	27.6	21.8	10.5	2.8
—	5	2	5.0	7.1	12.3	12.5	5.9	8.2	14.3	11.3
NA	NA	NA	4.5	3.4	3.1	1.6	2.9	3.3	6.5	3.6
5	14	28	100	100	100	100	100	100	100	100

Sources Chamber of Mines, *Annual Reports, 1928, 1938, 1948, 1958* and *1961*; Mennell (1961), p. 66; F. Wilson (1972), p. 108.

Table 6 *Declared Working Revenue, Working Costs and Working Profits (R), 1902–75*

Showing the average declared working revenue, working costs and estimated working profit per tonne milled for Transvaal and Orange Free State gold mines, members of the Chamber.

Year	Working revenue per tonne	Working costs per tonne	Working profit per tonne	Year	Working revenue per tonne	Working costs per tonne	Working profit per tonne
1902	4.63	2.83	1.82	1939	3.48	2.14	1.34
1903	4.38	2.72	1.64	1940	3.90	2.28	1.62
1904	4.24	2.68	1.57	1941	3.83	2.33	1.50
1905	3.95	2.59	1.38	1942	3.77	2.33	1.44
1906	3.80	2.45	1.38	1943	3.81	2.42	1.39
1907	3.74	2.29	1.46	1944	3.75	2.51	1.24
1908	3.46	1.98	1.48	1945	3.81	2.62	1.19
1909	3.19	1.89	1.27	1946	3.84	2.82	1.02
1910	3.14	1.94	1.15	1947	3.81	2.93	0.88
1911	3.08	1.98	1.05	1948	3.84	2.89	0.95
1912	3.20	2.06	1.10	1949	4.29	2.97	1.32
1913	3.06	1.97	1.05	1950	5.17	3.26	1.91
1914	2.92	1.88	0.99	1951	5.17	3.51	1.66
1915	2.89	1.92	0.93	1952	5.19	3.77	1.42
1916	2.94	1.99	0.90	1953	5.34	4.03	1.31

Year				Year			
1917	2.99	2.11	0.83	1954	5.61	4.26	1.35
1918	3.08	2.38	0.66	1955	5.93	4.45	1.48
1919	3.15	2.52	0.61	1956	6.31	4.73	1.58
1920	3.88	2.83	1.05	1957	6.93	5.00	1.93
1921	3.90	2.85	1.05	1958	7.24	5.18	2.06
1922	3.48	2.60	0.88	1959	7.70	5.01	2.69
1923	3.26	2.22	1.04	1960	8.16	5.13	3.03
1924	3.31	2.17	1.13	1961	9.05	5.57	3.48
1925	3.09	2.12	0.97	1962	9.54	5.72	3.82
1926	3.08	2.10	0.98	1963	9.92	5.88	4.04
1927	3.16	2.18	0.98	1964	10.40	6.06	4.34
1928	3.14	2.19	0.95	1965	10.80	6.33	4.47
1929	3.10	2.18	0.92	1966	11.14	6.63	4.51
1930	3.12	2.17	0.95	1967	11.03	6.79	4.24
1931	3.08	2.15	0.93	1968	11.10	6.94	4.16
1932	3.04	2.12	0.92	1969	11.36	7.07	4.29
1933	3.96	2.14	1.82	1970	11.24	7.34	3.90
1934	3.89	2.14	1.75	1971	12.36	7.88	4.48
1935	3.70	2.08	1.62	1972	16.25	8.79	7.46
1936	3.53	2.07	1.46	1973	23.93	10.51	13.42
1937	3.46	2.09	1.37	1974	34.70	13.18	21.52
1938	3.42	2.12	1.30	1975	34.45	16.71	17.74

Source Chamber of Mines of SA, *Eighty-sixth Annual Report, 1975.*

Table 7 Structure of Ownership of Orange Free State Gold Mines

Name of group	Number of mines group controls	Name of mine	Area from which Anglo mine originated	Mines in which Anglo holds minority interest
Anglo American Corp.	7	Western Holdings	SA Townships	
		Free State Geduld	Blinkpoort	
		Welkom	African & European	
		President Brand	African & European	
		President Steyn	African & European	
		Loraine	Wit. Extensions	
		Jeannette	Wit. Extensions	
Anglo-Transvaal	2	Virginia	—	None
		Merriespruit	—	None
Union Corp.	1	St Helena	SA Townships[a]	St Helena
JCI	1	Freddies Cons.	—	Freddies Cons.
Cons. Gold Fields	1	Free State Saaiplaas	—	FS Saaiplaas
Central Mining	1	Harmony	—	Harmony
General Mining	1	Riebeeck	—	Riebeeck

[a] Although developed on a property controlled by Anglo American, technical control over the St Helena mine was passed to Union Corp. prior to Anglo's take-over of SA Townships, hence the discrepancy of a Union Corp. mine on an Anglo property.

Sources The table was compiled from various points within the following: Graham (1964), Mennell (1961), and Gregory (1962).

Table 8   State Revenue from Gold and Uranium Mining, 1945–65[a]

Date	Revenue (£'000)
1945	20 141
1946	18 016
1947	11 366
1948	6321
1949	7407
1950	11 875
1951	22 680
1952	22 915
1953	16 219
1954	12 418
1955	14 721
1956	16 983
1957	16 532
1958	17 571
1959	18 576
1960	26 913
1961	36 279
1962	42 393
1963	53 751
1964	58 656
1965	60 350

[a] In South Africa uranium is mined as a by-product of gold from the same mines and, consequently, published figures for state revenue do not differentiate between the two.
Sources   1945–62: SA Bureau of Statistics, *Statistical Year Book, 1964*, p. R7; 1963–5: SA Dept. of Statistics, *South African Statistics, 1974*, p. 19.9.

Table 9 Selected Indices of Profitability on Gold Mines, 1966
(all values expressed in Rands)

Name of mine	Value of minerals[a]	Working costs[a]	Profits[a]	Total profits	Capital expenditure, inception to 1966	State participation in profits to 1966
Pre-Second World War mines						
				PART 1: GOLD MINES WITHIN THE ANGLO AMERICAN GROUP		
Brakpan[b]	—	—	—	—	6 122 737	5 927 192
Daggafontein	5.37	4.33	1.04	2 369 073	21 039 210	34 076 192
East Daggafontein	5.18	4.29	0.89	1 275 978	7 006 148	17 202
SA Land & Exploration	6.47	5.35	1.12	1 418 285	13 701 724	24 273
Post-Second World War mines						
Free State Geduld	27.44	7.82	19.62	35 933 303	57 256 407	25 756 914
Free State Saaiplaas	6.65	7.17	Loss	Loss	31 726 004	—
Loraine	10.19	8.16	2.03	2 233 192	45 664 965	—
President Brand	16.66	6.22	10.44	25 919 990	57 178 328	14 775 275
President Steyn	8.57	5.96	2.61	6 565 334	53 959 656	—
Welkom	9.01	5.77	3.24	7 047 686	36 906 637	—
Western Deep Levels	10.84	5.46	5.38	14 748 713	103 522 251	—
Western Holdings	18.98	6.18	12.80	34 344 555	45 894 467	40 169 475
Western Reefs	9.04	7.81	1.23	2 351 737	36 996 339	3 154 443
Vaal Reefs	13.08	8.10	4.98	10 956 335	53 649 235	2 779 497
				PART 2: GOLD MINES NOT WITHIN THE ANGLO AMERICAN GROUP		
Pre-Second World War mines						
East Geduld	5.72	4.21	1.51	1 954 202	7 517 359	593 370
Ellaton	—	—	—	—	6 364 544	—
Grootvlei	4.97	3.44	1.53	4 182 103	10 384 803	49 518
Marievale	6.11	4.06	2.05	2 435 131	7 958 108	—
New Kleinfontein	2.54	3.46	Loss	Loss	6 021 473	44 904

New State Areas	—	—	—	—	4 229 593	32 716 008
Rand Leases	3.58	4.04	Loss	Loss	9 389 493	413 389
Simmer and Jack	26.04	39.06	Loss	Loss	7 664 299	231 187
Spaarwater	9.90	8.47	1.43	191 857	5 216 570	—
Sub Nigel	6.10	5.72	0.38	306 237	9 871 964	362 894
Van Dyk	5.71	5.43	0.28	63 672	10 288 688	8828
Vlakfontein	10.34	6.75	3.59	2 343 430	11 045 077	—
Vogelstruisbult	5.67	5.28	0.39	352 998	14 679 798	27 162
Zandpan	10.03	9.51	0.52	259 970	16 174 007	—
Post-Second World War mines						
Blyvooruitzicht	16.79	8.96	7.83	13 720 615	47 338 449	23 759 390
Bracken	11.78	5.42	6.36	6 842 695	15 718 840	459 472
Buffelsfontein	13.66	7.99	5.67	13 710 150	71 913 081	1 756 477
Doornfontein	12.12	6.62	5.50	8 624 999	38 976 976	3 727 736
Freddies Cons.	13.28	8.74	4.54	3 537 368	40 498 317	—
Harmony	13.68	9.98	3.70	8 985 505	63 607 878	5 229 841
Hartebeesfontein	16.15	10.69	5.46	9 144 149	48 639 665	6 079 094
Kinross	—	—	—	—	10 845 784	—
Leslie	8.63	4.31	4.32	7 751 164	21 925 474	—
Libanon	8.56	6.08	2.49	3 878 890	26 801 971	33 799
Merriespruit	2.40	1.37	1.03	216 771	22 422 074	—
St Helena	11.47	4.43	7.04	16 826 392	34 738 971	5 790 539
Stilfontein	12.84	8.02	4.82	10 670 979	68 015 115	7 568 586
Virginia	11.14	8.91	2.23	4 126 040	50 804 823	—
West Driefontein	20.18	7.49	12.69	34 317 682	84 653 413	28 742 093
Western Areas	6.66	5.51	1.15	2 722 035	24 918 030	—
Winkelhaak	8.19	5.37	2.82	4 414 854	24 562 026	—

a per ton milled.
b If no data is presented in the first four columns it means the mine was not in production during the year.

Sources SA Dept of Mines, *Mining Statistics, 1966*, pp. 38–41; *Beerman's Financial Year Book of Southern Africa*, 1974 (vols I and II).

Table 10

Mine[a]	Group[b]	Ore milled '000 tons	Production kg	Grade g per ton	Working revenue per ton (R)
			PART 1: GOLD MINING STATISTICS, 1975		
1. West Driefontein	GFSA/Anglo	2638	59 357	22.50	82.30
2. East Driefontein	GFSA/Anglo	1461	25 577	17.61	62.63
3. Randfontein	JCI	837	11 654	13.92	48.03
4. Free State Geduld	Anglo	2287	37 804	16.53	60.60
5. Western Deep Levels / Western Ultra Deep levels	Anglo	3095	47 736	15.42	56.86
6. Blyvooruitzicht	Barlow Rand	1954	26 207	13.41	48.77
7. Western Holdings	Anglo	2999	41 207	13.74	50.10
8. President Brand	Anglo	2876	40 123	13.95	50.45
9. Kloof	GFSA	1327	15 152	11.42	41.77
10. St Helena	Union Corp.	2232	25 280	11.33	40.88
11. Hartebeesfontein	Anglo-Vaal	2807	32 560	11.60	43.23
12. President Steyn	Anglo	2519	27 031	10.73	39.67
13. Vaal Reefs	Anglo	6022	61 393	10.19	37.38
14. Buffelsfontein	Gen. Min.	3166	29 304	9.26	33.72
15. Doornfontein	GFSA	1379	13 688	9.93	36.55
16. Stilfontein	Gen. Min.	1768	14 637	8.28	30.21
17. Barberton	Gen. Min.	141	1466	10.40	40.77
18. Winkelhaak	Union Corp.	2015	14 860	7.37	26.32
19. Kinross	Union Corp.	1535	11 014	7.18	26.21
20. Libanon	GFSA	1311	10 663	8.13	29.54
21. Bracken	Union Corp.	1015	8069	7.95	28.68
22. Loraine	Anglo-Vaal	1086	7867	7.24	27.23
23. Western Areas	JCI	3447	22 581	6.55	24.32
24. Welkom	Anglo	2078	13 610	6.55	24.16
25 Wit. Nigel	Independent	224	1126	5.03	18.21
26. ERPM	Barlow Rand	1898	11 388	6.00	21.86
27. Freddies Cons.	Anglo	811	4400	5.43	20.43
28. Venterspost	GFSA	1391	7257	5.22	18.91
29. Harmony	Barlow Rand	5372	30 788	5.73	20.77
30. SA Land	Anglo	993	5136	5.17	18.85
31. Vlakfontein	GFSA	670	3290	4.91	18.30
32. Leslie	Union Corp.	1210	5685	4.70	17.52
33. Durban Deep	Barlow Rand	1877	7143	3.81	13.92
34. West Rand Cons. (gold & uranium sects.)	Gen. Min.	1851	6361	3.44	12.39
35. Grootvlei	Union Corp.	1699	5142	3.03	11.06
36. Cons. Main Reef ⎫ Crown / City Deep ⎭ Mines	Barlow Rand	1200	3955	3.30	12.18
37. Marievale	Union Corp.	1070	3985	3.72	13.66
38. Free State Saaiplaas	Anglo	1138	4914	4.32	16.63
39. East Daggafontein	Anglo	1010	1793	1.77	7.12
			PART 2: GOLD MINING STATISTICS, 1976		
1. West Driefontein	GFSA/Anglo	2468	55 754	22.59	75.52
2. East Driefontein	GFSA/Anglo	1771	36 083	20.37	67.63
3. Randfontein	JCI	944	15 997	16.95	56.27
4. Free State Geduld	Anglo	2149	34 704	16.15	55.41
5. Western Deep Levels / Western Ultra Deep Levels	Anglo	2941	44 532	15.14	50.67
6. Blyvooruitzicht	Barlow Rand	1854	23 269	12.55	42.12
7. Western Holdings	Anglo	3021	37 454	12.40	42.00
8. President Brand	Anglo	2994	36 815	12.30	41.98
9. Kloof	GFSA	1412	16 749	11.86	40.00
10. St Helena	Union Corp.	2260	26 164	11.58	38.60

Working costs per ton (R)	Working profit per ton (R)	Uranium production '000 tons	State assistance (R'000)	Total profit^c (R'000)	Tax and state share of profits (R'000)	Capital expenditure (R'000)	Total dividends declared (R)
17.38	64.92	732	—	181 183	105 445	12 610	65 482 044
18.55	44.08	—	—	67 561	—	22 203	39 944 155
16.94	31.09	—	—	26 903	—	14 509	—
16.22	44.38	—	—	105 188	64 872	7509	33 000 000
20.73	36.13	632	—	116 140	58 868	18 482	36 875 000
18.13	30.64	670	—	63 051	32 741	5803	22 800 000
15.49	34.61	—	—	109 804	67 850	6471	35 607 786
17.66	32.79	—	—	94 414	50 604	9937	35 100 000
21.57	20.20	—	—	29 607	7386	13 621	16 632 000
12.22	28.66	—	—	66 298	35 590	6542	24 062 500
20.01	23.22	2802	—	70 657	37 391	13 429	24 080 000
20.30	19.37	—	—	54 627	17 272	25 142	17 500 000
19.96	17.42	3659	—	111 350	42 644	30 927	33 250 000
20.13	13.59	3109	—	49 214	23 290	7149	19 800 000
19.02	17.53	—	—	25 935	12 749	4668	8 845 200
25.56	4.65	—	1371	10 156	211	6135	4 702 651
24.84	15.93	—	—	2333	40	2570	—
9.83	16.49	—	—	34 676	20 852	249	12 960 000
10.55	15.66	—	—	25 004	11 106	5735	9 720 000
16.39	13.15	—	—	18 771	4544	9728	7 937 300
11.50	17.18	—	—	18 287	10 983	—	7 280 000
24.67	2.56	*Profit: R87 000	—	5191	—	8205	964 019
15.55	8.77	—	—	32 190	2035	8561	20 959 614
17.15	7.01	—	—	15 695	5475	4105	6 737 500
19.78	− 1.57	—	229	53	43	645	—
20.59	1.27	—	4164	7156	81	5209	1 386 000
19.86	0.57	—	—	1185	—	3263	—
15.74	3.17	—	—	5762	Cr. 113	6764	2 525 000
13.95	6.82	3269	—	43 481	7054	14 417	20 701 181
17.10	1.75	—	—	2030	88	587	990 000
14.94	3.36	—	—	2666	1169	289	1 200 000
11.41	6.11	—	—	7809	4216	—	4 480 000
14.79	− 0.87	—	3280	2568	Cr. 19	2786	465 000
14.59	2.20	*Profit: R1152 000	3893	1289	59	840	566 500
8.03	3.03	—	—	5206	1638	1233	2 287 764
12.69	− 0.51	—	1327	1282	8	Cr. 83	—
8.73	4.93	—	—	5432	2747	—	2 340 000
14.40	2.23	*Profit: R26 000	—	5367	Cr. 41	9495	1 686 000
8.54	− 1.42	—	1337	− 44	23	444	—
21.14	54.38	1075	—	143 631	80 366	16 608	39 430 048
21.21	46.42	—	—	87 260	28 219	21 475	40 882 500
18.11	38.16	—	—	37 715	—	31 697	10 827 106
20.35	35.06	—	—	76 955	35 660	22 123	20 000 000
24.70	25.97	602	—	82 280	38 254	18 993	22 500 000
21.90	20.22	675	—	39 769	15 022	11 256	12 240 000
18.04	23.96	—	—	76 941	47 868	5526	23 238 766
20.15	21.83	—	—	66 069	12 718	40 278	23 868 000
24.70	15.30	—	—	23 447	3600	13 762	11 188 800
13.79	24.81	—	—	57 332	23 653	17 959	16 362 500

Mine[a]	Group[b]	Ore milled '000 tons	Production kg	Production Grade g per ton	Working revenue per ton (R)
11. Hartebeesfontein	Anglo-Vaal	2828	32 217	11.39	39.24
12. President Steyn	Anglo	2791	28 448	10.19	33.99
13. Val Reefs	Anglo	6572	66 004	10.04	33.37
14. Buffelsfontein	Gen. Min	3206	29 409	9.17	30.51
15. Doornfontein	GFSA	1367	12 057	8.82	30.43
16. Stilfontein	Gen. Min.	1893	16 429	8.68	29.11
17. Barberton	Gen. Min.	143	1200	8.39	28.31
18. Winkelhaak	Union Corp.	2015	15 616	7.75	26.12
19. Kinross	Union Corp.	1459	11 003	7.54	25.74
20. Libanon	GFSA	1365	10 289	7.54	25.72
21. Bracken	Union Corp.	998	7437	7.45	25.41
22. Loraine	Anglo-Vaal	1195	7897	6.61	21.83
23. Western Areas	JCI	3585	22 844	6.37	21.40
24. Welkom	Anglo	2130	13 432	6.31	21.30
25. Wit. Nigel	Independent	229	1376	6.01	19.70
26. ERPM	Barlow Rand	1843	11 031	5.99	20.10
27. Freddies Cons.	Anglo	1051	5704	5.43	18.43
28. Venterspost	GFSA	1313	6943	5.29	18.97
29. Harmony	Barlow Rand	5892	30 372	5.15	17.24
30. SA Land	Anglo	1061	5327	5.02	16.52
31. Vlakfontein	GFSA	700	3341	4.77	16.74
32. Leslie	Union Corp.	1170	5425	4.64	15.85
33. Durban Deep	Barlow Rand	1886	7935	4.21	14.07
34. West Rand Cons. (gold & uranium sects.)	Gen. Min.	1797	5217	2.90	9.95
35. Grootvlei	Union Corp.	1603	5607	3.50	11.75
36. Cons. Main Reef ⎱ Crown City Deep ⎰ Mines	Barlow Rand	837	2918	3.49	11.95
37. Marievale	Union Corp.	1081	3540	3.28	11.05
38. Free State Saaiplaas	Anglo	1210	3767	3.11	10.86
39. East Daggafontein[d]	Anglo	1208	2171	1.80	6.19
TOTALS					

Working costs per ton (R)	Working profit per ton (R)	Uranium production '000 tons	State assistance (R'000)	Total profit[c] (R'000)	Tax and State share of profits (R'000)	Capital expenditure (R'000)	Total dividends declared (R)
24.13	15.11	2790	—	49 475	25 001	7675	19 040 000
21.94	12.05	—	—	37 983	523	34 899	6 300 000
23.29	10.08	4233	—	79 200	22 644	31 794	20 900 000
22.32	8.19	3055	—	33 577	14 553	7912	9 900 000
22.90	7.53	—	—	11 387	2827	5386	2 948 000
27.89	1.22	—	2905	6392	479	1986	2 873 842
29.50	− 1.19	—	560	458	—	1399	—
11.46	14.66	—	—	30 756	19 364	130	9 120 000
13.15	12.59	—	—	18 944	8219	5008	5 760 000
19.44	6.28	—	—	9645	692	7684	3 571 785
12.97	12.44	—	—	12 977	8021	—	4 900 000
26.72	4.89	*Profit: R145 000	5613	366	—	5318	—
17.31	4.09	—	—	17 022	2150	8843	6 046 043
18.69	2.61	—	—	6669	408	5407	1 837 500
23.20	− 3.50	—	661	61	58	845	—
23.65	− 3.55	—	9263	3250	Cr. 1	4977	198 000
20.01	− 1.58	—	—	− 1154	—	1921	—
19.36	− 0.39	—	—	248	Cr. 51	2119	252 500
15.76	1.48	4215	—	39 027	2682	26 190	8 065 395
18.03	− 1.51	—	2180	915	24	153	82 500
15.54	1.20	—	—	1216	195	29	720 000
13.15	2.70	—	—	3331	1570	—	2 240 000
17.56	− 3.49	—	6498	540	—	1024	—
17.10	− 7.15	622	1620	2464	128	829	566 500
10.18	1.57	—	—	2493	678	202	915 106
14.42	− 2.47	—	2236	154	Cr. 8	162	—
9.20	1.85	—	—	2044	853	Cr. 23	1 350 000
16.37	− 5.51	*Profit: R128 000	—	− 2624	—	12 894	—
7.86	− 1.67	—	1849	− 130	73		—
				33 385	396 562		

*Uranium production figures unobtainable. Profit figures given to indicate scale of production.
[a] Mines are listed according to grades of ore based on 1976 figures, running from high to low grade.
[b] The following abbreviations have been used:

Anglo	Anglo American Corporation
Anglo-Vaal	Anglo Transvaal Mines Consolidated
Barlow Rand	Barlow Rand Ltd
Gen. Min.	General Mining and Finance Corporation
GFSA	Gold Fields of South Africa
JCI	Johannesburg Consolidated Investments
Union Corp.	Union Corporation

[c] Total profit is arrived at as follows:

1 Add profit from gold mining to
2 Profit from uranium production (if any) to
3 Profit from acid and pyrite production (if any) to
4 State assistance (if any) to
5 Net sundry profit.

Items 3 and 5 are not present in the table but are reflected in total profit.
[d] East Daggafontein withdrew from the Chamber during 1976 and is closing down.
Sources Chamber of Mines of SA, *Eighty-sixth Annual Report, 1975*, pp. 50–1, and Analysis of Working Results, October–December 1976, pp. 4–5; *GFSA Annual Report, 1974*, pp. 26–30; *Anglo American Corp. of SA, Annual Report, 1974*, pp. 70–4; Anglo American Gold Investment Co. Ltd, *Annual Report, 1974*, pp. 20–30; General Mining, *Annual Report, 1974*, pp. 41–3; Union Corp. Ltd, *Report and Accounts, 1974*, pp. 32–6; Barlow Rand Ltd, *Annual Financial Statement, 1974*, pp. 16–18; *South African Financial Gazette*, 4 March 1977, p. 7.

Table 11   *Gross Domestic Product in South Africa by Kind of Economic Activity, 1946–71*
(in percent)

Year	Agriculture	Mining	Manufacturing	Construction	Manufacturing and construction
1946	13.0	11.9	17.1	2.2	19.3
1947	15.6	10.5	17.3	2.7	20.0
1948	16.8	10.2	17.7	3.3	21.0
1949	14.5	11.7	18.7	3.3	22.0
1950	17.8	13.3	18.4	3.1	21.5
1951	18.5	13.2	18.4	3.3	21.7
1952	16.2	12.5	19.2	3.9	23.1
1953	17.0	10.8	20.7	3.3	24.0
1954	16.4	11.0	21.0	2.9	23.9
1955	15.1	12.3	20.4	2.8	23.2
1956	15.0	12.9	20.4	3.0	23.4
1957	14.3	13.2	20.2	3.0	23.2
1958	12.6	12.9	20.5	3.4	23.9
1959	12.5	13.4	20.1	3.3	23.4
1960	12.1	13.8	20.6	3.1	23.7
1961	12.2	13.3	21.2	2.8	24.0
1962	12.2	13.3	21.3	2.8	24.1
1963	12.2	12.8	22.0	3.0	25.0
1964	10.5	13.0	22.8	3.5	26.3
1965	10.2	12.7	23.5	4.0	27.5
1966	10.3	12.7	23.2	4.0	27.2
1967	11.7	11.8	22.6	4.0	26.6
1968	10.1	11.7	22.6	4.1	26.7
1969	9.6	11.5	23.0	4.4	27.4
1970	9.1	10.5	23.4	4.8	28.2
1971	9.6	9.3	23.0	5.0	28.0

Sources   SA Bureau of Census and Statistics, *Union Statistics for Fifty Years, (1910–1960)*, 1960; SA Dept of Statistics, *South African Statistics, 1972*, Pretoria, 1973; South African Reserve Bank, *Quarterly Bulletin*, March 1977.

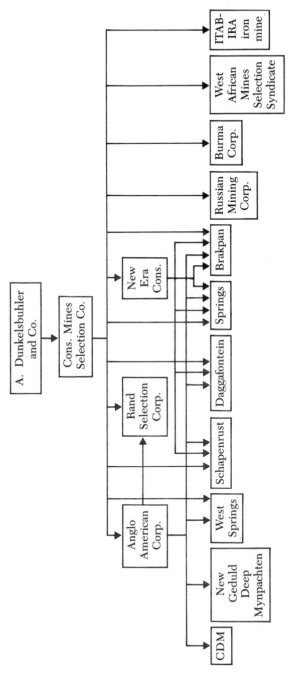

Figure 1   Control Structure in the Anglo American Group in 1918

Sources   Anglo American Corp. of SA, *Second Annual Report*, 31 December 1918, p. 3; Cons. Mines Selection Co., *Report of the Directors*, 31 December 1918, p. 4; Rand Selection Corp., *Report of the Directors*, 31 December 1918, p. 2.

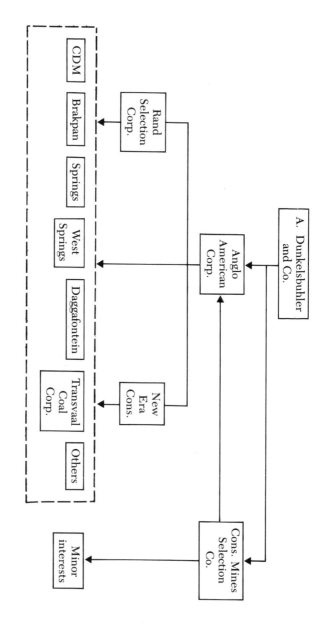

Figure 2   Control Structure in the Anglo American Group in 1923

Sources   Cons. Mines Selection Co., *Directors' Report*, 31 December 1922, and Minutes of the Extraordinary General Meeting, 17 October 1922, and Minutes of the Ordinary General Meeting in *The Mining World*, 28 May 1921; Anglo American Corp. of SA, *Fourth Annual Report*, 31 December 1920, Fourth Ordinary General Meeting, Minutes of the Proceedings, 27 May 1921, and *Seventh Annual Report*, 31 December 1923.

Figure 3   Control Structure (and Sales Channels) in the Diamond Industry Prior to 1929[a]

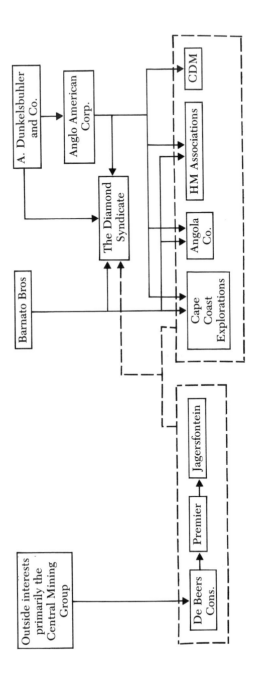

[a]Control routes are indicated by hard black lines; sales routes by dotted lines.

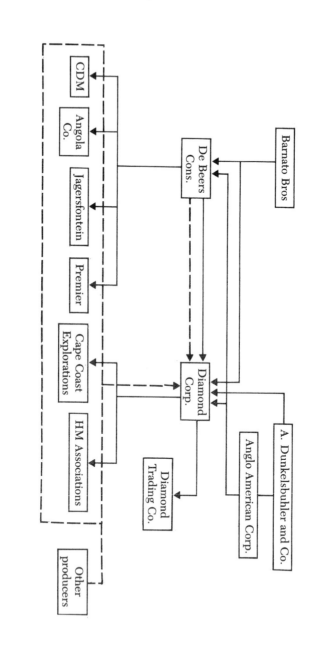

Figure 4   Control Structure (and Sales Channels) in the Diamond Industry Post-1929[a]

[a] Control routes are indicated by hard black lines; sales routes by dotted lines. (NB: The Diamond Producers' Association consisted of all the De Beers companies plus the Diamond Corp.)

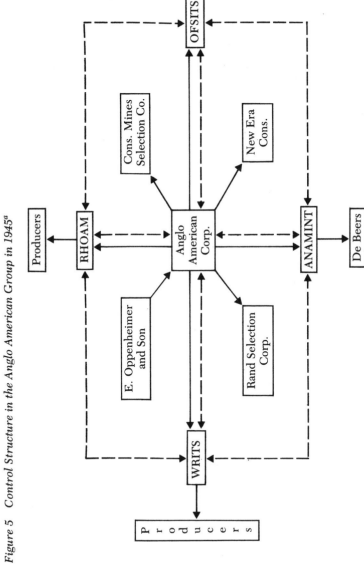

Figure 5   Control Structure in the Anglo American Group in 1945[a]

[a]Control routes are indicated by hard black lines; the rough path of shareholdings by dotted black lines.

APPENDIX 2

A Survey of the
Anglo American Group of Companies

INTRODUCTION

This appendix lists and provides information on 656 companies in the Anglo
American Group. The list is not a fully comprehensive record, but is the most
extensive public compilation of those companies involved with the Group up to
the end of 1976.

The appendix is divided into two parts. The first lists the most important 14
holding companies in the Group, isolating the 6 companies which form the
core of Group structure. Information on the cross-holdings among these 6, and
on some of the cross-holdings among the 14 companies, is also provided. A
diagram is included.

The second and major part of the appendix lists those companies which form
the bulk of the Anglo American Group. Documentation is presented, for the
sake of clarity, in four columns.

1 The first column provides the name of the company which forms a part of
   the Group. These names are presented in alphabetical categories, all the
   As, Bs, Cs, etc., being grouped together. The companies within each
   category—for example, within the As—are not placed in any order.
2 The second column provides the link with the Group: that is, the name of
   the holding company within the Anglo American Group, which holds Anglo's interest in the company named in column 1. Where more than one
   company is known to be involved the names are supplied. The holding
   arrangements within the Group structure are extremely complex and this
   column represents a somewhat simplified version (that is, intermediate
   holding companies have often been omitted). This has been done so as to
   be able to show as clearly as possible the links that exist between the
   companies mentioned in column 1 and those 14 companies which form the
   Group's inner circle. Thus column 2 provides the name of one of the 14
   companies (regardless of whether it has a direct or indirect holding) or, if
   the holding is through an important holding company which is not included
   in the 14, then that company is named in column 2. But in this latter
   instance the derivation to the 14 can still be found by looking up in column
   1 the name of the holding company mentioned in column 2, and thereby
   discovering its link with the 14. For instance, if in column 1 we have
   'Barnato Bros Ltd', then column 2 will give us the name of the Anglo Group

holding company, in this case 'JCI'. But 'JCI' is not part of the inner circle of 14 companies and therefore in order to discover its connection with the 14 (and thereby the connection of 'Barnato Bros') we look up 'JCI' in column 1: column 2 at that point shows AAC, De Beers, Randsel—the three companies in the inner core. Thus all companies presented in column 1 can ultimately be traced back to the inner 14.

3   Column 3 gives the size of the shares which the company named in column 2 holds in the company named in column 1. Sometimes, where the precise figure is not known, the terms 'Min[ority]' or 'Maj[ority]' are used. The term 'majority' does not necessarily mean that an interest of 51 per cent is held, but can also imply that effective control is exercised through a holding of less than 51 per cent. Where possible in these cases the means through which this control is exercised are given.

4   Column 4 provides some information, where possible, on the nature of activity of the company mentioned in column 1.

Finally, this survey was compiled from data relating mainly to Group activity in 1976. While all information contained herein is known to have been accurate then, a group the size of Anglo American is constantly expanding and changing and the Appendix does not reflect these changes. For instance, one company listed here in column 1, 'H. D. Development Ltd', has subsequently been placed in liquidation and its assets taken over by its holding companies, the A. A. C., Randsel and Charter (shown in column 2). Again, 'Boart and Hard Metal Products' (shown in column 1 and in column 2 in various other places) has recently changed its name to 'Boart International Ltd'. Caution should therefore be exercised in using the data presented in this Appendix.

THE ANGLO AMERICAN GROUP OF COMPANIES

The main holding companies in the Anglo American Group are as follows:

The Anglo American Corporation of South African (AAC)
De Beers Consolidated Mines (De Beers)
Charter Consolidated (Charter)
Rand Selection Corporation (Randsel)
Anglo American Investment Trust (ANAMINT)
Minerals and Resources Corporation (MINORCO)
Anglo American Gold Investment (AMGOLD)
Anglo American Industrial Corporation (AMIC)
Anglo American Coal Investment (AMCOAL)
Anglo American Properties (AMAPROP)
Zambian Copper Investments (ZCI)
Anglo American Corporation of Canada (AMCAN)
Anglo American Corporation Rhodesia (RHOAM)
Australian Anglo American (AUSTRAM)

Of these fourteen companies the most important are the first six: AAC, De Beers, Charter, Randsel, ANAMINT and MINORCO. These six companies form the inner core of the Anglo Group. They have holdings in each other as well as in the other eight companies. Their holdings in the fourteen top companies are as follows:

1 AAC holds interests in: De Beers, ANAMINT, AMGOLD, AMIC, AM-COAL, AMAPROP, Charter, MINORCO, AMCAN, RHOAM, AUSTRAM
2 De Beers holds interests in: AAC, Randsel, AMIC, AMAPROP, AMCAN, RHOAM, AUSTRAM
3 Randsel holds interests in: AAC, De Beers, ANAMINT, AMGOLD, AMIC, AMCOAL, AMAPROP, Charter, MINORCO, AMCAN, RHOAM, AUSTRAM
4 Charter holds interests in: AAC, ANAMINT, MINORCO, AMCAN, RHOAM, AUSTRAM
5 ANAMINT holds interest in: De Beers
6 MINORCO holds interests in: ZCI, RHOAM, AUSTRAM

These cross-holdings are represented in Figure 6. As can be seen, the big four holding companies are the AAC, De Beers, Randsel and Charter, followed by ANAMINT and MINORCO and then the remaining eight. *All the rest of the companies in which the Group participates throughout the world can, ultimately, be traced back to at least one of these fourteen holding companies.* Those remaining companies are listed below in alphabetical categories in column 1.

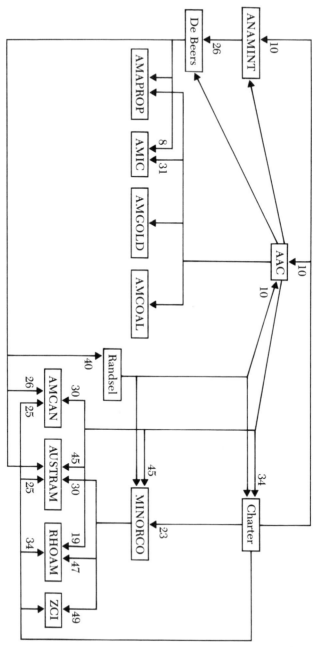

Figure 6   Cross-holdings Within the Anglo American Group

Name of company	Anglo holding company	Size of holding (%)	Nature of operation
African & European Investments Ltd	AAC	100	Holds coal interests
Anseld Holdings Ltd	AAC, Randsel	100	Holding co.
Anglo American Property Leasing Ltd	AAC	100	Holds property
Anmercosa Lands & Estates	AAC	100	Owns office blocks used by Group cos
Anmercosa Mozambique Oil Holdings	AAC	50	Oil and gas prospecting
Apex Mines	AAC (part of Gold Fields Group)	Min.	Supplies coal to Highveld Steel
Anglo American Corp. of Central Africa	AAC	100	Holds mining and industrial interests
Anglo American Prospecting (Rhodesia)	AAC, Randsel, RHOAM	Over 50	Prospecting
Anglo American Rhodesia Mineral Exploration	AAC, Randsel, RHOAM	Over 50	Prospecting
Anglo American International	AAC, Charter	50	Finance
Anglo Chemical Ore Co.	AAC, Charter	65	Mineral trading co.
Anmercosa Sales	AAC, Charter	100	Sells output of Group mines
Anglo American Corp. of the US	AAC, Charter, Randsel	Over 50	Holding US interests
Abrasive Grit Sales	ANAMINT, De Beers, JCI	About 33	Sales channel
Adamint Laboratories	De Beers	100	Diamond research
Apex Holdings Ltd	De Beers (through De Beers Ind. Corp.)	50	Holds interests in chemical cos
African Explosives & Chemical Industries	De Beers (through De Beers Ind. Corp.)	42.5	Manufactures explosives, chemicals, fertilizers, etc.

Name of company	Anglo holding company	Size of holding (%)	Nature of operation
Associated Mines (Malaysia)	Charter	49	
Argus Printing & Publishing Ltd	AAC, JCI and Charter (through Barlow Rand)	About 40	Newspaper group
Aluminum Investment Co.	AAC, Charter (through Barlow Rand)	10	Interests in light metals
African Wire Ropes Ltd	AMIC, AAC, Charter (through Barlow Rand)	6	Makes wire rope
Air & General Engineering	AAC, Charter (through Barlow Rand)	50	Makes refrigerator and air conditioning equipment
Ainsworth (Pty) Ltd	JCI		Engineering co.
Andcor	JCI	Over 50	
African Asbestos–Cement Corp.	JCI		
Agnew Lake Mines Ltd	AMCAN	10	Uranium mines
African Products Manufacturing Co. Ltd	AMIC	8.8	Processes maize to produce starch, glucose, etc.
Anglo-Transvaal Industries	AMIC		Part of Anglo-Transvaal Group
Anglo American Rhodesia Development	RHOAM	100	Holds property interests in Rhodesia (now Zimbabwe)
Anglo American Corp. of Botswana	MINORCO, Charter	100	Holds Botswana interests
Associated Manganese Mines of SA Ltd	AMIC	Min.	Controlled by Anglo-Vaal; has loan and share agreements with US Steel

Name of company	Anglo holding company	Size of holding (%)	Nature of operation
Anglo American Corp. do Brasil Limitada	AAC, AMGOLD	Maj.	Holding co. for Anglo's Brazilian interests
Anglo De Beers Forest Services (Lesotho) Ltd	De Beers	Maj.	Owns interests in Lesotho
Afrikander Lease Ltd	AAC	12.2	Gold mine
Anglo American Corp. Services	New Rhodesia Investments	100	
Anglo American (Rhodesian Services) Ltd	New Rhodesia Investments	100	
Appraised Securities Ltd	New Rhodesia Investments	100	
African Eagle Life Assurance Society Ltd	Randsel	75	Randsel acquired this insurance co. when it took over Schlezinger Group
Amalgamated Collieries of SA Ltd	AMCOAL	Maj.	Operates coal mine and owns Springfield Collieries
Anglo Power Collieries	AMCOAL	Maj.	Coal mine
African Gold & Base Metal Holdings Ltd	AAC	Maj.	Holding co. for some Anglo mining interests
African Loans & Investments	AAC	Maj.	Oppenheimer family involved
AMRHO Investments Ltd	AAC	Maj.	
Anglo American Corp. of SA (Portugal) SARL	AAC	Maj.	
Angloswazi Investments Ltd	AAC	Maj.	Holds some Anglo interests in Swaziland
Anglux Ltd, SA	AAC	Maj.	Registered in Luxembourg

Name of company	Anglo holding company	Size of holding (%)	Nature of operation
Ayer Hitah Tin Dredging Co.	Charter	Min.	Mines tin in Malaysia
Ansa Petroleum Beperk	AAC	Min.	
Anglo American Industrial Finance Co. Ltd	AMIC	100	Part of the AMIC Group cos
Anglo American Industrial Investments Ltd	AMIC	100	Part of the AMIC Group cos
Acme Timber Industries Ltd	AAC	Maj.	
Atkinson Oates Motors Ltd	McCarthy Rodway	Maj.	Retail motor firm
Anglo American (OFS) Housing Co. Ltd	AMAPROP	Maj.	Provides housing in OFS for employees of associated cos
Amaprop McCarthy Investments Ltd	AMAPROP, AAC	Maj.	
Anglo American Prospecting Co. Ltd	AAC	Maj.	Prospecting co.
Anglo American Prospecting Co. (South) Ltd	AAC	Maj.	Prospecting co.
Anglo American Prospecting Services Ltd	AAC	Maj.	Prospecting co.
Anmercosa Canadian Exploration Ltd	AAC	Maj.	Prospecting co. in Canada
Australian Anglo American Searches Ltd	AAC, AUSTRAM	Maj.	Prospecting co. in Australia
Australian Anglo American Ventures Ltd	AAC, AUSTRAM	Maj.	Prospecting co. in Australia
Anglo American Rhodesian Development Corp. Ltd	AAC	Maj.	Hires rolling stock to the Rhodesian Railways. Also ad-

Name of company	Anglo holding company	Size of holding (%)	Nature of operation
			ministers citrus and forest estates in Rhodesia
Anglo American Corp. Management & Services AG	AAC	Maj.	Service co. to the Group
Anglo American Corp. Services	AAC	Maj.	Service co. to the Group
Anglo American Gold Development Co. Ltd	AAC	Maj.	Service co. to the Group
Anglo American International (UK) Ltd	AAC	Maj.	
Anglo American International Services Ltd	AAC	Maj.	Provides services to Anglo's international division
Anglo American (Rhodesian Services) Ltd	AAC	Maj.	Provides services to Anglo's Rhodesian division
Anglo Botswana Services Ltd	AAC	Maj.	Provides services to Botswana division
Anglo Charter International Services Ltd	AAC	Maj.	Provides services to Charter Group
Anmercosa Computer Services	AAC	Maj.	
Anmersales AG	AAC	Maj.	
Australian Anglo American Services Ltd	AAC	Maj.	Provides services to Australian division
Blyvooruitzicht Mining Co.	AAC, AMGOLD, Charter, Randsel (administered by Rand Mines)	Over 33	Gold and uranium mining on the W. Rand
Buffelsfontein Mining Co.	AAC, AMGOLD, Randsel (administered by General Mining)	Over 33	Gold and uranium mine on Klerksdorp

Name of company	Anglo holding company	Size of holding (%)	Nature of operation
Balgray Collieries	AAC	Min.	Coal mine
Botswana Exploration & Mining Co.	AAC	100	Exploration and mining
Brakspruit Platinum	Charter, AAC, Barlow Rand	About 80	Involved in marketing platinum
Beralt Tin & Wolfram Mines (Portugal)	Charter	46	Mines wolfram in Portugal
Barlow Myers	Charter	49	Suppliers of engineering equipment
Barnato Bros	JCI	100	Diamond merchants
Barberton Iron & Steel Ltd	JCI	100	Engineering co.
Baffinland Iron	AMCAN (through Hudson Bay Mining & Smelting Co.)	19	Owns iron deposit on Baffin Island
Beaver Exploration	AMCAN (through Hudson Bay Exploration & Development)	100	Prospecting co.
Boart & Hard Metal Products	AMIC	100	Makes diamond drilling crowns, tungsten carbide steels. Has 100 subsidiaries in 28 different countries
Barlow Rand Ltd	AAC, Randsel, AMIC	About 20	Formed by a merger of Rand Mines & Thos. Barlow. Mining and engineering
Bindura Refining & Smelting Co.	RHOAM (through Rhodesia Nickel Corp.)	100	
Bwana M'Kubwa Mining Co.	MINORCO	49	Copper mine in Zambia

Name of company	Anglo holding company	Size of holding (%)	Nature of operation
Bamangwato Concessions	MINORCO	Min.	Owns Selebi-Pikwe copper/nickel mine in Botswana
Baluea Mines	MINORCO	13	Copper mine in Zambia
Barotseland Exploration Ltd	Zamanglo Exploration		Prospecting co. in Zambia
Botswana RST Ltd	Anglo American Botswana	Min.	Holds 85% of Bomangwato concessions
Boskop Areas (West Wits) Ltd	AAC	Min.	Prospecting co.
Blue Skies (Private) Ltd	New Rhodesia Investments	100	
Blesbok Colliery Ltd	AMCOAL	Maj.	Coal mine, subsidiary to AMCOAL
Bracken Mines Ltd	AAC, AMGOLD	Min.	Gold mine administered outside Group
Baffinland Iron Mines Ltd	Hudson Bay Mining	19	Owns iron deposit on Baffin Island
Blinkpan Koolmyne Beperk	AAC	Min.	Coal mine administered outside Group
Bruynzeel Holdings Ltd	AMIC	100	Holds a number of interests
Bruynzeel Plywoods Ltd	Bruynzeel Holdings	66.2	Manufactures veneers, plywood, blockboard, clipboard, etc.
Boart Diamond Products Ltd	Boart & Hard Metals	Maj.	Boart Group manufactures and markets various types of diamond and

Name of company	Anglo holding company	Size of holding (%)	Nature of operation
			tungsten carbide tipped drilling tools
Boart Drilling Ltd	Boart & Hard Metals	Maj.	as above
Boart Drilling & Contracting (Rhodesia) Ltd	Boart & Hard Metals	Maj.	as above
Boart Hard Metals Ltd	Boart & Hard Metals	Maj.	Carbide tipped drilling tools
Boart Hard Metals (Europe) Ltd	Boart & Hard Metals	Maj.	as for Boart Group
Boart Hard Metals (Canada) Ltd	Boart & Hard Metals	Maj.	as for Boart Group
Boart Products Rhodesia Ltd	Boart & Hard Metals	Maj.	as for Boart Group
Boart Tools Ltd	Boart & Hard Metals	Maj.	as for Boart Group
Boart International (Luxembourg) SAM	Boart & Hard Metals	Maj.	as for Boart Group
Bowater Associated Industries	AAC	Maj.	
Balamundi SA Ltd	SA Board Mills		Converts felt base paper into floor coverings, etc.
Barratts Industries Ltd	AAC	Min.	Industrial group in SA
Border Forests (Rhodesia)	AAC	Min.	
Bay Passage Investments Ltd	AMAPROP	Maj.	
Bryanston Hobart Shopping Centre Ltd	AMAPROP	Maj.	Shopping complex in J'burg
Bahamas International Trust Co. Ltd	AAC	Maj.	Finance co. based in Bahamas for world investment
British & Rhodesian Discount House Ltd	AAC	Maj.	Operates on money market

Name of company	Anglo holding company	Size of holding (%)	Nature of operation
Cons. Share Registers	AAC, Randsel	66.7	
Creative Homes Ltd	AAC, AMAPROP	About 50	Property developer around Cape Town
Carlton Centre Ltd	AAC, Randsel, AMAP-ROP	About 50	Building complex (shops, offices) in J'burg
Chemical Holdings Ltd	AAC	22.3	Holds chemical interests
Computer Sciences (SA) Ltd	AAC	70.5	Supplier of computing equipment
Cashew Investments Ltd	AAC, Randsel	100	Investment co.
Coke Producers (Pty) Ltd	AAC	Min.	Coal producers' selling organization
Cons. Diamond Mines of SW Africa	De Beers	97.9	Owns and mines the richest gem diamond field in the world
Central Selling Organization	De Beers	Maj.	Sells diamonds
Cons. Co. Bultfontein Mines	De Beers	58.8	Holds property leased to De Beers
Companhio des Diamantes d'Angola (Diamang)	De Beers	Min.	Prospecting and mining co. in Angola
Coronation Collieries	Randsel, AMCOAL	77.5	Coal mine
Charter France SA	Charter		
Cape Asbestos Co. Ltd	Charter	60.5	
Cape Asbestos Fibres	Charter (through Cape Asbestos)	Maj.	Markets output of mines
Cleveland Potash	Charter	50	Potash mine in the Midlands UK with ICI

Name of company	Anglo holding company	Size of holding (%)	Nature of operation
			(50%). For use in manufacturing fertilizers
Covenant Industries	Charter	37	Chemical sales company operating in East, West and Central Africa (with ICI)
Charter Overseas NV (Curaçao)	Charter	Maj.	Finances investment of Group outside sterling area
Chisangwa Mines Ltd	Charter, MINORCO	49	Zambian copper mine
Cape Portland Cement	AAC, Charter (through Barlow Rand)	Min.	Makes cement
Corner House Investment Co.	AAC, Charter (through Barlow Rand)	Maj.	Invests in mining and industry
Conning & Co. Ltd	AAC, Charter (through Barlow Rand)	Min.	
City Deep	AAC, Charter (through Barlow Rand)	100	Gold Mine
Cons. Main Reef	AAC, Charter (through Barlow Rand)	100	Gold mine
Crown Mines	AAC, Charter (through Barlow Rand)	100	Gold mine
Cornerhouse (Pty) Ltd	AAC, Charter (through Barlow Rand)	100	Owns office building of Rand Mines offices
Cons. Murchison (Tvl) Goldfields &Development Co.	JCI (part of Anglo Tvl Group) (JCI are technical advisers)	At least 15	Mines antimony concentrates and small quantities of gold
Conway Farm (Pty) Ltd	JCI	Maj.	Produces timber

Name of company	Anglo holding company	Size of holding (%)	Nature of operation
Christensen & Boart Oilfield Products Ltd	AMIC (through Boart & Hard Metals)	50	Provides drilling equipment for oil exploration and mining (mostly in SA)
Contractual Holdings (Zambia)	AMIC (through Boart & Hard Metals) & MINORCO	100	
Charter Properties (Pty) Ltd	RHOAM	100	Rhodesian property co.
Clay Products (Pty) Ltd	RHOAM	25	Manufactures clay products
Chilanga Cement	MINORCO (through Zambian Anglo American Ind. Corp.)	75	Produces cement
Chartered Exploration	MINORCO (through Zamanglo Exploration)	66	Mineral prospecting co.
Cons. Mines Holdings (Rhodesia) Ltd	New Rhodesia Investments	100	
Cape Industries Ltd	Charter	63.2	Manufactures building and insulation, light engineering and other products
Charter Cons. Investments Ltd	Charter	100	Issuing house in Charter Group
Cardium Holdings Ltd	De Beers Ind. Corp.	13.3	
Canadian Merrill Ltd	Hudson Bay Mining	23	Has oil and gas interests
Contractual Holdings	Boart & Hard Metals	Maj.	
Computer Advances (Pty) Ltd	Computer Sciences	100	Markets parent co.'s hardware
Central Reserves Ltd	AAC	Maj.	
Central Reserves (Rhodesia) (Private) Ltd	AAC	Maj.	

Name of company	Anglo holding company	Size of holding (%)	Nature of operation
Chemical Holdings Ltd	AAC	Min.	Manufactures and distributes chemicals to industry
Coronation Industrials Ltd	Tongaat Group	Maj.	Makes building materials
Carlton Hotels Ltd	AAC		Part of Carlton Centre complex
C. T. Bowring & Associates Holdings (SA) Ltd	AAC	Min.	
Cullinan Holdings Ltd	AAC		
Cabana Beach Development Ltd	AMAPROP	Maj.	Property development co. on Natal coasts
CDL Properties (Durban)	AMAPROP	Maj.	
Charter Properties Ltd	AMAPROP	Maj.	
Crescent Developments Ltd	AMAPROP	Maj.	
Cayman International Trust Co. Ltd	AAC	Maj.	Finance co. based in Cayman Islands for world investment
Compagnie Financière de Paris et des Pays-Bas	AAC		Finance co-formed with Banque de Paris et des Pays-Bas
Cape Verde Ltd	AAC	Min.	Prospecting co.
Compagnie Financière Eurafricaine	AAC	Maj.	General investment co.
Cello Securities Ltd			
Diamond Corp.	De Beers, AAC	100	Diamond selling co. Markets ⅔ of world's diamond production

Name of company	Anglo holding company	Size of holding (%)	Nature of operation
Dewhurst Farms Ltd	AAC, Randsel	Maj.	Distribution and sales co. for fresh produce
De Beers Holdings	De Beers	100	Holds De Beers's industrial interests, mainly through its interests in De Beers Ind. Corp.
De Beers Industrial Corp.	AMIC, De Beers	85	Holds most of De Beers's industrial interests
Diamond Producers' Association	De Beers	Maj.	Combination of South African producers, sells diamonds to Central Selling Organization
Diamond Purchasing & Trading Co.	De Beers, ANAMINT, JCI	77.5	Buys from the DPA (above) and Diamond Corp. and sells to the Diamond Trading Co.
Diamond Trading Co.	De Beers, ANAMINT, JCI	88	Sells diamonds to retailers
De Beers Botswana Mining Co. (Orapa Mine)	De Beers	85	Diamond mine in Botswana
D/K1 Diamond Mining Co.	De Beers	85	Diamond mine in Botswana
Debhold Canada	De Beers	100	Holds De Beers's interests in AMCAN
Durban Roodepoort Deep	AAC, Charter (through Barlow Rand)	100	Gold mine
Dryden Engineering Co.	AAC, Charter (through Barlow Rand)	40	Manufacturing and selling organization

Name of company	Anglo holding company	Size of holding (%)	Nature of operation
Down Town Real Estate Co.	JCI		Property dealer and developer
De Niza Mining Co.	AMCAN (through Hudson Bay Co.)	25	
Durham Industries of Canada	AMCAN (through Hudson Bay Co.)	100	
Dunlop (Zambia) Ltd	MINORCO (through ZAAIC)	25	Produces and sells tyres
Duncan, Gilbey & Matheson (Zambia) Ltd	MINORCO (through Zambian Anglo American Ind. Corp.)	24.5	
Delmas Ltd	General Mining		Colliery co. controlled by Gen. Min.
Daggafontein Mines Ltd	AAC, AMGOLD	Maj.	Gold mine administered by Anglo
De Beers Lesotho Mining Co.	De Beers	Maj.	Operates the Letseng-le-Terai diamond mine in Lesotho
Debhold (Canada) Ltd	De Beers Holdings	Maj.	Interested in Canadian mining and prospects
De Beers European Holdings SA	De Beers Holdings	Maj.	Interested in Australian Anglo American
De Beers Industrial Diamond Division Ltd	De Beers	Maj.	The outlet for sale of De Beers drilling and boart, holds De Beers patents for industrial diamonds
De Beers Industrial Diamond Division (Ireland) Ltd	De Beers	Maj.	Provides technical services to De Beers com-

Name of company	Anglo holding company	Size of holding (%)	Nature of operation
			panies in Ireland
Diacarb Ltd	Boart & Hard Metals	Maj.	
Debshan Ranches Ltd	Soetvelde	100	Owns an extensive cattle ranching operation at Gwelo, Rhodesia
Dawn Orchards Ltd	Soetvelde	100	Produces tomatoes, vegetables and fruit from the N. Transvaal
Duropenta Holdings	AE & CI	100	
Dorsic Holdings Ltd	SA Nylon Spinners	100	
David Whitehead & Sons (SA)	Tongaat Group	Maj.	Produces textiles
Elsburg Gold Mining Co.	JCI, AAC, AMGOLD, Randsel		W. Rand gold mine administered by JCI
Epoch Investments Ltd	AAC, Randsel	100	Investment co.
Euranglo (Pty) Ltd	AAC, Randsel, Charter	100	Holds 50% of Franco-SA Investment Co. with Banque de Paris et des Pays Bas
Ewing McDonald (Pty) Ltd	Randsel		
East Driefontein Mining Co.	Randsel	Min.	Gold Mine administered by Gold Fields
Elastic Rail Spike Group	Charter	Min.	Produces rails
Explosives (Zambia) Ltd	Charter	About 50	Manufactures explosives with ICI
Elevators & Engineering Ltd	Charter	25	Manufacturers

Name of company	Anglo holding company	Size of holding (%)	Nature of operation
East Rand Proprietary	AAC, Charter (through Barlow Rand)	Min.	Gold mine administered by Rand Mines
East Champ d'or Gold Mining Co.	JCI	Min.	Gold mine administered by JCI
East Daggafontein	AMGOLD	Min.	Gold mine administered by AAC
Elgin Metal Products	AAC, Charter (through Barlow Rand)	78	Produces stainless steel ware for domestic use
Engelhard Hanovia Inc.	AAC, Randsel, Charter (through HD Development)	70.1	Holds all Engelhard Group interests including gold refining and trading cos
Engelhard Minerals & Chemicals Ltd	AAC, Randsel, Charter (through Engelhard Hanovia)	66	Refines, fabricates and markets precious metals, especially platinum in the US
Engelhard Industries Ltd	AAC, Randsel, Charter (through Engelhard Hanovia)	Maj.	Holds industrial interests of Group
Engelhard Hanovia of SA Ltd	AAC, Randsel, Charter (through Engelhard Hanovia)	Maj.	Holds Group's SA interests
Eastern Forest Estate Ltd	RHOAM	100	Produces timber
Ellaton Gold Mining Co. Ltd	AAC	Min.	Mining finance co.
Eastern Transvaal Timber Co.	AAC	Maj.	
Exchange Buildings Ltd	AMAPROP	Maj.	
Egret Investments Ltd			

Name of company	Anglo holding company	Size of holding (%)	Nature of operation
Free State Geduld Ltd	AMGOLD, Randsel	Min.	Gold mine administered by AAC
Forest Industries & Veneers	AAC, AMIC, Randsel	70	Manufactures wood products. Also holds Peak Timbers
Finsh Diamonds (Pty) Ltd	De Beers	Maj.	Diamond mining co.
Ferranti Ltd	Charter	12.5	Large UK company
Freight Service Holdings	AAC, Charter (through Barlow Rand) and AMIC	77.2	Shipping co.
Ferreira Mines Ltd	AAC, Charter (through Barlow Rand)	100	Gold mine
Flourescent Lighting	JCI		JCI also participates in management of co.
Free State Development & Investment Co.	JCI		Finance and exploration co.
Francana Development	AMCAN	40	Holds Canadian interests, including 30% of Hudcan Development
Francana Oil & Gas	AMCAN (through Hudson Bay)	60	Oil and gas exploration and development co.
Francana Minerals	AMCAN (through Hudson Bay)	100	Produces soda sulphates and zinc
Founders Building society	RHOAM	12	Building society
Fitwaolo Mining Co.	ZCI		Copper mining prospect
Fibre Spinners & Weavers Ltd	Ropes & Mattings		Operates a grain bag mill

Name of company	Anglo holding company	Size of holding (%)	Nature of operation
Freddies Cons. Mines	AAC, AMGOLD	Maj.	Gold mine administered by Anglo
Free State Saaiplaas Gold Mining Co. Ltd	AAC, AMGOLD		Gold mine administered by Anglo
First Cons. Leasing Corp.	Premier Finance Corp.	Maj.	Specializes in the leasing of movable assets
Ferrous Scrap Distributors	Scaw Metals		
Flather Bright Steels Ltd	AAC	Maj.	
First Union General Investment Trust Ltd	AAC	Min.	General investment co.
G & W Holdings (Pty) Ltd	AAC, Randsel	About 30	Holds G & W Base and Ind. Minerals
Griqualand West Diamond Mining Co.	De Beers	72	De Beers leases the mining property to the co.
Geldenhuis Deep Mining Co.	AAC, Charter (through Barlow Rand)	100	Gold mine
Government Gold Mining Areas	JCI	Min.	Gold mine administered by JCI
Greatermans Stores Ltd	JCI	Maj.	Large retail group in southern Africa
Glencairn Holdings (Pty) Ltd	JCI		Finance and exploration co.
Great Northern Capital Corp.	AMCAN	27	
General Mining & Finance Corp.	Mainstraat Beleggings	50	Mining finance group in SA controlled by Federale Mynbou, but Anglo influential.

Name of company	Anglo holding company	Size of holding (%)	Nature of operation
			Gen. Min. controls Union Corp.
Guarantee Life Assurance Co. Ltd	African Eagle Life Assurance Society	100	African Eagle is the largest life assurer in SA
G & W Base & Industrial Minerals Ltd	G & W Holdings	100	Mines, processes and markets a wide range of industrial minerals to foundry, paint, plastic and other industries
G & W Industrial & Chemical Supplies	G & W Holdings	100	
Guarantee Life Properties Ltd	Guarantee Life Assurance	100	Holds property interests of Group
Gerencia Industrial Limitada	AAC	Maj.	
Gypsum Industries Ltd	Tongaat Group	14	
Gallo (Africa) Ltd	AAC	Min.	Produce records, sound equipment, etc.
Hollard Straat Ses Beleggings	AAC, Randsel	49	The holding co. for Anglo & Federale Mynbou (which owns 51% interests)
Harmony Gold Mining Co.	AAC, AMGOLD, Charter, Randsel	Maj.	Gold mine administered by Rand Mines
HD Development Ltd	AAC, Randsel, Charter	Maj.	Holds the Group's interest in Engelhard

Name of company	Anglo holding company	Size of holding (%)	Nature of operation
			Hanovia Inc. (71%)
High Level Gravels Ltd	De Beers	100	Diamond mining co.
Highveld Steel & Vanadium Co.	AAC, Randsel, AMIC, De Beers (through De Beers Ind. Corp.), Charter, JCI, Barlow Rand	51.8	Produces vanadium pentoxide, vanadium steel, rolled steel sections. Operates its own mines
Heatrae Group	Charter	Min.	Industrial group in the UK
Hume Ltd	AAC, Charter (through Barlow Rand)		Makes steel and concrete pipes. Has German partners
Henry Gould Ltd	AAC, Charter (through Barlow Rand)		Produces chrome
Hudson Bay Mining & Smelting Co. Ltd	AMCAN	34.8	Produces copper, zinc, silver, gold, cadmium, selenium, telunium and lead concentrates
Hudcana Development	AMCAN, Hudson Bay & Francana	100	Holding co. for Group interests in Canada
Hudson Bay Holdings	AMCAN (through Hudson Bay)	100	
Hudson Bay Exploration & Development	AMCAN (through Hudson Bay Mining & Smelting)	100	Prospecting and mining concern
Huletts Sugar Corp.	AMIC	11.8	Produces sugar
Hippo Valley Estates	RHOAM	25	Sugar cane planters and millers

Name of company	Anglo holding company	Size of holding (%)	Nature of operation
Hard Metal Tools Ltd	Boart & Hard Metals	100	
Horizon Holdings Ltd	MINORCO	Maj.	Holds MINOR-CO's interest in Trend Exploration
Haw Par Brothers International	Charter	13.3	Charter negotiated to take over London Tin Corp. which involved exchanging these shares
Hall, Longmore & Co.	De Beers Ind. Corp.	2	
Hartebeesfontein Gold Mines	AAC	Min.	Gold mine administered by outside group
Hudson Mining (Pty) Ltd	G & W Holdings	100	Do not confuse with Hudson Bay Mining and Smelting Co.
Hulett's Corp. Ltd	Tongaat Group	50	Sugar producer. Tongaat has control
Hypack Products Ltd	Tongaat Group	28	
Hogarths Ltd	AAC	Min.	
Isipingo Property Investment Co. Ltd	AAC, AMAPROP, Randsel, AMIC	75	Property development co.
Industrias de Caju Mocita (Mozambique)	AAC, Randsel	50	Grows and processes cashew nuts in Mozambique
Industrial Distributors Ltd	ANAMINT, De Beers, JCI	60	The Diamond Corp. and Diamond Producers Association sell industrial diamonds to this co.

Name of company	Anglo holding company	Size of holding (%)	Nature of operation
Industrial Distributors (Sales)	ANAMINT, De Beers, JCI (through Ind. Distributors)	100	Buys industrial diamonds from above co. and sells to the trade
Industrial Grit Distributors	ANAMINT, De Beers, JCI (through Ind. Distributors)	100	Does as above for diamond grit
Ingagne Colliery	AAC, Randsel	Maj.	Coal mine
International Pacific Corp. (Australia)	Charter	30	Merchant bank
Industex	AMIC	37.5	Makes rubber-impregnated industrial textiles
Iron Duke Mining Co. Ltd	RHOAM	100	Iron mine in Rhodesia
International Pipe & Steel Investments SA	De Beers (through De Beers Ind. Corp.) AAC	Min.	
Indumeni Coal Mines Ltd	AMCOAL		Coal mine administered by AAC
Illings (Pty) Ltd	AMIC	77.1	Imports and distributes Mazda cars, earth-moving equipment, cranes, hydraulic excavators & mechanical handling equipment
Industrial Metal Products (1972) Ipcorn Ltd.	AMIC	Maj.	
Inter-Mine Services OFS (Pty) Ltd	AAC		Supplies stores to Anglo Group mines in SA
Ironstone Minerals Ltd	Highveld Steel	100	Part of Highveld Steel & Vanadium Group

Name of company	Anglo holding company	Size of holding (%)	Nature of operation
Industrias de Caju, Antenes SARL	Industrias de Caju Mocita (Mozambique)	100	Processes cashew nuts in Mozambique
Johannesburg Cons. Investments Ltd (JCI)	AAC, De Beers, Randsel	50	Major mining finance house now part of the Anglo Group
J. L. Clarke & Co	Randsel, AMIC	33.3	
JCI General Engineering Ltd	JCI	100	Engineering co. making mining equipment, structural steelwork and precision engineering and agricultural equipment
Jeannette Gold Mines Ltd	AAC, AMGOLD	25	Gold mine, administered by Anglo
John B. Clarke Motor Co.	McCarthy Rodway	Maj.	Retail motor firm
Kriel Coal Mining Co.	AAC, Randsel		Coal mine in SA
Koffiefontein Diamond Mine	De Beers	Maj.	Diamond mine in SA
Kimberley Engineering Ltd	De Beers (through De Beers Ind. Corp.)	50	Engineering concern 50% owned by Anglo-Vaal
Kanshansi Copper Mine	MINORCO		Zambian copper mine
Konkola Mining Co.	ZCI		Copper mine in Zambia
Kasempa Minerals	MINORCO (through ZAMANGLO Exploration Ltd	Maj.	Prospecting co. operating in Zambia
Kalahari Investments Ltd	MINORCO, Anglo American Botswana, ZCI	100	Holds interests in Makgadikgadi Soda &

Name of company	Anglo holding company	Size of holding (%)	Nature of operation
			Bamangwato Concessions
Kenya Fertilizers Ltd	Charter	50	50% of fertilizer co. held by ICI
Kadola Mines Ltd	Charter	33.6	Mine in Zambia
Kinross Mines Ltd	AMGOLD		Gold mine, administered by others
Kloof Gold Mining Co.	AMGOLD		Gold mine administered by Anglo
Karina (Private) Ltd	AAC	Maj.	
Kenilworth Centre (Pty) Ltd	AMAPROP	Maj.	Owns office and shopping complex in Cape Town
Kaffrarian Metal Holdings	AAC	Maj.	Prospecting co.
Kiln Products Ltd	AAC	Min.	
Loraine Gold Mining Co.	AMGOLD	16	Gold mine
Libanon Gold Mining Co.	AMGOLD	Min.	Gold and uranium mine
La Lucia Property Investment Co.	AAC, AMAPROP, Randsel (through SA Townships)	55	Developing 330 acres (133 ha) of land on N. coast of Natal
LTA Engineering Co. Ltd	AMIC, AAC, Randsel, Boart & Hard Metals	40	1 of the 2 largest construction and civil engineering groups in SA
Lennings Holdings (Pty) Ltd	Randsel, JCI, AMIC		General engineering
Leesbak Investments (Pty) Ltd	AMIC (indirect)	100	Owns office premises

Name of company	Anglo holding company	Size of holding (%)	Nature of operation
Leo Computer Bureau	AAC (through Barlow Rand)	Maj.	
LHL Engineering Ltd	AAC (through Barlow Rand)	26.4	Makes equipment for ambulances, fire engines, refrigeration units, etc.
L. & F. Metter (Pty) Ltd	AAC (through Barlow Rand)	Min.	Structural engineering, building, construction, plant sales, etc.
Louw's Creek Mining Timber Ltd	JCI	100	Produces timber for mines
Lubimbi Coal Areas	RHOAM	50	Coal mine in Rhodesia
Lytton Minerals Ltd	AMCAN, Hudson Bay Mining	67	
Lydenburg Platinum Ltd	AAC, JCI	Min.	Platinum mine
Longyear International BV	AMIC (through Boart & Hard Metals)	75	Manufactures and sells drilling equipment worldwide and does contract drilling
Lydenburg Holdings Ltd	AAC	Maj.	General investment
Leslie Gold Mines Ltd	AAC, AMGOLD	Min.	Gold mine administered by other group
Lynnedeale's Motors Ltd	McCarthy Rodway	Maj.	Retail motor firm
Leymac Distributors Ltd	McCarthy Rodway	Maj.	Retail motor firm
Mainstraat Beleggings (1965) Eiendoms Bpk	AAC, AMIC, Randsel, De Beers Ind. Corp.	50	50% owned by General Mining, invests in engineering

Name of company	Anglo holding company	Size of holding (%)	Nature of operation
			and heavy industry
Messina (Transvaal) Development Co.	AAC	9.2	Copper mining, but also some industry, property and loan finance
Mondi Valley Paper Co. Ltd	AAC, AMIC, JCI, Randsel	85.3	Owns large ground wood-pulp paper mills
McCarthy Main Holdings Ltd	AMIC, Randsel, AAC	50	Motor dealer, with earth-moving equipment and engineering cos as subsidiaries
Motor Assemblies Ltd	Through McCarthy Main Holdings	15	Assembles motor vehicles
Metair Holdings (Pty) Ltd	Through McCarthy Main Holdings	40	Holds 53% of Airco Engineering
Mozambique Fisheries Ltd	AAC, Randsel	45	Fishing co.
Main Place Holdings	AAC, JCI	Maj.	Property holding co. in J'burg
Marine Diamonds	De Beers (through CDM of SWA)	36.2	Off-shore diamond mining co.
Middelburg Steel & Alloys (Pty) Ltd	Charter, AMIC, Barlow Rand	70	Holds interests in RMB Alloys, Southern Cross Steel, Palmiet Chrome Corp., Thos. Beglie & Co.
Mwinilunga Mines	Charter, ZCI	Min.	Zambian copper mine
McKechnie Brothers (SA) Ltd	Through Barlow Rand	10	Engineering co.

Name of company	Anglo holding company	Size of holding (%)	Nature of operation
Milsell Chrome Mines	Barlow Rand (through TC Lands)	Min.	Chrome mine
MITAC (Pty) Ltd	AMIC (through Boart & Hard Metals)		Management consultants
Madziwa Mining Co. Ltd	RHOAM (through Rhodesia Nickel)	100	Nickel mines in Rhodesia
Mazoe Citrus Estates Ltd	RHOAM	100	Citrus farms
Merchant Bank (Zambia) Ltd	MINORCO (through ZAIIC)	20	Merchant bank in Zambia
Metal Fabricators of Zambia Ltd	MINORCO (through Zambian Anglo American Ind. Corp.)	10	Metal manufacturers in Zambia
Makgadikgadi Soda Ltd	Through Kalahari Investments	Min.	Soda mine in Botswana
Mulfulira Copper Ltd	MINORCO	Min.	Zambian copper mine
Marina da Gama Ltd	AMAPROP		Property developer in Cape Town
Metals & Minerals Investment Corp. Ltd	Randsel	49	Investment trust co. with interests in metal and mineral producers
Morupule Colliery Ltd	Anglo American Botswana	80	Botswana coal mining co.
Messina Rhodesia Investments	RHOAM	Min.	Base metal mining co. in Rhodesia
Mindrill Ltd	Through Boart & Hard Metals	100	
Metkor Investments Ltd	Through IPSA	Min.	Investments in engineering firms
McCarthy Rodway Ltd	Through McCarthy Main Holdings	Maj.	Largest retail motor organization in SA
Mazeppa Investments Ltd	Through McCarthy Rodway	Maj.	Motor retailing co.

Name of company	Anglo holding company	Size of holding (%)	Nature of operation
McCarthy's Affiliated Investments	Through McCarthy Rodway	Maj.	
Metair Investments Ltd	Through Metair Holdings	72	Manufactures air-conditioning and refrigerator equipment and truck bodies
Morelands Foods & Feeds Ltd	Through Tongaat Group	Maj.	
Majoram Holdings Ltd			
Matte Smelters Ltd	Union Platinum, Johnson Matthey	Maj.	Concentrates platinum group metals
Minas del Otono, SA	Lytton Minerals	48	Copper mining co. in Mexico
Marico Mineral Co. Ltd	Vereeniging Refractories	100	Supplies raw material to parent co.
Mopani Magnesite Ltd	Vereeniging Refractories	About 50	Mines Magnesite
New Central Witwatersrand Areas Ltd	AAC	Maj.	Mining finance co. holding interests in De Beers, AAC, Randsel, JCI, AMGOLD
Natal Anthracite Colliery	AMCOAL	Min.	Coal mine
Newcastle Platberg Colliery	AMCOAL	Min.	Coal mine
Natal Ammonium Collieries	AMCOAL	Min.	Coal mine
New Jagersfontein Mining & Exploration Co. Ltd	De Beers	67.7	Diamond mining co.
Northern Lime Co. Ltd	De Beers Ind. Corp., Charter, Barlow Rand (Rio Tinto owns about 10%)	30	Produces marble chips and dust and sells to Marble Line & Associated

Name of company	Anglo holding company	Size of holding (%)	Nature of operation
			Industries Ltd in which it has interests
New Largo Colliery	AMCOAL, Randsel	Maj.	Coal mine, supplies ES-COM
Natal Coal Exploration	Randsel, AMCOAL	40.3	Prospecting co.
N'Changa Cons. Copper Mines Ltd	ZCI	49	Holds the copper mining and refining interests of Anglo in Zambia
National Milling Co. (Zambia)	Charter	50	Milling concern in Zambia
National Fund Holdings	Barlow Rand, JCI	16	Central Acceptances had control
National Carpets Ltd	JCI	14	Manufactures carpets
Nedsual	AAC, De Beers	Min.	Formed out of a merger of Nedbank (controlled by the Old Mutual), UAL (controlled by Anglo) and Syfrets (controlled by Anglo). One of the largest banking and financial services groups in SA
Nefic Ltd	Nedsual	Maj.	Specialist general bank
NEFIC Acceptances Ltd	NEFIC	Maj.	Merchant bank
Nedsual Economic Unit Ltd	Nedsual	Maj.	Provides economic information to cos

Name of company	Anglo holding company	Size of holding (%)	Nature of operation
New State Areas Ltd	JCI	Maj.	Land and township co.
New Imperial Mines Ltd	AMCAN	10.6	Canadian copper mining co.
Ndola Lime Co.	Zambian Anglo American Ind. Corp. (ZMAIC)	50	
Northern Breweries Ltd	ZAAIC, SA Breweries	49	Monopoly over Zambian liquor industry
National Finance Corp. of SA	AAC	Min.	Operates on the money market
National Board of Executors	Nedsual	Min.	Nedsual has largest single holding
New Middleridge Ltd	AAC	Maj.	Prospecting co.
New Rhodesia Investments Ltd	AAC	100	A holding company for Anglo's Rhodesian interests other than those held by RHOAM
Natal Tanning Extract Co. Ltd	AAC		Owns forests and 3 factories to produce tanning extract from bark
Orange Free State Investment Trust	AMGOLD	Maj.	Holds Anglo's gold mining interests in OFS
Orama Holdings Ltd	Cons. Diamond Mines SWA	84.7	Holds diamond interest
Overseas & Rhodesian Investment Co. Ltd	Randsel, RHOAM, AAC	Maj.	Holding co. for some Anglo interests in Rhodesia
Oranje Koelkamers Ltd	AMIC	50	Produces and distributes

Name of company	Anglo holding company	Size of holding (%)	Nature of operation
			meat and dairy produce
Orange Free State Land & Estate Co. Ltd	AMIC	Maj.	Property co. operating in OFS
Oriole Investments Ltd	AAC		
Orlop Investments Ltd	New Rhodesia Investments	100	
Olympic Motors Ltd	McCarthy Rodway	Maj.	Retail motor firm
President Brand Mining Co.	AMGOLD	Maj.	Gold mine in OFS adminis- tered by Anglo
President Steyn Mining Co.	AMGOLD	Maj.	Gold mine in OFS adminis- tered by Anglo
Petrangol Consortium	AAC, De Beers, JCI, Barlow Rand, General Mining	67.5	Holds a 25% stake in the output of a pro- ducing oilfield in Angola
PGM Brakspruit Ltd	Charter, AAC, Barlow Rand, General Mining	Over 80	Buys platinum from Rusten- burg Plats and resells to En- gelhard Miner- als & Chemical Corp.
Premier (Transvaal) Diamond Mining Co.	De Beers	98.4	Mines dia- monds
Protea Holdings Ltd	Randsel	15	Has interests in chemicals, medicines, scientific in- struments, metal products
Potgietersrust Platinum Ltd	Randsel, AAC, JCI	Maj.	Part of the new Union Plats Group

Name of company	Anglo holding company	Size of holding (%)	Nature of operation
Pretoria Portland Cement Co.	Charter, Barlow Rand	26.4	Cement producer
Prospecting (?) (full name not known)	Charter		Prospecting venture in Madagascar
Platinum Prospecting Co.	Charter, General Mining	At least 25	Platinum prospecting co.
Printing Investments Ltd	JCI	100	Holds Swan Press, also Wallack's
Palabora Mining Co. Ltd	JCI	7	Copper mine controlled by Rio Tinto
Phalaborwa Engineering Co.	JCI	Maj.	Engineering concern
Premier Portland Cement Co.	RHOAM	7	Rhodesian subsidiary of Pretoria Portland which owns 49%
Premier Finance Corp.	AAC	Maj.	Provides medium-term finance
Peak Timbers Ltd	AAC	Maj.	Owns forests in Swaziland
Prospecting Ventures Ltd	AAC	Maj.	Prospecting co.
Prairie Investments Ltd	MINORCO	100	Owns 51% of Engelhard Minerals & Chemicals
Premier Finance Corp.	Randsel	100	A finance company, part of Schlezinger Group
Prolux Paint Holdings	AE & CI	100	Holdings in paint manufacturers
Pan Textiles Ltd	SA Nylon Spinners	100	
Parcs Motors Ltd	McCarthy Rodway	Maj.	Retail motor firm

Name of company	Anglo holding company	Size of holding (%)	Nature of operation
Rhochar Holdings Ltd	AAC, Randsel	100	Holds AAC's and Randsel's interests in Charter
Rand Mines	Barlow Rand	Maj.	Merger between Rand Mines & Thos. Barlow led to Barlow Rand being formed
Rhodes Fruit Farms Ltd	AAC, Randsel, De Beers	Maj.	Fruit and wine farms controlled by Anglo
Rhodesian Nickel Corp.	RHOAM, AAC, Randsel	85	Holds interests in Rhodesian nickel mine
Rhodesian Acceptances	RHOAM, AAC, Randsel	About 50	Merchant bank in Rhodesia
Rand Mines Holdings	Barlow Rand, AAC, Randsel, Charter	Over 80	Holds interests in Rand Mines Engineering Investments, TC Lands and others
Rhokana Corp.	MINORCO	Min.	Copper mining co. in Zambia
Rathsdown Ltd	Charter	Min.	Industrial group in the UK
Roan Cons. Mines	ZCI	Min.	Copper mining co. in Zambia
Rio Tinto-Zinc Corp.	Charter, JCI	About 15	UK mining group
Rand Mines Engineering Investments Ltd	Rand Mines Holdings, Rand Mines, TC Lands	100	Holds a large number of Barlow Rand's engineering interests
Rand Mines Properties	Rand Mines Holdings, Rand Mines	Maj.	Holds gold properties

Name of company	Anglo holding company	Size of holding (%)	Nature of operation
Rand Mines Property Brokers	Rand Mines Properties	100	
Ready Mixed Concrete (SA) Ltd	Barlow Rand	33.3	Operates ready-mix concrete plants
Rheem SA Ltd	AMIC, Engelhard Hanovia (SA)	45	Makes steel drums
Randfontein Estates	JCI	Min.	Gold mine administered by JCI
Rustenburg Platinum Mines	JCI	Maj.	Part of the Union Plats Group
Ropes & Mattings Ltd	AMIC	14	Textile group in SA
Rhodesia & Nyasaland Forest Enterprises Ltd	RHOAM	100	Timber producer
Rhodesian Diamond & Carbide Ltd	RHOAM	40	
Rhodesian Iron & Steel Corp.	RHOAM	8	Produces iron and steel
Ridgeway Hotel Ltd	Zambian Anglo American Ind. Corp.	30	Hotel group in Zambia
Rhokana Copper Refinery	ZCI	Min.	Copper refinery in Zambia
Rioden Investments Ltd	AAC	20	Prospecting co.
RNFE (Private) Ltd	AAC	Maj.	
Rhodesian Alloys Ltd	AAC	Min.	
Refractory Minerals Ltd	Vereeniging Refractories	100	Supplies raw material to parent co. Operates in Rhodesia
Rand Carbide Ltd	AE & CI	68	
St. Helena Gold Mining Co.	AMGOLD, Randsel	20	Gold mine administered by Union Corp.

Name of company	Anglo holding company	Size of holding (%)	Nature of operation
Southvaal Holdings Ltd	AMGOLD, Randsel	Maj.	Gold holding company
SW Africa Co.	AAC, Randsel	Min.	Produces vanadium and lead; administered by Gold Fields Group
South African Breweries Ltd	AAC, AMIC, JCI, Randsel, Barlow Rand	31.6	Largest brewery group in SA, with interests in liquor, food, hotels and industry
Soetvelde Ltd	AAC, SA Townships, AMCOAL	Over 33	Holds Anglo's agricultural land interests. Over 51 000 morgen
Stellenbosch Wine Trust	SA Breweries, JCI	48	Holds wine interests
Swaziland Iron Ore Development Co.	AAC, Randsel	Maj.	Owns an iron ore mine in Swaziland
Standard Bank of Angola	AAC	Min.	Angolan branch
Standard Bank of Mozambique	AAC	Min.	Mozambican branch
Société Minière d'Anglade	Charter, AAC	40	Co. mines scheelite deposits in France
Société Minière de Maurétanie	Charter, AAC	44.6	Co. mines copper in Mauretania, Charter administers the mine. Co. uses the AAC patented Torco process to treat the ore
Société Minière et Met. de Penarroya	Charter	Min.	French mining co.

Name of company	Anglo holding company	Size of holding (%)	Nature of operation
South West Finance Corp.	De Beers	100	Holds Oppenheimer family's rights to diamonds in Namibia
Synthetic Diamond Co.	De Beers	100	Holds synthetic diamond interests
Societá Nazionale Sviluppo Impresse Industriale	De Beers, Charter	Min.	A leading Italian finance and investment co. in which the Banque de Paris and the French Bernberg group also participate
Sea Diamonds Ltd	Cons. Diamond Mines	52.9	A holding co. in De Beers
South African Nylon Spinners (Pty) Ltd	De Beers Ind. Corp.	37.5	Spins continuous filament fibres from imported polymers. ICI holds 25%, the SA govt owns 37.5%
Stewarts & Lloyds of SA Ltd	De Beers Ind. Corp., Randsel, AMIC	Min.	Makes tubes, borehole pumps, windmills, etc.
South African Titan Products	AE & CI	40	Controlled by Titan Products (UK)
Southvaal Holdings Ltd	Randsel, AMGOLD	Min.	Holds interests in Anglo's Vaal Reefs gold mine
South African Townships Mining & Finance Co. Ltd	Randsel	92.9	Has interests in gold, diamond and base metal mining, industry and property

Name of company	Anglo holding company	Size of holding (%)	Nature of operation
Sabel Developments Ltd	SA Townships	100	Shopping centre in Belleville, Cape Town
South African Coal Estates	Charter, Randsel, AM-COAL	58	Coal mining co.
Selection Trust	Charter	27	UK mining house with large copper, gold, diamond and molybdenium interests in Africa, Australia and N. America. Charter largest shareholder
Swaziland Collieries Ltd	Charter, Barlow Rand	87.4	Has coal mines in Swaziland
Shell Transport & Trading Co. Ltd	Charter	About 10	Part of the Shell group (Royal Dutch Shell Petroleum)
Stormill (Pty) Ltd	Barlow Rand	100	Industrial township in Transvaal
South Wales Group Ltd	Barlow Rand	33.3	Heavy engineering group holding company in the UK
South African Forest Investments Ltd	Barlow Rand, AMIC	100	Timber producer with saw-milling and forestry interests in Transvaal
South African Shipping Finance Co. Ltd	Barlow Rand	Min.	Owns Rand Bank Ltd and other interests
Steelbrite Ltd	JCI	Almost 50	Furniture manufacturer

Name of company	Anglo holding company	Size of holding (%)	Nature of operation
			controlled by JCI
South African Minerals Corp.	JCI	Maj.	Base metals company
Standard Charter Bank Group	AAC, JCI	Min.	JCI holds a share in the Standard Bank (London) Ltd which owns the Standard Bank Investment Corp. (in which AAC has an interest) which owns the Standard Bank of SA
Shannon Sawmills Ltd	JCI		Administered by JCI
Sunningdale Farm Ltd	JCI		Controlled by JCI
Sylvite of Canada Ltd	Hudson Bay Mining	100	Mines potash and supplies it to Terra Chemicals
Scaw Metals Ltd	AMIC	100	Produces ferrous and non-ferrous castings, rolled steel products, etc.
South African Board Mills	AMIC	Min.	Paperboard producer
Stafford Mayer Co. (SA) Ltd	AMIC	24.5	Holds coal, sugar and industrial interests. Owns 68% of SA Board Mills
Stone & Allied Industries	AMIC	100	Owned 100% by Orange Free State Lane &

Name of company	Anglo holding company	Size of holding (%)	Nature of operation
			Estate Co., in which AMIC has a majority share
Shaft Sinkers Ltd	LTA	Maj.	Engaged in shaft-sinking across the world
Simoona Estates Ltd	RHOAM	100	Farmland in Rhodesia
Spes Bona Exploration & Mining Ltd	RHOAM	31.5	Mining and exploration in Rhodesia
Salfontein Gold Mining Co.	AMGOLD	Min.	Gold mine
Sentrust Bpk	AAC	Maj.	Finance house
Schlezinger Insurance & Institutional Holdings Ltd (SII)	Randsel	Maj.	Interests in life insurance, property development and banking. One of the largest financial groups in SA
Sorec Ltd	Randsel	47	Controls part of the property development interests of SII, of which it is a subsidiary
Springbok Colliery Ltd	South African Coal Estates	100	Coal mine controlled by AM-COAL
South African Mines Selection Ltd	AAC	Maj.	Holding co. for mining interests
St Andrews Securities Ltd	AAC	Maj.	
South African Land & Exploration Co. Ltd	AMGOLD		Gold mine administered by Anglo

Name of company	Anglo holding company	Size of holding (%)	Nature of operation
Scandiamant Ak-tiebolag	De Beers	25	Composed of 3 cos manufacturing synthetic diamonds in SA, Ireland, Sweden
Strikine Copper Ltd	Hudson Bay Mining	32	Owns copper deposits in British Columbia
Shangani Mining Corp.		Maj.	
Springfield Collieries Ltd	AMCOAL	Maj.	Coal mine administered by Anglo
Standard Bank Investment Corp.	AAC	Min.	See Standard Charter Bank Group and Standard Banks of Angola and Mozambique
Southridge Ltd	AAC	Maj.	Prospecting co.
Swakop Exploration Ltd	AAC	Maj.	Prospecting co. in Namibia
Syndicat de Recherches de Nord-Andriamena	AAC	Min.	Prospecting co.
Safmot Ltd	McCarthy Rodway	Maj.	Retail motor firm
Southampton Assurance Co. of Rhodesia Ltd	African Eagle Life Assurance Society	100	Part of the Group's Rhodesian operations
Tsumeb Corp.	AAC, SWA Co.	Min.	Lead and zinc mine in Namibia
Transalloys (Pty) Ltd	AAC, Randsel	65	Produces ferro-manganese. Phillip Bros of Switzerland is also

Name of company	Anglo holding company	Size of holding (%)	Nature of operation
			involved (owns 35%)
Tidal Diamonds Ltd	Cons. Diamond Mines	54	Holding co. for De Beers
Tiger Oats & National Milling Co. Ltd	AMIC, Randsel, JCI	Min.	Basic food processor
Transvaal Cons. Lands Ltd	Charter, Barlow Rand	About 40	Holds mineral rights, colliery and financial interests
Tronoh Mines (Malaysia) Ltd	Charter	29.7	Owns 2 tin mines in Malaysia
Trade & Transportation Services Ltd	Charter	8	UK co.
Trans-Atlas Holdings Ltd	Barlow Rand		Has a majority holding in Cons. Stonecrushers Ltd which dominates the crushed stone and sand market in the Transvaal
Transvaal & Delagoa Bay Ltd	TC Lands	96	Holds Douglas Drift Colliery and other interests (e.g. Rand Mines Engineering)
Tedelex Ltd	Barlow Rand	Min.	Makes and distributes electrical household goods (e.g. hifis, radios, fridges)
Toyota (SA) Ltd	JCI	Min.	Holds franchise for Toyota vehicles
Teba Trust (Pty) Ltd	JCI	Maj.	Finance and exploration co.

Name of company	Anglo holding company	Size of holding (%)	Nature of operation
Terra Chemicals International	Hudson Bay Mining	15	Operates a chemical complex from the US. Sylvite of Canada supplies its potash.
Terra Nova Exploration	Hudson Bay Exploration	33	Prospecting co.
Tombill Mines Ltd	Hudcana Development	38	Holds 40% of Francana Minerals
Thompson Ramco (SA) Ltd	AMIC	45	Produces motor components. 51% is held by TRW Inc. of US
Trojan Mining Co. Ltd	Rhodesian Nickel Corp.	100	Rhodesian mining co. (nickel)
Tanganyika Concessions Ltd	RHOAM	Min.	
Tubemakers of SA Ltd	Stewarts & Lloyds of SA	100	Holds S. & L.'s tubemaking interests in SA
Tubemakers of Rhodesia Ltd	Stewarts & Lloyds of SA	100	Holds Rhodesian interests
Tube & Pipe Industries Ltd	Stewarts & Lloyds of SA	100	Holds associated tube interests
Trend Exploration	MINORCO	57	Has oil interests in Canada and Indonesia
Townsview Estates Ltd	Randsel	Maj.	Provides technical and managerial services to Schlezinger Group's property cos
Thaton Ltd	AAC	Maj.	
The Sungei Besi Mines Ltd	Charter	Min.	Tin Mine in Malaysia

Name of company	Anglo holding company	Size of holding (%)	Nature of operation
Transvaal Coal Corp.	AMCOAL	Maj.	
Trans-Natal Coal Co. Ltd	AMCOAL	Min.	Coal mine
The Deep Drilling Co. Ltd	Boart & Hard Metals	Maj.	
Transvaal Vanadium Co. (Pty) Ltd	Highveld Steel & Vanadium	Maj.	
Tongaat Group Ltd	AAC	Min.	Produces sugar, food, clothes, and is involved in property and construction
Tongaat Sugar Ltd	Tongaat Group	Maj.	Produces sugar
Tongaat Investments Ltd	Tongaat Group	Maj.	Property and electrical engineering interests
The Rhodesian Milling Co.	RHOAM	Min.	
The Discount House of SA Ltd	Nedsual	Maj.	Operates in the SA money market
Tuli Exploration Ltd	AAC	Maj.	Prospecting co.
Triomf Fertilizer Ltd	AE & CI	49	Manufactures fertilizers
Umhlanga Beach	AMAPROP	Maj.	Holiday centre on N. coast of Natal
United Transport Holdings	AAC, AMIC, Randsel	40	Owns buses, commercial vehicles and cars for hire. United Transport (UK) owns 60%
Umgala Collieries Ltd	AMCOAL	Min.	Coal mine
Ultra High Pressure Units	De Beers	50	Produces synthetic diamonds

Name of company	Anglo holding company	Size of holding (%)	Nature of operation
Union Acceptances Holdings	Nedsual	Maj.	Holds merchant banking interests
Union Platinum Mining Co. Ltd	AAC, JCI	Maj.	Platinum mining co. which also controls Rustenburg Plats, Waterval Plats & Potgietersrust Plats
Union Corp.	General Mining, Charter	Min.	Has been taken over by General Mining
Union Steel Corp. Ltd	AMIC	13.1	Controlled by ISCOR, produces steel products, etc.
USCO Aluminium Corp. Ltd	Union Steel Corp.	Maj.	Operates an aluminium wire and conductor plant
Union Carriage & Wagon Co.	General Mining, Mainstraat Beleggings	Min.	Biggest single supplier of railway coaches and electric locomotives to SA Railways and other rail networks
Unitor (Zambia) Ltd	Zamanglo Ind. Corp.	20	
Ultra High Pressure Units (Ireland) Ltd	De Beers	50	Produces synthetic diamonds in Ireland plant
Virginia Merriespruit Investment Co. Ltd	Charter, AAC, Barlow Rand, Engelhard Hanovia (SA)	82	Kennecott Copper of US owns 10% of the co.
Virginia (Orange Free State) Gold Mining	Virginia Merriespruit Investment Co.		Gold mine administered by

Name of company	Anglo holding company	Size of holding (%)	Nature of operation
Co. Ltd			Anglo-Vaal Group
Vaal Reefs Ltd	AMGOLD, Randsel	Maj.	Gold mine administered by Anglo
Venterspost Ltd	AMGOLD	Min.	Gold mine administered by Gold Fields
Vierfontein Collieries Ltd	De Beers Ind. Corp., African & European	28.5	Supplies coal to one of ESCOM's power stations
Van Dyke's Drift Colliery	TC Lands		Coal mine
Vryheid Coronation Colliery	Coronation Colliery	Maj.	Coal mine administered by AMCOAL
Vereeniging Refractories Ltd	AMCOAL, AMIC	66.7	Manufactures refractories, silica, bricks, etc. Has a number of subsidiaries
Vereeniging Cons. Mills Ltd	AMCOAL	Min.	Produces foodstuffs, cattle feed, etc.
VE Exploration Ltd	AMCOAL	Maj.	Prospecting subsidiary of AMCOAL
Vereeniging Tiles Ltd	Vereeniging Refractories	Maj.	Manufactures tubes, etc.
Vitro Clay Pipes Ltd	Vereeniging Refractories	50	Shares market with Cullinan Refractories
VPC Ltd	LTA	42	Handles turnkey heavy industrial projects
Vanderbijl Engineering Corp. Ltd	AAC	Min.	Controlled by ISCOR. UK

Name of company	Anglo holding company	Size of holding (%)	Nature of operation
			cos. involved Associated Electrical Engineers, Vickers, & Ashmore Benson Pease & Co. Also Mesta Machine Co. of US. Produces heavy mechanical equipment
Vecor Heavy Engineering	Vanderbijl Engineering	Maj.	Subsidiary of Vanderbijl
Vosa Valves Ltd	Stewarts & Lloyds of SA	100	
Veldmaster (Pty) Ltd	Union Steel Corp.	Maj.	Produces agricultural discs and earth-engaging parts
Valley Exploration & Mining Co. Ltd	AAC	Maj.	Prospecting co.
Western Holdings Ltd	AMGOLD, AAC, Randsel	Maj.	Gold mine administered by Anglo
Welkom Gold Mining Co.	Randsel, AAC, AMGOLD	Maj.	Gold mine administered by Anglo
West Witwatersrand Areas Ltd	AMGOLD, Randsel, AAC	20.1	Holds West Rand gold interests. Control by Gold Fields, Anglo influential
Western Deep Levels Ltd	AMGOLD, AAC, Randsel, Charter.	Maj.	Gold mine administered by Anglo
Western Reefs Ltd	AAC, Randsel, AMGOLD	Maj.	Klerksdorp gold mine administered by Anglo

Name of company	Anglo holding company	Size of holding (%)	Nature of operation
Western Areas Ltd	AAC, Randsel, AM-GOLD	Maj.	Gold mine administered by JCI
West Driefontein Gold Mining Co. Ltd	AMGOLD, AAC, Randsel	Min.	Gold mine administered by Gold Fields Group
Wankie Collieries Ltd	AAC, RHOAM, Randsel	Maj.	Large coal field in Rhodesia
Williamson Diamond Mining Co.	De Beers	50	Owns large diamond field in Tanzania together with Tanzanian govt
Waterval (Rustenburg) Platinum Mining Co. Ltd	JCI, AAC	Maj.	Part of the new JCI-controlled Union Platinum Group of mines
Witbank Collieries Ltd	Charter, Barlow Rand	Maj.	Controlled by Rand Mines for Barlow Rand
Werff Brothers Ltd	Charter	40	UK co.
Welgedacht Exploration Ltd	Barlow Rand	Maj.	Administered by Rand Mines
Winterveld (TCL) Chrome Mines Ltd	Transvaal Cons. Lands		Chrome mine in Barlow Rand Group
Weyerhauser (SA) Ltd	Barlow Rand, SA Forest Investments	66.6	Makes corrugated cardboard containers. Weyerhauser (US) holds 33.3%
Witwatersrand Gold Mining Co.	JCI	Maj.	Land and township co.
White Pass & Yukon Ltd	AMCAN	25.6	Provides transport services in Yukon,

Name of company	Anglo holding company	Size of holding (%)	Nature of operation
			British Columbia
Western Bank Ltd	Randsel	Min.	Controlled formerly by Anglo, now by Barclays Bank with Anglo increasing its interests in Barclays
West End Property Co. Ltd	Anglo American Botswana	100	Owns a multistorey office building, Botsalano House, in Gaborone, Botswana
Whitehorse Copper Mines Ltd	AMCAN, Hudson Bay Mining	41.6	Copper mining co. in Canada
Winkelhaak Mines Ltd	AAC, AMGOLD	Min.	Gold mine
Western Ultra Deep Levels Ltd	AAC, AMGOLD	30	Mining finance co. controlled by Anglo
Witwatersrand Deep Ltd	AAC	Min.	Mining finance house
Warbler Investments Ltd	AAC	20	Prospecting co.
Western Decalta Petroleum	Hudson Bay Mining	38	
Witbank Coal Holdings Ltd	AMCOAL, AAC	Maj.	Holding co. for some Anglo coal interests
Wendt GMBH Ltd	Boart & Hard Metals	Maj.	
W. S. Craster (Private) Ltd	Scaw Metals		
Zandpan Ltd	Randsel, AAC, AMGOLD	Min.	Gold and uranium mines administered by Anglo Vaal
Zinchem Ltd	AAC, AMIC, Randsel	100	Produces zinc dust

Name of company	Anglo holding company	Size of holding (%)	Nature of operation
Zuinguin Natal Ltd	African & European, Randsel, AMCOAL	57.5	Coal co. controls Indumeni Coal Co. as well
Zululand Oil Exploration Co.	Engelhard Hanovia, Barlow Rand		Has on- and off-shore concessions in Zululand. Gulf Oil doing exploration
Zinc Oxides of Canada Ltd	Hudson Bay Mining	100	Holds 100% of Durham Industries of Canada
Zambian Anglo American Industrial Corp. (ZAAIC)	MINORCO	100	Holds Anglo Group's industrial and agricultural interests in Zambia
Zambia Copper Investments	MINORCO	49.9	Holds Anglo's mining interests in Zambia
Zambia Clay Industries Ltd	Zamanglo Ind. Corp.	22	
Zamanglo Exploration Ltd	ZCI	60	
Zambian Broken Hill Mining Co. Ltd	MINORCO	Maj.	Lead and zinc mine in Zambia
Zamanglo Australia (Pty) Ltd	MINORCO	100	Owns 30% of Australian Anglo American
Zambia Breweries Ltd			Previously Northern Breweries. See 'N'

Sources   Company Reports:

Anglo American Corp. of South Africa, *Annual Reports,* 1970–6
De Beers Cons. Mines, *Annual Reports.* 1970–6
Charter Cons., *Annual Reports,* 1970–6
Rand Selection Corp., *Annual Reports,* 1970–6
Anglo American Investment Trust, *Annual Reports,* 1970–6
Mineral and Resources Corp., *Annual Report,* 1976
Anglo American Gold Investment, *Annual Report,* 1976
Anglo American Industrial Corp., *Annual Reports,* 1970–6
Anglo American Coal Investments, *Annual Report,* 1976
Anglo American Properties, *Annual Reports,* 1975–6
Zambian Copper Investments, *Annual Reports,* 1973–6

Financial Mail, Johannesburg: September 1968–February 1970, January 1975–August 1976; *Financial Gazette,* Johannesburg: September 1968–February 1970.

APPENDIX 3

A Survey of the
International Links of the Anglo American Group

INTRODUCTION

This appendix presents the links between companies in the Anglo American Group and some of the more important European, American and Japanese companies. Some governments with direct links with Anglo American companies have also been included. This list is not a fully comprehensive record and is compiled from information relating to Group activity in 1976.

Documentation is presented, for the sake of clarity, in the following way.

1. The first line of an entry is set in **bold type** and shows the company or group with which the Anglo Group is linked (e.g. American Metal Climax) and the country of origin of that company or group (e.g. the US).
2. The second line is set in SMALL CAPITALS and shows the holding company within the Anglo Group which is the other pole of the linkage (e.g. Charter Consolidated). Where two or more Anglo companies are involved these are given. In cases where the Anglo Group is known to be involved but the name of the holding company itself is not known, or where a large number of Anglo companies are involved, the term 'Anglo Group' is used.
3. Subsequent lines, set in text type, specify the precise nature of the connection between the Anglo Group and the international Group with which it is connected, e.g. joint holdings in a third company and the nature of that company's association with the other two; the provision of financial support; loans; etc. Where more than one connection is known to exist these are given. Where the connection is through holdings in other companies, those connecting companies are *italicized*. Where holdings exist in connecting companies, the size of the holdings, where known, is given as percentages. These percentages should, however, be treated with some caution as they are constantly varying. When possible, cross references have been made.

Abbreviations of the names of some of the Anglo Group companies mentioned in the appendix are as follows:

AAC   Anglo American Corporation of South Africa Ltd
Randsel   Rand Selection Corporation Ltd
AMIC   Anglo American Industrial Corporation Ltd
AMCAN   Anglo American Corporation of Canada Ltd

UAL   Union Acceptances Ltd
JCI   Johannesburg Consolidated Investments Ltd
DEBINCOR   De Beers Industrial Corporation Ltd
AE & CI   African Explosives & Chemical Industries Ltd
ZCI   Zambian Copper Investments Ltd
RHOAM   Rhodesian Anglo American Ltd
LTA   LTA Engineering Co. Ltd

Air Reduction Inc. (of the US)   AAC, RANDSEL   Air Reduction holds 35% of *Transalloys (Pty) Ltd* in which the AAC holds 38.5% and Randsel holds 16.5%. *Avesta Jernverks*, a Swedish company, also holds 10% of Transalloys.

Aluminium Co. of Canada (SA) Ltd, Alcan (SA), Alusuisse   RAND MINES, TC LANDS   Alcan holds 15% and Alusuisse holds 33.3% of *Aluminium Investment Co.*, in which Rand Mines holds 7.5% and TC Lands holds 2.5%.

American Metal Climax (Amax) (US)   CHARTER CONS. ZCI   Charter holds 27% of *Selection Trust*, which holds 11.5% of Amax. Amax owns *Roan Selection Trust* which, together with ZCI (an Anglo Group company), controls half of the Zambian copper industry. (AMAX AND ANGLO ARE EXTREMELY CLOSE.)

Apeldoorn NV (Holland)   AMIC   Apeldoorn owns 40% of *Apeldoorn— Lighthouse Net and Twine (Pty) Ltd* in which *Ropes and Mattings Ltd* holds 60%. AMIC holds 12.5% of Ropes and Mattings.

Ashmore Benson, Pease & Co. (UK)   AAC   Major holdings together in *Vanderbijl Engineering Corp.*

Banca Commerciale Italiane   AAC   Financial links with Anglo Group holding companies.

Banque de Paris et des Pays-Bas   AAC, CHARTER CONS.   Financial links. Also, Banque de Paris holds 50% in *Franco-South African Investment Co.*, in which Charter also participates. Through this company's connections Charter has gained holdings in *Société Minière de Mauritanie, Sociétié Minière d'Anglade*. Also Charter, AAC, De Beers and Banque de Paris formed a syndicate to acquire a controlling interest in a leading Italian investment and finance company, *Società Nazionale Sviluppo Inpresse Industriale*. Finally, together with UAL this company formed the finance committee for the *Zambese Consorcio Hydro-Electrico* which won the contract to build the Cabora Bassa Dam in Mozambique.

Barclays Bank DCO   AAC, CARLTON CENTRE LTD   Barclays are bankers to the AAC and other Group companies. H. Oppenheimer and S. Spiro of Anglo American are on the board of Barclays DCO; Barclays holds 10% of *Carlton Centre Ltd.*

Bethlehem Steel Corp. (US)   CHARTER CONS. JCI   Charter and JCI have holdings in *Rio Tinto Zinc Corp.* which together with Bethlehem Steel holds 50% of the *British Newfoundland Corp.* responsible for the building of the $1000m Canadian Churchill Falls Power Project. JCI and Charter have holdings in Rio Tinto Zinc Corp.

Botswana, government of   DE BEERS CONS., ANGLO GROUP   The Botswana government holds about 15% in the *Orapa Diamond Mining Co.* and 15% in the *DK/1 Diamond Co.,* both of which are controlled by De Beers Cons. The government also holds 15% in the *Botswana Roan Selection Trust,* jointly controlled by the Anglo and *Amax* Groups. Botswana RST is the company which controls the Selebi-Pikwe copper and nickel mine in Botswana.

Bowater Paper Corp. (UK)   AAC, AMIC, RANDSEL, JCI   Bowater Paper holds 14.9% of *Mondi Valley Paper Co. Ltd,* and has option to increase this to 25%. The remainder of the shares in Mondi are held by: AAC (31%), AMIC (22.1%), Randsel (13.3%) and JCI (18.7%). Bowater provides the technical and management services to Mondi Valley.

British & Commonwealth Shipping Group (Cayzer Group)   AAC, RANDSEL, AMIC, JCI   Cayzer has an interest in *Southern Sun Hotels Corp.* in which *South African Breweries* holds 55%. Anglo Group holdings in SA Breweries are: AAC (2%), Randsel (1.8%), AMIC (2.8%), JCI (15.3%).

British Steel Corp. (BSC)   AMIC, RANDSEL   Following the nationalization of the British steel industry, the southern African interests of the BSC were handed over to *International Pipe and Steel Investments South Africa Ltd* (IPSA), in which the BSC had a 30% holding, the South African state corporation, ISCOR, and two of its associates, *African Gate Holdings* and *Mellor Investments,* held 40% and Anglo Group companies held 10%. IPSA holds at least 51% of *Dorman Long Africa Ltd, Stewarts and Lloyds of South Africa Ltd* and *Vanderbijl Engineering Corp.* Both Dorman Long and Stewarts and Lloyds have subsidiaries in Rhodesia.

British Ropes Ltd   AMIC, RAND MINES ENGINEERING INVESTMENTS (RMEI)   *African Wire Ropes Ltd* is an associated company of British Ropes. AMIC holds 3.1% of African Wire and RMEI (a wholly owned subsidiary of the *Barlow Rand Group* in which Anglo group companies have substantial holdings) holds 3%.

Bureau de Récherche Géologique et Minière (France)   CHARTER CONS. The two companies are part of a copper prospecting consortium in Zaïre. The *Zaïrean government* also participates.

Chile, government of   CHARTER CONS.   The Chilean government development agency has formed a prospecting company, called *Empresa Nacional de Minera,* with Charter.

Christensen Diamond Products   BOART & HARD METALS PRODUCTS LTD These two companies each own 50% of *Christensen–Boart Oilfield Products (Pty) Ltd.* Boart & Hard Metals is 100% owned by AMIC.

Commonwealth Development Corp.   AAC   An original shareholder, together with the AAC, *Guest Keen and Nettlefolds* (not subsequently) the *Swaziland government* in *Swaziland Iron Ore Development Co. Ltd.*

Commonwealth Engineering   MAINSTRAAT BELEGGINGS   Commonwealth Engineering established *Union Carriage & Wagon Lt.,* control of which was subsequently handed over to the Anglo Group (through its 50% holding in Mainstraat Bel.) and *General Mining.*

Computer Sciences Corp. (US) ANGLO GROUP CSC, which is the largest software supplier in the US, holds 49% in *Computer Sciences South Africa Ltd,* in which the Anglo Group has a 51% holding.

Cory Mann George (UK) AMIC, RAND MINES Cory Mann George has a holding in *Freight Services holdings,* in which AMIC holds 19.3% and Rand Mines (part of the Barlow Rand group) also has an interest.

Crèdit Foncier Franco-Canadian (associate of Banque de Paris) HUDSON BAY MINING & SMELTING CO. LTD, AMCAN These three companies established various holding companies for their joint interests. Two of these are *Francana Development* (40% owned by AMCAN, 60% by CFFC) and Hudcana Development (10% owned by AMCAN, 60% by Hudson Bay Co. and 30% by CFFC).

Deutsche Bank HIGHVELD STEEL & VANADIUM CORP. CHARTER CONS. The Bank has provided large loans for Highveld Steel (£20m) and Charter (£12m). Also involved in financing other projects with Anglo Group companies, probably the most important of which is the establishment with Anglo, *Daimler-Benz, Bosch, General Motors, IBM, Universal Lead, Barclays Bank,* the *Luxembourg Credit Bank,* the *Swiss Banking Company* and *Rothmans South Africa* of a development bank, the bank for the *Economic Development for Equatorial and Southern Africa* (EDESA).

Dunlop Ltd ZAMBIAN ANGLO AMERICAN INDUSTRIAL CORP. (ZAAIC) Zaaic holds 25% of *Dunlop (Zambia) Ltd,* which is controlled by Dunlop.

Eastern Stainless Steel (US) RAND MINES, CHARTER CONS., AMIC, ENGELHARD HANOVIA OF SOUTH AFRICA Eastern Stainless Steel holds 15.2% of *Middelburg Steel and Alloys (Pty) Ltd,* which is controlled by the Anglo Group through Rand mines (52.5%), Charter (6.3%), AMIC (13.8%), Engelhard (3.7%). The SA government's *Industrial Development Corp. (IDC)* holds 8.4%.

Filatures Prouvost Masurel et Cie (France) AMIC This French company is an associate of *Ropes and Mattings Ltd.*

First National City Bank New York ANGLO GROUP Has financial and other links with the Anglo Group.

Gebsenkirshener Bergwerks Aktiengesellschaft (Germany) ANMERCOSA MOZAMBIQUE OIL HOLDINGS Anmercosa holds 50% of an oil consortium, in which the German company has a 10% holding and the *Société Nationale des Pétroles d'Aquitaine* holds 40%. The consortium has oil and gas rights over two concession areas (about 36 000 sq. km/1400 sq. miles) in Mozambique.

Imperial Chemical Industries (ICI) DEBINCOR, CHARTER CONS. ICI has a 12.5% direct holding and a 30% indirect holding—through *Apex Holdings (Pty) Ltd,* in which it has a 50% interest—in AE & CI. DEBINCOR has a 12.5% direct holding and a 30% indirect holding (through its 50% interest in *Apex Holdings*) in AE & CI. ICI also hold 25% of *South African Nylon Spin-*

ners (Pty) Ltd, in which DEBINCOR has a 37.5% interest and the state-owned *IDC* has a 37.5% interest. ICI and Charter each hold 50% in *Cleveland Potash Co. Ltd.* ICI holds about 63% and Charter around 37% in *Covenant Industries Ltd.* Covenant Industries Ltd, in association with the *Zambian government (through INDECO),* has an explosives factory in Zambia, and the company also owns a fertilizer factory in Kenya.

Isakwajima Heavy Industries (IHI Japan) LTA IHI has technical contracts with *Integrated Steelworks Engineering Co (Pty),* which is owned (43%) by *VPC Ltd,* in which LTA has a 42% holding.

International Nickel Co. of Canada Ltd JCI International Nickel has a long-term contract to buy the total output of nickel from *Rustenburg.*

Iran, Government of CHARTER CONS. Through its *Industrial Development and Renovation Organization* the Iranian government has, together with Charter, formed a copper prospecting company.

Johnson Matthey (UK) JCI Johnson Matthey is the refiner and sole marketing agent for the platinum group metals produced by *Rustenburg Platinum Mines Ltd,* controlled by JCI.

Kennecott Copper (US) AAC, CHARTER CONS., RAND MINES, HARMONY GOLD MINING CO. Kennecott holds 10% of *Virginia-Merriespruit Investment Co.,* in which the AAC holds 10%, Charter holds 8%, Rand Mines 12%, and Harmony Gold Mining Co. (32.5% owned by Anglo Group companies) holds 50%. The *Anglo-Vaal Group* also holds 10%.

Kleinwort Benson AMIC Kleinwort Benson holds 33.3% of *J. L. Clarke & Co.* in which AMIC has a 33.3% interest.

Klöchner and Co. (Germany) AMIC Klöchner owns *National Materials Service Corp. (Pty) Ltd.* together with the *Union Steel Corp.* in which AMIC has a 13.1% holding.

KZO (a Dutch chemical combine) AE & CI *Rand Carbide,* a subsidiary of AE & CI, holds 41.7% of *Holland Electro-Chemical Industries,* which is a subsidiary of KZO.

Lazard Frères ANGLO GROUP, NEDSUAL Acts on an agency basis for the Anglo Group in various spheres. Has a small holding in Nedsual (formed out of a merger between Nedbank, UAL and Syfrets), in which Anglo has important holdings.

Lease Plan International Corp. (US) JCI Lease Plan International has a substantial interest in *Lease Plan International Corp. of South Africa Ltd,* in which JCI has a minority interest.

Manbré and Gartons (UK) AMIC Manbré and Gartons controls *African Products Manufacturing Co.,* in which AMIC holds 8.8%.

Mesta Machine Cmpany (US) ANGLO GROUP Mesta was an original shareholder with the Anglo Group and other companies in *Vanderbijl Engineering Corp.*

Metropolitan Vickers (UK)   ANGLO GROUP   Vickers was an original shareholder in *Vanderbijl Engineering Corp.* in which the Anglo Group has an interest.

Mitsubishi (Japan)   ZCI   *N'Changa Consolidated Copper Mines Ltd* obtained a $10m loan from Mitsubishi and *Mitsui* in April 1969. N'Changa is owned by ZCI.

Mitsui (Japan)   CHARTER CONS.   Mitsui forms part of a copper prospecting consortium with Charter and others in Zaïre.

Morgan Grenfell (UK)   AAC   Supplied a portion of the original capital when the AAC was formed in 1917. This banking house has financed a number of Anglo Group projects over the years and has close links with the Group.

Morgan Guaranty (US)   AAC   This banking house also involved as above with Anglo. Morgan Grenfell is the leading member of the Morgan Group's British activities.

Nalco Chemical Co.   AE & CI   Nalco holds 50% of *Anikem (Pty) Ltd*, in which AE & CI holds 50%.

Newmont Mining Corp. (US)   AAC, RHOAM, HIGHVELD STEEL & VANADIUM CORP.   Newmont Mining supplied a portion of the original capital when the AAC was formed in 1917. It also participated in the formation of RHOAM in 1928, supplying engineering services as well as capital. Newmont has participated in *Zambian Anglo America*'s copper mining activities. It also holds 10% of Highveld Steel. (NEWMONT IS AN IMPORTANT US CONNECTION.)

P. & O. Shipping Group (UK)   UAL   The two companies together formed a new company *P. & O.—UAL Shipping and Finance Ltd.* UAL, now part of *Nedsual*, was controlled by the Anglo Group.

Petrofina Group (Belgium)   AAC, DE BEERS CONS. MINES, JCI, RAND MINES   Petrofina holds 50% of the *Angolan Oilfields Ltd.* 25% of Angolan Oilfields was held by the *Portuguese government* and 25% by a consortium, *Petrangal Consortium*, in which the Anglo Group had a 32.5% holding (AAC 18.75%, De Beers 6.25%, JCI 5%, Rand Mines 2.5%).

Quebec Mattagami Minerals Ltd (Canada)   AMCAN   Petrofina holds 80% of the refinery serviced by the field. Quebec Mattagami, which has a large holding in *Agnew Lake Mines Ltd*, sold a 10% interest in Agnew Lake to AMCAN, which is 84.4% owned by the Anglo Group.

Rheem International Inc. (US)   AMIC, ENGELHARD HANOVIA   Rheem International holds 55% of *Rheem South Africa (Pty) Ltd.* AMIC holds 30% of Rheem SA and Engelhard Hanovia holds 15%. Rheem SA makes steel drums.

Rio Tinto Zinc Corp. (UK)   CHARTER CONS., JCI   Charter holds about 12–13% of Rio Tinto and JCI also has a holding. Rio Tinto controls the *Palabora Mining Co.* in which JCI has a 7% interest. Rio Tinto also controls the *Rössing*

Open-Cast Mining Project in Namibia, in which *Sentrust* has a stake. Sentrust is controlled by *Central Mining*, in which Anglo has about a 40% holding. Rio Tinto and Anglo co-operated closely in Zambian copper mining. (RIO TINTO IS AN IMPORTANT UK CONNECTION.)

Rothschilds ANGLO GROUP The closest contacts between Rothschilds and the Anglo Group are through the AAC, De Beers Cons., RHOAM and Charter. Historically the financial and other links between Rothschilds and Anglo have been exceptionally close. (A VERY IMPORTANT EUROPEAN CONNECTION.)

Royal Dutch Shell Petrol Group (UK, Holland) CHARTER CONS. Charter holds 8% of *Shell Transport and Trading Ltd*, a Shell Group company. *General Mining*, in which the Anglo Group has a 40% interest, holds about 20% of *Trek-Beleggings* in which *Shell South Africa Ltd* had a holding.

Selection Trust (UK) CHARTER CONS. Charter holds 27% of Selection Trust. This is the largest single holding. *Union Corp.*, in which Charter has a 10% interest and which is now controlled by *General Mining* (in which Anglo has a 40% interest) also has a holding in Selection Trust. It is through its holding in Selection Trust that the Anglo Group has acquired a share in *Amax*.

C. G. Smith Group (UK) AMIC C. G. Smith and *Tongaat Sugar Co.* each hold, indirectly, 21% of and exercise joint control over *Hulett's Corp. Ltd*. AMIC owns 12% of Hulett's.

Société Générale du Belge (Belgium) RHOAM, DE BEERS Société Générale has a holding in *Tanganyika Concessions*, in which RHOAM participates, and in *Diamang* (a diamond concern in Angola), in which De Beers participates.

Société Nationale des Pétroles d'Aquitaine (France) ANMERCOSA MOZAMBIQUE OIL HOLDINGS, DE BEERS For the connection between Société Nationale and Anmercosa see *Gebsenkirschener Bergwerks. Aquitaine South West Africa*, a subsidiary of Société Nationale, and *De Beers Oil Holdings*, a subsidiary of De Beers, are prospecting together in Namibia.

Société Recherche Minérale (Sicily) LTA *Mining and Engineering Technical Services*, which is 100% owned by *Shaft Sinkers Ltd*, a subsidiary of LTA, has a holding with Société Recherche in a sulphur mine in Sicily.

Somic (UK) AMIC Somic holds 30% of *Somic Africa (Pty) Ltd*, in which *Ropes and Mattings* holds 70%. AMIC holds 12.5% of Ropes and Mattings.

Standard Bank Group (UK) (Standard Chartered Group) ANGLO GROUP, JCI, AAC, RAND MINES *The Standard Bank (London)* owns 86% of the *Standard Bank Investment Corp. (STANBIC)* in which Anglo has a holding, probably around 8%. STANBIC owns 100% of the *Standard Bank of South Africa Ltd*. JCI has a holding in the *Standard Bank (London)*. The Anglo Group also has holdings in the *Standard Bank of Angola* and the *Standard Bank of Mozambique* in which the *Standard Chartered Group Ltd*—which owns the Standard Bank (London)—has a 30% holding. The Standard Banks in Angola and Mozambique act as bankers to the AAC in these countries. The Standard Group also has holdings in *Central Acceptances*, in which Rand

Mines has an interest, and in *National Fund Holdings,* in which the Anglo Group (through Rand Mines and JCI) has a 16% interest.

Standard Oil of Indiana (US)   CHARTER CONS.   A member of the copper prospecting consortium in Zaïre, with Charter and other companies.

Stewarts and Lloyds   See *British Steel Corp.*

Swaziland, government of   AAC   The Swazi government holds 20% of *Swaziland Iron Ore Development Co.,* which Anglo controls. See also *Commonwealth Development Corp.*

Tanzania, government of   DE BEERS CONS.   The Tanzanian government holds 50% of the *Williamson Diamond Mining Co.,* in which De Beers has a 50% holding.

Leon Templesman of New York (US)   CHARTER CONS.   These two companies and others form a copper prospecting consortium in Zaïre.

Titan Products (UK)   AE & CI   Titan controls *African Titan Products (Pty) Ltd,* in which AE & CI has a 40% holding.

Union Bank of Switzerland   ANGLO GROUP   The Bank has financial links with a number of Anglo Group companies.

United Kingdom, government of   ANGLO GROUP   The state-owned BP's branch in South Africa, *BP South Africa,* has a holding in *Trek-Beleggings* in which *General Mining* has a 20% holding. (The Anglo Group owns about 40% of General Mining.) The *Royal Dutch Shell Group* is also interested in Trek-Beleggings. Anglo's links with the UK government can also be traced through the *British Steel Corp.* and the *Commonwealth Development Corp.*

United States Natural Oil Resources   RAND MINES   Natural Oil has an agreement with Rand Mines for off-shore oil prospecting in a concession area off Plattenberg Bay. Rand Mines, which used to be 30% owned by Anglo, is now tied to the Anglo Group through the *Barlow Rand Group.*

United States Steel Corp. (US Steel)   AMIC   US Steel holds 31% of *Ferralloys,* a subsidiary (69% ownership) of *Associated Manganese Mines of South Africa Ltd,* in which AMIC has a holding.

United Transport Ltd (UK)   ANGLO GROUP   United Transport holds 60% of *United Transport Holdings Ltd,* in which the Anglo Group has a 40% interest.

Van Hattum en Blankevoort NV (Holland)   LTA   Van Hattum owns 50% of *United Harbour Contractors (Pty) Ltd,* in which LTA has the other 50%. The Anglo Group controls LTA through a 40% holding.

Volvo and Mazda cars (Sweden and Japan)   MCCARTHY MAIN HOLDINGS   *Lawson Motors Group,* which holds the franchise for Volvo motor vehicles, pooled their 200 marketing outlets with the 100 marketing outlets of *Illings (SA) (Pty) Ltd,* which holds the Mazda vehicles franchise. (In addition, there is a 10% share exchange agreement between the two companies.) The Anglo Group holds 50% of McCarthy Main Holdings which holds 90% of Illings (SA).

Weyerhauser (US) BARLOW RAND   Weyerhauser holds 33.3% of *Weyerhauser South Africa* in which Barlow Rand is interested (33.3%). *South African Forest Investment Ltd,* in which Barlow Rand (through Rand Mines) is interested, holds the remaining 33.3% of *Weyerhauser SA.*

Zambia, government of   ZCI, ANGLO AMERICAN CORP. OF CENTRAL AFRICA, CHARTER CONS.   The Zambian government, through its *Mineral Development Corp. (MINDECO),* owns 51% of *N'Changa Cons. Mines,* in which the Anglo Group, through ZCI, has a 49% interest. (These are the copper mines owned by Anglo prior to nationalization.) The Anglo American Corp. of Central Africa holds the management contracts for these (N'Changa) mines. ZCI owns 12.2% of *Roan Cons. Mines* in which the Zambian government through *MINDECO* has a 51% holding and *Amax* has a 36.8% holding. (See Amax. (These are the former *Roan Selection Trust* copper mines.) The Zambian government, through its *Industrial Development Corp. (INDECO)* has an interest in the explosives plant built in association with *Covenant Industries.* Charter Cons. holds 37% of Covenant. (See ICI.) Charter and other Anglo Group companies have other interests together with *INDECO.*

Sources   Company Reports:

Anglo American Corp. of South Africa, *Annual Reports* 1970–6
De Beers Cons. Mines, *Annual Reports,* 1970–6
Charter Cons., *Annual Reports,* 1970–6
Rand Selection Corp. *Annual Reports,* 1970–6
Anglo American Investment Trust, *Annual Reports,* 1970–6
Mineral and Resources Corp. *Annual Report* 1976
Anglo American Gold Investment, *Annual Report,* 1976
Anglo American Industrial Corp., *Annual Reports,* 1970–6
Anglo American Coal Investments, *Annual Report,* 1976
Anglo American Properties, *Annual Reports,* 1975–6
Zambian Copper Investments, *Annual Reports,* 1973–6

Financial Mail, Johannesburg: September 1968–February 1970, January 1975–August 1976; *Financial Gazette,* Johannesburg: September 1968–February 1970.

Bibliography

OFFICIAL PUBLICATIONS

South Africa

Board of Trade and Industries, Report no. 94, *The Engineering Industry in South Africa* (Pretoria, 1929).

Board of Trade and Industries, Report no. 282, *Investigation into Manufacturing Industries in the Union of South Africa* (Pretoria, 1946).

South African Bureau of Census and Statistics, *Union Statistics for Fifty Years, 1910–1960* (Jubilee Issue, Pretoria, 1960).

South African Bureau of Statistics, *State of South Africa: Economic, Financial and Statistical Year Book for the Republic of South Africa, 1968–1977* (inclusive) (Da Gama Publishers, Johannesburg).

South African Bureau of Statistics, *Statistical Year Book, 1964–1966* (inclusive) (Pretoria).

South African Department of Statistics, *South African Statistics; 1965, 1972, 1974, 1976 and 1978* (Pretoria).

Stadler, J. J., 'Some Aspects of the Changing Structure of the South African Economy since World War II', *South African Statistics, 1968* (Bureau of Statistics, Pretoria).

Steyn, G. J. J. F., 'Some Aspects of the Development of the Domestic and Foreign Trade of the Republic of South Africa during the Post-War Period', *South African Statistics, 1970* (Department of Statistics, Pretoria).

South African Department of Statistics, *South West Africa Survey, 1967*, and *South West Africa Survey, 1974* (Pretoria).

Kotze, Sir R. (Government Mining Engineer), Memorandum on the Far East Rand (Department of Mines, 1916).

South African Department of Mines, *Annual Reports, 1954, 1960, 1968–1969* (Pretoria).

South African Department of Mines, *Secretary for Mines Annual Report 1970* (Pretoria).

South African Department of Mines, *Mining Statistics, 1966–1973* (inclusive) (Pretoria).

South African Department of Planning, *Economic Development Programme for the Republic of South Africa: 1968–1973* (Pretoria, 1968) and *Economic Development Programme for the Republic of South Africa: 1972–1977* (Pretoria, 1972).

South African Reserve Bank, *A Statistical Presentation of South Africa's Balance of Payments for the Period 1946 to 1970* (Pretoria, March 1971).

South African Reserve Bank, *Annual Economic Report, 1973* (Pretoria).

South African Reserve Bank, *Quarterly Bulletin of Statistics*, December 1959–December 1973 (inclusive) (Pretoria).

South African Reserve Bank, 'Post-War Growth and Structural Changes in the South African Economy', *Quarterly Bulletin* (Pretoria, September 1971).

Union of South Africa, *Official Year Book of the Union of South Africa*, no. 1 (1917), no.

2 (1918), no. 3 (1919), no. 8 (1925), no. 13 (1930–1), no. 17 (1934–5), no. 18 (1937), no. 20 (1939), no. 22 (1941), no. 23 (1946), no. 24 (1948), no. 26 (1950), no. 27 (1952–3), no. 29 (1956–7).

Union of South Africa, *Official Year Book of the Union and of Basutoland, Bechuanaland Protectorate and Swaziland*, no. 12 (1927–8).

Report of the Transvaal Labour Commission: Together with Minority Report, Minutes of Proceedings and Evidence (Johannesburg, 1903).

Report of the South African Native Affairs Commission, 1903–1905, Cmd. 2399 (London, 1905).

Union of South Africa, Report of the Economic Commission (Pretoria, 1914).

South West Africa, Report of the Administrator, 1919 (U.G40, 1920).

Report of the Inderdepartmental Committee on the Social, Health and Economic Conditions of the Urban Natives (Pretoria, 1942).

Report of the Witwatersrand Mine Native Wages Commission on the Remuneration and Conditions of Employment of Natives on the Witwatersrand Gold Mines 1943 (UG 21/1944, Pretoria).

Union of South Africa, Report of the Commission of Enquiry into Policy Relating to the Protection of Industries, 1958 (Pretoria, UG 36/1958).

Report of the Committee re. Foreign Bantu (Froneman Report) Pretoria, 1962 (incomplete photocopy).

Report of the Commission of Enquiry into South West African Affairs, 1962–63 (Odendaal Commission) (RP no. 12, 1964).

Report of the Commission of Inquiry into the Regulation of Monopolistic Conditions Act 1955, RP 64/1977.

Golden Jubilee of the Union of South Africa, *Our First Half Century, 1910–1960* (published by SA Government, Johannesburg, 1960).

United Nations Organization

Statistical Office of the United Nations, *Supplement to the World Trade Annual, 1970*, vol. 3 *(Africa)* (UNO, New York).

COMPANY PUBLICATIONS, CIRCULARS, PRESS RELEASES AND RELATED DOCUMENTS

AE & CI Ltd, *Annual Report, 1972, 1973* (Fiftieth Anniversary Issue) and *1974*.

AE & CI, *Basics Anonymous* (Johannesburg, 1972).

AE & CI, press releases, 1971–6 (various).

African and European Ltd, *Report of the Directors, 1920–1925* (inclusive).

African Explosives and Chemical Industries Ltd, *This Is AE & CI* (Johannesburg, 1973).

African Land and Investment Company, *Eighteenth Annual Report*, 31 March 1920, pp. 6–7.

African Loans and Investments Ltd, Notice Convening the First Annual General Meeting (9 May 1961).

Anglo American Coal Investments Ltd, *Annual Report, 1976*.

Anglo American Corp. of South Africa Ltd, *Annual Reports, 1918–1926, 1954–1960* and *1970–1979* (inclusive).

Anglo American Corp. of South Africa Ltd, Minutes of the Proceedings at the Fourth Ordinary General Meeting (31 December 1920), Seventh Ordinary General Meeting (27 May 1924), Eighth Ordinary General Meeting (16 May 1925) and Nineteenth Ordinary General Meeting (16 May 1936).

Anglo American Corp. of South Africa Ltd, *Chairman's Statement, 1954, 1956, 1971–1979* (inclusive).

Anglo American Corp. of South Africa Ltd, 'Circular to Members: Proposed Merger of

Orange Free State Investment Trust Limited with West Rand Investment Trust Limited by means of a Scheme of Arrangement' (Johannesburg, 1 May 1972).

Anglo American Corp. of South Africa Ltd, press releases, 1969–76 (various).

Anglo American Corp. of South Africa Ltd, *A Career in South Africa: Attractive Opportunities for all Graduates Interested in Mining* (Johannesburg, c.1953).

Anglo American Corp. of South Africa Ltd, *Gold in the Transvaal: Mines of the Anglo American Corporation Group* (undated).

Anglo American Corp. of South Africa Ltd, *The Orange Free State Gold Fields* (1959).

Anglo American Corp. of South Africa Ltd, *Western Deep Levels: Deepest Mine of the Future* (undated).

Anglo American Corp. of South Africa Ltd, *Western Deep Levels Ltd: The Story of a Great New Gold Mine* (undated).

Anglo American Gold Investment Co. Ltd, *Annual Reports, 1972–1976* (inclusive).

Anglo American Gold Investment Co. Ltd, press statements, 1972–4 (various).

Anglo American Industrial Corp. Ltd, *Annual Reports, 1970–1977* (inclusive).

Anglo American Industrial Corp. Ltd, 'Circular to Members regarding the acquisition of the entire issued capital of Engelhard Enterprises of Southern Africa' (Johannesburg, 11 April 1973).

Etheridge, D. A. (Manager, Gold Division, Anglo American Corp. of South Africa), 'Wages, Productivity and Opportunity', paper delivered to the Conference on Closing the Wage Gap (South African Institute of Race Relations in association with South African Institute of Personnel Management, Johannesburg, January 1973).

Anglo American Industrial Corp. Ltd, 'Circular to Members regarding proposed offer to members of Boart and Hard Metal Products SA Limited to acquire their shares' (Johannesburg, 11 August 1969).

Anglo American Investment Trust Ltd, *Annual Reports, 1970–1977* (inclusive).

Anglo American Properties Ltd, *Annual Reports, 1975* and *1976*.

Barclays National Merchant Bank Ltd, 'Circular to Shareholders of Barclays National Bank Limited and Western Bank Limited' (Johannesburg, 6 February 1975).

Barlow Rand Ltd, *Annual Financial Statement, 1974*.

Barlow Rand Ltd, *Annual Reports, 1972–1976* (inclusive).

Barlow Rand Ltd, news release, June 1971–December 1974 (various).

Barlow Rand Ltd, news release: 'Announcement by Barlow Rand Limited and The South African Breweries Limited to Acquire the 39 million 102 thousand 979 Barsab Investment Trust Limited shares not indirectly owned by them' (Johannesburg, 16 October 1972).

Barlow Rand Ltd, news release: 'Joint Announcement between Barlow Rand Limited and Union Corporation Limited to Integrate their Companies into a new Group called "Unicorp Barlows Limited"' (Johannesburg, 15 July 1974).

Thos. Barlow and Sons Ltd, News Releases, January 1971–June 1971 (various).

Beerman's Financial Year Book of Southern Africa, 1974, vols I and II (R. Beerman Publishers, London, 1974).

Central Mining and Investment Corp. Ltd, *Report of the Directors* (including Report of the Consulting Engineer, Report of the Manager and Report of the Proceedings at the Ordinary General Meeting), *1919–1925* (inclusive) and *1932*.

Chamber of Mines of South Africa, *First Annual Report, 1889* (Witwatersrand Chamber of Mines) and *Eighty-sixth Annual Report, 1975* (inclusive).

Chamber of Mines, *The Mining Survey, 1946, 1969* and *1971*.

Chamber of Mines of South Africa, *Gold in South Africa* (Public Relations Department Series no. 163, undated).

Charter Consolidated Ltd, *Annual Reports and Accounts, 1970–1977* (inclusive).

Charter Consolidated Ltd, *Statement by the Chairman Mr. S. Spiro, 1972–1976* (inclusive).

Charter Consolidated Ltd, press statements, 1970–4 (various).

Charter Consolidated Ltd, press statement: 'Charter's Oil Drilling Programme in North Sea Begins' (London, 16 July 1974).

City Developments Ltd, 'Prospectus of City Developments Limited, the name of which is to be changed to Anglo American Properties Limited' (24 November 1970).

Consolidated Diamond Mines of South West Africa Ltd, *Annual Reports, 1920–1926* and *1972–1974* (inclusive).

Consolidated Diamond Mines of South West Africa Ltd, *Diamond Mining in the Desert* (Johannesburg, undated).

Consolidated Diamond Mines of South West Africa Ltd, 'Disciplinary Code Ovambo Employees'.

Consolidated Gold Fields of South Africa Ltd, *Report of the Directors* (including Manager's Report, Consulting Engineer's Report and Report of the Proceedings at the Ordinary General Meeting), *1917–1920* (inclusive) and (Gold Fields of South Africa Ltd) *Annual Reports, 1973, 1974, 1976* and *1978*.

Consolidated Gold Fields Ltd, *Consolidated Gold Fields: Ten Years of Expansion* (London, December 1968).

Consolidated Mines Selection Co. Ltd, *Report of the Directors* (including Minutes of the Ordinary General Meeting), *1917–1922* (inclusive).

De Beers Consolidated Mines Ltd, *Annual Reports, 1896–1900, 1918–1926, 1970–1977* (inclusive).

De Beers Consolidated Mines Ltd, Minutes of the Ordinary General Meeting, 1898–1900 (inclusive) and 1924.

De Beers Consolidated Mines Ltd, press releases, January 1970–December 1974 (various).

De Beers Industrial Corp. Ltd, *Annual Reports, 1972–1974* (inclusive).

General Mining and Finance Corp. Ltd, *Annual Reports, 1973* and *1974*.

General Mining and Finance Corp. Ltd, press release: 'Proposed Offer to Acquire Issued Shares of Union Corporation Limited' (Johannesburg, 30 September 1974).

General Mining and Finance Corp. Ltd, 'Prospectus of General Mining and Finance Corporation Limited' (Johannesburg, 3 April 1975).

Gold Fields of South Africa, *Annual Report, 1974*.

Gold Fields of South Africa Ltd, *Chairman's Review, 1973* and *1974*.

Gold Fields of South Africa Ltd, 'Offer by Gold Fields of South Africa Limited for Union Corporation Limited' (Form of Acceptance Document, 26 September 1974).

Hagart, R. B., Speech to the Society of Investment Analysts (London, June 1959).

Highveld Steel and Vanadium Corp. Ltd, *Annual Report, 1977*.

Koch, H. C. (President of the Transvaal and Orange Free State Chamber of Mines), 'The Gold, Uranium and Coal Mining Industries of South Africa' (lecture delivered at Stellenbosch University, 10 April 1958).

McKie Brothers, Van Velden and Co. (Stock and Share Brokers), 'Anglo American Gold Investment Co. Ltd. (AMGOLD), Gold Fields of South Africa Ltd (GFSA): A Comparison of their Prospects as Longer Term Investments' (Johannesburg, 21 March 1974).

McKie Brothers, Van Velden and Co. (Stock and Share Brokers), 'Rand Selection Corporation Limited' (Johannesburg, 5 March 1973) and 'Rand Selection Corporation Limited' (Johannesburg, 5 February 1974).

Martin and Co. (Stock and Share Brokers), 'Anglo American Properties' (Johannesburg, 17 October 1972).

Martin and Co. (Stock and Share Brokers), 'De Beers—A Short History' (Johannesburg, undated).

Martin and Co. (Stock and Share Brokers), 'De Beers Consolidated Mines: a comprehensive review of the world's leading diamond producer' (Johannesburg, December 1971).

Martin and Co. (Stock and Share Brokers), 'The Consolidated Diamond Mines of South-West Africa Limited' (Johannesburg, 7 October 1971).

Martin and Co. (Stock and Share Brokers), 'Western Bank Limited' (Johannesburg, 18 February 1974).

Mercabank, 'Manufacturing', *Focus on Key Economic Issues,* no. 20, March 1978.

Mercabank, 'The Southern African Market', *Focus on Key Economic Issues,* no. 12, July 1975.

Mineral and Resources Corp. Ltd, *Annual Reports, 1974, 1976* and *1977.*

The Nedbank Group, *South Africa, An Appraisal: the soverign risk criteria* (Johannesburg, 1977).

Nedbank and Syfrets—UAL Holdings Ltd (Nedsual), *Annual Report, 1973/4.*

New Consolidated Gold Fields Ltd, *Report of the Directors* (including Manager's Report, Consulting Engineer's Report, and Report of the Proceedings of the Ordinary General Meeting, 1921–1926 inclusive).

Optima (a quarterly review published by the Anglo American Corp., De Beers and Charter Consolidated Groups of Companies), vol. 1, no. 1, June 1951—vol. 27, no. 3, 1978 (inclusive).

Rand Mines Ltd, Circular to Shareholders: 'Proposed Merger of Rand Mines Limited with Thos. Barlow and Sons Limited by means of a Scheme of Arrangement' (Johannesburg, 2 June 1971).

Rand Mines Ltd, news releases, January 1971–June 1971 (various).

Rand Mines Ltd, 'Scheme of Arrangement for the Proposed Merger of Thos. Barlow and Sons Limited and Rand Mines Limited' (Johannesburg, 26 April 1971).

Rand Selection Corp. Ltd, *Report of the Directors, 1918–1924* (inclusive) and *Annual Reports, 1970–1976* (inclusive).

Scaw Metals Ltd, *Scaw Metals* (Johannesburg, undated).

Schlesinger Insurance and Institutional Holdings Ltd, 'Merger of Schlesinger Insurance and Institutional Holdings Limited and Rand Selection Corporation Limited by way of a Scheme of Arrangement in terms of the Companies Act (Act No. 61 of 1973)' (5 November 1974).

S. W. Silver and Co., *Handbook to South Africa* (London, 1891).

Standard Bank Investment Corp., *Standard Bank Review* (Johannesburg, December 1975).

Standard Bank Ltd, *Director's Report and Accounts* for the year ended 31 March 1972.

Standard Bank of South Africa Ltd, *National Income and Production Indices, 1946–1959* (Johannesburg).

Syfrets and UAL Holdings Ltd, 'Circular to Members and Notice of Extraordinary General Meeting relating to the Merger of Nedbank Ltd, Nedfin Ltd and Syfrual' (Johannesburg, 22 November 1973).

Syfrets Trust Company Ltd, 'Rand Selection Corporation' (Investment Research Department Document, Johannesburg, 2 August 1971).

Syfrets Trust Company Ltd, *Annual Report, 1973.*

Union Acceptances Ltd (UAL), *Chairman's Statement, 1972.*

Union Acceptances Ltd (UAL), press releases, 1972–73 (various).

Union Acceptances Ltd (UAL), *Scope for Investment: South Africa's Growing Economy* (Johannesburg, November 1969).

Union Acceptances Ltd (UAL), 'Sentrachem Limited' (Confidential Investment Research document, 24 April 1974).

Union Corp. Ltd, *Report and Accounts, 1974.*

Union Corp. Ltd, *Union Corporation Limited: Group and Associated Companies* (Johannesburg, undated).

Union Corp. Ltd, 'Offer by Union Corporation Limited to acquire the entire issued share capital of Carlton Paper Corporation Limited' (Johannesburg, 11 December 1972).

Union Corp. Ltd, 'Statement by your Directors in Response to the Offer by Gold Fields of South Africa Limited (GFSA): Reasons for Rejecting the GFSA Offer' (Johannesburg, 7 October 1974).

Vereeniging Estates Ltd, *Annual Reports, 1970–1974* (inclusive).
Volkskas, *Finance and Trade Review,* Pretoria (December 1969).
West Rand Investment Trust Ltd, *Annual Report, 1971.*
Western Bank Ltd, *Annual Report, 1974.*
Wilson, W., 'Attitudes Towards Black Employees' (Address to Chamber of Mines by Anglo American Deputy Chairman, September 1972).
Zambia Copper Investments Ltd, *First Annual Report and Accounts* to 30 June 1970 and *Annual Reports, 1971–1976* (inclusive).
Zambian Anglo American Ltd, *Annual Reports, 1970–1973* (inclusive).
Zambian Anglo American Ltd, 'Circular to Members regarding Proposals for the Expansion and Development of the Company' (Bermuda, 11 July 1974).

NEWSPAPERS AND PERIODICALS

The Cape Argus, Johannesburg (daily paper) (1966–77, occasional issues).
The Cape Times, Cape Town (daily paper) (1966–77, occasional issues).
Commerce and Industry, vol. III, no. 7 (January 1941).
The Economist, London (1970–6, occasional issues).
The Economist, 'Kruger's Golden Rand: A Survey of Gold and South Africa' (22 March 1975).
Financial Gazette, South Africa (1968–March 1977) (weekly paper, inclusive).
Financial Mail, South Africa (weekly paper) (29 May 1959–25 May 1962, inclusive; June 1962–August 1968, occasional issues; September 1968–December 1978, inclusive).
Financial Mail, Special Report, 'Lesotho: Ten Years of Independence' (24 September 1976).
Financial Mail, Special Survey, 'AE & CI' (11 April 1974).
Financial Mail, Special Survey, 'Carlton Hotel: Innkeeper International' (24 November 1972).
Financial Mail, Special Survey, 'The Changing Face of Barclays' (30 January 1976).
Financial Mail, Special Survey, 'Coalplex' (8 September 1978).
Financial Mail, Special Survey, 'FVB: Men—Money—Management' (19 June 1970).
Financial Mail, Special Survey, 'Gauging JCI's Mettle' (25 September 1970).
Financial Mail, Special Survey, 'Gold: The Winter of Our Discontent' (13 August 1976).
Financial Mail, Special Survey, 'Inside the Anglo Power House' (4 July 1969).
Financial Mail, Special Survey, 'Lean Years for Coal' (13 December 1968).
Financial Mail, Special Survey, '1961–66: The Fabulous Years: The Story of the Republic that Investors Built' (14 July 1967).
Financial Mail, Special Survey, 'South African Breweries: Focus on You' (27 July 1979).
Financial Mail, Special Survey, 'South West: Calm Amidst the Storm' (20 August 1965).
Financial Mail, Special Survey, 'The Standard: Regrouping for Growth' (11 February 1972).
Financial Mail, Special Survey, 'Steel: Dialogue or Disorder' (23 July 1971).
Financial Mail, Special Survey, 'Swaziland's Independence: Tribalism with a Difference' (30 August 1968).
Financial Mail, Special Survey, 'Top Companies' (an annual survey of the top 10 companies in South Africa measured by gross assets, profits, market capitalization and turnover) (1968–78, inclusive).
Financial Mail, Special Survey, 'Bottoms Up! A Survey of the Liquor Industry' (28 November 1975).
Financial Mail, Supplement, 'Breakthrough!' (a survey on coal) (5 March 1976).
Financial Mail, Supplement, 'The Changing Face of Property' (7 September 1973).
Financial Mail, Supplement, 'Chemicals: Formula for the Future' (18 June 1976).
Financial Mail, Supplement, 'General Mining: A Sense of Direction' (5 October 1973).
Financial Mail, Supplement, 'Gold' (17 November 1972).
Financial Mail, Supplement, 'Kruger Millions' (6 February 1976).

Financial Mail, Supplement, 'The Property Hive—Still Very Much Alive' (10 October 1975).

Financial Mail, Supplement, 'South West Africa' (2 March 1973).

Financial Mail, Supplement, 'Through a Glass Darkly: A Special Survey on Property' (10 September 1976).

Financial Times, London (1973–8, inclusive).

Forbes, Special Report: Spotlight on International Business, 6 July 1981, pp. 83–91.

The Mining World, London (weekly) (1919–26, inclusive).

Rand Daily Mail, Johannesburg (daily paper) (1966–77, occasional issues).

South African Mining and Engineering Journal (1950–76, occasional issues).

South African Mining and Engineering Journal, 'General Mining 75th Anniversary' (30 December 1970).

South African Mining and Engineering Journal,' 80th Anniversary Issue, Johannesburg Consolidated Investment Company Limited' (29 September 1969).

The Star, Johannesburg (daily paper) (1966–77, occasional issues).

Sunday Express, Johannesburg (weekly paper) (1966–77, occasional issues).

Sunday Times, Johannesburg (weekly paper) (1966–77, occasional issues).

Sunday Tribune, Durban (weekly paper) (1968–77, occasional issues).

BOOKS, ARTICLES AND DISSERTATIONS

Adam, H. (1971) *Modernising Racial Domination* (University of California Press, Berkeley).

Adler, T. (ed.) (1977) *Perspectives on South Africa* (University of the Witwatersrand, Johannesburg).

Althusser, L. (1969) *Fox Marx* (Allen Lane, Penguin Press, London).

Althusser, L. and Balibar, E. (1970) *Reading 'Capital'*, trans. B. Brewster (New Left Books, London).

Amery, L. S. (ed.) (1909) *The Times History of the War in South Africa, 1899–1902*, vol. 6 (S. Low, Marston & Co., London).

Angove, J. (1910) *In the Early Days: The Reminiscences of Pioneer Life on the South African Diamond Fields* (Handel House, Johannesburg and Kimberley).

Arrighi, G. (1967) *The Political Economy of Rhodesia* (The Institute of Social Studies, series major, vol. xvi, The Hague, Mouton).

Arrighi, G. (1970) 'International Corporations, Labour Aristocracies and Economic Development in Tropical Africa', in R. Rhodes (ed.), *Imperialism and Underdevelopment: A Reader* (Monthly Review Press, London and New York).

Arrighi, G. (1971) 'The Relationship between the Colonial and Class Structures', (mimeo, Dakar).

Aylward, A. (1878) *The Transvaal of Today: War, Witchcraft, Sport and Spoils in South Africa* (Blackwood and Sons, London).

Baran, P. (1970) 'On the Political Economy of Backwardness', in R. Rhodes (ed.), *Imperialism and Underdevelopment: A Reader* (Monthly Review Press, London and New York).

Baran, P. and Sweezy, P. (1973) *Monopoly Capital: An Essay on the American Economic and Social Order* (Pelican Books, Harmondsworth).

Barber, J. 'Rhodesia and Inter-State Relationships in Southern Africa', C. Potholm and R. Dale (eds), in *Southern Africa in Perspective: Essays in Regional Politics* (Free Press, New York).

Beckingham, D. O. (1972) 'The Group in Industry: A View of Diversification', *Optima*, vol. 22, no. 3 (September).

Behrman, J. (1969) 'Some Patterns in the Rise of the Multinational Enterprise', Graduate School of Business, University of North Carolina (Research Paper no. 18).

Behrman, J. (1970) *National Interests and the Multinational Enterprise: Tensions Among the North Atlantic Countries* (Prentice-Hall, New York).

Bell, P. (1971) 'On the Theory of Imperialism', *The Review of Radical Political Economics*, vol. 3, no. 1.

Bellairs, K. F. (1889) *The Witwatersrand Goldfields: A Trip to Johannesburg and Back* (Chapman, London).

Bender, G. (1972) 'Angola: History, Insurgency and Social Change', *Africa Today*, vol. 19, no. 1.

Benson, M. (1977) *The African Patriots* (Faber & Faber, London).

Bergman, L. F. (1968) 'Technological Change in South Africa's Manufacturing Industry, 1955–64', *South African Journal of Economics*, vol. 36.

Berle, A. (1954) *The 20th Century Capitalist Revolution* (Harcourt, Brace and World, New York).

Bienefeld, M. and Innes, D. (1976) 'Capital Accumulation and South Africa', *Review of African Political Economy*, no. 7 (September–December).

Black, R. A. L. (1958) 'Mechanization in South Africa's Mining Industry', *Fact Paper no. 57* (South African Department of Mines, May).

Black, R. A. L. (1960) 'The Development of South African Mining Methods', *Optima*, vol. 10, no. 2 (June).

Bleloch, W. (1901) *The New South Africa* (Heinemann, London 1901).

Bonner, P. L. (1979) 'The 1920 Black Mine Workers' Strike: A Preliminary Account', in B. Bozzoli (ed.), *Labour Township and Protest* (Ravan Press, Johannesburg).

Bozzoli, B. (1975a) 'The Roots of Hegemony: Ideologies, Interests and the Legitimation of South African Capitalism', D.Phil. dissertation (University of Sussex).

Bozzoli, B. (1975b) 'Origins, Development and Ideology of Manufacturing in South Africa, *Journal of Southern African Studies*, vol. 1, no. 2 (April).

Bransky, D. (1974) 'The Causes of the Boer War: Towards a Synthesis', paper delivered to the Workshop on the Social and Economic History of South Africa (Oxford University).

Bundy, C. (1972) 'The Emergence and Decline of a South African Peasantry', *African Affairs*, vol. 71, no. 285 (October).

Bundy, C. (1974) 'Passing through a Period of Stress: The Transkei Peasantry, 1890–1914', paper presented to the Workshop on the Social and Economic History of South Africa (Oxford University).

Burawoy, M. (1972) *The Colour of Class on the Copper Mines: From African Advancement to Zambianization*, Zambian Papers no. 7, Institute for African Studies (University of Zambia).

Burnham, J. (1960) *The Managerial Revolution* (Indiana University Press, Bloomington).

Busschau, W. J. (1936) *The Theory of Gold Supply* (Oxford University Press, London).

Busschau, W. J. (1947) 'The Expansion of Manufacturing Industry in the Union' (a Review Article of Report no. 282 of the Board of Trade and Industries), *South African Journal of Economics*, vol. 13, no. 3 (September).

Cartwright, A. P. (1964) *The Dynamite Company* (Purnell, London).

Cartwright, A. P. (1965) *The Gold Miners* (Purnell, London).

Chambers, S. P. (1952) 'Sources of Capital for Industry', *Optima*, vol. 2., no. 3 (September).

Christie, R. (1977) ' "Slim Jannie" and the Forces of Production: South African Industrialization 1915–1925', Institute of Commonwealth Studies, University of London, Seminar Paper.

Clarke, D. (1977) 'Foreign African Labour Inflows to South Africa and Unemployment in Southen Africa', paper delivered at Workshop on Unemployment and Labour Reallocation (University of Natal, Pietermaritzburg, March).

Clarke, S. (1977) 'Marxism, Sociology and Poulantzas's Theory of the State', *Capital and Class*, no. 2.

Clarke, S. (1978) 'Capital, Fractions of Capital and the State: "Neo-Marxist" Analyses of the South African State', *Capital and Class*, no. 5.

Clarke, S. *et al.* (eds) (1981) *One Dimensional Marxism* (Allison and Busby, London).

Cockram, G. M. (1976) *Vorster's Foreign Policy* (Academica, Pretoria).
Conference on Natural Resources and National Welfare: The Case of Copper (1974), Lusaka, Zambia, July (collected papers, University of Zambia).
Coombs, C. A. (1957) 'The Growing Role of the New York Money Market', *Optima*, vol. 7, no. 1 (March).
Davies, R. (1976) 'Mining Capital, the State and Unskilled White Workers in South Africa, 1901–1913', *Journal of Southern African Studies*, vol. 3, no. 1 (October).
Davies, R. (1977) 'Capital, the State and White Wage Earners: An Historical Materialist Analysis of Class Formation and Class Relations in South Africa, 1900–1960', D.Phil. dissertation (University of Sussex).
Davies, R., Kaplan, D., Morris, M. and O'Meara, D. (1976) 'Class Struggle and the Periodisation of the State in South Africa', *Review of African Political Economy*, no. 7 (September—December).
Davies, R. and Lewis, D. (1976) 'Industrial Relations Legislation: One of Capital's Defences', *Review of African Political Economy*, no. 7 (September—December).
de Brunhoff, S. (1976) *Marx on Money* (Urizen Books, New York).
de Clercq, F., Hemson, D., Innes D. and Legassick, M. (1977) 'Capital Restructuring and the South African State: The Case of Foreign Labour', paper delivered to CSE Conference (Bradford University).
de Clercq, F. and Legassick, M. (1978) 'Capitalism and Migrant Labour in Southern Africa: The Origins and Nature of the System', paper delivered to the ECA/MULPOC Conference on Migratory Labour in South Africa (Lusaka).
de Kiewiet, C. W. (1937) *The Imperial Factor in South Africa: A Study in Politics and Economics* (Cambridge University Press, London).
de Sousa Ferreira, E. (1972) 'International Capital in Namibia: Tsumeb and the CDM', paper delivered to the Namibia International Conference (Brussels).
Dobb, M. (1963) *Studies in the Development of Capitalism* (Routledge and Kegan Paul, London).
Doxey, G. V. (1961) *The Industrial Colour Bar in South Africa* (Oxford University Press, London).
Drummond, I. M. (1974) *Imperial Economic Policy, 1917–1939: Studies in Expansion and Protection* (George Allen and Unwin, London).
Fanon, F. (1965) *Studies in a Dying Colonialism* (Monthly Review Press, New York).
Fanon, F. (1970) 'The Pitfalls of National Consciousness—Africa', in R. Rhodes (ed.), *Imperialism and Underdevelopment: A Reader* (Monthly Review Press, London and New York).
Farnie, D. A. (1956) 'The Mineral Revolution in South Africa', *South African Journal of Economics*, vol. 24, no. 56.
Fetter, F. A. (1941) 'The Pricing of Steel in South Africa', *South African Journal of Economics*, vol. 9, no. 3 (September).
Finlay, W. (1976) 'South Africa: Capitalist Agriculture and the State', B.Soc.Sci. (Hons) dissertation (University of Cape Town).
First, R. (1961) 'The Gold of Migrant Labour', *Africa South*, vol. 3 (April—June).
First, R. (1964) *South West Africa* (Penguin African Library, London).
First, R. (1972) 'The Bantustans: The Implementation of the Odendaal Report' (paper delivered at Namibia International Conference, Brussels).
First, R., Steele, J. and Gurney, C. (1973) *The South African Connection: Western Investment in Apartheid* (Penguin African Library, London).
Food and Agriculture Organisation (1977). *Namibia: Prospects for Future Development* (Rome).
Francis, E. V. (1939) *Britain's Economic Strategy* (Jonathan Cape, London).
Frank, A. Gunder. (1970a) 'On the Mechanisms of Imperialism: The Case of Brazil' in R. Rhodes (ed.), *Imperialism and Underdevelopment: A Reader* (Monthly Review Press, London and New York).
Frank, A. Gunder. (1970b) 'The Development of Underdevelopment', in R. Rhodes

(ed.), *Imperialism and Underdevelopment: A Reader* (Monthly Review Press, London and New York).

Frankel, S. Herbert (1938) *Capital Investment in Africa: Its Course and Effects* (Oxford University Press, London).

Fraser, M. and Jeeves, A. (eds) (1977) *All That Glittered: Selected Correspondence of Lionel Phillips 1890–1924* (Oxford University Press, Cape Town).

Furtado, C. (1967) *Development and Underdevelopment: A Structural View of the Problems of Developed and Underdeveloped Countries* (University of California Press, Berkeley and Los Angeles).

Gann, L. H. (1965) *A History of Southern Rhodesia: Early Days to 1934* (Chatto and Windus, London).

Germond, R. C. (1967) *Chronicles of Basutoland* (Morija, Sesuto Book Depot).

Gervasi, S. and Lowenstein, C. (1972) 'Southern Africa in the World Economy', (Institute of Commonwealth Studies, Oxford).

Ginsberg, D. (1974) 'The Formation of an African Migrant Labour Force on the Diamond Fields: 1867–1900', paper delivered at the Workshop on Social and Economic History of South Africa (Oxford University).

Ginsberg, D. (1975) 'The Black Flag Rebellion of 1875: A Study of Intra-Class Conflict and Co-operation' (MA dissertation, University of Sussex).

Girvan, N. (1973) 'Multinational Corporations and Dependent Underdevelopment in Mineral-Export Economies', Seminar Paper, Institute of Development Studies.

Glanville, E. (1888) *The South African Gold Fields* (Sonnenschein, London).

Goldblatt, I. (1971) *History of South West Africa from the beginning of the Nineteenth Century* (Juta's, Cape Town).

Graham, M. R. (1964) 'The Gold Mining Finance System in South Africa with Special Reference to the Financing and Development of the Orange Free State Gold Field up to 1960', Ph.D. thesis (University of London).

Gregory, T. (1962) *Ernest Oppenheimer and the Economic Development of Southern Africa* (Oxford University Press, London).

Guelke, A. (1974) 'Africa as a Market for South African Goods', *Journal of Modern African Studies*, vol. 12, no. 1 (March).

Guy, J. (1974) 'The Origins of Migrant Labour in Lesotho', University of Lesotho (mimeo).

Hagart, R. B. (1952) 'The Changing Pattern of Gold Mining Finance', *Optima*, vol. 2, no. 4 (December).

Hagart, R. B. (1976) 'The Formative Years; A Recollection', *Optima* vol. 17, no. 3 (September).

Hamish, E. (1974) 'Copper—Working in the Messina District', *Journal of the South African Institute of Mining and Mentallurgy*, vol. 74, no. 6 (January).

Harries, P. (1976) 'Labour Migration from the Delagoa Bay Hinterland to South Africa: 1852–1895', Institute of Commonwealth Studies, University of London, Collected Seminar Papers no. 21, *The Societies of Southern Africa in the 19th and 20th Centuries*, vol. 7.

Hemson, D. (1978) 'Trade Unionism and the Struggle for Liberation in South Africa', *Capital and Class*, no. 6 (Autumn).

Hepple, A. (1974) *Press under Apartheid* (International Defence and Aid, London).

Hobsbawm, E. J. (1972) *Industry and Empire* (Penguin Books, Harmondsworth).

Hobson, J. A. (1900) *The War in South Africa* (London).

Hobson, J. A. (1902) *Imperialism: A Study* (London).

Hobson, J. A. (1928) *The Evolution of Modern Capitalism* (George Allen and Unwin, London).

Hocking, A. (1973) *Oppenheimer and Son* (McGraw-Hill, Johannesburg).

Holloway, J. and Picciotto, S. (eds) (1978) *State and Capital: A Marxist Debate* (Edward Arnold, London).

Horner, D. and Kooy, A. (1979) 'Conflict on South African Mines, 1972–1979', Saldru Working Paper no. 25.

Horowitz, D. (1969) *Empire and Revolution: A Radical Interpretation of Contemporary History* (Random House, New York).

Horrell, M. (1967) *South West Africa* (South African Institute of Race Relations, Johannesburg).

Horwitz, R. (1967) *The Political Economy of South Africa* (Wiedenfeld and Nicolson, London).

Houghton, D. Hobart (1973) *The South African Economy* (Oxford University Press, Cape Town).

Houghton, D. Hobart and Dagut, J. (eds) (1972) *Source Material on the South African Economy 1860–1970*, vols. I, II and III (Oxford University Press, Cape Town).

Innes, D. (1975) 'The Role of Foreign Trade and Industrial Development in South Africa', in J. Suckling, R. Weiss and D. Innes, *Foreign Investment in South Africa: The Economic Factor* (Africa Publications Trust, London).

Innes, D. (1976) 'The Mining Industry in the Context of South Africa's Economic Development', Institute of Commonwealth Studies, University of London, Collected Seminar Papers no. 21, *The Societies of Southern Africa in the 19th and 20th Centuries*, vol. 7.

Innes, D. (1977) 'The Exercise of Control in the Diamond Industry of South Africa: Some Preliminary Remarks', in T. Adler (ed.), *Perspectives on South Africa* (University of the Witwatersrand, Johannesburg).

Innes, D. (1978) 'Imperialism and the National Struggle in Namibia', *Review of African Political Economy*, no. 9.

Innes, D. (1981a) 'Capitalism and Gold', *Capital and Class*, no. 14.

Innes, D. (1981b) 'South African Capital and Namibia', in R. Green, K. and M. Kiljunen (eds), *Namibia, The Last Colony* (Longman, London).

Innes, D. and Malaba, L. (1978) 'The South African State and Its Policy vis à vis Supplier Economies', paper presented at the ECA/MULPOC Conference on Migratory Labour in Southern Africa (Lusaka).

Innes, D. and O'Meara, D. (1976) 'Class Formation and Ideology: The Transkei Region', *Review of African Political Economy*, no. 7.

Innes, D. and Plaut, M. (1978) 'Class Struggle and the State', *Review of African Political Economy*, no. 11.

Innes, D. and Plaut, M. (1979) 'Class Struggle and Economic Development in South Africa: The Inter-war Years', Institute of Commonwealth Studies, University of London, Collected Seminar Papers no. 24, *The Societies of Southern Africa in the 19th and 20th Centuries*, vol. 9.

International Labour Office (1973), *Multinational Enterprises and Social Policy* (ILO, Geneva).

Jann, A. (1954) 'Southern Africa as a Field for Swiss Capital', *Optima*, vol. 4 no. 3 (September).

Jeeves, A. H. (1975) 'The Control of Migratory Labour on the South African Gold Mines in the Era of Kruger and Milner', *Journal of Southern African Studies*, vol. 2, no. 1.

Johns, S. (1973) 'Opposition in Southern Africa: Segments, Linkages and Cohesion', paper presented to the Workshop on Southern Africa at Dalhousie University.

Johnstone, F. (1970a) 'Class Conflict and Colour Bars in the South African Gold Mining Industry', University of London, Collected Seminar Papers, *The Societies of Southern Africa in the 19th and 20th Centuries*, vol. 1.

Johnstone, F. A. (1970b) 'White Prosperity and White Supremacy in South Africa Today', *African Affairs*, vol. 69, no. 275.

Johnstone, F. A. (1976) *Class, Race and Gold* (Routledge and Kegan Paul, London).

Kallaway, P. (1974) 'Preliminary Notes Toward a Study of Labour on the Diamond Fields of Griqualand West', paper delivered at the Workshop on the Social and Economic History of South Africa (Oxford University).

346   Bibliography

Kane-Berman, J. (1972) *Contract Labour in South West Africa* (South African Institute of Race Relations, Johannesburg).
Kane-Berman, J. (1978) *Soweto: Black Revolt, White Reaction* (Ravan Press, Johannesburg).
Kantor, B. and Kenny, H. (1976) 'The Poverty of Neo-Marxism: The Case of South Africa', *Journal of Southern African Studies*, vol. 3, no. 1.
Kaplan, D. (1976a) 'An Analysis of the South African State in the "Fusion" Period, 1932–1939', Institute of Commonwealth Studies, University of London, Collected Seminar Papers no. 21, *The Societies of Southern Africa in the 19th and 20th Centuries*, vol. 7.
Kaplan, D. (1976b) 'The Politics of Industrial Protection in South Africa', *Journal of Southern African Studies*, vol. 3, no. 1.
Karis, T. and Carter, G. (1977) *From Protest to Challenge: A Documentary History of African Politics*, vols I, II and III (Hoover Institution Press, Stanford).
Kaunda, K. D. (1974) *Southern Africa: A Time for Change* (Lusaka, 26 October).
King, W. (1962) 'South Africa's Growing Money Market', *Optima*, vol. 12, no. 3 (September).
Kuhn, R. (1978) 'A History of the African Labour Movement circa 1924 to 1946 with special reference to the 1946 African Mineworkers' Strike', BA (Hons) dissertation (University of Cape Town).
Laclau, E. (1971) 'Feudalism and Capitalism in Latin America', *New Left Review*, no. 67 (May–June).
Lall, S. (1973) 'Transfer-Pricing by Multinational Manufacturing Firms', *Oxford Bulletin of Economics and Statistics*, vol. 35, no. 3 (August).
Lamb, B. (1975) 'Sharpeville: The Realignment of Nationalist Forces in South Africa, 1950–1960', MA dissertation (School of Oriental and African Studies, University of London).
Lambert, R. (1978) 'Black Working Class Resistance in South Africa, 1950–1961: A Historical Materialist Analysis', MA thesis (University of Warwick).
Lazar, L. (1972) *Namibia* (Africa Bureau, London).
Leftwich, A. (ed.) (1974) *Economic Growth and Political Change in South Africa* (Allison and Busby, London).
Legassick, M. (1971) 'The Frontier Tradition in South African Historiography', Institute of Commonwealth Studies, University of London, Collected Seminar Paper no. 12, *The Societies of Southern Africa in the 19th and 20th Centuries*, vol. 2.
Legassick, M. (1974a) 'Capital Accumulation and Violence', *Economy and Society*, vol. 3, no. 3.
Legassick, M. (1974b) 'Legislation, Ideology and Economy in Post-1948 South Africa', *Journal of Southern African Studies*, vol. 1, no. 1 (October).
Legassick, M. (1974c) 'South Africa: Forced Labour, Industrialisation and Racial Discrimination', in R. Harris (ed.), *The Political Economy of Africa* (Boston).
Legassick, M. and Innes, D. (1977) 'Capital Restructuring and Apartheid: A Critique of Constructive Engagement', *African Affairs*, vol. 76, no. 305.
Legassick, M. and Wolpe, H. (1976) 'The Bantustans and Capital Accumulation in South Africa', *Review of African Political Economy*, no. 7.
Legum, C. (1976) *Vorster's Gamble for Africa: How the Search for Peace Failed* (Rex Collings, London).
Legum, C. (ed.) (1977) *Africa Contemporary Record, 1976: Annual Survey and Documents* (Rex Collings, London).
Leistner, G. (1973) 'The Economic Problems and Policies of South Africa's Neighbouring Black African States', South African Institute of International Affairs (Pretoria).
Lenin, V. I. (1969) *British Labour and British Imperialism: A Compilation of Writings by Lenin on Britain* (Lawrence and Wishart, London).
Lenin, V. I. (1973a) *Collected Works*, vol. 23 (Progress Publishers, Moscow).
Lenin, V. I. (1973b) *Imperialism, the Highest Stage of Capitalism* (Foreign Language Press, Peking).

Lenin, V. I. (1973c) *Lenin on Imperialism and Imperialists* (Progress Publishers, Moscow).

Lerumo, A. (1971) *Fifty Fighting Years* (Inkululeko Press, London).

Letcher, O. (1936) *The Gold Mines of Southern Africa: The History, Technology and Statistics of the Gold Industry* (the Author, Johannesburg, and Waterlow and Sons, London).

Lewis, J. (1978) 'The New Unionism: Industrialization and Industrial Unions in South Africa, 1925–1930', in E. Webster (ed.), *Essays in Southern African Labour History* (Ravan Press, Johannesburg).

Lewsen, H. (1976) 'Black Trade Unions in South Africa: Their Role and Potential', MBA Research report (University of the Witwatersrand).

Lichtheim, G. (1971) *Imperialism* (Allen Lane The Penguin Press, London).

Limebeer, A. (1951) 'The Group System of Administration in the Gold Mining Industry', *Optima*, vol. 1, no. 1 (June).

Lipton, M. (1974a) 'White Farming: A Case Study of Change in South Africa', *Journal of Commonwealth and Comparative Politics* (March).

Lipton, M. (1974b) 'South Africa: Authoritarian Reform?', *World Today* (June).

Lomas, P. K. (1955) 'Industrial Profits since the War', *South African Journal of Economics*, vol. 23.

Lombard, J., Stadler, J. and Van der Merwe, P. (1968) *The Concept of Economic Co-operation in Southern Africa* (Econburo, Pretoria).

Luxembourg, R. (1971) *The Accumulation of Capital* (Routledge and Kegan Paul, London).

MacConachie, H. (1967) 'Progress in Gold Mining over Fifty Years', *Optima*, vol. 17, no. 3 (September).

Magdoff, H. (1969) *The Age of Imperialism: The Economics of U.S. Foreign Policy* (Modern Reader Paperbacks, New York and London).

Mandel, E. (1968) *Marxist Economic Theory*, vols. I and II (Merlin Press, London).

Mandel, E. (1970) 'The Laws of Uneven Development', *New Left Review*, no. 59 (January–February).

Marais, G. (1960) 'The Value of the Ottawa Agreement between the Union of South Africa and the United Kingdom Reconsidered', *Finance and Trade Review*, vol. II.

Marquard, L. (1971) *A Federation of Southern Africa* (Oxford University Press, London).

Marx, K. (1970) 'The Eighteenth Brumaire of Louis Bonaparte', in K. Marx and F. Engels, *Selected Works* (Lawrence & Wishart, London).

Marx, K. (1971) *A Contribution to the Critique of Political Economy* (Lawrence & Wishart, London).

Marx, K. (1973) *Grundrisse* (Pelican Marx Library, London).

Marx, K. (1974) *Capital*, vols. I, II, III (Lawrence & Wishart, London).

Marx, K. and Engels, F. (1970) *Selected Works* (Lawrence & Wishart, London).

Matthews, J. W. (1887) *Incwadi Yami, or Twenty Years' Personal Experience in South Africa* (S. Low, Marston, Searle and Rivington, London).

Mennell, C. S. (1961) 'The Changing Character of the South African Mining Finance Houses in the Post-War Period', MBA thesis (University of Pennsylvania).

Meyer, F. (1952) 'The Development of the Iron and Steel Industry in South Africa', *South African Journal of Economics*, vol. 20, no. 2.

Molteno, R. (1971) *Africa and South Africa* (Africa Bureau, London).

Moorsom, R. (nd) 'Proletarianisation and the Formation of Worker Consciousness: background to the contract workers' strike in Namibia, 1971–1972' (mimeo).

Moorsom, R. (1977a) 'Underdevelopment and Class Formation: the origin of migrant labour in Namibia, 1850–1915', in T. Adler (ed.), *Perspectives on South Africa* (University of the Witwatersrand, Johannesburg).

Moorsom, R. (1977b) 'Underdevelopment, Contract Labour and Worker Consciousness in Namibia, 1915–1972', *Journal of Southern African Studies*, vol. 4, no. 1.

348   *Bibliography*

Murray, R. (1971a) 'Internationalization of Capital and the Nation State', *New Left Review*, no. 67 (May–June).

Murray, R. (1971b) 'The Namibian Economy: An Analysis of the Role of Foreign Investment and the Policies of the South African Administration', *The Role of Foreign Firms in Namibia* (Africa Publications Trust).

Murray, R. (1972) 'Underdevelopment, the International firm and the International Division of Labour', Seminar Paper (Institute of Development Studies).

Morris, M. (1976) 'The Development of Capitalism in South African Agriculture: Class Struggle in the Countryside', *Economy and Society*, vol. 6, no. 3.

Nkrumah, K. (1966) *Neo-Colonialism: The Last Stage of Imperialism* (International Publishers, New York).

Noble, J. (1875) *Descriptive Handbook of the Cape Colony: Its Condition and Resources* (Juta, Cape Town and London).

Noble, J. (ed.) (1892) *Illustrated Official Handbook of the Cape and South Africa* (Juta, Cape Town).

O'Connor, J. (1970) 'The Meaning of Economic Imperialism', in R. Rhodes (ed.), *Imperialism and Underdevelopment: A Reader* (Monthly Review Press, London and New York).

Officially Contributed, 'The Development of the use of Electricity in South Africa', *South African Journal of Economics*, vol. 16, no. 4 (December 1948).

O'Meara, D. (1975a) 'The 1946 African Mineworkers' Strike and a Political Economy of South Africa', *Journal of Commonwealth and Comparative Politics* (March).

O'Meara, D. (1975b) 'White Trade Unionism, Political Power and Afrikaner Nationalism', *South African Labour Bulletin*, vol. 1, no. 10 (April).

O'Meara, D. (1977) 'The Afrikaner Broederbond 1927–1948: Class Vanguard of Afrikaner Nationalism', *Journal of Southern African Studies*, vol. 3, no. 2 (April).

Oppenheimer, H. F. (1950) 'The Orange Free State Goldfields', *South African Journal of Economics*, vol. 18.

Oppenheimer, H. F. (1954) 'The Union's Group Mining System', *Mining and Industrial Magazine* (September, Johannesburg).

Oppenheimer, H. F. (1967) 'Sir Ernest Oppenheimer: A Portrait by His Son', *Optima*, vol. 17, no. 3 (September).

Oppenheimer, H. F. (1974) 'South Africa after the Election', *African Affairs*, vol. 73, no. 293 (October).

Palmer, G. F. D. (1954) 'Some Aspects of the Development of Secondary Industry in South Africa since the Depression of 1929–1932', *South African Journal of Economics*, vol. 22.

Palmer, G. F. D. (1958) 'The Development of the South African Money Market', *South African Journal of Economics*, vol 26.

Pearsall, C. W. (1937) 'Some Aspects of the Development of Secondary Industry in the Union of South Africa', *South African Journal of Economics*, vol. 5, no. 4 (December).

Phimister, I. (1974) 'Rhodes, Rhodesia and the Rand: Mining in Southern Rhodesia, 1890–1902', *Journal of Southern African Studies*, vol. 1, no. 1 (October).

Poulantzas, N. (1973) *Political Power and Social Classes* (New Left Books, London).

Prinsloo, D. S. (1976) *South West Africa: The Turnhalle and Independence*, Study Report no. 4 (South African Foreign Affairs Association).

Ranger, T. O. (ed.) (1968) *Aspects of Central African History* (Heinemann, London).

Reader, W. J. (1970) *Imperial Chemical Industries: A History*, vol. I, *The Forerunners, 1870–1926* (Oxford University Press, London).

Richards, C. S. (1944) 'The Task Before Us: With Special Reference to Industry', *South African Journal of Economics*, vol. 12, no. 3 (September).

Richards, C. S. (1951) 'Devaluation and Its Effects on the Gold Mining Industry', *Optima*, vol. 1, no. 1 (June).

Richardson, P. (1977) 'The Recruitment of Chinese Indentured Labour for the South African Gold Mines, 1903–1908', *Journal of African History*, XVIII, I.

Rodney, W. (1974) *How Europe Underdeveloped Africa* (Tanzania Publishing House, Dar-es-Salaam).

Rostow, W. W. (1960) *The Stages of Economic Growth: A Non-Communist Manifesto* (Cambridge University Press, Cambridge).

Rothschild, K. (ed.) (1971) *Power in Economics* (Penguin Modern Economic Readings, London).

Roux, E. (1966), *Time Longer than Rope* (V. Gollancz, London).

Sammel, H. B. 'African Loans and Investments: Analysis' (undated document).

Sammel, H. B. 'E. Oppenheimer and Son Ltd' (confidential document, undated).

Sammel, H. B. Letter to Mr H. Oppenheimer (2 September 1966).

Schauder, H. (1946) 'The Chemical Industry in South Africa Before Union (1910)', *South African Journal of Economics*, vol. 14, no. 4 (December).

Seers, D. (1970) 'The Meaning of Development', *Communication Series no. 44* (Institute of Development Studies).

Segal, R. and First, R. (eds) (1967) *South West Africa, Travesty of Trust* (Audré Deutsch, London).

Selwyn, P. (1973) 'Core and Periphery: A Study of Industrial Development in the Small Countries of Southern Africa', Discussion Paper no. 36 (Institute of Development Studies).

Serfontein, J. H. P. (1976) *Namibia?* (Fokus Suid, Pretoria).

Simons, H. J. and Simons, R. E. (1969) *Class and Colour in South Africa: 1850–1950* (1969) (Penguin African Library, London).

Smith, R. (1971) *Dialogue with South Africa* (Liberian Writers Series II).

South African Institute of Race Relations, *A Survey of Race Relations in South Africa, 1966–1977* (annual survey, inclusive) (Johannesburg).

Speck, S. (1972) 'Malawi and the Southern African Complex', in C. Potholm and R. Dale (eds), *Southern Africa in Perspective* (Free Press, New York).

Spence, J. E. (1968) *Lesotho: The Politics of Dependence* (Oxford University Press, London).

Spence, J. E. (1972) 'South African Foreign Policy: The "Outward Movement"', in C. Potholm and R. Dale (eds), *Southern Africa in Perspective* (Free Press, New York).

Stein, M. (1979) 'Black Trade Unionism during the Second World War: The Witwatersrand Strikes of December 1942', paper delivered at the Institute of Commonwealth Studies, University of London.

Stevens, R. (1972) 'The History of the Anglo-South African Conflict over the Proposed Incorporation of the High Commission Territories', in C. Potholm and R. Dale (eds), *Southern Africa in Perspective* (Free Press, New York).

Sunkel, O. and Faivovich, E. (1974) 'Transnationalization, National Disintegration and Reintegration in Contemporary Capitalism: An Area for Research', Internal Working Paper no. 18 (Institute of Development Studies).

Tarbuck, K. (ed.) (1972) *Rosa Luxemburg and Nikolai Bukharin: Imperialism and the Accumulation of Capital* (Allen Lane, London).

Trapido, S. (1971) 'South Africa in a Comparative Study of Industrialization', *Journal of Development Studies*, vol. 3, no. 3 (April).

Tregenna-Piggott, J. V. (1975) 'The Structure and Performance of South African Manufacturing Industry', (mimeo, University of Natal).

Vaitsos, C. (1974) 'Power, Knowledge and Development Policies: Relations Between Transnational Enterprises and Developing Countries', Seminar Paper (Institute of Development Studies).

van den Berghe, P. (1967) *South Africa: A Study in Conflict* (University of California Press, Berkeley).

van der Horst, S. T. (1942) *Native Labour in South Africa* (Oxford University Press, London).

van Onselen, C. (1976) *Chibaro: African Mine Labour in Southern Rhodesia 1900–1933* (Pluto Press, London).

Walker, E. (1957) *A History of Southern Africa* (Longman, London).

Wellington, J. W. (1967) *South West Africa and its Human Issues* (Oxford University Press, London).

Williams, M. (1975) 'An Analysis of South African Capitalism—Neo-Ricardian or Marxism?', *Bulletin of the Conference of Socialist Economists* (March).

Williams, M. (1978) *South Africa, the Crisis of World Capitalism and the Apartheid Economy* (Winstanley Publications, London).

Wilson, F. (1972) *Labour in the South African Gold Mines, 1911–1969* (Cambridge University Press, London).

Wilson, F. (1976) 'International Migration in Southern Africa', SALDRU Working Paper no. 1, (May).

Wilson, M. and Thompson, L. (eds) (1979) *The Oxford History of South Africa,* vols. I and II (Oxford University Press, London).

Wincott, H. (1957) 'Institutional Investment in Britain', *Optima,* vol. 7, no. 1 (March).

Wolpe, H. (1972) 'Capitalism and Cheap Labour Power in South Africa: From Segregation to Apartheld', *Economy and Society,* vol. 1, no. 4.

Index

Abex Corporation of America, 197
Act of Union (1910), 68
Administration of Persons to the Union
  Regulation Act (1913), 68
Aero Marine Investments, 210
Aerflo (Pty) Ltd., 178
African Eagle Life Assurance Society,
  217, 221
African and European Investments, 133,
  134
African Explosives and Cape Industries
  (AE & CI), 207, 211, 221; in manufac-
  turing, 175, 176; merger of, 211–12;
  1960s–1970s industrial activity, 199–
  202
African Explosives and Cape Industries
  Rhodesia, 201
African Explosives and Industries Ltd.
  (AE & I), 124–26
African Mine Workers' Union, 143
African National Congress of South Africa
  (ANC), 128, 172–74
African Wire Ropes, 178
Agriculture, 118, 119, 128
Air Reduction, 200
Albatros-Fisons, 201
Albu, G. & L., House of, 47, 55
ALCAN, 234
Althusser, L., 19, 20
'Althusserian Marxism' (Clarke *et al.*), 19
American-South African Investment
  Trust, 148
American Metal Climax (AMAX), 234
Anglo-Alpha Cement, 179
Anglo American Coal Investment (AM-
  COAL), 221, 233
Anglo American Construction, 204
Anglo American Corporation of Bots-
  wana, 233

Anglo American Corporation do Brazil
  Limitada, 233
Anglo American Corporation of Canada,
  233
Anglo American Corporation of Central
  Africa, 233
Anglo American Corporation of Rhodesia,
  233
Anglo American Corporation of South Af-
  rica, *see* Anglo American Group
Anglo American Corporation of South Af-
  rica (Portugal), 233
Anglo American Corporation of the
  United States, 233
Anglo American Gold Investments (AM-
  GOLD), 221, 233
Anglo American Group (and Anglo
  American Corporation of South Africa),
  221, 230, 231, 236; centralization in
  manufacturing under (1970s), 208–15;
  centralization in mining under (1970s),
  212–15; as channel for British and U.S.
  capital, 92; concentration of power of,
  in gold (postwar), 155–57; concentration of power of, in other mining (postwar), 157; control established by,
  97–98, 101–2; De Beers taken over by,
  97–117, 192; expansion of gold mining
  under, 132–38; Far East Rand, tables,
  87, 88; Far East Rand gold field and,
  87–93; financial and property interests
  of, 206–7; formed, 16, 91–93; industrial
  associates of, 200–5; industrial portfolio
  of, 193; industrial subsidiaries of, 194–
  200; as leader in gold (1950s), 184; in manufacturing (1950s), 174–77, 181, 183; monopoly of, in industry and finance,
  188–228; and Namibian diamonds, 98–

351

Nalco Chemicals, 202
Namibia, 238–39
National Bank of South Africa, 91
National Board of Executors, 215
National Bolts and Rivets, 179
National Finance Corporation, 148, 149,
181
National Income: from manufacturing,
119, 120; *see also* Gross domestic prod-
uct
Native Administration Act (1927), 128
Native Affairs Commission (1905), 68
Native Affairs Department, 64–65
Native Labour Department, 52
Native Labour Regulation Act (1913), 68–
69
Native Labour (Settlement of Disputes)
Act of 1953, 145
Native Land and Trust Act (1936), 129
Native Lands Act (1913), 67, 68
Native Laws Amendment Act (1937), 129
Native Recruiting Corporation, 80
Native Service Contract Act (1932), 128
Nedbank, 216, 221
Nedfin bank, 221
Nedsual (Nedbank and Syfrets-UAL
Holdings), 215–19
New Era, 103
New Era Consolidated, 101
Newmont Chemical, 195
Newmont Mining Corporation, 91, 234
Nobel, 125
Nobel-Dynamite Trust, 119–20, 124
Nobel-Kynochs Co., 124
Northern Lime, 214

Odendaal Commission, 238–39
Oil imports, 191
Old Mutual, 215–17, 219
Ottawa Agreement (1932), 123
Oppenheimer, Ernest, 55, 134, 229;
achievements of, in Gregory's view,
13–14; appointed to De Beers board,
106; and decentralization, 136; on diamond production (1932), 107–8; and
forming Anglo American, 91–93; and
jack hammer, 85; manufacturing and,
181–83; as member of Parliament, 111;
and Namibian diamonds, 98–101; 1920
report of, on gold interests, 97; on productivity increases, 86; and publishing,
205; and reduction in price of diamonds, 105–6; registering Anglo
American in South Africa, 109; strength
of, 93

Oppenheimer, Harry, 99, 106, 111, 229–
31; on Anglo American, 92; and industrial control, 194; manufacturing and,
183; and post-World War II financing of
gold mining operations, 147
Oppenheimer, Louis, 137, 229
Oppenheimer, Nicholas, 229, 231
Oppenheimer family, 90, 103, 229–31;
and Afrikaner sharing, 158; in control
of richest gold fields, 90–91; in control
(1920s), 102; expansion of, 97–98; *see
also* Anglo American Group
Oppenheimer Group, *see* Oppenheimer
family; Anglo American Group
Oppenheimer and Son (Hocking), 14
Oppenheimer and Son, E., 137, 230–32
Orange Free State Investment Trust, 137

Pacsa (company), 210
Pact (government), 122, 123, 126
Pan Africanist Congress, 174
Pass Law (1895), 58, 61, 62
Pass laws, 129, 174; reformed (1900s), 63,
64
Poulantzas, N., 19, 20
Permanent Alloy Castings, 178
Phalaborwa, 221
Phillips, Sir Lionel, 82, 123
Phillips and King, Messrs, 21
Polyfos, 202
Porges and Co., Jules, 36
Premier (Transvaal) Diamond Mining
Co., 40, 90, 103
Premier Portland Cement Company
(Rhodesia), 177
Pretoria Portland Cement Co., 120, 177,
204
Productivity: of blacks in gold mines, 84–
86; mechanization and postwar, 152–
54; 1960s, 188–90
Project Engineering, 178

Raine Engineering Co., 198
Rand Carbide, 201–2
Rand Mines Co., 55, 159, 213, 214, 218
Rand Mines Holdings, 214
Rand Mines Properties, 206, 214, 221
Rand Native Labour Association (NLA),
61–63, 65
Rand Selection Corporation, 97, 101,
103, 193, 205, 216, 217, 221, 230;
formed, 90; postwar, 158
Recession: 1907–1909, 40; 1920–1921,
100; 1970s, 208; *see also* Depression
Redbury Holdings, 210